Academic Motherhood in a Post-Second Wave Context

Challenges, Strategies, and Possibilities

Academic Motherhood in a Post-Second Wave Context

Challenges, Strategies, and Possibilities

Edited by

D. Lynn O'Brien Hallstein
and Andrea O'Reilly

DEMETER

DEMETER PRESS

Published by:
Demeter Press
c/o Motherhood Initiative for Research and
 Community Involvement (MIRCI)
140 Holland St. West, P.O. 13022
Bradford, ON, L3Z 2Y5
Telephone: 905.775.9089
Email: info@demeterpress.org
Website: www.demeterpress.org

Demeter Press logo based on Skulptur "Demeter" by Maria-Luise Bodirsky
<www.keramik-atelier.bodirsky.edu>

Cover Artwork: Richard Hallstein
Cover/Interior Design: Luciana Ricciutelli

Printed and Bound in Canada

Library and Archives Canada Cataloguing in Publication

    Academic motherhood in a post-second wave context : challenges, strategies and possibilities / edited by D. Lynn O'Brien Hallstein and Andrea O'Reilly.

Includes bibliographical references.
ISBN 978-0-9866671-9-0

    1. Women college teachers—Social conditions. 2. Women in higher education—Social conditions. 3. Motherhood. 4. Working mothers. 5. Work and family. I. Hallstein, D. Lynn O'Brien II. O'Reilly, Andrea, 1961-

LB2332.3.A23 2012   378.0082   C2012-901998-4

This book is dedicated to Adrienne Rich for her groundbreaking work in Of Woman Born: Motherhood as Experience and Institution, *which laid the foundation for both feminist maternal scholarship and books like this one that continue her project of teasing out the nuances of institutionalized motherhood and the potential of mothering to be empowering for women.*

Table of Contents

SECTION TWO: STRATEGIES

SECTION THREE: POSSIBILITIES

Acknowledgements

We would like to express our appreciation to the following people who helped to bring this book to life. Special thanks to Renée Knapp, Randy Chase, and Tracey Carlyle. Special thanks are due to Demeter Press's production editor, Lucianan Ricciutelli, who was copied on email exchanges between Lynn and Andrea about the cover art and "figured out" what we really wanted.

Our deepest appreciation to the contributors to this volume for their steadfast commitment to seeing this book come to life and for their willingness to share both their ideas and stories about what it means to be and think as academic mothers.

Lynn is also grateful for her feminist academic mentors, Julia T. Wood and Sonja K. Foss, both of whom mentored her as a graduate student, taught her how to write, and who continue to be a part of her academic life. Their contributions and lingering legacies were ongoing as the book developed and came to fruition.

Andrea would also like to thank the Social Science Research Council of Canada for its support of her research on academic motherhood. Thank you as well to Melissa Nurse for her careful proofreading of my chapter. Thank you as always to my MIRCI family for providing the safe and sustaining "homplace" that makes possible my maternal scholarship.

Last, but not least, we would like to thank our families. For Lynn, as always, she is grateful for Jean-Philipp's, Joshua's, and Michel's support for and respect of her need to be a mother-academic. And, finally, to her father and cover artist, Richard Hallstein for his ability to be and think as a feminist-father-cover-artist. Academic motherhood would be much easier if everyone had such a father.

For Andrea, thank you as always to my children, Casey, Erin and Jesse, my partner Terry, my sister Jennifer and my mother Jean; in believing in me, I was able believe in myself.

Academic Motherhood in a Post-Second Wave Context

Framing the Conversation

D. LYNN O'BRIEN HALLSTEIN AND ANDREA O'REILLY

THE COMPLEXITIES OF BEING both a professional and a mother[1] have garnered much attention recently in both public and academic forums. The subject of motherhood and employment, particularly for educated professional women, for example, has emerged on the public agenda in the United States and Canada over the last ten years. Moreover, with the publication of best-selling books such as Ann Crittenden's *The Price of Motherhood* and Sylvia Ann Hewlett's *Creating a Life: Professional Women and the Quest for Children*, individuals as diverse as talk-show hosts, policy makers, magazine writers and newspaper columnists are also discussing the complexities of mothering and working. Headlines ask: "Can women really have it all? A career and family?" and terms and phrases such as "the biological clock," "the mommy tax," "the price of motherhood," "time crunch," and the "on-track/off track career," may be heard in everyday conversations. These concerns and concepts are not new; the "second-shift," "the double day," and "the pink ghetto" have been studied for more than twenty-five years by scholars and policy-makers. What is new, however, and what has captured the interest of the media and the general public, is that the women now under discussion can, by virtue of their privileged status as the first generation of college-educated baby boomer women, "have it all": an education, a career, and a family.

At the foundation of this new conversation, then, is the recognition that the "girls who had it all"—young women who are the first generation of women to benefit from the large-scale social and political changes brought about by second wave feminisms—are now both mothers and professionals. In 2005, *Newsweek* also captured the essence of this new

1

conversation when the magazine devoted its cover story to exploring how contemporary women are managing their lives as second-wave beneficiaries once they become mothers. The feature article opens with the following question: "What happened when the girls who had it all became mothers?" ("Mommy Madness"). In short, at the heart of the *Newsweek* cover story and the larger conversation across cultural institutions is the understanding that many contemporary women, whether any individual woman identifies as a feminist or not, are second wave beneficiaries—they have benefited from and taken advantage of second wave feminism's successes in terms of opening up access for girls and women in both educational and professional institutions. And, as such, contemporary women, at least privileged women, have a new and different set of issues to address than their mothers had before them. Daphne de Marneffe, in fact, argues that unlike their own mothers—women mothering in the second wave—contemporary women need to solve a new problem, "namely, how to take advantage of the access women had gained in the workplace while not shortchanging their desire to mother" (64).

For most women but especially academic women, solving this new post-second wave problem is not without its difficulties, particularly in regard to managing the intensive and unbounded demands of academia, children, and family-life management and the tensions that arise as a result of trying to manage it all. Indeed, in the last few years, *The Chronicle of Higher Education* has published articles that explore the difficulties graduate student women recognize will come with being both an academic and a mother. Titles such as, "Grad Students Think Twice About Jobs in Academe" (June) or "Finding a Parent-Friendly Place" (Kajitani) have been covered recently. In fact, Megan Kajitani, a career advisor for graduate students at a California research university, reports that, weekly, she is asked the following questions by graduate students: "Is it really possible to balance children and the tenure track? Would a non-faculty position in academe make it easier to be an involved parent?" and, "Should I just leave the ivory tower if I want a career and children?" (par. 1). She continues, "Often, the student posing the question was a 30ish woman trying to figure out if she could have kids and remain in academe. Sometimes, it was a 30ish man tired of spending more time in the lab than with his family" (par. 1). In short, as more and more women have entered academia in North America, questions are emerging, to paraphrase de Marneffe, about how to take advantage of the access women have gained in academia while not shortchanging many women's desire to mother.[2]

We suggest that 30ish graduate students are asking these questions specifically because they recognize, often even before they become mothers, that mothering and professing simultaneously seems incompatible if not impossible. While we do not believe doing so is impossible, we will suggest in this book that being a mother and a professor is fraught with a complex set of challenges and difficulties, primarily because of the new and unique context within which academic women and mothers find themselves today. In fact, we believe that 30ish graduate students and academic mothers across disciplines are asking these questions because the context in which they find themselves is shaped by three, often competing and/or contradictory, forces or features: contemporary women's status as post-second wave beneficiaries, the intensive and unbounded career-path and ideal worker norms of academia that center on achieving tenure and promotion, and the demanding and also unbounded requirements of the contemporary ideology of "good mothering," intensive mothering. Indeed, we argue that, when these three factors converge—when post-second wave beneficiaries *are both* mothers and professors—a distinct-to-academia "perfect storm" of difficult and almost-impossible-to-meet challenges for academic mothers emerges. To put it another way, we are arguing and will show in this introduction that, despite the fact that academia is a liberal and progressive institution, academic mothers are living, working, and mothering at the intersection of three shaping forces that create a unique-to-academic-mothers set of challenges when they try to have and manage "it all," which also make academia a more challenging profession for women who are or want to become mothers.

As such, we also suggest in this book that understanding academic motherhood requires continuing to ask and answer the very questions being asked today by 30ish graduate students to explore more fully the challenges, strategies, and possibilities academic mothers are currently facing, implementing, and thinking about as they mother and profess. To do so, however, requires a new framework to explore the complexities of academic mothers' lives, a framework that is laid out and detailed in the next three sections of this introduction. In fact, section one describes this new framework and situates contemporary women's post-second wave split subjectivity within the context of both the intensive mothering ideology and an emerging neo-traditional family configuration. Section two details academia's intensive and unbounded career-path requirements, expectations, and ideal-worker norms and the ways that all three penalize academic women once they become mothers, in a manner that is more pronounced than most other professions. Finally, section three provides an overview of the chapters that follow and briefly describes the overarching sections of the book—challenges, strategies, and possibilities—that are the main area of foci for exploring academic motherhood within our post-second wave context.

WHY NOW? UNDERSTANDING CONTEMPORARY WOMEN'S POST-SECOND WAVE SPLIT SUBJECTIVITY

Contextualizing *why* so many 30ish academic women are asking the kinds of questions that they are *now* is important to understanding more fully contemporary academic motherhood-the ideas, institutional assumptions, and organizing systems that shape academic women's understanding of motherhood within academia—and mothering—a woman's desire to mother and her actual practices of mothering. Indeed, we suggest that the questions are being asked at this time precisely because academic motherhood is now unfolding within a post-second wave context. When we use the term "post-second wave," we mean to suggest "after second wave feminism" or "as a result of second wave feminism," and, unlike much popular writing, we do not employ the term to mean that we live in a post-feminist context, implying that all gender problems have been solved via second wave feminism. In fact, we mean that our contemporary context is one that is simultaneously split between newfound gains for women—especially for middle-class women with class, race, and sexuality privileges—and old family-life gender patterns and assumptions that discipline both men and women.

More specifically, because they are the first generation of women who are second-wave beneficiaries, contemporary women are living within a cultural milieu that Peggy Orenstein, for example, calls "half-changed," where young women grow up with new expectations about what it means to be female while, simultaneously, traditional patterns, particularly around family life and parenting, remain unchanged. Or, as Julia T. Wood puts it, American women's lives are in a "transitional time" between new roles and expectations and persisting and deeply held traditional gender values and roles (17). Thus, women's post-second wave split subjectivity is simultaneously divided between real and tangible gender similarity with men and problematic and oppressive gender assumptions primarily connected to family-life issues.

Intriguingly, then, recognizing that contemporary women have a post-second wave split subjectivity reveals the ways that, on one hand, the lives of women without children have become more and more similar to the lives of men without children, while, on the other hand, simultaneously recognizing that becoming a mother fundamentally changes that similarity and, equally important, changes women's lives in ways that most often do not affect many men's lives after they become normative fathers. Shari Dworkin and Faye Wachs describe well the post-second wave similarity between men's and women's lives. Today, as they suggest, drawing on the work of Michael Kimmel and speaking in relation to professional life and individual self-care: "As has been noted by Kimmel (2000), at the turn of the millennium, men's and women's lives are becoming 'more similar,' at least for the most advantaged. For the privileged, most professions are gender-neutral,[3] and women and men are routinely employed in the same professions, enjoy the same leisure activities, and engage in similar rituals of selfcare" (120). In other words, as gender roles and expectations have changed for both men and women, single or unencumbered—unencumbered with or from children—men's and women's lives are now "more similar," as long as both men and women adhere to the norms and institutional assumptions of professional organizations, including the male organizing systems that undergird academia.

Interestingly, another striking consequence of second-wave beneficiaries' lives is that most educated and class-privileged mothers, including academic mothers, either lay the groundwork for an academic career or establish a career before they become mothers. As Andrea O'Reilly (*Mother Outlaws*) argues, "Today, for the majority of middle-class women, motherhood is embarked upon only after a career is established, when the woman is in her thirties" (9). Equally important, most young women, not just academic women, seem to ground this decision in the post-second wave choice to "do it all." As Susan Douglas and Meredith Michaels' work suggests, educated women are taught the post-second wave middle-class premise that contemporary women now have the choice to "do it all," as long as they make good choices (5). We suggest that it is now a common post-second wave belief that making good choices in the context of academia means making the "choice" to become a mother after an academic career is established, at the "right time" on the tenure-and-promotion career clock.

This new post-second wave context and new cultural assumptions and beliefs about the "correct" choices for academic women, however, are difficult and complex because lingering "old" gender assumptions about women emerge once all women, including academic women, become mothers. And, these old gender assumptions contradict and challenge the similarity that now exists between unencumbered men and women. Indeed, feminist writers and scholars (Crittenden; Hayden and O'Brien Hallstein; Hirshman; O'Brien Hallstein "Second Wave Silences"; O'Reilly *Mother Outlaws*, *Twenty-first Century Motherhood*; Orenstein; Warner; Williams; Wood) have all shown that, even though second wave feminism opened up access to educational and professional contexts for at least already privileged women, women still have primary responsibility for childcare and childrearing once they have children. Popular writers (Crittenden; Hirshman; Wolf), for example, all argue that this is the case even when women work and across class lines. As Linda Hirshman puts it: "the assignment of responsibility for the household to women applies in every social class" (11). Ann Crittenden also reveals that women's responsibility for childrearing and care also emerges even if a couple shared household labor before the arrival of a child. As she puts it: "Before the arrival of the first child, couples tend to share the house work fairly equally. But something about a baby encourages the resurgence of traditional gender roles" (25).

Ironically, then, many women today, particularly those who are college educated, middle-class and professional, may not actually encounter overt gender discrimination until they become mothers. As Crittenden puts it, "Many childless women under the age of thirty five believe that all the feminist battles have been won" (88). But, as Crittenden continues, "once a woman has a baby, the egalitarian office party is over" (88). Contemporary women's subjectivity, then, is split between newfound gains as unencumbered women (women without children) and old gendered expectations when women become mothers. Thus, at the core of women's post-second wave split subjectivity is a key tension between women's post-second wave freedom from key pre-second wave gender discrimination as unencumbered women and ongoing gender-based discrimination once women become mothers.

INTENSIVE MOTHERING: FUELING POST-SECOND WAVE SUBJECTIVITY AND BACKLASH

Today, the contemporary ideology of good mothering, what Sharon Hays first named as *intensive mothering*, is at the heart of the dominant childrearing ideology that disciplines women into these "old" gender-based expectations, and, by extension, men who adhere to normative fathering roles that place the burden of childrearing on mothers. Feminist scholars (Douglas and Michaels; Hays; O'Brien Hallstein, "Second Wave Silences"; O'Reilly, *Mother Outlaws*) argue, in fact, that intensive mothering, or what Douglas and Michaels recently named the *new momism*, is one of the most byzantine sights of tension between old and new gender beliefs. Consequently and ironically, then, even though contemporary women believe that they now have the choice to mother or not, feminist scholars (Douglas and Michaels; Hays; O'Brien Hallstein "Second Wave Silences"; O'Reilly *Mother Outlaws*) also suggest that there is very little choice in terms of *how* to mother. Indeed, as Sharon Hays first suggested, "If you are a good mother, you *must* be an intensive one. The only 'choice' involved is whether you *add* the role of paid working woman" (italics in the original 131).

Intensive mothering, as feminist academics (Douglas and Michaels; Hays; O'Reilly *Mother Outlaws*) have established, rests on at least three core beliefs: 1) children need and require constant and ongoing nurturing by their biological mothers who are single-handedly responsible for meeting these needs; 2) in meeting those needs, mothers must rely on experts to guide them; and 3) mothers must lavish enormous amounts of time and energy on their children. As such, embedded within these core principles is the demand that good mothers are unbounded by or unencumbered from all other life obligations when they mother. In short, good mothers should always put their children's needs before their own, their work, or anything else. Therefore, even though not all women practice intensive mothering, as Hays argues, it is the *proper* ideology of contemporary mothering that all women are disciplined into and judged against, across race and class lines, even if not all women actually practice it and many mothers work.[4]

In putting their children's needs before their own, intensive mothers also participate in what Sara Ruddick first described as *maternal thinking*. According to Ruddick, maternal thinking refers to the "intellectual capacities [the mother] develops, the judgments she makes, the metaphysical attitudes she assumes, and the values she affirms in and through maternal practice" (24). Mothers, in short, as O'Reilly (*Twenty-first Century Motherhood*) has recently argued, are the ones who do the maternal thinking: the remembering, worrying, planning, anticipating, orchestrating, arranging, and co-ordinating of and for the household (*Twenty-first Century Motherhood*). It is mothers who remember to buy the milk, plan the birthday party and worry that the daughter's recent loss of appetite may be indicative of anorexia. Although the father may sign the field trip permission form or buy the diapers, it is the mother, in most households, who reminds him to do so. Delegation does not make equality and, equally important, delegation also continues to require that mothers have the psychological responsibility for remembering, managing, and executing the household, family life, and childrearing (O'Reilly, *Twenty-first Century Motherhood*). And, this kind of work is never ending and difficult to simply "turn off" at work. As a result, maternal thinking is constant and ongoing; it is another component of intensive mothering that is without boundaries. Thus, intensive mothering now plays a key role in reinforcing the tension contemporary women live with between their newfound similarity with unencumbered men's lives and old, family-life gender-based discrimination once they become mothers.

Although they do not use the language of *women's split subjectivity*, Douglas and Michaels' work supports our contention that intensive mothering is one of the lynchpins of contemporary women's post-second wave subjectivity and reveals how the new momism works as a new, post-second wave sophisticated backlash ideology. Douglas and Michaels clearly recognize the complexity of contemporary mothers' split subjectivity when they discuss how both postfeminism and second wave backlash are embedded in the new momism. In terms of postfeminism—the idea that feminism is no longer needed because second wave feminism "solved" gender inequity and, as a result, women can now "have it all"—Douglas and Michaels suggest that the new momism "has become the central, justifying ideology of what has come to be called 'postfeminism'" (24). While they are disdainful of postfeminism, Douglas and Michaels also argue: "Postfeminism means that you can now work outside the home even in jobs previously restricted to men, go to graduate school, pump iron, and pump your own gas, as long as you remain fashion conscious, slim, nurturing, deferential to men, and become a doting selfless mother"

(25). The new momism, then, simultaneously recognizes the post-second wave newfound similarity that exists between unencumbered men's and women's lives and reinforces an oppressive pre-second wave gendered-based understanding of family life that continues to place the burden of responsibility for childrearing and family life on mothers once children arrive. Thus, and equally important, as Lynn O'Brien Hallstein (*White Feminists*) argues, rather than simply eroding second wave gains, the new momism is a sophisticated post-second wave backlash ideology that simultaneously recognizes and refutes second wave feminist gains and further entrenches contemporary women's split subjectivity.

NEO-TRADITIONAL FAMILIES: THE NEW POST-SECOND WAVE FAMILY CONFIGURATION

We believe that one result of contemporary mothers'—including academic mothers'—post-second wave split subjectivity is that a "new" normative family configuration is emerging, a family arrangement that Miriam Peskowitz first described as a *neo-traditional family*. Neo-traditional families appear to be new and even progressive because many contemporary, privileged heterosexual families have both an educated and professional mother and father. This family configuration continues to be problematic, however, since the basic foundation of pre-second wave family roles and responsibilities still hold once children arrive: mothers continue to be primary caregivers of children in this "new" family type. In other words and to tie it to academic women specifically, while unencumbered academic women have benefited in real and important ways from second wave feminism, once academic women become mothers, many of those women adopt neo-traditional family configurations that continue to place the primary responsibility of household labor and caregiving on them, even as they maintain their full-time employment within academia. In new and complex ways, then, while contemporary women's lives have been freed from a *domestic destiny* as mothers, academic women's lives have not been freed from *domestic responsibility* in their homes. Equally important, neo-traditional families are the new norm for many academic women, and this "new" norm also creates complexity and tension for academic women, because it demands that women simultaneously meet the intensive demands of the new momism while also meeting the intensive and exacting norms and expectations of academia.

ACADEMIA: LIBERAL PERCEPTIONS, UNENCUMBERED EXPECTATIONS

Any discussion about the norms and expectations of academia must begin with an acknowledgement that, as a professional institution, academia in North America, as Jamie Huff et al. in this volume and Anna Agath-angelou and L. H. M. Ling also argue, is primarily considered a liberal and progressive institution both politically and socially, particularly in regard to women. While we concur that, in general, academia has been progressive in terms of opening its doors to women and implementing progressive policies to eliminate much gender biases, we believe that it is crucial to qualify the extent to which academia *as an institution* is liberal. Indeed, we believe that it is better to conceptualize academia as liberal to the level that an academic adheres both to the premise of be-ing unencumbered by family obligations and to the ideal-worker norms that continue to structure and shape career-path and professional success within academia. When any academic fails to adhere to these norms they are penalized; however, because women academics continue to have more childrearing responsibility as women, academic mothers are penalized by these norms of academia far more than normative academic fathers. Consequently, as we detail next, academia reinforces rather than chal-lenges women's split subjectivity—whether intended or not—while also demanding that academic mothers adhere to the institutionalized unen-cumbered-by-family-life norms that drive career-path success in academia and, subsequently, make academia as an institution not nearly as liberal and progressive for academic mothers as many believe.

Childrearing Responsibilities: Impeding Career Progress

Recent studies of both academic women and mothers (Mason and Goulden, "Do Babies Matter?", "Do Babies Matter (II)?"; Wolfinger, Mason, and Goulden), for example, reveal that gender discrimination more generally and specifically against academic mothers continues to be widespread in academia, primarily due to women's ongoing caregiv-ing responsibilities. Indeed, even though more and more women are completing Ph.D.s and are entering the academic "pipeline," academic mothers do not have gender equity with male academics, including male academics who also have children. Mary Ann Mason and Marc Goul-den ("Do Babies (II)"), for example, argue that "Even though women make up nearly half of the Ph.D. population, they are not advancing at the same rate as men to the upper ranks of the professoriate; many are dropping out of the race" (11).

The primary reason women are dropping out or "leaking out of the pipeline" is because having children penalizes academic mothers far more than it does normative academic fathers, while sometimes having children even benefits academic fathers. Mason and Goulden ("Do Babies (II)") even wryly argue "'Married with children' is the success formula for men, but the opposite is true for women, for whom there is a serious 'baby gap'" (11). More pointedly, in their earlier essay, Mason and Goulden also note "there is a consistent and large gap in achieving tenure between women who have early babies and men who have early babies [having a baby prior to five years after a parent completes his or her Ph.D.], and this gap is surprisingly uniform across the disciplines and across types of institutions" ("Do Babies Matter?" 24). They also note, "surprisingly, having early babies seems to help men; men who have early babies achieve tenure at slightly higher rates than people who do not have early babies" (24). The opposite is the case for women who have early babies. Consequently, Mason and Goulden ("Do Babies Matter?") find that women with early babies often "do not get as far as ladder-rank jobs" and often make family-work choices that "force them to leave the academy or put them into the second tier of faculty: the lecturers, adjuncts, and part-time faculty" (24).

Moreover, Mason and Goulden's general findings are also confirmed by The American Association of University Professors (AAUP). In their 2001 "Statement of Principles on Family Responsibility and Academic Work," the AAUP reveals

> although increasing numbers of women have entered academia, their academic status has been slow to improve: women remain disproportionately represented within instructor, lecturer, un-ranked positions; more than 57 percent of those holding such positions are women while among full professors only 26 percent are women; likewise among full-time faculty women, only 48 percent are tenured whereas 68 percent of men are. (55)

Even though more women are earning their doctorates, as Alice Fothergill and Kathryn Feltey also note, "the structure of tenure-track jobs has not changed in any real way to accommodate them" (17). Perhaps this is why, they continue, "the number of women in tenure track jobs has *declined*: from 46 percent in 1977 to 32 percent in 1995" (17). This research on motherhood in academia shows, as noted by Angela Simeone, that:

> marriage and family, while having a positive effect on the [academic] careers of men, has a negative effect on the progress of women's careers. Married women, particularly with children are more likely to have dropped out of graduate school, have interrupted or abandoned their careers, be unemployed or employed in a job unrelated to their training, or to hold lower academic rank. (12)

Indeed, "university settings have been found to be so hostile to women," as Fothergill and Feltey observe, "that the 'Ivory Tower' has been called the 'Toxic Tower'[5] by some in academia" (9). Thus, the research is clear: academic norms regularly have harmful effects on academic women's careers once they become mothers.

Ideal-Worker Norms: Creating a Maternal Wall for Academic Mothers

Academic mothers also face the same maternal wall that other professional women face. Joan Williams' groundbreaking work in *Unbending Gender: Why Family and Work Conflict and What To Do About It*, for example, explores how the ideal-worker theory shapes professional and managerial workplaces, including academia. Williams argues that the ideal worker is the unencumbered worker—unencumbered by family responsibilities—and that this idea is based on a traditional, heterosexual, married-couple model of men as paid at work and women at home tending to children and family-life issues. Based on this theory, professional institutions assume and expect the ideal worker to: work uninterrupted across their career with no time off for family responsibilities, prioritize career success, and change work hours and even geographic location as needed to advance a career. Even though this theory is based on traditional, heterosexual, and gender norms, it still applies across professional institutions, including academia.

Because women, including academic women, still have more responsibility for childcare, rearing, and family-life management, Williams concludes that mothers face a maternal wall because they are unable to meet these ideal-worker norms. In fact, Williams defines the maternal wall as "bias and stereotyping that affect mothers in particular as opposed to women in general" (97). The maternal wall manifests itself in both obvious and subtle ways to include negative competence assumptions (once mothers, women are regarded as less committed to their careers), negative prescriptive stereotyping—both benevolent and hostile—(as mothers, it is assumed that women are or should be more feminine and maternal and be devoted to family; and, if they are not, then, they are viewed as too masculine) and attribution bias (the assumption that if mothers are away from or late to work, then, it is because of their children) (97). The maternal wall, Williams continues, is made up of three inter-connected practices that, in her words, "drive mothers out of the workforce of their 'own choice'"; they are: "the executive schedule (extensive overtime), the marginalization of part-time workers, and the expectation that workers who are 'executive material' will relocate their families to take a better job" (70).

Clearly, the literature described above reveals that women's childrearing responsibilities and the maternal wall impede academic mothers' ability to be successful within academia's ideal-work norms. Even so, many academics—male and female, professors and administrators—continue to believe that academia as a professional institution is better for women in general and mothers specifically. These beliefs are so persistent that it would almost be counter intuitive to suggest otherwise and even heresy to argue academia may be more problematic in key ways for academic mothers than other professions, especially law and medicine. We are willing, however, to make that heretical argument in order to continue to clarify the extent to which academia is liberal and progressive for unencumbered men and women *rather than academic mothers* and to continue to reveal the ways academia as an institution further reinforces rather than challenges academic women's post-second wave subjectivity.

Is Academia Really Better for Mothers than Other Professions? Not Always

When comparing professions, it is important to remember that all professional women have been largely unsuccessful in their attempts to wed motherhood with a career. A study cited by Crittenden, for example, shows that fewer than 20 percent of college-educated baby boomer women have managed to achieve both motherhood and a career by their late thirties or forties; another study shows "that baby boomer women without children have been twice as successful in achieving a career as the women with children" (32). Sylvia Hewlett's study, reported in her best selling book, *Creating a Life*, found that "across a range of professions, high achieving women continue to have an exceedingly hard time combining career and family: thirty-three percent of high-achieving woman and forty-nine percent of ultra-achieving women are childless at age 40; (this compares to twenty-five percent of high-achieving men and nineteen percent for ultra-achieving men)" (86). Hewlett concludes that "the more successful the woman, the less likely it is she will find a husband or bear a child. For men the reverse is true. The more successful the man, the more likely he is to be married with children" (42). Investigating professions as diverse as medicine, law, business and government service, Crittenden concludes that while women were entering these professions in record numbers, few women were represented at the senior levels of the profession and most of these women were childless.

Even though all professional women face barriers wedding motherhood and professional life, academic mothers actually seem to face more challenges than women in other professions, particularly law and medicine. A significant, and to many a surprising, finding of Hewlett's research, for example, was the fact that female academics have the highest rate of childlessness (43 percent) (97). Likewise a 1988 Canadian Association of University Teachers report stated that "of all the professions, that of university teaching is the one in which women have the least number of children" (cited in Dagg and Thompson 84). Teresa M. Cooney and Peter Uhlenberg in their 1989 article "Family-Building Patterns of Professional Women: A Comparison of Lawyers, Physicians and Post-Secondary Teachers," developed from a study of United States 1980 State Census of the Population, similarly found that lawyers and teachers are more likely to be childless than are physicians and that physicians tend to have more children than lawyers or teachers do (752). After ten years of marriage, the rate of childlessness among lawyers and teachers is approximately 25-30 percent greater than that among physicians. And among those aged 35-39, teachers are significantly more likely than both physicians and lawyers to be childless. And post-secondary teachers in this age group have fewer children than both lawyers and physicians: the mean number of children for women with children is, for physicians: 2.18, for lawyers: 1.93, and for post-secondary teachers: 1.80.

Significantly, Nicholas Wolfinger, Mary Ann Mason and Marc Goulden in their 2008 article "Alone in the Ivory Tower: How Birth Events Vary Among Fast-Track Professionals" found that these statistics have remained largely unchanged over the last two decades. Their review of the 2000 census PUMS (Public Use Micro Sample) shows that "physicians have the highest rate of birth events followed by attorneys and academics" (i). Moreover, their study also shows that:

> Male physicians and lawyers are the most likely to have babies in the household, whereas women faculty are the least likely. Female physicians, male faculty and female lawyers are in the middle. Although female physicians and lawyers have a higher rate of birth events than male faculty from ages 30-39, male faculty from ages 25-29 and from ages 40-44 have more babies in the household. Nevertheless, both male and female faculty have fewer babies than do members of other professions. Finally, all groups except faculty family have the most birth events in their early thirties. For female faculty the peak years are the late thirties. Note also that these patterns of birth events diverge substantially for those of the male and female population in general. (8)

Furthermore, "while faculty overall are less likely than physicians to have a baby in the household, the disparity is larger for women than men, with female faculty 41 percent less likely than female physicians to have had a recent birth event. Female lawyers are also less likely than female physicians to have a baby in the household, with 23 percent lower odds" (11). In other words, the number of children a professional has is determined by gender—professional men have more babies than professional women—and, among women, *by profession*—the number of children is determined by the profession within which a woman works.

Accounting for the Baby Disparity among Professions

The above studies analyze the data to determine reasons for this disparity in birth events among female professionals. The key variables appear to be marriage, income, and the training required for each profession. Wolfinger, Mason and Goulden's study shows that "female faculty is less likely to be married than female physicians: 61 percent of female faculty and 59 percent of female lawyers are partnered, compared to 70 percent of physicians. Female faculty is the most likely (13 percent) of the three professions to be separated, divorced or widowed" (12). However, what also needs to be asked is: Why do female faculty have lower rates of marriage and higher rates of separation and divorce?

The first variable is related to income differences among the three professions. In relation to income, female professors earn less than both lawyers and physicians: starting salaries for physicians is about US $120,000, $60,000 for a lawyer, and $51,000 for a professor (Wolfinger, Mason and Goulden, 5). This higher income, as Wolfinger, Mason and Goulden explain, enables female physicians "to pay for childcare or provide their partners with the opportunity to be stay-at-home fathers" (12). Similarly, Cooney and Uhlenberg found that

> for women aged 35-39, marriage is associated with a 17 percent *increase* in income for female physicians while it relates to a 19 percent and 15 percent *loss* in income for lawyers and teachers respectively. (736)

Moreover, "for female physicians aged 35-30 who live alone with children, they earn 17 percent less, whereas teachers and lawyers earn 27 percent and 31 percent less respectively" (756). In other words, and, as Cooney and Uhlenberg explain, "not only does it appear that women physicians experience relatively small losses in their human capital investments and relatively large net gains when they marry and/or have children, but also women physicians who follow these family paths earn higher incomes, on average, than women lawyers and teachers who completely forgo such family roles" (756). Again, what needs to be asked and what will be considered below is why the profession of medicine, as compared to those of law and post-secondary teaching, allow for not only higher numbers of children for women but also higher incomes when married and less of a salary decrease when single.

Another variable or piece of the puzzle is the training required for professions or, as Cooney and Uhlenberg describe it, the different struc-tured career paths among academic, legal, and medical professions. As Cooney and Uhlenberg observe, "lawyers who enter in law firms and teachers who accept university appointments typically work in a position for five to seven years before being considered for partnership or tenure respectively. In contrast, after their training, physicians move almost immediately into a group or private practice, or gain hospital privileges" (757). Moreover, as Cooney and Uhlenberg go on to explain, "Women lawyers and teachers may delay marriage, remarriage or childbearing until they have passed their major career hurdles" (757). A similar explanation is offered by Wolfinger, Mason and Goulden. They write:

> The unique career structure of academia offers no good op-portunity to take time out to have children. After four to eight years in graduate school, assistant professors have about six years to publish or perish. Only after tenure and promotion from assistant to associate professor are faculty assured of job security. The median doctorate recipient is already 33 or 34 years of age; after a probationary assistant professorship, close to 40. In terms of career development this would be an ideal time for female professors to start their families, but biologically they are already past prime childbearing age. (4)

Indeed, as Mason elaborates further in a 2003 interview, "Academic women are expected to work hardest during their tenure-track years, precisely when their biological clocks are ticking the loudest … these busy career-building years are also the most likely the reproductive years" (cited in Wilson 3).

Academic women's fertility is also affected by kinds of jobs available in academia. According to Wolfinger, Mason and Goulden, another impediment to academic fertility is the paucity of well-paid part-time professional options that allow an academic mother to "stay in the game" or maintain her professional status while also mothering. As they describe the issue:

> Academics who want to work less than full-time generally must resort to the reduced pay and status of adjunct professorships. In contrast, both medicine and law presumably offer more op-portunities for part-time employment.... Not all lawyers [for example] aspire to have high-powered corporate careers. Also the failure to make partner is not as catastrophic as failing to get tenure: one can simply move to another law firm. Faculty usually has to relocate if they do not get tenure but wish to remain in academia. (4)

Finally, the highly specialized training of academe makes it nearly impossible for a professor in the humanities or liberal arts to find employment outside of the university upon graduation; a physician or lawyer would likely be able to find well-paying work outside of their profession—in government, the non-profit sector, consulting and so forth: in contrast, a Ph.D. in medieval history has only a university to turn to for employment. Indeed, as is often joked in Liberal Arts Ph.D. programs across North America: it is either a spot in a university or one in the welfare line. In academe there are few if any "off ramps" to well-paid part-time academic work or to full-time work outside of university teaching. Indeed, as Kathleen Christensen, director of the Workplace, Workforce and Working Families at the Alfred P. Sloan Foundation comments: "There is only one genuinely legitimate career path in the academy. It's very rigid, up or out, and you have to get on and stay on or you're penalized if you deviate" (qtd. in Wilson 3).

The literature reviewed above reveals that the relatively low wages of professors, lower rates of marriage for academics, and the lengthy and highly specialized career path of post-secondary teaching all support our contention that the structure of academia and concurrent norms make academia, in several key ways, more challenging for mothers in general and specifically in comparison to law and medicine. However, we would suggest yet another contributing factor that is unique to academia—one not fully considered in the above articles and that has particular relevance to the concept of women's post-second wave split subjectivity we are exploring in this introduction—is that the unbounded nature of academic work is incompatible with motherwork-caregiving, family-life management, and the psychological responsibility of caregiving. In other words, we are suggesting that the unbounded culture of academic work *in relation to* the unbounded nature of motherwork are incompatible and create unique-to-academic mothers almost-impossible-to-meet conflicting and contradictory requirements for success *as both mothers and academics*.

Before further substantiating this claim, it is important to clarify a key place where academia is actually less demanding than law and medicine: the number of hours worked each week. In the articles noted previously, the authors argue that hours worked, in addition to income, marriage and career path, is a key variable in determining the likelihood of women having children in the legal, medical, and academic professions. Wolfinger,

Mason and Goulden report that "in contrast to their male counterparts, working long hours is associated with decreased fertility among professionals. Most notably, putting in 40-49 hours a week lowers the odds of women fast-track professionals having a baby by 37 percent; working 50-59 hours a week decreases the odds by 54 percent and working 60 more hours deceases them by 63 percent" (11). However, they go on to say that "among female professionals, faculty work the least, with a median 40 hours per week; physicians work the most, with a median work of 50 hours; and lawyers are in the middle, at 45 hours" (11). Significantly, while overall increased hours are associated with decreased fertility, female professors with the fewest work hours have the lowest rate of fertility.

Cooney and Uhlenberg's study reveals a similar inconsistency. Their study reveals that "physicians, on average, work five to ten more hours per week than are lawyers. Teachers are working the fewest hours" (754). However, "although physicians and their husbands," Cooney and Uhlenberg write, "work more hours than other professional women and their husbands, they are still more likely to have children, and more of them, than these other couples" (754). These numbers suggest that it is not the hours worked that determine fertility but the nature of the work done and whether such is computable with motherhood.

The Unbounded Nature of Academia

We also believe, given these numbers, that it is *the specific culture of unboundedness* of academic work and not the hours undertaken to perform this work that also makes academia particularly incompatible with motherwork. Indeed, the work of academia, more so than law and medicine, lacks clear boundaries and, rather than make "juggling it all"—career, children, and family—easier, this lack of boundaries actually makes it more challenging. In a 2001 bulletin, for example, the American Association of University Professors noted "The lack of a clear boundary in academic lives between work and family has, at least historically, meant that work has been all pervasive, often to the detriment of the family" (qtd. in Ward and Wolf-Wendel 1).

Moreover, in their 2004 article "Managing Complex Roles in Research Universities" Kelly Ward and Lisa Wolf-Wendel consider three theoretical models—role conflict, ideal worker and male clockwork—to examine what has been termed *the unboundedness of academic culture* that makes university work particularly incompatible with motherhood. The first, role conflict, they explain, "posits that individuals have limited time and energy, and adding extra roles and responsibilities necessarily creates tensions between competing demand and a sense of overload" (Marshall and Barnett qtd. in Ward and Wendel 1). The second theoretical framework, ideal worker, they argue is particularly prevalent in academe as it requires, in their words, "a singleness of purpose that parenthood does not always allow" (3). The third explanation, male clockwork, as discussed above, assumes "an idealized trajectory of a faculty career (i.e. from graduate school, to assistant, associate, full professor, in direct succession) may not describe the actual or expected career of an academic woman. For some women, the balance between work and family disrupts the standard timetable for the ideal career trajectory" (3). Though the word *unboundedness* is not used by Ward and Wolf-Wendel, the concepts and terms of their three-explanation model—singleness of purpose, overload, standard timetables—speak to and further confirm the unboundedness of academic work.

When most professors do their work, unlike many other professions, much of that work is not done at the workplace or office. Professors do not normally work set hours in an office as most professionals do: their work is done in the evenings, and on weekends, and often undertaken at home. As well, university teaching is less task-driven than other careers: unlike law or medicine where the work and its completion are clearly defined and marked as when a course case or a surgery is concluded, academic work has less clearly defined boundaries of completion: there are always more articles to read to develop an academic essay and another student waiting to discuss their assignment. Moreover, university teaching, unlike most careers, is composed of three very distinct jobs—teaching, including graduate supervision, research and university service—and all are tasks that not only are never-ending but require different, and often conflicting, skills and scheduling. As well, the reflection and writing needed for scholarly research, the foremost demand of university teachers on the tenure track, requires large and uninterrupted blocks of time for it to be undertaken and completed successfully.

Finally, in academe there are less definable measures of achievement: a professor dedicated to teaching will still have students who fail their course, and a professor committed to scholarly excellence and who is awarded research funding is always aware that there other, more prestigious grants, that should be applied for. Indeed, the academic career, as Lotte Bailyn of the Massachusetts Institute of Technology acutely observes is,

> paradoxical. Despite its advantages of independence and flex-ibility, it is psychologically difficult. The lack of ability to limit work, the tendency to compare oneself primarily to the excep-tional giants in one's field, and the high incidence of overload make it particularly difficult for academics to find satisfactory integration of work with private life.... It is the *unbounded* na-ture of the academic career that is at the heart of the problem. Time is critical for professors, because there is not enough of it to do all the things their jobs require: teaching, research, and institutional and professional service. It is therefore impossible for faculty to protect other aspects of their lives. (qtd. in "State-ment of Principles on Family Responsibilities and Academic Work" 220)

We would suggest, then, that it is the "unboundedness" of academic work that is particularly incompatible with motherhood because the lack of clear boundaries between work and family makes it difficult for academic mothers to manage "it all."

The unboundedness of academia is compounded, however, by the requirement of being disembodied—that the body and its functions, particularly reproductive functions and the life-cycles associated with it (pregnancy, birthing, nursing, and providing ongoing sustenance to self and others) are to be kept separate from intellectual life for career-path success. As we have tried to sketch above, because of the ideal-worker norms, the long time of training, which coincides with women's repro-ductive timeline, and the limitless nature of the work of academe, ideal academic workers must be disembodied to be successful. These require-ments have worked for men because of the traditional gendered divi-sion of labour in homes and society: normative men have had women to do the necessary home/family/body work that all people require to live. Without children, women are able to function as disembodied and unencumbered workers more or less like men (although, it is crucial to note that all women still do more community/family work, i.e., look after elderly/have more self-body work to do/community work, etc.) if they are not mothers. But once they become mothers, such unencumbered and disembodied work is impossible because mothers are embodied because of pregnancy, childbirth, nursing, and the physical care that is required of children, but especially young children. Moreover, because mothering requires embodiment not just to be a good mother but to insure the welfare of children, when meeting these demands, it is especially hard for academic mothers to continue to do the disembodied cerebral job of the mind in terms of reading, thinking, and writing that is required for the life of an "intellectual."

Of course, academic mothers can try to fake an unencumbered disembodied self by passing as a non mother, i.e., being in the "motherhood closet" or, if a mother is economically privileged, then, she can "download" such work to others by buying reproductive caregiving, usually from other less privileged women. Of course, only privileged women are financially able to "down load" carework to others; as well many intensive mothers are reluctant to do so as such fundamentally violates the norms of intensive mothering. Thus, the unbounded nature of academia also requires a disembodiment, both of which are fundamentally at odds with the unbounded nature of the intensive mothering ideology and mothers' embodiment that begins first with pregnancy and continues throughout the life-cycle of children.

Thus, ironically, there is an "unbounded" culture at the heart of academia that is similar to the unbounded demands at the heart of the intensive mothering ideology, such that the norms of academic life are incompatible with the norms of intensive mothering. In short, we are suggesting that academic mothers' *specific* post-second wave subjectivity has two contradictory and impossible demands to be "unbounded." On one hand, the unbounded nature of academia demands and requires unencumberedness from family-life and childrearing responsibilities and disembodiment at its core for professional and career success. And, on the other hand, ironically, post-second wave intensive mothering stipulates that "good" mothers must be without boundaries when it comes to their mothering and maternal thinking, which demands and requires at its core that good mothers are unencumbered by professional work, or at least that mothers act as if they are when they are mothering their children. To put it another way: intensive mothering suggests that good mothers act like they are unencumbered by work demands, even when they are encumbered by professional life, while academia suggests good academics act like they are unencumbered by motherwork, even when they are encumbered by those demands.

WHAT ARE ACADEMIC MOTHERS TO DO?

As we have tried to show in this introduction, exploring academic motherhood more fully requires a new framework that contextualizes academic motherhood within women's post-second wave subjectivity and intensive mothering, the specific structures and career-path norms of academia, the unique and surprising ways academia, in fact, makes it more difficult for professional women to be both academics and mothers, and, finally, in relation to the ways that these factors create a "perfect storm" of difficulty when these factors converge such that academic mothers are living and thinking within two almost-impossible-to-meet requirements both to mother and profess intensively and without boundaries.

In the context of academia, then, as this introduction has revealed, having this new framework is crucial to exploring in more complex and nuanced ways the "perfect storm" that has emerged as a result of the daily tensions academic mothers face in our "post-second wave feminist" cultural milieu and academic context. Clearly, our post-second wave context necessitates answering the kinds of questions being asked by post-second wave graduate students—"Is it really possible to balance children and the tenure track?" "Would a non-faculty position in academe make it easier to be an involved parent?" and "Should I just leave the ivory tower if I want a career and children?"—because, implicitly, the focal point of these questions is the key tensions post-second wave academic mothers face between newly gained gender equity for unencumbered women and old gender-based discrimination against academic mothers specifically and between the unbounded nature of both academia and intensive mothering. Indeed, these kinds of questions are some of the most crucial questions that need to be addressed now, specifically *as mothers* within academia.

But, these are not the only kinds of questions that need to be addressed if we hope to understand academic motherhood—the ideas, institutional assumptions, and organizing systems that shape academic women's understanding of motherhood within academia—in all its complexities, nuances, and sources of tension between the old and the new, between academic mothers' conflicting demands of unboundedness. Indeed, *as academics* we also need to ask and answer the following theoretical question in order think through academic motherhood: what are the various different intellectual ideas that can be used to continue to understand better the challenges, strategies, and possibilities that exist for academic mothers as they manage their post-second wave split subjectivity? Asking and answering questions about being an academic and a mother and questions grounded in theoretical ideas will allow us to use a new framework for exploring academic motherhood, and doing so also allows us to understand more fully the challenges, strategies, and possibilities that currently exist when academic mothers detail what it means *to be* an academic mother and *to think* about academic motherhood.

ACADEMIC MOTHERHOOD: CHALLENGES, STRATEGIES, AND POSSIBILITIES

To explore thoroughly what it means to be an academic mother and to think about academic motherhood, then, necessitates multifaceted and interdisciplinary approaches to delve into the personal and institutional challenges academic women face; requires varied strategies to manage those challenges and tensions, and necessitates looking at different theoretical possibilities for how we think about and understand what it means to be and think as academic mothers within our post-second wave context. In short, we need both personal narrative—mothers' lived experiences as academic mothers—*and* academic theories and ideas to unpack the complexities academic mothers face and live each day. To do so, then, rather than rely on only personal narrative or intellectual ideas/research, all the contributors here draw on and utilize intellectual ideas or theories to help them frame their discussion of academic motherhood. Moreover, with only two exceptions, contributors also utilize narratives—either their own and/or those of other academic women—in their use of academic ideas.

Of course, the use of narrative in feminist thinking, critical inquiry, and/or political action has been a hallmark of much feminist scholarship. Indeed, from the early days of 1960s and 1970s North American feminism, the idea and slogan, "the personal is political," focused feminists on listening to and theorizing women's lives from their own stories and narratives. Moreover, much feminist work (Belenky et al.; Gilligan;

Harding; Hirsch) in the late 1980s and early 1990s was grounded in women's narrative, voices, and "ways of knowing." Within the context of motherhood studies, however, it was Adrienne Rich in *Of Women Born* who first intertwined her own experiences as a mother of three boys, her own narrative and stories (e.g., her oft-noted Vermont vacation), to help her think through and explore motherhood and mothering. This book, then, is situated within both the long history of feminist use of narrative and Rich's landmark approach in contributors' use of narrative and theory.

As such, this book explores how *both* research and narrative can inform contemporary understandings of academic motherhood, particularly in regard to understanding the post-second wave institutional and personal challenges of academia, strategies of resistance and empowerment for academic mothers, and considers the possibilities presented when various different theoretical ideas and perspectives are or can be utilized in the service of understanding motherhood in academia. Thus, while previous collections such as *Mama, PhD* (Evans and Grant) and *Parenting and Professing* (Hile Bassett) examined being a mother academic from narrative or "lived experience" and others, "Mothers in the Academe" in the *Journal of the Association for Research on Mothering* explored mother academics' experiences from a theoretical perspective, to our knowledge, this is the first book both to utilize the idea of a post-second wave split subjectivity as the overall framework for exploring this topic area and to incorporate both narrative and theory to strengthen the interdisciplinary dialogue among academic motherhood, intellectual ideas, and personal narrative.

OVERVIEW OF CHAPTERS

To explore our contemporary post-second wave complexities, this book looks at and is organized around three area of foci: both the personal and specific institutional *challenges* academic women face, the multifaceted *strategies* different academic women have implemented to manage those challenges, and investigates different theoretical *possibilities* for how we think about and understand what it means to think as academic mothers. In short, the collection of essays here, written by academic women from various different disciplines, at different stages of their academic careers, and from diverse locations from within academia, is devoted to this exploration of challenges, strategies, and theoretical possibilities. Thus, this book explores how *both* research and narrative can inform contemporary understandings of academic motherhood, particularly in regard to understanding the institutional and personal challenges of academia, strategies of resistance and empowerment for academic mothers, and considers the possibilities presented when various different theoretical ideas and perspectives are or can be utilized in the service of understanding academic motherhood today.

CHALLENGES

The chapters in *Challenges* explore the multifaceted challenges academic mothers face. The two kinds of challenges addressed in the following chapters are institutional/structural and personal. In short, each chapter in this section investigates the various structural and personal adversity academic mothers face daily. The first three chapters investigate the personal challenges academic mothers face as they negotiate the competing demands of family and work life; while the last four chapters consider such from an institutional/structural context.

In "Spies Like Us: The Lives of Double Agents Evolving Identities and Strategies of Mothers in Academe," the chapter that opens the section, Bethany Crandell Goodier explores the stories women tell about the experience of being both professor and mother and the strategies they use to maintain their professional and good mother identities at work and at home. Employing narrative interviewing techniques, Goodier interviewed twenty mother/professors from liberal arts institutions in the southeast at various stages of their careers with children ranging from eight months to eighteen years. She argues that while the women she interviewed strived to create a coherent sense of self that embraces the multifaceted elements of their lives, significant competition to this coherence exists not only from societal expectations of the separation of spheres and cultural norms surrounding motherhood and professionalism, but their own internalization of these norms. Drawing on the work of Anthony Giddens, Goodier argues the professor/mothers in this study limit the opportunities to resist dominant narratives and hegemonic influences surrounding motherhood by reinforcing (and recreating) the very systems that constrain them through the way they talk about work and home.

The following chapter "'We Shoot Our Wounded': Pregnancy, Mothering and PPD on the Tenure Track," Kerri Kearney, with the assistance of a co-author, Lucy Bailey, presents a narrative account of Kearney's experiences with pregnancy and post-partum depression (PPD) while in a tenure-track faculty position. The narrative explores the implications of her body's betrayal to a PPD diagnosis within an institution in which pregnant, mothering, and fragile bodies just don't "fit" (Pillow). The authors highlight how academic context shapes women's experiences with PPD, the particular vulnerability of non-tenured mothers, and the importance of recognizing PPD as one of many complexities of academic mothering—a condition not always recognized as such, even by other academic mothers. At a broader level, Kearney's experiences offer insights for organizational practices in emphasizing the importance of creating supportive institutional spaces for those struggling with any illness or frailty—universal human conditions that lurk around the corner for all of us.

In the third chapter, "'You Can Slip One in Between Your Thesis and Comps': Unanticipated Consequences of Having a Baby in Graduate School," Serena Patterson reveals that having a baby in graduate school seemed like a good idea at the time. People had babies all the time; how hard could it be? Twenty years later, the author looks back at and takes stock of the difficulties she faced as a graduate student mother and the long-term consequences of her decision to have a baby during graduate school. Each phase of academic life, including comprehensive exams, coursework, a clinical internship, dissertation, landing a position and teaching in a community college for fifteen years, has both shaped, and been shaped by, motherhood. Hers is a personal narrative, set within the Canadian academic landscape from the 1980s to the present.

In "Balancing Work and Family in Higher Education: Best Practices and Barriers," Heather Wyatt-Nichol, Margarita Cardona, and Karen Drake examine the tenure rate among women with young children and consider explanations for the disparities. They examine family friendly policies among a variety of U.S. colleges and universities that have been recognized for their best practices, specifically parental leave, child-care, tenure-clock stop, and active service-modified duties. They also integrate this best practices approach with results of a recent quality of life in academia survey conducted by the authors through the University of Baltimore Work/Life Balance Initiative, funded by a grant from ACE/Alfred

P. Sloan Foundation. They conclude that policies designed to eliminate or minimize structural inequality will only be effective through supportive organizational cultures and leadership that is held accountable through performance measures.

In the fifth chapter, "Solving the N Puzzle: Memoir of a Mother-Scholar," Carolyn Barber's autoethnographic memoir focuses on her three and one-half years as a graduate school mother-scholar in a Ph.D. program. Barber argues that the term *mother-academic* appears to encompass a combination of social and professional roles, with the hyphen acting as a pivot bar offering reassurance that these two roles operate in balance, never encroaching on one another. In her chapter, however, Barber shows how the hyphen is "deceitful," because it does not reveal the all-consuming, dueling nature of motherhood and academic work. She also details how hard she tried to separate these roles, because she felt she needed to and others expected her to do so in order to succeed in academia. In the end, however, as Barber reveals, she decided to "opt out" of academia rather than risk further depletion of her physical and mental health.

The following chapter, "'Which June?' What Baby?: The Continued Invisibility of Maternity in Academia," by Laura J. Beard explores the challenges that academic mothers face at the institutional or structural level, focusing particularly on some of the discriminatory microinequities that make academic career paths more difficult for academic mothers. The article draws in part from Beard's own experiences as an academic mother, in part from the experiences of colleagues at her university (many of whom did interviews available in an archive in the Women's Studies Program), and also from the experiences reported in published articles and documents, including the reports from the Modern Languages Association's Committee on the Status of Women in the Profession. She examines the inequities that exist within our academic culture and the ways in which women sometimes participate (willingly or unwillingly) in perpetuating those inequities and concludes with suggestions for making academic systems more welcoming environments for academic mothers. Michele L. Vancour in "Academic Mothers Climb the Ladder of Promotion and Tenure: One Rung at a Time," similarly examines the relationship among motherhood, role balance and health-promoting behaviors. Through in-depth interviews with seventeen academic faculty mothers of preschool children at four public universities in New England, the author uncovered challenges inherent in women's daily balancing acts, especially as these mothers pursued tenure and promotion while negotiating childcare and heavy course loads. She suggests that institutionalized family-friendly programs, policies and practices will facilitate women's progress along their career trajectory.

The final chapter in this section, by Linda Ennis, "Contract-Faculty Mothers On the Track To Nowhere," explores the lived experience of contract-faculty mothers in the Canadian university system, as opposed to tenured-faculty, for the purpose of providing a voice for these women and to give them the credibility that they seem to lack in this academic setting. Using in-depth interviews from fifteen participants, Ennis argues that her interviewees reveal that there is a two-tiered system operating in academia in the way of tenured-faculty's needs and interests taking precedence over contract-faculty, as well as a general prejudice against contract-faculty mothers on the "mommy track." These findings also included a discussion as to why they entered academia as contract-faculty and despite their oppressive situation, the reasons they remained.

STRATEGIES

The chapters in *Strategies* detail academic mothers' attempts to manage and sometimes confront the challenges academic mothers face. The authors in this section reveal various different kinds of strategies or approaches to being academic mothers. In the first chapter, "I Should Have Married Another Man; I Couldn't Do What I Do Without Him: Intimate Heterosexual Partnerships and their Impact on Mothers' Success in Academe," Andrea O'Reilly explores women's partnered heterosexual relationships and the role they play in determining mothers' success as academic workers. O'Reilly argues that the highly gendered scripts of the normative wife and husband role serve to hinder women's employment success. In particular, O'Reilly maintains that, in order to make successful academic careers possible for mothers, it is just as critical to challenge patriarchal marriage as it is the masculinist culture of academe; likewise, she argues that women must secure gender equity in the home as well as in the workplace. Sharing stories of four academic mothers, the article examines how and why traditionally gendered partnerships, particularly as they are manifested in the normative wife role, hinder a mother's success in academe. Conversely, the article shows how and why domestic relationships modeled on gender equity work to enhance such.

In "From Motherhood, Through Widowhood: The Path to Receiving the Academic Hood," Yvonne Redmond-Brown Banks asks and
answers: What is the true nature of the experience when one becomes a
widow while in pursuit of an academic-hood? Redmond-Brown Banks
provides insight, through personal narrative about the challenges faced
while mothering in academia as a widow. Her story chronicles the impact of her grief, and the lessons learned along the journey with her two
young children. The details of her unfolding grief are intertwined as she
discusses the dissertation process, the impact of keeping her full-time
job, loneliness, the voices of her children, and the overlapping influences
of each. Referencing the many cues taken from her children, as they
shared in the experience of her pursuit, allows Redmond-Brown Banks
to open the dialogue further by putting forth strategies that may help
other women who find themselves entering academia under the label of
both *widow* and *mother.*

Challenging the perceived notion that non-tenure track jobs are dis-
empowering to academic mothers, Jill M. Wood, in her chapter, "Non-
Tenure-Track Academic Work: The 'Mommy Track' or A Strategy for
Resistance?," argues that the oppressive nature of non-tenure track work
(for mothers, especially) has been well documented, but that the freeing
possibilities of such work has not yet been well established. Using radi-
cal-cultural feminist theory, Wood suggests that academic mothers who
seek to embrace their maternal desire can use non-tenure track positions
to subvert current discourses that dictate what it currently means to be a
mother in the academy. Wood's chapter weaves together feminist theory,
personal narrative, and literature on institutional barriers that serve to
keep tenure track mothers in their "place" in the University in order to
reconceptualize non-tenure track academic work as a possibility for a
subversive, transformative, and empowering life choice.

The following chapter, written by Laurie J. C. Cella, "Demeter on Strike:
Fierce Motherhood on the Picket Line and the Playground," describes
Cella's experience as a graduate student balancing the expectations of
academic life with new motherhood. In her narrative, Cella examines the
various pressures to become the "successful" graduate student with the
equally daunting expectations to be a "good" mother to her son Cody,
and in doing so, provides several strategies she developed in order to
successfully manage these unrealistic expectations for academic mothers.
First, Cella argues that academic mothers need to understand that their

work pace will shift, and they need to be prepared to let go of their pre-conceived notions of a "fast-paced" academic. Second, she underscores the importance of "mother mentors," who can provide honest, realistic advice to a new academic mom. Finally, Cella believes that creating a strong community of academic mothers who are able to support and encourage each other will give young female graduate students and untenured professors the support and confidence they need to challenge the masculine norms of academic culture.

In "Re-Writing the Script," Jennifer Hauver James begins with a personal narrative about two significant moments in the author's life as an academic mother when two impossible ideals—the junior faculty member who devotes her life to establishing her career and the mother who devotes her life to nurturing and tending to her children's every need—became crystal clear to her. Using a feminist post-structural lens, James critically reflects on the gendered understandings that serve to substantiate these two ideals. She then engages in critical autobiographical inquiry to examine the ways in which she has internalized both ideals and may act upon herself to sustain, alter or resist them. In so doing, she articulates her struggle to resist prevailing narratives and discusses strategies for naming ourselves as academic mothers.

Joanne Minaker, in "Being a Mother Academic: Or, I Didn't Get a Ph.D. to Become a Mom," thinks reflexively about the relationship between motherhood and academia. She employs a personal experiential and sociological perspective to provide the lens through which she explores what it means to be a mother academic. Written while on maternity leave from a tenured university position, the paper offers a unique vantage point from which to trace her mothering journey and work inside of academia. She argues that while the two identities and positions are mutually exclusive, mothering and academic life, are mutually reinforcing; each informed the other in direct and subtle ways. The following chapter by Rachel Epp Buller "Integrating the Personal and the Professional," also argues against the tenure track as the singular path to academic greatness. In a narrative approach based on her own experiences, Buller demonstrates how the alternative path of the independent scholar can offer more diverse work options and provide far more flexibility than the tenure track. Buller outlines concrete steps for other scholars seeking to work outside the academy and presents her own integration of personal and professional interests as one possible strategy.

In "Halving It Both Ways: Co-Parenting in an Academic Couple," Karen Christopher and Avery Kolers explore individual and institutional level strategies for navigating and resisting the gendered university. They situate their own personal experiences attempting to resist both a neo-traditional family configuration and ideal-worker norms within the theory of the university as a gendered organization. They find that the flexibility offered by faculty positions facilitates co-parenting to some degree, but also requires continual resistance to the gendered model of the ideal worker. They conclude with implications and recommendations, but warn that some putative improvements to university policies and practices may exacerbate gender and class inequalities among university faculty.

Finally, Marta McClintock-Comeaux, in "Great Expectations for Moms in Academia: Work/Life Integration and Addressing Cognitive Dissonance" begins by presenting one woman's narrative navigating the motherhood/academia journey. In an effort to explore and understand the complexities of embracing multiple roles, the chapter moves to an analysis of several work/life integration theories, including: the expansive hypothesis, the scarcity hypothesis, the ideal worker theory, and the intensive mothering lens. The author hypothesizes that the competing tensions of conflicting, overwhelming expectations specific to women result in cognitive dissonance. The chapter concludes with strategies that could be employed and changes that could be made that would alleviate some of the stress created by cognitive dissonance for academic moms.

POSSIBILITIES

Unlike the *Strategies* section, in the final section of the book, *Possibilities*, contributors primarily focus on rethinking intellectual ideas and/or theoretical approaches to understanding academic motherhood. All of the authors in this section do so in the hopes of thinking through both the problems and/or challenges of current theories and/or specific ideas in order to continue to refine how we can or should theorize academic motherhood.

In "Autonomy in a Chilly Climate: Authority, Self-Confidence, and Resistance," Sylvia Burrow shows that a climate in which mother academics are not considered serious academics can erode self-confidence, introducing doubt over child or career choices while undermining authority and integrity. Burrow takes a philosophical approach revealing costs of impaired self-confidence for autonomy, understood as a capacity for self-determination that is developed through and deeply affected by social relations. Her article points toward resistance as a means of cultivating autonomy: through resisting masculine stereotypes and ideals of the model scholar, academic mothers can regain or advance autonomy.

The next chapter, by D. Lynn O'Brien Hallstein, "Being and Thinking Between Second and Third Wave Feminisms: Theorizing a Strategic Alliance Frame to Understand Academic Motherhood," explores the contemporary tensions that she sees as a feminist maternal scholar who has one foot in second and one foot in third wave feminisms. She does so with an eye toward laying a theoretical foundation for an alliance between feminist maternal scholarship and third wave intersectionality, between her second and third wave commitments, as a means to think more carefully about what theoretical possibilities can exist to help us better understand academic motherhood. She ultimately argues that an alliance or partnership between feminist maternal scholars and intersectional thinkers requires feminist maternal scholars to incorporate more intersectional principles to move beyond the additive approach to understanding women's lives and to begin to acknowledge the intra-women oppression that permeates contemporary maternity. Conversely, she also argues that intersectional work must recognize that the ideological and material reality of contemporary maternity requires a strategic focus on gender and feminism, capital "F" feminism, while also suggesting an alliance perspective requires an eradication of the younger-older, matrophobic generational structure that undergirds third wave intersectionality. Finally, she concludes with a preliminary discussion of what a future alliance, grounded in a politics of accountability, must entail theoretically as we begin to develop specific strategies of resistance against the barriers and challenges that impede academic mothers.

Employing an autoethnographic approach, Amber Kinser examines the limits of feminism and academic training in offering women a sense of clarity and stability in motherhood, and the possibility of living fully anyway in "The Cost of an Education: Exploring the Extended Reach of Academe in Family Life." She grapples with the isolation of families holding academic knowledge while surrounded by a pervasive U.S. "mythos" of parenting that stands counter to that knowledge. In uprooting the mythos and exposing the unnecessary constrictions that lay beneath its surface, Kinser works to separate maternal worth from adult obsession about and intrusion into children's lives and to foster a sense of greater comfort amidst the messiness of academic family life.

While, in "Basketball, Skating, and Scholarship: Or How to do Research from the Bench, the Rink, and the Car," Elizabeth Podnieks discusses how her work as an Associate Professor of English and maternal scholar has influenced her role as a mother to two children who respectively play basketball and figure-skate an average of five times a week. Her chapter focuses on her sense of self as an empowered academic mother and maternal academic, and on how her research in Modernist Life Writing and Motherhood Studies intersects in positive and rewarding ways with her life as a mother. Through a theoretical reading of mothering in academe coupled with a personal narrative exploring her experiences editing and writing maternal texts while raising her children, she considers the symbiotic, challenging, and ultimately empowering consequences that emerge from the conflation of her domestic and professional, private and public, maternal and academic selfhoods, drives, and passions.

Masako Kato, in "Academic Mother Crossing Linguistic and Cultural Borders," offers a self-reflective account of her experiences as a Japanese mother and as a linguistic anthropologist during her dissertation research. It specifically looks into the complicated relationship between the responsibilities of mothering and working, and the ways in which they affect her identity and ideological orientation. While recalling and analyzing the challenges of managing these responsibilities during fieldwork, the author explores the constructive nature of academic motherhood. The author finds that being a mother and a researcher worked collaboratively to enhance her abilities in each role and allowed her to successfully finish the research because it gave her opportunities to constantly have a dialogue with her informants and herself. She then suggests a possibility of academic motherhood: that motherhood and work are not in a conflicting relationship but in a dialogic relationship which strengthen and maximize the success of both.

In "Mothers in Law: Re-thinking Equality to Do Justice to Children in Academia," Isabelle Martin and Julie Paquin explore the divide between the legal discourse on women's rights to work and their own personal experiences and needs as academic mothers. Drawing upon their experience as mothers, graduate students and legal scholars, they identify some of the limitations in the capacity of current Canadian legal conceptions of equality to provide appropriate solutions to the problems faced by academic mothers. They conclude that many of the challenges faced by mothers could be addressed by reframing the legal understanding of equality in a way allowing for the full recognition of the relational aspects of parenthood, and describe the possibilities to support academic mothers and transform academia deriving from such a transformation of the notion of equality.

The final chapter of the book, written by Jamie Huff, Sarah Coté Hampson, and Corinne M. Tagliarina, "Liberalism's Leaky Legacy: Theory and the Narratives of Graduate Student Mothers," explores contemporary liberal theory and the structure and discourses of academia. Using in-depth interviews with 34 graduate student mothers, conducted at the University of Connecticut, the authors connect three theoretical frameworks with the lived narratives of the women interviewed in order to critique the liberal architecture of academia, which they believe has failed graduate student women. They suggest that their interviewees demonstrate that pregnancy and mothering present graduate students with a complicated situation in which the academy's liberal basis makes effective maternity policy a difficult achievement. Additionally, they argue that the silence of those women who have "leaked" from the academic pipeline has not been adequately addressed by existing academic policies, and the authors shed light on what academia loses when it does not retain the distinct voices of mothers.

CONCLUSIONS

Taken as a whole, the 24 chapters in this book reveal that academic motherhood within our post-second wave context is and will remain challenging. Indeed, the chapters reveal that contemporary motherhood is neither straightforward nor simple. The chapters, in fact, have considered the ongoing specific challenges academic mothers have faced, the strategies they have developed to negotiate the challenges of their post-second wave split subjectivity, and new intellectual possibilities for how we think about contemporary academic motherhood, while revealing that much more work needs to be done and that the conversation within a post-second wave context must continue.

Even so, we think that two general conclusions emerge from the book about where and how feminist maternal scholars can focus attention if they want to challenge and change key issues that face academic mothers.

First, we believe that the chapters reveal that it is now time to focus on maternal empowerment or *empowerment specifically for mothers*. When we use the term *maternal empowerment*, we mean a state or place in which mothers are or may be empowered. But what do we mean when we theorize upon or lobby for maternal empowerment? We suggest that maternal empowerment is best understood as an oppositional stance that seeks to counter and correct the many ways that the intensive mothering ideology causes mothering to be limiting or oppressive to women. Earlier, we suggested that intensive mothering is at the heart of mothers' post-second wave split subjectivity and entails at least three core beliefs: 1) children need and require constant and ongoing nurturing by their biological mothers who are single-handedly responsible for meeting these needs; 2) in meeting those needs, mothers must rely on experts to guide them; and 3) mothers must lavish enormous amounts of time and energy on their children. As such, embedded within these core principles is the demand that good mothers are unbounded by or unencumbered from all other life obligations when they mother. In short, good mothers should always put their children's needs before their own, their work, or anything else.[6]

In addition to requiring the kind of unboundedness discussed earlier in this chapter, intensive mothering specifically and motherwork in general are oppressive to women because both necessitate the repression or denial of the mother's own selfhood; as well, it assigns mothers all the responsibility for mothering but gives them no real power from which to mother while also demanding limitless devotion to children. Such "powerless responsibility," to use Adrienne Rich's term, denies a mother the authority and agency to determine her own experiences of mothering, while also discouraging any legitimate form of boundary setting for the mother to take care of herself. As well, it results in most women mothering alone in the isolation of their home, feeling overwhelmed and exhausted, as many of chapters in this book detail. Moreover, since no mother can achieve idealized motherhood, women bring to their lived experiences of mothering self-recrimination, anxiety, doubt, and guilt, which are only further encouraged by the institutionalized career-path norms and ideal-worker expectations of academia. In turn, mothers who do not seek to achieve idealised motherhood, either by choice or circumstance, are labelled 'unfit' mothers who will find themselves and their mothering under public scrutiny and surveillance. Finally, in defining mothering as private and non-political work, patriarchal motherhood restricts the way mothers can and do affect social change through feminist childrearing and maternal activism.

Maternal empowerment, whether it be termed feminist (Gordon; Glickman; Green; O'Reilly, *Mother Outlaws*), outlaw (O'Reilly, *Mother Outlaws*; Rich), radical (Copper), rebellious (Douglas and Michaels), or hip (Gore) seeks to confer to mothers the agency, authority, authenticity and autonomy denied to them in patriarchal motherhood (O'Reilly, 2004a, 2004b, 2006a, 2006b, 2007, 2008). As Fiona Green has observed ("Feminist Mothers," "Developing a Feminist Motherline"), empowered or outlaw mothers, "seek to live Rich's emancipatory vision of motherhood and, driven by their feminist consciousness, their intense love for their children and the need to be true to themselves, their families, and their parenting, [these] feminist mothers choose to parent in a way that challenges the status quo" ("Feminist Mothers" 130). Erica Horwitz's study (2003, 2004) on empowered mothering reveals that the practice of outlaw motherhood may be characterized by seven themes: The importance of mothers meeting their own needs; being a mother does not fulfill all of a woman's needs; involving others in their children's upbringing; actively questioning the expectations that are placed on mothers by society; challenging mainstream parenting practices; not believing that mothers are solely responsible for how children turn out; and challenging the idea that the only emotion mothers ever feel toward their children is love.

Central to each theme and act of maternal empowerment is a redefinition of motherhood from a feminist-maternal perspective. "Good" mothers in patriarchal motherhood, for example, are defined as white, middle class, married, stay at-home moms, while "good" mothers from a politic of maternal empowerment are drawn from all maternal identities and include lesbian, non-custodial, poor, single, older, and "working" mothers. Likewise, patriarchal motherhood limits family to a patriarchal nuclear structure wherein the parents are married and are the biological parents of the children, where the mother is the nurturer and the father is the provider. Unlike the patriarchal perspective, however, the maternal empowerment perspective embraces a variety of family structures including single, blended, step, matrifocal, same-sex, and so forth. Further, as patriarchal motherhood characterizes childrearing as a private, non-political undertaking, maternal empowerment foregrounds the political-social dimension of motherwork; more specifically, it challenges traditional practices of gender socialization and performs anti-sexist childrearing practices so as to raise empowered daughters and empathetic sons. Finally, for many mothers, maternal empowerment becomes expressed as maternal activism. Mothers, by way of maternal activism, use their position as mothers to lobby for social and political change. Whether it is in the home or in academia at large, expressed as anti-sexist childrearing or maternal activism, from this perspective motherwork is redefined as a social and political act through which social change is made possible. Simply put, we suggest that the aim of maternal empowerment is to reclaim the power denied to mothers in patriarchal motherhood generally and specifically within academic motherhood.

The second general conclusion we draw from the chapters in this book is that we must eradicate neo-traditional family configurations. Indeed, we view the absence of a sustained analysis on gender inequity in our homes-the "new" neo-traditional family configuration-and the ideology of gender essentialism that supports and legitimizes it as the "Achilles' Heel" of both the contemporary maternal empowerment movement and academic motherhood. As the chapters here reveal, while family-friendly government policies and workplace practices are certainly desired and needed, they will only serve to empower mothers if their progress is matched in the private sphere. Moreover, as the results from O'Reilly's (in progress) large qualitative study on mother academics and her chapter in this volume suggest, it seems that gender equity in the home is more often a determinant of employment success than family friendly policies in the workplace. When asked what enabled them to achieve success in academia, the overwhelming majority of respondents identified not workplace policies but the support of their partners: "I couldn't have done it without him." Or, as historian Jodi Vandenberg-Davis remarked: "Women who have reached full professor seem to share a common characteristic: husbands who stay at home for part of the child-rearing years, work part time, or at the very least are not in jobs that require a great deal of travel." "These familial adaptations" she continues, "may prove to be more important than the rather minimal institutional adaptations." However, as Christopher and Kolers' chapter reveals, even when dual-academic couples try to co-parent, they face enormous challenges and burdens.

Ongoing gender essentialism, even though it may present itself in more sophisticated, even "feminist" ways, however, must be recognized as that which underpins post-second wave motherhood and gives rise to its many oppressive practices and tensions for contemporary women's post-second wave split subjectivity. But what does all of this mean for a theory and politic of maternal empowerment? The challenge, as we see it, is to determine how best to affirm the necessary work of social reproduction, in all of its stages and embodiment; it must be acknowledged that it is mothers who do this work, often to their own detriment, while insisting that culture, and that includes fathers, must likewise assume responsibility for motherwork and take on its tasks in both thought (i.e., the maternal thinking and psychological responsibility for managing and executing family life described above) and action. What is needed, in other words, is a re-positioning of the word *mother* from a noun to a verb so that the work of mothering is rendered separate from the identity of mother; that care is divested of biology such that family configurations can be based on the caregiving that is necessary to sustain families rather than gender roles based on biology. In the context of the scholarship and activism on maternal empowerment such requires that we move from a politic of maternalism to that which Judith Stadtman Tucker perceptively defines as a "feminist ethic of care" framework:

> As with maternalism, feminist care ethic designates caring for others as an essential social function. But rather than valorizing maternal sensitivity and altruism as a vital resource, feminist care ethic aims to liberate caregiving from its peripheral status and reposition it as a primary human activity. (212)

She goes on to explain that, "For proponents of the contemporary mothers' movement, grounding the agenda in an ethic of care opens up the possibility of developing a *gender neutral* approach to social policy and an opportunity to expand the language of care as a public good beyond the maternalist paradigm" (212, emphasis added).

The feminist ethic of care perspective redefines "motherhood issues"–maternity leave, childcare, flextime, workplace discrimination against mothers, and the societal devaluation of carework to name but a few—*as parental and family concerns*. In so doing, the 'feminist ethic of care' paradigm displaces and dislodges the gender essentialist framework which constructs and constitutes contemporary western motherhood and neo-traditional family configurations. Perhaps this reframing in tandem with the new post-second wave framework suggested here will not automatically result in gender equity in our homes; however, both make such more probable and achievable. A gender neutral approach not only makes progressive social policy—from parental leave to flextime—available to fathers, thus allowing for their active participation in the social reproduction of households; more importantly, it makes carework for men and masculinity normative. In other words, if carework is degendered and if such is reinforced by workplace and governmental policy, not only will more men do reproductive labor, this work, as a result, will no longer be viewed or defined as women's calling and vocation. And, one primary consequence that would likely emerge is that neo-traditional families would be challenged.

While the chapters in this book begin to reveal just how complex and multifaceted achieving these two key changes will be in our post-second wave context, we believe these changes are both warranted and possible. In short, we believe that the ongoing conversation this book suggests reveals that it is now time to use a new framework that aims to work toward maternal empowerment for mothers in general and academic mothers specifically, while also finding ways to eradicate neo-traditional family configurations. It is past time to acknowledge that mothers need empowerment not for their children *but for themselves*, and academic mothers are no different. As the second decade of the twenty-first century unfolds, we hope that our new framework and the conversation that has begun in this book will prove valuable to academic mothers and, hopefully, non-normative fathers as we continue to advocate for maternal empowerment for mothers and non-normative family configurations.

[1]In this chapter, we primarily discuss *mothers* rather than *mothers and fathers* or *parents*. We are sensitive to the issue of using inclusive and/or gender-neutral language when talking about family-life issues as a means to challenge rather than reinforce gender stereotypes and norms. Moreover, as feminist maternal scholars, one of our most important goals is to have more gender-neutral family configurations. As a result, we also hope to have more co-parenting family configurations rather than the neo-traditional family configurations we discuss later in this chapter. However, because this book is devoted to the exploration of academic motherhood (almost all of the contributors are academic mothers, with

the exception of Christopher and Kolers' excellent chapter on the current barriers to co-parenting because of the masculine ideal worker norms that undergird academia) and we ultimately hope this book offers a challenge to neo-traditional family configurations, we primarily focus on gender-specific issues in regard to mothers and motherhood as a way to detail thoroughly just how much academic motherhood is replete with gender assumptions and norms that are not gender inclusive now. When we can, however, we employ gender-inclusive language.

[2]We believe it is important to note that we recognize that not all women wish to become mothers. Indeed, many women are happily childless by choice. Moreover, intellectually, we want to resist essentializing women by suggesting that it is "normal" for women to desire to become mothers. Equally important, when we do describe "women's desire to mother" or "a woman's desire to mother," we mean only those women who wish to become mothers rather than all women in general.

[3]Clearly, as the review of the underlying male organizing assumptions of academia detail later in this chapter and various chapters in the book also reveal, we do not agree with Dworkin and Wachs' suggestion that professions are "gender neutral." Rather, we believe that professions, including academia, are currently equitable for unencumbered professional men and women as long as both adhere to the assumptions and norms of the profession. The moment a woman becomes a mother, however, that gender equity is challenged because of the underlying male organizing assumptions. Even so, we do concur with Dworkin and Wachs' larger point in this quote about the post-second wave similarity that now exists for professional men and women who are unencumbered.

[4]The work of contemporary feminist scholars also makes it clear that the intensive ideology is based on a racial hierarchy that privileges white women and devalues and sanctions black women's mothering practices. Indeed, feminist scholars (Douglas and Michaels; Hays; O'Reilly, *Mother Outlaws*) argue intensive mothering is based on white privilege, even though many black women have resisted intensive mothering through community and other mothering practices and they have been sanctioned as a result. Indeed and sadly, the practices of other and community mothering are viewed as "deviant" within the intensive mothering ideology because these practices challenge and resist the belief that bloodmothers can only care for children, refuse the practice of mothering only in isolation, and defy the notion that mothers must lavish all their attention on their

children at their own expense. Thus, these "deviant" mothering practices challenge intensive mothering ideologies, even though they are viewed as problematic within the intensive ideology and many black women have been vilified for these practices, particularly in terms of discussions of welfare mothers (Douglas and Michaels).

[5]Consequently, as we note later, a significant, and to many a surprising, finding of Sylvia Hewlett's research was the fact that female academics have the *highest* rate of childlessness (43 percent) (97). Likewise surprising, is the scarcity of research on mothers in the academe. "The inclusion of women in academia as subjects of research on work and family/parenting," as Alice Fothergill and Kathryn Feltey note, "has occurred only recently—and only in a limited way" (9).

[6]Moreover, as O'Brien Hallstein suggests in *White Feminists*, intensive mothering as we know it today is also a uniquely post-second wave ideology of mothering that simultaneously incorporates and refutes second wave feminism.

WORKS CITED

Agathangelou, Anna and L. H. M. Ling. "An Unten(ur)able Position: The Politics of Teaching for Women of Color in the U.S." *International Feminist Journal of Politics* 4.3 (2002): 368-98.

Belenky, Mary R., Blythe Clinchy, Nancy Goldberger and Jill Tarule. *Women's Ways of Knowing: The Development of Self, Voice, and Mind.* New York: Basic Books, 1986.

Collins, Patricia H. "The Meaning of Motherhood Black Culture and Black Mother Daughter Relationships." *Double Stitch: Black Women Write about Mothers and Daughters.* Ed. by Patricia Bell-Scott, Beverly Guy-Sheftall, Jacqueline Jones Royster, Janet Sims-Wood, Miriam DeCosta-Willis and Lucie Fultz. Boston: Beacon Press, 1991. 42-60.

Cooney, Teresa M. and Peter Uhlenberg. "Family Building Patterns of Professional Women: A Comparison of Lawyers, Physicians, and Post Secondary Teachers." *Journal of Marriage and Family* 51 (August 1989): 749-758.

Copper, Baba. "The Radical Potential in Lesbian Mothering of Daughters." *Maternal Theory: Essential Readings.* Ed. Andrea O'Reilly. Toronto: Demeter Press, 2007. 186-193.

Crittenden, Ann. *The Price of Motherhood: Why the Most Important*

Job the World is Still the Least Valued. New York: Henry Holt and Company, 2001.

de Marneffe, Daphne. *Maternal Desire: On Children, Love, and the Inner Life*. New York: Little, Brown and Company, 2004.

Douglas, Susan J. and Meredith Michaels. *The Mommy Myth: The Idealization of Motherhood and How It Has Undermined Women*. New York: Free Press, 2004.

Dworkin, Shari L. and Faye Linda Wachs. *Body Panic: Gender, Health, and the Selling of Fitness*. New York: New York University Press, 2009.

Evans, Elrena and Caroline Grant. *Mama, PhD: Women Write About Motherhood and Academic Life*. New Brunswick, NJ: Rutgers University Press, 2008.

Fothergill, Alice and Kathryn Feltey. "'I've Worked Very Hard and Slept Very Little': Mothers on the Tenure Track in Academia." *Journal of the Association for Research on Mothering* 5.2 (Fall/Winter 2003): 7-19.

Gilligan, Carol. *A Different Voice: Psychological Theory and Women's Development*. Cambridge, MA: Harvard University Press, 1982.

Glickman, Rose L. *Daughters of Feminists: Young Women with Feminist Mothers Talk About Their Lives*. New York: St. Martin's Press, 1993.

Gordon, Tuula. *Feminist Mothers*. New York: New York University Press, 1990.

Gore, Ariel, and Bee Lavender. *Breeder: Real Life Stories from the New Generation of Mothers*. Seattle, WA: Seal Press, 2001.

Green, Fiona. "Feminist Mothers: Successfully Negotiating the Tensions Between Motherhood and Mothering." *Mother Outlaws: Theories and Practices of Empowered Mothering*. Ed. Andrea O'Reilly. Toronto: Women's Press, 2004. 31-42.

Green, Fiona J. "Developing a Feminist Motherline: Reflections on a Decade of Feminist Parenting." *Journal of the Association for Research on Mothering* 8.1,2 (Winter/Summer 2006): 7-20.

Harding, Sandra. *Whose Science? Whose Knowledge? Thinking from Women's Lives*. New York: Cornell University Press, 1991.

Hayden, Sara and D. Lynn O'Brien Hallstein. *Contemplating Maternity in an Era of Choice: Explorations into Discourses of Reproduction*. Lanham, MD: Lexington Press, 2010.

Hays, Sharon. *The Cultural Contradictions of Motherhood*. New Haven: Yale University Press, 1996.

Hewlett, Sylvia Ann. *Creating a Life: Professional Women and the Quest for Children*. New York: Miramax, 2002.

Hile Bassett, Rachel. *Parenting and Professing: Balancing Family Work with an Academic Career*. Nashville: Vanderbilt University Press, 2005.

Hirsch, Marianne. *The Mother/Daughter Plot: Narrative, Psychoanalysis, Feminism*. Bloomington: Indiana University Press, 1989.

Hirshman, Linda R. *Get to Work: A Manifesto for Women of the World*. New York: Viking, 2006.

Horwitz, Erika. *Mothers' Resistance to the Western Dominant Discourse on Mothering*. Ph.D. Thesis. Simon Fraser University, Vancouver, British Columbia, 2003.

Horwitz, Erika. "Resistance as a Site of Empowerment: The Journey Away From Maternal Sacrifice." *Mother Outlaws: Theories and Practices of Empowered Mothering*. Ed. Andrea O'Reilly. Toronto: Women's Press, 2004. 43-58.

Dagg, Anne Innis, and Patricia J. Thompson. *MisEducation: Women and Canadian Universities*. Toronto: Ontario Institute for Studies in Education, 1988.

June, Aubrey Williams. "Grad Students Think Twice About Jobs in Academe." *Chronicle of Higher Education*. Retrieved Feb. 24, 2011. <http://chronicle.com/article/Grad-Students-Think-Twice/1453>.

Kajitani, Megan Pincus. "Finding a Parent-Friendly Place." *Chronicle of Higher Education*. Retrieved Feb. 24, 2011. <http://chronicle.com/article/Finding-A-Parent-Friendly/46855>.

Mason, Mary Ann and Marc Goulden. "Do Babies Matter (Part II)? Closing the Baby Gap." *Academe* 90.6 (Nov./Dec. 2004): 10-15.

Mason, Mary Ann and Marc Goulden. "Do Babies Matter? The Effect of Family Formation on the Lifelong Careers of Academic Men and Women." *Academe* 88.6 (Nov./Dec. 2002): 21-27.

"Mommy Madness." *Newsweek* 21 Feb. 2005: 42-49.

O'Brien Hallstein, D. Lynn. *White Feminists and Contemporary Maternity: Purging Matrophobia*. New York: Palgrave, 2010a.

O'Brien Hallstein, D. Lynn. "Public Choices, Private Control: How Mediated Mom Labels Work Rhetorically to Dismantle the Politics of Choice and White Second Wave Feminism." Sara Hayden and D.

Lynn O'Brien Hallstein, Eds. *Contemplating Maternity in an Era of Choice: Explorations into Discourses of Reproduction.* Lanham, MD: Lexington Books, 2010b: 5-27.

O'Brien Hallstein, D. Lynn. "Second Wave Silences and Third Wave Intensive Mothering." Amber E. Kinscr Ed. *Mothering and Feminism in the Third Wave.* Toronto: Demeter Press, 2008a: 107-116.

O'Brien Hallstein, D. Lynn. "Second Wave Successes and Third Wave Struggles." *Women's Studies in Communication* 31.2 (Summer 2008b): 143-150.

O'Reilly, Andrea, ed. *Mother Matters: Motherhood as Discourse and Practice.* Toronto: Association for Research on Mothering, 2004a.

O'Reilly, Andrea. *Toni Morrison and Motherhood: A Politics of the Heart.* Albany: SUNY Press, 2004b.

O'Reilly, Andrea, ed. *Mother Outlaws: Theories and Practices of Empowered Mothering.* Toronto: Women's Press, 2004c.

O'Reilly, Andrea. "Between the Baby and the Bathwater: Some Thoughts on a Mother Centered Theory and Practice of Feminist Mothering." *Journal of the Association for Research on Mothering* 8.1&2 (Winter/Summer 2006a): 323-330.

O'Reilly, Andrea. *Rocking the Cradle: Thoughts on Motherhood, Feminism, and the Possibility of Empowered Mothering.* Toronto: Demeter Press, 2006b.

O'Reilly, Andrea, ed. *Maternal Theory: Essential Readings.* Toronto: Demeter Press, 2007.

O'Reilly, Andrea. *Feminist Mothering.* Albany: SUNY Press, 2008.

O'Reilly, Andrea. *Twenty-First Century Motherhood: Experience, Identity, Policy, Agency.* New York: Columbia University Press, 2010.

Orenstein, Peggy. *Flux: Women on Sex, Work, Kids, Love, and Life in a Half-Changed World.* New York: Double Day, 2000.

Peskowitz, Miriam. *The Truth Behind the Mommy Wars: Who Decides what Makes a Good Mother?* Emeryville, CA: Seal Press, 2005.

Pillow, Wanda S. *Unfit Subjects: Educational Policy and the Teen Mother.* New York: Routledge, 2004.

Rich, Adrienne. *Of Woman Born: Motherhood as Experience and Institution.* 2nd ed. New York: W.W. Norton, 1986.

Ruddick, Sara. *Maternal Thinking: Toward a Politics of Peace.* Boston: Beacon Press, 1989

Simeone, Angela. *Academic Women Working Towards Equality.* South

Hadley, MA: Bergin and Garvey Publishers, 1987.

Stadtman Tucker, Judith. "Rocking the Boat: Feminism and the Ideological Grounding for the Twenty-First Century Mothers' Movement." *Feminist Mothering*. Ed. Andrea O'Reilly. Albany, New York: SUNY Press, 2008. 205-219.

"Statement on Principles on Family Responsibility and Academic Work," The American Association of University Professors, 2001.

Vandenberg-Davis, Jodi. Personal comment, 2008.

Ward, Kelly and Lisa Wolf-Wendel. "Academic Motherhood: Managing Complex Roles in Research Universities." *Association for the Study of Higher Education* 2003: 1-17.

Warner, Judith. *Perfect Madness: Motherhood the Age of Anxiety.* New York: Riverhead Books, 2005.

Williams, Joan. *Unbending Gender: Why Family and Work Conflict and What To Do About It.* Oxford: Oxford University Press, 2000.

Wilson Robin. "How Babies Alter Careers for Academics: Having Children often Bumps Women off the Tenure Track a New Study Shows." *The Chronicle of Higher Education* December 5, 2003: 1-7.

Wolf, Naomi. *Misconceptions: Truth, Lies, and the Unexpected on the Journey to Motherhood.* New York: Anchor Books, 2003.

Wolfinger, Nicholas, Mary Ann Mason, Marc Goulden. "Alone in the Ivory Tower: How Birth Events Vary Among Fast-Track Professionals." Paper presented at the 2008 Annual Meeting of the Population Association of America, New Orleans, LA, 2008.

Wood, Julia T. *Gendered Lives: Communication, Gender, and Culture.* 7th ed. Belmont: Wadsworth, 2007.

I. Challenges

Spies Like Us

The Lives of Double Agents Evolving Identities and Strategies of Mothers in Academe

BETHANY CRANDELL GOODIER

> *Double agents lie for a living.*
> —Alison Pearson

I T WAS THE FIRST DAY OF A BRAND NEW SEMESTER and I looked the part of a prepared, accomplished assistant professor. My freshly cleaned hair was pulled into a low ponytail, complementing my casually professional black pants and plum colored cardigan sweater set selected especially for this tone setting day. A fresh coat of lip-gloss graced my lips and I smiled brightly as I made my way to the front of the classroom. I chatted easily with the students I knew from previous semesters while I flipped on the computer and lowered the screens around the large lecture hall. I Inhaled deeply as I turned to open my folder with class lists and lecture notes and thought, "Okay, Goodier—you can do this. Just keep going. No one in this room knows what your life is *really* like. Just keep up the act. You'll be fine."

Only thirty minutes earlier I was sitting my car, head bent over the steering wheel sobbing. The morning was rough, the first time at daycare for my six-month-old child and the first day of school for my four-year-old. I had changed clothes twice (once for spit up on the shoulder, the second for pancake syrup lovingly transferred during a morning hug) and made two return trips home before even hitting the highway. My son had been wrenched from my neck like a frightened cat at daycare and my daughter's subtle look of disappointment when I couldn't stay "just a little longer like the other mommies" had broken me. The tears welled in my eyes as I pulled into my parking space in the garage, wondering whether I was making the right choices in my life. Was my work really this engaging ... this important? Was it worth all of this? As I watched the occasional student or faculty member hurry past, oblivious to my turmoil, I wondered if I was truly as alone as I felt. I found myself looking in car windows as I walked through the garage, searching out other "double agents;" academic mothers who cried in their cars, then donned their cloaks and masks of professionalism to hide the chaos before reaching their offices or classrooms.

Extant research on women in academe suggests that integrating motherhood and successful career is beyond challenging.[1] One study found that of tenure track men and women who have children early in their careers, the men are 38 percent more likely to have earned tenure within twelve to fourteen years (Mason and Goulden). And while many institutions have adopted tenure clock stoppages and some version of modified duties in the case of birth or adoption, most "continue to support and value procedures and evaluative measures based on a progressive, linear, and seamless career model" (Townsley and Broadfoot 137). Lisa Wolf-Wendel and Kelly Ward cite Williams: "In the academic profession the 'ideal worker' is one who, in essence is 'married' to his work, leaving little time for bearing and raising children" (113). As a graduate student, I remember a respected, senior faculty member telling me that women who had children in academe had "wasted their Ph.D." and "stolen a spot" from more deserving (i.e., childfree) candidates. While male faculty members seemed able to balance academic careers and children quite easily, evidence of women with successful academic careers and thriving families was limited. Though support for their existence is beginning to increase, the prevailing attitude in the academy still suggests motherhood is for those who are not serious about their careers (e.g. non-tenure track appointments, instructors, adjuncts).

Nonetheless, as I navigated the demands of my career and early motherhood, I began to sense that there was a "secret society" of double agents; women attempting to integrate the worlds of professor and mother and break free of the stereotypes (and research findings) that suggest they cannot co-exist. This chapter examines the narratives of twenty such women, mother/professors at various stages of their careers with children ranging from eight months to eighteen years. Using techniques of narrative interviewing, I explore the stories these women tell about the experience of being both professor and mother and the strategies they use to maintain their "professional" and "good mother" identities both at work and at home. Using the technique of value identification in narrative discourse (Vanderford, Smith, and Harris), I also identify underlying values inherent in the narratives of these women that limit or promote change.

METHOD

I began this study by contacting other academic mothers via email and Facebook to request their participation. After receiving an overwhelming number of positive responses, I scheduled interviews with those I knew personally and increased my sample with women suggested by my participants during these meetings. Because of the variation in workload and expectations for tenure among different institutions, I decided to interview women from Liberal Arts institutions with teaching, service and research expectations and loads similar to my own. I recognize that this is but one "type" of academic mother and that my study is limited by this choice. My intention is for this study to serve as a starting point for future research and discussion among all types of academic mothers.

All of these interviews were positioned as "coffee talks": engaged, personal meetings where we talked about the lived experience of being both professor and mom.[2] Following the work of many feminist researchers, I sought not to interrogate my participants, but to engage them in conversation throughout our interview. I used a moderately scheduled interview guide, but allowed the conversation to flow naturally, sharing my own stories and reflections about each topic. This technique minimizes, as Jenny Nelson argued, "perceived authority of the interviewer" and "provides the respondent with a comfortable format by which she can relate her story" (228). Open-ended prompts were used to elicit more detail when appropriate (e.g., Why do you say that? Tell me more about that experience; How did you feel about that? etc.). Each interview lasted 45-150[3] minutes and all were recorded and later transcribed for analysis.

Twenty women were interviewed for this study, ranging in age from 31 to 55. All had at least one child living at home between the ages of eight months and eighteen years and all but two had spouses or partners who shared (though not all equally) parenting responsibilities. Participants came from four Liberal Arts institutions in the southeast and all were in tenured (n=10) or tenure track (n=9) positions with the exception of one who served as the director of a graduate program in a non-tenure track position.[4] All but three women were affiliated with departments in schools of Humanities and/or Social Sciences and twelve serve or recently served in some administrative role (e.g. department chair, associate chair, program director, etc.). Though I acknowledge issues of race and class have a significant influence on the construction of identity, I did not request participants to identify race, class or religion during these interviews.[5]

Data from these interviews was transcribed and later reviewed using two separate techniques for analysis.[6] First, to understand how these women made sense of their identities as both "professionals" and "mothers"[7] and to identify the strategies used to maintain these identities, I adopted a ground theory approach that allowed categories to emerge from the data. I identified common themes and points of difference between participant's narratives and created schemes for interpreting and classifying these themes. Second, I reviewed the data again using the Value Identification in Narrative Discourse technique developed by Marsha Vanderford, David Smith and Willard Harris (1992)[8] to examine the underlying values[9] represented in their narratives.

RESULTS

As I reviewed the transcripts, I found that participants told similar stories about their experiences of being professor/mother and made sense of these identities in similar ways. Additionally, while each certainly adopted strategies unique to position and personality, many of these women shared similar strategies for balancing the expectations of these roles and for maintaining a strong sense of competence as both professor and mother. The values inherent in their narratives suggest both limitations and potential for change.

Stories

While each woman's experience was unique, their stories shared common themes. Specifically, they 1) conveyed confidence that being a professor and a mother made them better in each role and 2) confirmed that institutional support (or the lack of it) influences the way they approach their lives as mother/professors.

Roles Intertwined

The first common theme that emerged in the narratives of my participants was the belief that, despite the occasional challenges, being a professor and a mother made them better in both roles. Though none were asked this question directly, 18 of the 20 participants at some point in the interview explicitly stated that they felt they were better mothers and professors because of their participation in each role. As one participant stated, "Being a professor and a mom are totally linked. I can't imagine being one without being the other. Each one is better because of the other." When asked what characterizes the ideal mother and ideal professor, one woman noted,

> I think they have a lot of qualities in common—whether you are a professor or a mom you are giving all the time—and as I get older I realize what I do is who I am and so as the kids get older that becomes more important and what I do becomes more relevant for them. I can bring my work to their classroom and having kids makes me a more engaged professor—I am more respectful of their lives outside the classroom because I have one too!

During our conversation, I asked one of the participants who had been a professor for many years before having children how things had changed. She responded:

> I am a better professor now than I ever was before kids. Maybe I don't grade as quickly, but I see things differently. I see my students differently and in some strange way I care more about being an effective teacher and scholar. I just feel more invested. I know I'm a better mom than I would be if I wasn't a professor. No—I can't go on every field trip or plan every class party, but I help my children think more critically about the world—they are exposed to so many unique experiences here at [institution]. I love that!

These same respondents were also very conscious of their position as role models for not only their own children, but also their students. "I want to be a role model that women can work and have meaningful careers.... I want to contribute to the home and to the finances and I want my son and daughter to see that." Another stated, "I think it is an important part of what I do—to model how it is entirely possible to have a job—a demanding job that you really like but also have a family that works. You don't have to have one or the other."

Institutional Issues

A second theme common to the narratives of all participants was the relative lack of institutional support for combining the roles of mother and professor. Though most acknowledge the policies and procedures at their institutions have improved in recent years,[10] all of the women interviewed shared stories about reactions to their pregnancies, challenges in navigating institutional policy or obtaining modified duties after the births/adoption of their children, and/or messages intrinsic to the organizational culture that constrained their performance of professor/mother.

The most prominent theme in these narratives was the negative, inappropriate, and often unethical and illegal reactions of chairs and deans to the news of participant's pregnancies. All but one[11] of the participants interviewed had "funny stories" to share about how and when they disclosed the news to their supervisors. Most centered on the reactions of the chair and his/her immediate focus on how to "solve the problem" of scheduling and whether or not these pregnancies were planned. These reactions ranged from the inexplicably rude: "my boss actually asked me if I considered abortion as an option," to the humorous "I think she was totally shocked because she said, 'well how did that happen?' I looked at her for a minute to see if she really wanted an answer." Most indicated more concern for the needs of the department than the individual in their initial reactions to the news. One participant said, "I told my chair and he said: 'That's great news! How long do you have to be gone and who is going to cover your classes for you?'" Another shared a detailed narrative of her disclosure:

> Well, first my chair asked me if I got pregnant on purpose—that was the first question he asked me. And then he went into this sort of convoluted thing about how we could solve the scheduling problem—he told me that maybe we could—I was teaching four classes at the time, but maybe we could do a Tuesday/Thursday schedule so that I could have my baby and still get paid and still come back right away. And so he thought I would have a four course load, and maybe take a one course break for administra-

tive duty and maybe we could use some of those independent studies I did as banked classes so I would be responsible for two classes that fall and he was very happy with this thought and I said okay, but, but (pause), I do not think that will work because I am having a baby. I am not just going on a hike. I am having a baby!

Still others told stories of their challenges regarding the lack of institutional policy on pregnancy and adoption. One explained,

So there were no policies on maternity when I got pregnant and when I told people I was expecting they were like, "great—get a few people to cover your class and be back after two weeks." Yeah—two weeks. So that's what I did. They made it clear that there was no policy that protected me from this. Now I know that there is, but my chair then—she had no desire to protect me on this one—it made her life easier if I went back as soon as possible so she didn't try to find out what I could do from HR *or anything. And I told her I was having a lot of trouble—bleeding a lot, not getting any sleep, experiencing some post partum depression and she basically said, "Wow, that's rough, but what can we do? We don't have maternity leave. I need you back at work."*

When discussing her quick return to the classroom, another participant explained: "I had no tenure. I had no power. I had no feet to stand on. There was no policy here at [institution]. What else could I do?"

Four of the participants interviewed experienced challenges negotiating policies because of their unique roles as administrators during their pregnancies. "It's great that we have all these policies now, but no one seems to have considered how they will work for people in administration—it's like they are expected to be immune from the desire to get pregnant or adopt." One professor in an administrative role acknowledged the reaction she received regarding her child's birth was supportive in theory, but difficult in practice: "I got a lot of supportive nods, but the university is not really supportive. No one in my position had ever done this and no one knew how to handle it. I didn't get the accommodations I needed at the time."

Similarly, ten of the participants noted challenges in the implementation of institutional policies related to parenthood: "So another woman in my department got pregnant a month earlier than me and she got this great modified duties arrangement. My chair said, 'I already gave her the course break' like there was only one and that was all he could do." Another noted, "Who your chair is matters—the policies are there, but I don't think they really want you to use them. I actually heard people say 'we don't want people to get too good of a deal'—like having a baby is some sort of vacation! If your chair isn't supportive, you're screwed. They have to fight for you."

Participants also told stories about messages about parenthood implicit in the organizational culture. One noted, "Everything *seems* very family friendly here, but when you look below the surface there are things that make you wonder—meetings really early or late in the day, comments made by others about where you are at certain times or how you structure your day—not to mention the tenure system in general." Regarding implicit messages about children and childbirth, one participant recalled:

> *There are lots of legendary stories you hear around here about [name] who had a c-section on Friday and was back to work on Monday or so and so who was running two weeks after her child was born, or someone bringing their newborn to class in a snuggly so that they wouldn't miss a day of teaching—what is that all about? Are we trying to say that's a good thing? That this is what we should aspire to be?*

Thus, these stories reveal much about the institutional issues and messages around pregnancy and childbirth. Most of the women experienced great difficulty navigating the system and the explicit and implicit messages about motherhood suggest that having children is acceptable as long as it doesn't interfere with your work or change the system in any way.

Strategies. In addition to common stories, the women I interviewed also shared similar strategies, both practical and intellectual, for successfully integrating motherhood and a life in the academy. While it is beyond the scope of this chapter to explore all of the strategies cited, three were most prominent: 1) prioritizing; 2) redefining boundaries; and 3) reframing identity.

Prioritizing

Fourteen participants identified strict prioritizing as one of their strategies for integrating both roles. More specifically, prioritizing included identifying tasks or areas of responsibility most relevant to their personal and professional objectives. Notably, all but two participants explicitly stated that their children were their "highest priority" and that all decisions about work and home flowed from what was best for them. Of the fourteen women who shared narratives of prioritizing, the most common areas of focus were: 1) picking the children up from school/being home when they arrived (e.g. "I just feel like it is my job to pick them up at 3:00"); 2) putting "nutritious meals" on the table (e.g. "I feel the need to put something relatively healthy on the table most nights"); 3) being "present" when they were with their children (e.g. "I am very task oriented, but when I am with her I just try to be present—be present and enjoy who she is at this moment"); 4) affording their children opportunities for growth outside of school (e.g. "I don't want my kids to not do soccer or gymnastics or baseball or whatever because of my work"); and 5) setting aside family hours (e.g. "Between 5:00 and 8:00 it's family time—no work, no email, no nothing. We hold that time sacred"). Tasks or areas identified as low on the priority list (though not mentioned by all participants) were: 1) cleaning the house (e.g. "there is a lot more dust on the floors"); 2) exercise (e.g. "I try to make time to exercise, but it is the first thing that goes if someone needs to meet or the kids get sick")[12]; 3) taking care of themselves (e.g. "It's scary—I am so focused on the kids health and nutrition, but I don't really take very good care of myself. Sometimes I eat M&M's for lunch because that's all I have time for").

Not surprisingly, requirements for tenure and promotion often drove professional priorities, with time most often prioritized for 1) research/writing or scholarly work (e.g. "I block time to write every week"); 2) enhancing teaching (e.g. "I want to make sure I am the best I can be in the classroom and that takes time"); 3) service to the department/institution (e.g. "I think it's important to be a good departmental and institutional citizen—I try to participate in the life of the department wherever I can"). Noted as relatively low on their list of priorities were: 1) meetings without a significant purpose (e.g. "I hate those meetings where we just go over things we could have covered in email—those drive me nuts"); and 2) attendance at "extra" events (e.g. "You know it's tough to convince myself to pay a babysitter to go to graduation or night time and weekend events—we don't really get paid enough to do all that and it doesn't really count for anything like tenure or promotion or whatever—so it's hard").

Redefining Boundaries

A second strategy described by every participant was the redefinition of the boundaries between work and home. One explained it this way,

> *It's sort of a blessing and a curse, but when you are a professor the lines between your work life and your home life are necessarily blurry. We are always thinking, always reflecting, and ultimately always working. You can't turn it off. At the same time, I don't stop being a mom when I go to work. The two are connected. I work at home and I bring kids to the office. I am always thinking about my research—always. And sometimes when I teach I use my kids as examples. So for me, the two are always connected. Both are central to who I am.*

For some, the blurring of boundaries came out of necessity (e.g. not enough time to grade at work; child's day off not in line with university calendar, no childcare available). Often, they worked at home or brought children into the office because of factors beyond their control and with limited resources (both personal, institutional and societal) to address the situation. For others, the decision to blur these lines was quite purposeful. One woman noted, "Oh I am very purposeful about bringing those two worlds together. I think it is important. To change the culture to be truly family friendly, we have to blur those lines for people. We have to show them you can be both a good professor and a good parent." When I mentioned that another participant had cited one of the women I interviewed as a role model for integrating the roles of professor and mother on campus she responded,

> *You know it is interesting that you say someone saw me on campus with [child's name] because I was very conscious about that. I wanted to have my kids on campus. I wanted to change the culture of our department. I wanted to make that generational transition between the old men in our department and the newer*

faculty…it was always in my mind to make him visible. I didn't really want to show how hellish it was some days (laughs), but I did want people to see me bring him to campus.

Of course, the women also acknowledged the "shadow side" of re-defining these boundaries recognizing they probably "worked more" because of their willingness to integrate these two spheres. One woman noted, "It's probably bad in some ways. I am sure I work more than I would in a 9:00-5:00 job where I could just leave things there at the end of the day, but I wouldn't change it." Another acknowledged, "Sometimes I think the flexibility hurts us—we will bring a child to campus rather than saying—no, I am taking the day to be with my child and I am not going to feel bad about it. We should be able to do that—we work weekends, nights, all hours of the day. We shouldn't feel bad about it." Remarkably, nine of my participants gave examples of blurring the boundaries between home and work by choosing to work under what might normally be considered extreme conditions such as teaching from hospital beds before or after the birth of a child, teaching while hemorrhaging from a miscarriage (later hospitalized), telephone interviewing candidates while in labor, attending meetings two days after childbirth, stopping on campus to send class cancelation notice on the way to the hospital, taking a phone call from the Chair while in active labor, and teaching with a baby in a snuggly five days after delivery. One woman reflected,

Part of it is the message from the institution—"Don't miss class! I know you are having a baby, but someone better be in that classroom!" which makes it your responsibility. The other side of that is that we don't want to be the "that" girl—the one who had a baby and then let everything else fall aside. You know? I also think we have a lot of respect for our students—for our work—and we don't want to let that go.

For many of the participants, blurring the boundaries between work and home created both opportunities and constraints. Many reported working beyond the anticipated "40-50 hour week" and often reported feeling "guilty" for not being more productive while their children were young.

59

Reframing

A third strategy found in these narratives was the process of reframing of their identities as both academics and mothers. One participant openly acknowledged this process:

> *You know I think one of the things I did after I became a mom was to sort of re-story myself or maybe reframe the way I thought of myself—both as a professor and a mother. I was no longer this hard core academic with grand plans of significant scholarly activity and a chairship by 35. But I wasn't this doting mother who wanted only to spend time with her kids either. I have changed who I think I am, but also who I want to be—and I think that's a good thing.*

Still others were equally clear that their definitions and expectations of themselves had evolved as they became mothers and professors, though less explicitly aware of the process. When asked if you could be both the ideal professor and the ideal mom, one participant responded:

> *No! I say no too quickly. You know—it's hard. You can't have it all, but I am increasingly convinced that I don't want it. Having children means that I can not be the academic I thought I was going to be when I started graduate school. To be that person, means not being able to be the mother I want to be. But I am not dissatisfied with the academic I have become. I like my career even though it is so not like I thought it was going to be. It's not what I was trained to be, but I am happy with it; very happy with it.*

In sum, the stories told by these professor mothers explicitly emphasized confidence in the blending of these two roles, challenges in navigating institutional policies and norms, and highlighted strategies of prioritizing, redefining boundaries, and reframing. These themes were consistent and pervasive throughout the interviews, but I was concerned that they revealed only the superficial areas of connection between my participants. By examining the underlying values inherent in these narratives I hoped to find both points of connection to these themes as well as any areas of contradiction. It is to the discussion of the implicit values inherent in their stories that we now turn.

Underlying Values

In addition to using grounded theory to identify common themes in the stories of my participants, I also used the VIND technique to identify the underlying terminal and instrumental values present in their stories. This technique involves searching the narratives for implied or explicit statements of value such as how something "should" be or what mother/professors "ought" to do. I searched for actions that were repeated, praised and/or condemned, justifications for behavior, actions that were identified as blocking a goal, cause/effect relationships in plot lines, and actions that lead to the achievement of terminal values. The intent of this analysis was to identify underlying values that limited or promoted change. Two major (and sometimes contradictory) value categories emerged from this level of analysis: 1) intensive mothering and 2) professionalism.

Intensive Mothering

Sharon Hays coined the term "intensive mothering" in reference to an ideology of mothering that "advises mothers to expend a tremendous amount of time, energy, and money in raising their children." Lynn O'Brien Hallstein, citing Susan Douglas and Meredith Michaels, Sharon Hays and Andrea O'Reilly, argues this ideology is characterized by three core beliefs: "1) children need and require constant and ongoing nurturing by their biological mothers who are single-handedly responsible for meeting these needs; 2) in meeting those needs, mothers must rely on experts to guide them; and 3) mothers must lavish enormous amounts of time and energy on their children" (143). With the exception of two participants, the underlying values that emerged from the analysis of the narratives of the mother/professors demonstrated a profound acceptance of these core beliefs of intensive mothering.

First, all but two participants in this study indicated they felt it was their or their partner's responsibility as parents to care for and nurture their children. While all participants had some form of hired (e.g. nanny, occasional babysitter, after school program) or unpaid caregivers (e.g. neighbors, friends),[13] all but two indicated some discomfort with this practice. One participant stated, "I just don't like it. We are supposed to raise our kids. It's our job. I don't like leaving them with babysitters or sending them to aftercare. If [husband's name] or I can pick them up, we should—and we do." Another said,

> *This is the first year that [child's name] is in an afterschool pro-*
> *gram. It makes me want to cry, but she loves it! I have no problem*
> *with them being in school, but once the school day is over, I feel*
> *like, okay, it's time for one of us. One of us needs to go and get*
> *them because they are ours and we need to take care of them....*
> *I don't know why I feel guilty about leaving them in aftercare—I*
> *just feel like at three o'clock it is my job to take care of her.*

Even the strategy of prioritization mentioned earlier reveals a great deal about their adherence to the ideology of intensive mothering. They prioritize being highly attentive and engaged rather than simply "good enough" mothers.

In addition to feeling as though it was their or their partner's responsibility to care for their children, participants seemed to adhere to the second tenant of intensive mothering: reliance on experts. Seventeen of the women in this study referenced seeking or accepting the advice of experts in childrearing. Most often, this advice came from books, consults with teachers, or medical professionals.[14] One explained, "Of course, the first thing I did when I found out I was pregnant was go find a book—such an academic! That's what we do." Another said, "Oh the books I read—books on hormonal teenagers, books on kids with OCD, books on this, books on that." Additionally, several acknowledged following the "rules" about breastfeeding religiously after the birth of their children. One woman, for example, noted: "We were obsessed with feeding them on a schedule. We wouldn't let the babysitter give them a bottle so we would come home to two screaming children with the babysitter just serenely rocking the two of them, one in each arm, but the book said to feed them every three hours and we weren't going to deviate from that." Others highlighted the value they placed on teacher and medical expert advice. One participant stated, "I think I take what the teachers say too much to heart, but you know they are the experts on kids so if they say little Johnny isn't living up to some standard then I get worried." Notably, references to physicians, developmental psychologists, psychiatrists or other medical experts appeared over 150 times across 20 interview transcripts.

Finally, the women in this study also demonstrated (though to a lesser degree than the first two) a belief in the third tenet that mothers must expend enormous amounts of time and energy (not to mention money) on their children. All of my participants indicated a desire to have "quality" time with their children, where the focus was primarily on meeting the needs of the child. One participant explained, "I feel like the hours from 5:00-8:00 is their time. I try not to do any work, answer any emails. I focus exclusively on them." When discussing her weekly routine, another participant explained how she had to remind herself to focus on her child at home, "On the days where I stay home with [name] I am not teaching, but I might do a few things on the computer while she is tooling around and I sometimes have to stop myself and say 'don't do this right now. Do this while she is napping. Be present with her at this moment'." Over half of my participants echoed this need to be "present" in the moment. One stated, "Sometimes I am thinking about what I need to be doing at work, but then I realize I really need to be here—to be more present—to get into reading the book and doing the voices in the book." Several acknowledged the importance of saving some energy for their children at the end of the day: "There are days where I am just exhausted. I don't have an ounce of energy left and yet I feel like I need to go home and focus on the kids. It's not fair that my students get all my attention. So, on those days I muscle through and focus what's left of my energy on them."

Another area where participants devoted large amounts of time and energy on their children was as volunteers at school or in afterschool activities. Sixteen of the twenty participants reported some involvement or volunteering in their child's classroom (e.g. room mom, reading tutor, supervising field trips, serving as officer on parent/teacher association). While many participants reported becoming involved because it aligned with their philosophies of education (e.g. "parents should be involved with their children's schools") others acknowledged becoming involved out of guilt or a sense of responsibility. One woman noted, "There is this sort of bending over backwards to be the class mom and prove you can do it—prove you can work and be a good mom."

Participants were also equally committed to their children's after-school activities. Thirteen participants reported their children were involved with at least one (though typically more) after-school activities that required coordination and parental participation. When asked why she continues to manage a particularly complex schedule of after-school activities throughout the week, one woman stated, "I don't want my desire to work to be the reason they can't be involved in things—so yes, sometimes I kill myself to make sure they have those opportunities, but

I don't want them to miss out because I want a full life. They should have a full life too." Another explained, "I want them to have time to explore their interests. Sometimes that means I spend more time in the car or managing schedules, but it gives them a chance to try things out. I think that's important."

Finally, sixteen of the participants acknowledged difficulty taking time out for them during what "should be" family time (e.g. weekends, evenings). One woman explained, "Sometimes I write on Saturday mornings. I feel awful about it though. I hate to leave when we could all spend time together. My husband is totally supportive about it—he tells me to take the time I need, but I am so bad. I feel so bad about it." Another explained why she doesn't leave to go exercise in the afternoon when her spouse gets home, "I am not going to choose to do that on my own—if you tell me to do it, I might, but to choose not to be with the kids so that I can exercise—well that would mean I wasn't a good mom—that I didn't like spending time with them." Another agreed stating, "It just feels like if I said I wanted to go do something by myself on the weekends then that meant something was wrong. That I didn't like spending time with them." Notably, all of the women who indicated this discomfort, said their spouses/partners did not share this challenge. "[Husband's name] has no problem leaving to go exercise or run an errand or whatever. Doesn't faze him a bit. I don't think men think about it the same way." Another stated, "[Name] makes sure he makes time to exercise, even if that means less time with the kids. He makes the time. He tells me to do it too, but it's just harder for me to do. I can't hire a babysitter so I can go exercise. I just can't bring myself to do it."

Professionalism. Another value underlying these narratives was the importance of a strong professional image or "face" at work. Despite the espoused benefits of the flexibility of a faculty career and the ways in which boundaries have been redefined and often blurred between home and work, there was a pervasive valuing of the professional over the personal throughout their stories. For example, when asked why she continued teaching while having a miscarriage one associate professor acknowledged, "I just didn't feel right about cancelling class for that—it seemed like it was my choice to be pregnant and my responsibility to deal with its loss. I didn't want it to affect my job." When asked about bringing her children to the office when they were young, one full professor acknowledged, "I wanted to break the boundaries—I wanted people to see my children at the office, but I was also self conscious about the "mommification" of the job. I didn't bring [child's name] to department meetings or things like that." Another noted,

> I think having your kids around is great, but there are times where it is wholly unprofessional—hiring meetings, faculty meetings, stuff like that. We all have to bring our kids to class sometimes or to the office sometimes, but I think, on the whole, you should avoid bringing them to meetings or class whenever you can. I mean, no one in the corporate world would even consider bringing a baby to a board meeting!

Notably, fourteen of the women in this study admitted they were careful about the audience with whom they disclosed personal information.

> I look at the audience—I mean if it is a group of faculty that are cool with the fact that I choose to pick up my kids at 3:00 then I will say that is why I can't meet then, but if it's not—if it's a group that would roll their eyes—then I just say I have a prior commitment.

In contrast, all but three of those women said they did not hide their mothering role or responsibilities from their students. "I have no problem talking about my kids, using them as examples, or things like that. I don't do it every day, but they are a part of my life and I have no problem acknowledging that for students." Another stated,

> I absolutely tell students that is why I can't meet with them at 3:30—I give them all my available time, I let them know I will do anything to help them, but at 3:30, I am a mom and I make no apologies for that. I think it is good for them to have that role model.

Several participants mentioned the importance of male colleagues who talked openly about their parenting responsibilities. "It helps that my male colleagues are open about their desire to be good parents as well and bring their kids to work. It makes it more ok for me to do the same." Nonetheless, other participants acknowledged the gender inequality surrounding perceptions of professionalism: "It's different for men and women—men are somehow given more latitude—they are presumed professional. We have to prove it. And every time we leave for pick up or cancel class for sick kid, we lose a little credibility." Another noted,

If one of my male colleagues brings his children to class or a meeting, everyone talks about what a great dad he is, but I hear those same colleagues talk about women who bring their children to meetings in derogatory ways. I am not a great mom when I bring my kids to class. There really is a double standard there.

DISCUSSION

This study began with the intent to identify other "double agents" in academe; to provide a space for authentic conversation among professor/mothers about the experience of performing these often conflicting roles. What emerged from my interviews, however, was not a pervasive sense of bifurcation; these women were not seeking to maintain their double agent status or conceal their identities as professor/mothers. Instead, they actively sought strategies for constructing integrated, coherent narratives of selves as professor/mothers in ways that made each role stronger. As they spoke, I was reminded of Sarah Jane Tracy and Angela Tretheway's argument for a "crystallized" sense of self; one that allows us to "speak about, understand, and experience the self in more appropriately politicized and layered ways" (186). They argue:

By conceiving of identities as ongoing, emergent, and not entirely predictable crystals, people are forced to acknowledge a range of possible selves embodied in a range of contexts—even as they are constrained by discourses of power. The crystallized self suggests that there are always new facets that are themselves neither real nor fake, but are materially and symbolically relevant and ready to be polished, cleaved, or transformed (189).

The women in this study seem to have adopted this way of perceiving their experience. On the whole, they did not talk about their roles as professors and mothers in separate or distinct ways. They see their lives as multifaceted, complex, and amorphous. They acknowledged that at any given moment one aspect of their life may be more prominent (e.g. the birth of a new baby, the year leading up to tenure review), but that all remain core to their sense of self and performance in each role.

Nonetheless, significant competition to this coherence exists not only from societal expectations of the separation of spheres and cultural norms surrounding motherhood and professionalism, but our own internalization of these norms. We limit our opportunities to resist these dominate narrative and hegemonic influences surrounding motherhood by reinforcing (and recreating) the very systems that constrain us through the way we talk about work and home. According to Anthony Giddens, "language use is embedded in the concrete activities of day to day life and is in some sense partly constitutive of those activities" (xvi). As human agents and social systems engage in the process of mutual constitution, the language we use helps to create and re-create the very system we hope to resist. Framing babysitters and aftercare as "other people raising our children" constitutes a reality that supports intensive mothering and denies the very real economic and professional realities that make this an impossible goal. The "guilt" reported by many women when they spoke of taking time out for themselves reinforces the dominate narrative that "good mothers" are self-sacrificing and should not want to be away from their children. The description of an ideal professor as one that is "fully engaged, prepared, up to date, passionate about the subject matter and willing to do anything for the student" or teaches while miscarrying or from her hospital bed is equally problematic.

There appear, however, to be cracks in the facade. While all but two of the women in this study demonstrated a tendency to adopt an ideology of mothering consistent with intensive mothering, they were always reflexive about this choice (e.g. "I know it doesn't make sense," "this completely goes against my feminist sensibilities," "it's crazy to think it has to be all my responsibility," "I know they don't need all my undivided attention"). This acknowledgement, coupled with a growing awareness of the limitations of an intensive mothering ideology and the contradictions it creates for mothers who integrate paid work with parenting, suggests perhaps a shift towards a new ideology of mothering for these women. Notably, the two women whose analysis of underlying values did not suggest an ideology of intensive mothering or overwhelming concern for professionalism suggest a potential shift in the ways some women think and speak about motherhood in academe. In fact, references to these two women made by other participants during our interviews suggest they may already serve as models for resisting "intensive mothering."[15]

CONCLUSIONS

Several lessons emerge from these conversations. First, we must question or at least discuss more openly the dominant narratives of mothering and professionalism. Every woman interviewed spoke about being a "good mom" and while each definition of that term was unique, most were laden with expectations consistent with the ideology of intensive mothering. Perceptions of "professionalism" are heavily influenced by the masculinized organizing norms of the worlds of business and the academy. Since language is constitutive of reality, we must begin to question those whose language or terminology creates or re-creates a reality that constrains us. We need to create moments of reflexivity (both public and personal) that allow us to consider, critique and question our decisions as well as those things we do not label as choices.

Second, we must continue to question institutional policies and actors—even when they are our friends and other mothers—who continue to construct motherhood as a personal/private choice and therefore, not something to which institutions should respond (see O'Brien Hallstein). Similarly, we should examine our own practices to identify what examples we set for other mother/professors. We are part of the cultural system that reinforces the underlying values of intensive mothering and professionalism. If I argue for modified duties for new parents, but then don't apply for them—or worse, accept but then work just as much as I did while I have them—then I perpetuate the system that makes it difficult for new professor/mothers to create a more integrated life. When we tell heroic stories of the women who were back in the classroom two days after birth with the baby in a sling, we create an iconic (though unrealistic) image to which other women may aspire. We should instead, tell the stories of mothers who took advantage of tenure stoppages and modified duties, completed their tasks effectively, grew professionally, but also took the time required to adjust to parenthood. We should spotlight those who know how to say no, those who take care of themselves personally and professionally; those who don't believe being a good professor or mother is all about sacrificing the self in the process.

Third, while the participants in this study acknowledge institutions have come a long way in creating tenure clock stoppages and modified duty policies in response to the needs of academic parents, there is still a great deal of work to be done in this area. Susan Finkel, Steven Olswang, and Nian She found that while faculty support the *idea* of tenure stoppages and maternity leave or modified duty arrangements, most believed that utilizing these policies would hurt them professionally. Arlie Russell Hochschild suggests institutions must not only adopt policies, but create organizational climates which are unequivocally supportive of their use. Several of the women in this study acknowledged being told that using these policies would suggest they were "not serious" about their careers or would "minimize their earning potential" because they were earning tenure a year later than their cohorts. They acknowledged the institutional climate and more specifically, the support of their chair and other senior faculty as central to their decision to utilize existing policies. Similarly, we should educate those who do not understand the purpose or intent of these policies (e.g. those who describe modified duties as a semester off or suggest professors use their sabbaticals to care for newborns rather than requesting modified duties) and openly question those who deny the need for or efficacy of these policies. Those who create and administer these policies must consider how they will be implemented for female administrators as well. Accepting a position in academic administration should not negate your opportunities to use these policies. We need to work towards policy changes at institutions respect parent's individual choice and institutional requirements. More boldly, perhaps we should reconsider a tenure system that forces women to decide between parenting and their careers with rigid timelines (e.g. childbearing years are also tenure earning years).

It has been four years since that day in the car. Since then, I have been tenured and promoted, published reasonably well, recognized for my teaching and service and even recently appointed as chair of my department. Nonetheless, I still find myself glancing in car windows as I walk through the garage, searching for other mothers trying to balance/integrate/juggle the demands of these often conflicting roles. Occasionally I see one—usually early in her career—car seat properly installed in the back, quickly fixing her makeup and jumping out of the car when she notices me. I smile, nod encouragingly, and try to let her know that she is not alone; that we are all double agents in this world of academe and motherhood. For me, the greatest benefit of this study was that opportunity for that connection; the recognition that so many women are experiencing the same trials and tribulations, joys and successes. Most important, I was surprised at how hearing the crystallized narratives of other women helped me embrace the complexity and multi-faceted nature of my own story. It made me more aware of the influence the ideologies of intensive mothering and professionalism on my daily life and the ways my own language sometimes reinforces this hegemonic influence and constrains my own actions and agency. While I am aware that these findings are limited to liberal arts institutions and can not be generalized to the academy in general, it gives me hope for the future of the new professoriate.

[1]For some examples see Bailyn; Fletcher and Bailyn; Fogg; Fothergill and Feltey; Gatta and Roos; Kerber; O' Laughlin and Bischoff; Philipsen; Williams; Wilson.

[2]Fifteen of these interviews were face to face. Five were conducted by telephone or Skype.

[3]Because of scheduling challenge, two interviews took place over two separate meetings.

[4] Length of service ranged from two to eighteen years.

[5]Though I recognize this study would be richer if a discussion of race and class were included, my primary focus was on the experience of academic mothers regardless of race and class. Because of my methodological choice of conversational interviewing, I opted not to include discussions of race and class in these interviews though I expect future research would seek to explore these issues in more depth.

[6]This is consistent with much of the research grounded in feminist standpoint theory which embraces multiple methods as a means of understanding womens' experiences (see Doughtery and Krone; Litwin and O'Brien Hallstein; O'Brien Hallstein).

[7]From this point forward, I refer to participants as professor/mothers or mother/professors. I interchange these terms to highlight the dynamic nature of these roles and the ways in which one is often privileged over the other is specific circumstances.

[8]Developed to facilitate data analysis in their study of the values in physician and patient narratives before and after an ethics education project,

the Value Identification in Narrative Discourse (VIND) technique, makes the process for identifying values explicit. The researcher is able to identify both terminal and instrumental values by focusing on the narrative elements of characters and actions. The authors propose a series of rules for analyzing each element, identifying how terminal and instrumental values are imbedded in the descriptions of behaviors, goals, obstacles, justifications, labels, emotions, and relationships present in the story (see Vanderford, Smith and Harris 129-130).

[9]Like Vanderford, Smith and Harris, I draw on the definition of "values" from Bruce Gronbeck and Ralph T. Eubanks: "'basic orientation toward life,' or 'a concept of the desirable,' which 'transcendentally guides actions and judgments across specific objects and situations...'" (cited in Vanderford, Smith and Harris 129).

[10]Many of the women interviewed explained they participated on committees to build these policies and lobbied for changes to existing policies to make them more user friendly and equitable.

[11]It is worthy to note that this participant had the youngest children and thus, the reaction of her chair may reflect the changes in institutional policy and practice or may signal a shift in general attitude and culture regarding pregnancy in academia.

[12]It is worthy to note that three of my participants were adamant that exercise was extremely high on their priority list and five others spoke of their spouses strong commitment to daily or rigorous exercise. On the whole, however, exercise was identified as the "priority that loses priority" when things come up. One participant noted, "I block time for exercise on my calendar, but nine times out of ten I cancel it because something comes up or I need the time for a meeting or something. I can't seem to hold that time like I do with other things."

[13]It is important to note that participants varied greatly in the frequency of use of caregivers. Some had routine help (e.g. same hours every week) while others hired when necessary. It became apparent in our discussions that frequency of use depended on finances, need, and individual comfort level.

[14]It is important to note here that five of the women in this study identified at least one of their children as having "special needs" requiring medical or psychiatric attention.

[15]Future research should focus on the specific language and practices these women employ that shape perceptions of mothering and professionalism.

Specifically, what makes them less likely to "buy in" to the ideology of intensive mothering and resist dominant narratives of professionalism.

WORKS CITED

Bailyn, Lotte. "Academic Careers and Gender Equity: Lessons Learned from Mit." *Gender, Work, and Organizations* 10 (2003): 137-53.

Dougherty, Debbie S. and Kathleen Krone. "Overcoming the Dichotomy: Cultivating Standpoints in Organizations through Research." *Women's Studies in Communication* 23.1 (2000): 16-40. Web. 5 Jan. 2008.

Douglas, Susan and Meredith Michaels. *The Mommy Myth: The Idealization of Motherhood and How It Has Undermined Women*. New York: Free Press, 2004.

Finkel, Susan K., Steven Olswang and Nian She. "Childbirth, Tenure and Promotion for Women Faculty." *The Review of Higher Education* 17.3 (1994): 259-70.

Fletcher, Joyce, and Lotte Bailyn, eds. *The Equity Imperative: Redesigning Work for Work-Family Integration: Organizational, Cultural, Critical and Individual Perspectives*. Mahwah: Lawrence Erlbaum, 2005.

Fogg, Piper. "Family Time: Why Some Women Quit Their Coveted Tenure Track Jobs." *Chronicle of Higher Education* 13 June 2003.

Fothergill, Alice and Kathryn Feltey. "I've Worked Very Hard and Slept Very Little: Mothers on the Tenure Track in Academia." *Journal for the Association of Research on Mothering* 5.2 (2003): 7-19.

Gatta, Mary L. and Patricia A. Roos. "Balancing Without a Net in Academia: Integrating Family and Work Lives." *Equal Opportunities International* 23 (2004): 124-42. Web. 5 March 2010.

Giddens, Anthony. *The Constitution of Society*. Berkeley: University of California Press, 1984.

Hays, Sharon. *The Cultural Contradictions of Motherhood*. New Haven, CT: Yale University Press, 1996.

Hochschild, Arlie Russell. *The Time Bind: When Work Becomes Home and Home Becomes Work*. New York: Metropolitan Books, 1997.

Kerber, Linda. "We Must Make the Academic Workplace More Humane and Equitable." *Chronicle of Higher Education* 18 March 2005: B6-B9.

Litwin, Anne Helaine, and Lynn O'Brien Hallstein. "Shadows and Silences: How Women's Positioning and Unspoken Friendship Rules in

Organizational Settings Cultivate Difficulties among Some Women at Work." *Women's Studies in Communication* 30.1 (2007): 111-142.

Mason, Mary Ann and Marc Goulden. "Do Babies Matter? The Effect of Family Formation on the Lifelong Careers of Academic Men and Women." *Academe Online* 88 (2002). Web. 5 January 2008.

Nelson, Jenny. "Phenomenology of Feminist Methodology: Explicating Interviews." *Doing Research on Women's Communication: Perspectives on Theory and Method*. Eds. K. Carter and C. Spitzak. Norwood, NJ: ABLEX, 1989. 221-41.

O'Brien Hallstein, Lynn D. "Silences and Choice: The Legacies of White Second Wave Feminism in the New Professoriate." *Women's Studies in Communication* 31.2 (2008): 143. Web. 3 March 2010.

O'Laughlin, Elizabeth and Lisa Bischoff. "Balancing Parenthood and Academia: Work/Family Stress as Influenced by Gender and Tenure Status." *Journal of Work Family Issues* 26 (2005): 79-106.

Pearson, Alison. *I Don't Know How She Does It: The Life of Kate Reddy, Working Mother*. New York: Random House, 2002.

Philipsen, Maike Ingrid. *Challenges of the Faculty Career for Women*. The Josey-Bass Higher and Adult Education Series. San Francisco: Josey Bass, 2008.

Townsley, Nikki C. and Kristen J. Broadfoot. 'Care, Career and Academe: Heeding the Calls of a New Professoriate." *Womens Studies in Communication* 31.2 (2008): 133-143.

Tracy, Sarah Jane and Angela Tretheway. "Fracturing the Real Self Fake Self Dichotomy: Moving toward 'Crystallized' Organizational Discourses and Identities." *Communication Theory* 15.2 (2005): 168-95.

Vanderford, Marsha L., David H. Smith, and Willard S. Harris. "Value Identification in Narrative Discourse: Evaluation of Hiv Education Demonstration Project." *Journal of Applied Communication Research* 20.2 (1992): 123-60.

Williams, Joan. "How the Tenure Track Discriminates against Women." *Chronicle of Higher Education* (2000): B10.

Wilson, Robin. " Rigid Tenure System Hurts Young Professors and Women, University Officials Say." *Chronicle of Higher Education* 7 October 2005: A12.

Wolf-Wendel, Lisa, and Kelly Ward. "Academic Life and Motherhood: Variations by Institutional Type." *Higher Education* 52.3 (2006): 487-521.

"We Shoot Our Wounded"

Pregnancy, Mothering and PPD on the Tenure Track

KERRI S. KEARNEY AND LUCY E. BAILEY

Rock-a-bye baby in the tree top.
When the wind blows the cradle will rock.
When the bough breaks, the cradle will fall.
And mommy will catch it, baby and all.[1]

I HAVE NEVER SUNG THIS LULLABY to my children with the original ending of "and down will come baby, cradle and all" (see Taylor). After all, what child wants to drift off to sleep with the image of impending doom stuck in her little head? Becoming a mother well after professional success, I believed not in the ability for women to have it all, but for women with good support and lots of energy to have *some* of whatever they wanted. So, although I had chosen to be both a working professional and a mother, I would of course be ready to catch my babies should they fall.

During my first two years as faculty at a research university, I listened with some curiosity but no real understanding to the "feminists" discuss the challenges of negotiating "it all"—with many situating their concerns against the backdrop of the ever-ticking tenure clock. I really wanted to relate but I didn't. I believed that competence, not mere biological designation as male or female, determined professional success. I often had, after all, worked my way into the good ole boys network—confident, all business, the kind of girl the guys would confide in. At the time, I didn't worry about tenure; I was confident in my ability to do my job and assumed the rest would take care of itself. As Andrea O'Reilly (2006) reflects on her experiences in academia, "I firmly believed that if I just continued to work hard, all would be fine." Looking back, she adds, "I am [now] amazed at both my defiance and naïveté" (77). How the mighty fall.

Through the act of writing and publishing this narrative about my experiences, I have chosen words over silence (Lorde) and action over passivity; however, as an academic scholar new to feminism, I also knew my limited knowledge of the feminist literature might mute the potential contributions of my reflections. There existed a real possibility of missing significant connections, marginalizing important points, or expressing something unintended. Perhaps as one sign of how my experiences with PPD changed me, I asked for help from a friend, colleague, and feminist scholar who served as co-author in this reflective process. And this is not unusual; women's experiences often benefit from shared processing, regardless of the names that rest on manuscript bylines (Dickens and Sagaria; Kochan and Mullen). However, this work remains an autoethnographic narrative, or a study of "one's own culture and oneself as a part of that culture," (Patton 85; Goodall; Hayano) and, as such, the focus goes back and forth between looking through an "ethnographic wide-angle lens, focusing outward on social and cultural aspects of ... personal experience," and looking inward, "exposing a vulnerable self that is moved and may move through, refract, and resist cultural interpretations" (Ellis and Bockner 739). Presented within an autoethnographic framework, this narrative of my experiences with PPD remains wholly my own, and only one possible interpretation of my experiences.

Among the questions I have confronted in choosing to publicly process my experiences echoes Lee Murray's thoughts about her work. Murray reflected, I know that making my story "available in the public domain, I need to assume everyone has the potential to read my work and know my secrets ... [I wonder if] the telling ... [will] be an opportunity to recreate myself and gain new insight that is not possible through introspection itself? ... Will the telling provide healing?" (130). In addition to these possibilities, I have also considered how the telling might help others. Will it *matter* to another woman who may encounter similar struggles? Will it *matter* in how we think about and work within academic culture? In how we think about PPD? These are my questions and my hopes.

In this narrative, I consider how the ideal of intensive mothering (O'Brien Hallstein; O'Reilly 2003) shapes both the experiences and evaluations of contemporary mothers who in particularly stigmatized ways fail to fit this ideal. My experiences with pregnancy and post-partum depression (PPD) while on the tenure track highlight how significant institutional, political and social factors in academia can shape academic women's experience with the ideal of intensive mothering. For untenured women, the traditional seven-year span of tenure-track time profoundly shapes their experiences with mothering ("Mothering in the Academy"), and mothering profoundly shapes their academic experiences. The PPD that can affect women in the wake of childbirth is a significant yet less recognized dimension of this phenomenon for academic mothers. Finally, as an organizational scholar, I draw from the embodied knowledge gained from my experiences to consider more broadly the culture of academia and the implications for all who work within it.

My initial guiding belief about academic culture was that gender mattered very little in enacting or assessing professional competence. But several experiences shifted this belief as the tenure clock relentlessly ticked away the months toward the organizational decision that would determine my professional future. First, I became unexpectedly and undeniably female—I got pregnant after two years in my faculty position. Then I gave birth and grappled with two encounters of post-partum depression (PPD), all while on the tenure track. These experiences forced me to acknowledge that gender is a powerful institutional force. I can boil this uncomfortable realization down to babies ... one of the few remaining wholly female territories in humanity today. But, like other professional women, pertinent aspects of my story began well before I entered the workplace.

PRE-TENURE TRACK: THE INFLUENCE OF EARLY TRAINING AND EXPERIENCE

From childhood, I was taught in both subtle and overt ways that femininity is best "covered" in organizational environments. I was the middle kid of three girls born to a stay-at-home mother and a father who, given few childhood advantages, still worked his way to financial and professional success. He was a strong authoritarian presence even in his frequent absences from the daily work of raising a family. I wonder now how truly disconcerted my father was when he fathered three girls; he was, after all, a man who openly stated, even years later, that he stopped teaching agricultural education "the year they let the girls in." His response was to raise us to compete like men, to work like men, to never need to depend on a man and, in order to do all of this, to attain the top levels of formal education. Although my mother quietly portrayed the very model of intensive mothering, willing to discount her own needs on behalf of her children (as defined by O'Brien Hallstein; O'Reilly 2006; and others[2]), my father's message was that professional success meant handling things like a man: De-emphasize the feminine. And, in my family, good performance was rewarded.[3]

All of these guidelines seemed very clear to me, even capable of living in concert, until I was a married professional. As marital guidance my father encouraged me to be at home when my husband returned from work, dinner on the table, with a smile on my face. My mother, offering no advice to the contrary, seemed to agree. But I wondered how I was to navigate those expectations with the demands of my professional commitments? What did that mean for having children? But I do believe this approach made sense to my father; it was the best path he could see for us—ensuring our ability to care for ourselves while my mother modeled the appropriate wife and mothering role. Within the proper circumstances (i.e., marriage and raising a family), we were, I suppose, intended to smoothly transform into suitable wives and mothers. And I don't know, even today, what a better path would have been. As is the case with all parents, their decisions were bound by time and context, and those decisions became significant for shaping my perspectives on balancing work and family.

With dual careers and dual incomes, my husband and I were three years into raising our family, happily co-parenting two young children, when fate intervened with sudden pregnancy—my own. For the professional me, it meant damage control. Pregnant on the tenure track—a clearly delineated seven-year period that determines the academic's future—should you or shouldn't you? Must you choose between family, mothering, and tenure? All these questions academic women have asked for decades become irrelevant if you are already surprisingly, unexpectedly pregnant at 39 years old. Instead, the question for the professional me became how I could quietly slip this third baby into my life when I was already clearly visible in the academic environment (Hochschild; Ward and Wolf-Wendel). T–5.5 years to tenure ... for the very first time, a ticking tenure clock suddenly became audible in my mind.

T − 5.5 YEARS TO TENURE (FALL 2005): FEMALE BODIES IN MASCULINE INSTITUTIONAL SPACE

Thoroughly absorbing both childhood and cultural messages that femininity and professionalism were incompatible I worried that my pregnant body would be a distraction—would signify my weakened professionalism in a competitive academic environment. I worked to offset the "problem" through sheer competency. So when, early in my pregnancy, the baby tested positive for Down Syndrome and a specialist diagnosed cleft lip, I grieved while researching the facts, selecting a surgeon and making preparations. When my husband emotionally checked out of what had become a totally overwhelming pregnancy to him, I soldiered forward with two small children and my rapidly burgeoning belly. In addition to my "regular" teaching and research load, I chaired a lectureship, took over a major grant, joined committees, ushered students along in their dissertations, revised program materials, and was on and off airplanes for consulting jobs external to the university. I was a pregnant woman on the tenure track, hear me roar!

At seven months pregnant, my body protested. Lack of attention to my own physical needs put me in the hospital, exhausted and with pneumonia. Never one to quit just because things became hard, I pushed on, juggling the grant's demands from my hospital bed with a Smartphone and no one the wiser. The moment I was released from the hospital, I was back on the job, anxious to reclaim my professionally appropriate persona. Within two months I delivered a healthy baby girl whose cleft lip was repaired eleven weeks later. Shortly after her surgery, I was diagnosed with post-partum depression (PPD), which was not at all unusual for an "older" mom who had a "difficult" pregnancy; as a result, I was placed on a mild anti-depressant. This was a blur of demands to navigate amidst pregnancy, childbirth, and mothering my other two children, but my successful negotiation of the competing needs made the following academic year a strong one for me.

T − 3 YEARS, 5 MONTHS (AUGUST, 2007): TOWARD A BUILDING STORM

When my youngest daughter was fifteen months old, my general practitioner took me off the anti-depressants with little evident concern. I gladly cast aside the drugs so often associated with women and weakness and hurried back to the more comfortable and organizationally-acceptable pressure of my to-do list. One more appointment to check off the list. Another "girl thing" to keep quiet. I barely even paused for a single breath in the doctor's office. Early training runs deep: competent, professional, and back to work. Tick, tock continues the clock.

By that fall, the grant that I led grew from a budget of $300,000 to 1.3 million dollars—at that time, the largest in the college—which I managed alongside my other research and teaching demands. With the grantor's tendency to work at all hours, I was literally on call 24 hours a day; he became a fulltime management job in himself—a fourth child pulling at my skirts. I often juggled a baby, with a toddler at my side, while my fingers flew across a keyboard balanced in my lap. It was a precarious balancing act, 24/7, and with no time or attention to myself, and without really processing the effects on my body, I became increasingly exhausted. And I began to struggle with the fear that I was failing on all fronts. Three months after going off the anti-depressant, in October of that year, I felt verbally attacked by a tenured male faculty member, looming over me, unhappy with how I handled the grant. With my background in business and organizational consulting, I didn't do things the right or the traditional academic way. Suggestions of mismanagement and that I was too "friendly" with the grantor flew. After all, how else could I have grown the grant the way that I did? My response to these accusations? I cried. And I submitted two resignations—one for the grant and one for my faculty position; both were refused, although eventually, and to my profound relief, I was allowed to depart from the grant.

Did I know something was wrong with me then? Certainly I should have. In my previous career, I was well accustomed to negotiating philosophical differences with others, including angry men intent on intimidation. Nothing in my work history would have foretold that I would panic in that set of circumstances. But I only remember the desire to hide, to seek safety. Unbeknownst to me or others around me, a rebound of the postpartum depression had been slowly wrapping its arms around me—silent, stealthy, and deadly. And none of us, least of all me, would realize that until many more months slipped away.

T – 3 YEARS, 8 MONTHS (NOVEMBER, 2007): BRINGING OUT THE HAZMAT SUIT

In her qualitative study of women living with PPD, Verta Taylor reports that the condition incites a "web of distressing emotions," from a pernicious blend of "sadness, hopelessness, worthlessness and loss" (45) to feelings of numbness and despair. For some women, PPD is simply a "dark cloud" (47). For me, those months of unknowingly living with advancing PPD were like wearing a full hazmat suit—outside of which everything and everyone seemed to be at a strange distance. The sense of isolation was confusing and eventually terrifying. Had I been able to articulate my struggle then, to expose my internal dialogue, it would have sounded something like:

> *I push harder—I want to be a part of the scenes of my life and I am trying, running hard, really I am, but I can't reach you, can't reach where you are—right where you are standing. I see people I* know *I* love *but I don't* feel *anything beyond the same level of compassion or concern that I would feel for a stranger. Even if I touch you with my bare hand—no heat, no breath from your body reaches me. There is little feeling in my world now. I can recognize emotion in your face but I can't internalize it, can't feel myself connect to it in any way. I hear myself silently scream "I am in here alone, please help me." I am a survivor, and I will fight my way through. Never let them see you sweat. Never* show weakness.

Burgeoning fear, an urgent need to seek safety from some undefined threat and a relentless clanging of my fight or flight instinct permeated my days and nights. All access to human emotion was eventually lost to me and, in my decisions and actions, I became rational and "cold." I fought for control through characterizing my new world as normal and manageable; I told myself I had finally become the real me.

As time passed and rebounding PPD wrapped me more tightly in its grasp, much of my memory of events become empty gaps: vague flashes of conversations with students whose faces are out of focus or missing and scattered classroom memories, despite teaching evaluations that establish I was there. I functioned in full faculty mode all the while, in what Raspin, in her description of PPD, calls a "trance state" (124). I also fought my unfolding reality in the personal spaces of my life, making rapid, *easy,* deliberate, and seemingly rational decisions to disconnect from those who tried to come too dangerously close to my internal world; this included separating from my husband without hesitation or any real feelings about the decision. The exception was my relationship with my children; I had deeply internalized the concept of intensive mothering as the right path. And I fully accepted that, if necessary, I would sacrifice myself for them. In some ways my *willingness* to sacrifice myself to mothering was my only remaining grasp on being a "suitable mother." I practiced an utter and, in many ways, ingrained avoidance of my own needs as my body gave way to illness—and a complete erasure of me.

T − 3 YEARS TO TENURE (JUNE 2008): THE STRANGER IN MY MIRROR

From my medical records I know that I called my obstetrician's office myself, at the beginning of summer, when my youngest daughter was two. On a Friday, I reported myself as in trouble, please help me, there's something terribly, terribly wrong. By that afternoon, I was pacing back and forth in my living room ranting in anger, loaded to the gills on a doctor-prescribed valium-like drug intended to "bridge" me to Monday, but unable to sit down. Out of control. Totally past coping. Suicidal. Undiagnosed, uncontrolled rebound PPD had finally blown apart all my best defenses and coping skills.

My next clear memory is from the following Monday at the doctor's office where I was temporarily placed on a medical hold by an openly dismayed doctor who offered repeated apologies for my current state. Knowing there was, indeed, a problem but wanting to maintain control and not over-dramatize the issue, I assured my doctor that I would make an appointment with a psychologist who was experienced with treating PPD. If I had something to help me until then, I would get it all under control. I was given a cocktail of drugs that allowed me to return to my scheduled day, which I did, arriving only fifteen minutes late to my next meeting with apologies to those present. I do not remember feeling distressed or anxious about the medical hold—from inside my hazmat suit, I characterized it as a rational response by the doctor. For me, it was simply an additional challenge I needed to overcome to efficiently return to my real responsibilities.

My next clear memory, from an unknown number of days later—overwhelming pain and grief. Sobbing on the couch of my kids' playroom. Feeling bruised, battered, and certain I wouldn't survive. I repeated one question over and over: "But where is my husband?" The drugs were beginning to do their job. They were slowly reconnecting my emotions to my conscious world. But my last moments of real, of connected, of lucid understanding were ten months old. I simply couldn't understand the links among where I was, what I felt, and the decisions I made that, even today, I cannot really, fully relate to me. Ten months to process and try to understand. To try to make right somehow. Ultimately it was too much. Overload. I spiraled back into numbness of a different kind. I was fully, painfully connected now but I could see no clear way through this. Barely hanging on by the jagged remnants of my acrylic fingernails.

What remains striking to me today is that from deep in the fog of those summer days, I could and did still find my children. Although I recognized the fragility of my state and internalized anew the many criticisms of my traditional extended family and the larger culture, I believed that, no matter what, my children needed me. Strangely, by idealized mothering standards, some may have judged me as a better mother during this time, less inhibited about play and hyper-attuned to meeting my children's desires and needs. Bedtimes were about tucking them in their little beds, reading stories, and passing out hugs and kisses. Mealtimes were simple but the moments after filled with games, uninhibited dancing to the radio that now piped through ceiling speakers in our new house—the one without a husband—and sweet, sweet laughter. These experiences contrasted starkly with the exhaustion that overtook me once my children were safely settled at school or with their father … exhaustion that led me to crawl into my bed to hide until I believed my children needed me yet again.

It seems important to note that the totality of my experience of PPD, and that which Sally Raspin reported in her narrative about PPD, is at odds with common media representations. My PPD occurred just after two U.S. mothers severely neglected or attacked their own children; their diagnosis, as reported by the national media, was PPD. While each of my doctors was clear that there is much we still do not understand about PPD, a mother's inclination to harm her children was explained as a type of post partum *psychosis* undifferentiated from post partum *depression*.[4] Taylor's explanation of PPD as a form of "gender deviance" (36) might help explain society's fascination with the most dramatic and damaging of PPD-related incidents: Women's experience of darkness and despair in the wake of childbirth violates cultural prescriptions for motherhood and thus becomes a compelling draw for voyeuristic audiences. But I believe that equally damaging to understanding the complexity of women's experiences with PPD in all its expressions is the reductive and simplistic representations that women simply lose control. In fact, PPD has a component that must be diagnosed and treated chemically—my doctors compared PPD to diabetes, a disease that also requires chemical treatment and cannot be simply "powered through." With PPD, it is not a simple matter of giving up or claiming control. This was a difficult truth I struggled to accept so that I could begin to forgive myself for what I initially perceived as my personal weakness; only then did I begin to truly heal.

While I have come to understand that my indoctrination into mothering has a scholarly term—intensive mothering—and is an ideal that is taught to women across both class and racial lines (O'Brien Hallstein), I continue to look for an additional explanation for my ability to mother while so thoroughly ravaged by PPD. Why was it the perceived needs of my mothering role that broke through the fog? The most compelling explanation for me is the concept of maternal instinct—I credit some type of biologically-based force that pushed me to mother, daily, robotically, and often carefully, checking each key step in my own mind. Maternal instinct is a construct feminists have problematized for years, one of many efforts to combat biological essentialism that has long reduced women's skills and behavior to the ineffable and inevitable workings of nature. Just as Taylor's study of PPD details, experiences deemed biological are processed and lived through social categories. Yet as I acknowledge the extent to which PPD stripped me of any sense of myself, and consider it within the framework of intensive mothering, it is not a question of whether I prioritized my children or me—there was no me. And while, after a great deal of analysis of my experience, an explanation of biologically-driven maternal instinct feels inadequate, I have not yet found a better way to make sense of my experiences.

I was single with three kids and still on the tenure track. But for how long? And against what odds? The person in the mirror looked familiar but I gazed at her only briefly; she was someone from a past life whom I forgot the moment I looked away. And the ticking tenure clock and passage of time barely registered; achieving tenure seemed far beyond my immediate battlefield.

T – 2 YEARS, 10 MONTHS TO TENURE (FALL 2008): THE GENDERED FRAILTIES OF THE BODY AND ACADEMIA

During that summer, still the summer my youngest daughter was two, three wonderful doctors supported me as my PPD cycled in and out of control. I was not under contract at the university and I did not call in to report my condition. At a deep level I sensed and understood—in some ways had been prepared from the cradle for just this type of service: There was no space for my very female experiences in the narratives of autonomy, professionalism and rationality that govern academia. Higher education is a profoundly gendered institution, built on an array of assumptions about competition, getting credit for work, building an individual reputation in youth, negotiating "scarce" time, and actively "minimizing" family life (Hochschild 126-127). PPD not only violates cultural prescriptions concerning women's roles and motherhood (which perhaps evokes fear and hinders other academic mothers' support and feelings of affinity), it also violates the professional academic workplace: it intrudes messily with the emotional, the personal, the gendered, the unpredictable, and the unspoken in space constituted by the Cartesian mind/body split (Grosz).

And, though I could have never articulated this at the time, at some level I must have recognized, as Murray did in her work, that if I told my secret, there was "no turning back or taking back. I [would be] left wide open to absorb the reactions of others. Part of what [got] in the way of my telling [was] the expected response of the listener" (130). Indeed, the listener's response seemed utterly predictable as I, too, had been raised and trained in a culture in which people experience masculine values as normative and idealized, and I was struggling with the confusing collapse of once clear, tidy, and comforting boundaries. Yet my embodied experiences were beginning to render the fabricated and absurd nature of that divide strikingly clear to me, even as I recognized the divide and its accompanying values still governed my academic workplace. As Gareth Morgan expressed, "so long as organizations are dominated by ... patriarchal values, the roles of women in organizations will always be played out on 'male' terms" (219), including by women anxious not to discuss that which may threaten their viability in a very gendered organizational arena.

And yet, in August, as my children were two, four and six, and as my tenure clock entered its fourth year, summer was ending and I had to return to work. I was shaky, fearful, with minimal stamina and a sense of impending doom. But I simply had no choice. I was alone and now living in a harsh and full-color reality. I feared that as I was still healing someone would judge me as an inadequate mother and try to take my children from me. And, in keeping them with me, I feared the implications for my children of having a less than ideal mother. I also had to fight to retain my career—all the while knowing that three of my seven designated tenure years had already passed. Nothing was stable; nothing was certain; everything seemed at risk.

Now back at work, my hazmat suit seemed to be replaced by a cloak of invisibility, of nonexistence, of a different kind of isolation than that which I experienced from within the hazmat suit. I sensed there was no space to express what I was negotiating. No one stuck their heads into my office for casual conversation. Some colleagues looked the other way when I walked down the hall, responded only briefly, or were painfully but minimally polite when required. My offers to assist with departmental efforts seemed to be set aside or simply not needed. My primary interactions with colleagues took place in formal meetings from which I could not be omitted. I am struck now that my body—intrusive and pregnant merely two years earlier—now felt utterly invisible. In his study of privilege, power, and difference, sociologist Allan Johnson reminds us of the significance of visibility in human experience, writing, "of all human needs, few are as powerful as the need to be seen, included, and accepted by other people" (58). Indeed.

Feeling deeply hurt and a gnawing fear about how to navigate an increasingly unfamiliar and unfriendly workplace, and with growing pressure from my extended family to "get your act together" and "to be the [traditional] mother I know you can be," my hard-earned control of PPD became fragile and I could not forestall a deepening descent. My doctors recommended I take medical leave from the university and, with some relief, growing acceptance that I couldn't do it alone, and yet fear of the implications, I agreed. Once I made that decision, I no longer had a choice about whether to tell. And yet I predicted what the listener's response might be in this context. In addition to my failure to fit the intensive mothering ideal, I feared that articulating this failure, my failure to control my own body, would pose an even greater risk to my career than any of my private struggles had.

Significantly, although I received the support of individual administrators, I discovered that no institutional mechanism existed to assist faculty members who take medical-related leave. As it was after the birth of my child, during my six weeks of medical leave I never was truly away from the demands of the university—not physically, electronically, or emotionally. Medical leave from the university, I found, was a pretty but false illusion, like working "part-time," something O'Reilly (2006) calls "another one of the ironies of university life" (79). During my medical leave, I received little support with courses or dissertation advisees and, as I acknowledged this reality and withdrew further into myself, there was little obvious need for support and, therefore, little help came from those who may have been willing. And many may not have noticed my struggles, pressured by their own responsibilities, focusing only on the flurry of demands that faced them or, equally possible, noticing but just not knowing what to say. From my position within this competitive and individualistic culture, I didn't feel I had any real options but to find the needed strength within *me*—the determination to persevere, to push through. I was an untenured woman socialized to believe in the importance of cloaking female sex status with masculine competence, with children who needed me, with complex collegial relationships, and with a stigmatized and little understood condition that violated every norm of academic professionalism.

When I returned to the university six weeks later, I felt isolated and out of the loop. But, seeing few choices, I trudged forward in baby steps. I healed and became strong. In February 2009, my children's father and I celebrated a medical declaration of full recovery from PPD—finally real, doctor-affirmed freedom from a terrible battle. With a deepened understanding of the intricacies of PPD and of our relationship, my husband and I reunited. But I told almost no one at the university. I sensed there would have been no celebration on my behalf.

My experiences with PPD in an academic role exemplify feminists' arguments that social context shapes experiences deemed biological, in this case, women's experiences with mothering and with the uniquely embodied experience of PPD. And though I consider surviving those dark days a monumental success—this is not what success looks like in academia. As O'Reilly states, "Had I been willing to cleave off my maternal self and 'pass' as a non-mother, my stay in academia would have been less difficult" (2006: 76). Indeed, to navigate academia properly, I would have had to hide many more of my experiences in the wake of my daughter's birth. Yet such cleaving and passing were impossible. PPD did not give me that choice, even though I recognized that the condition likely symbolized to others the presumed weaknesses of women's bodies, or more accurately, the human frailties that lurk around every corner for all of us, man or woman—the complex nexus of circumstances that might transform any of us, in an instant, from competent professionals to the wounded and hunted. Just as my pregnancy "did not fit" (Pillow) in the academic workspace, the physical and emotional reverberations of PPD were at odds with all that the culture embodied: autonomy, rationality, certainty, competitiveness, and competency. These gendered experiences in a gendered organization finally helped me understand my feminist colleagues' perspectives that seemed, at one time, abstract and intangible, even as suspicious efforts to escape some modicum of their own professional responsibility: Gender does in fact matter, in profound cultural, institutional and personal ways.

And while the implications of this gendered cultural issue extend well beyond higher education, it has particular implications in academia because we relentlessly subject faculty and students to evaluation, comparison and ranking, and, in the case of faculty, we sometimes see ourselves somehow removed from or immune to the messy human issues that plague the general population as a whole. Academic culture encourages faculty to maintain psychological facades, or exhibit organizationally acceptable emotions, behaviors, gestures and verbal statements (Hewlin), in part because it is, after all, a masculine, professional culture. It has been called a "cult," in which the rules and norms are so heavily inscribed that those who leave must actively work to "deprogram" their thinking and adjust to the "outside" culture (Benton[5]). While eccentricity is welcomed, there is no institutional space for weakness: Losing control is perceived as an utterly feminine construct.

T − 1 YEAR, 10 MONTHS TO TENURE (FALL 2009): POST PPD-ME: REDEFINING MY ROLE AND MYSELF

After many months of recovery and reflection, I realized that one workplace complexity I was navigating was that I simply did not remember much of what occurred two years earlier, while I worked and interacted with my colleagues with undiagnosed and untreated PPD, and while I was disconnected from everything that makes up me. Whole conversations were lost from my memory and I found at times that colleagues were inexplicably angry, waiting for me to make amends or to address some event or conversation that occurred during a time for which I had no recollection. At these moments I felt like I was walking through a room wired with invisible explosives. Now free of the distorting vision of the hazmat suit and the work of processing the consequences of a condition that I could not have foreseen or controlled, I realized that however flawed the institutional resources for supporting mothering labor and no matter the responses to my medical condition, my own responses also had consequences within this culture. I was learning how to navigate my changed perspective within the scripts governing a masculine work culture in which, I, too, had been socialized.

T – 1 YEAR, 6 MONTHS TO TENURE (DECEMBER 2009): IT'S JUST *OUR* CULTURE: "WE SHOOT OUR WOUNDED"

Two comments about academic culture made during the following months have stayed with me. In both cases, I believe these constructive reflections were offered to help me depersonalize some of my experiences and gain additional perspective on academic culture. The first was the insight that in higher education "we shoot our wounded"—a comment referring to the competitive, masculine nature of academic work, an environment that, in this reference, culls out its weaker members through deliberate gunfire rather than waiting on natural selection. The second and related comment was uttered in a separate conversation, and I have come to recognize it as having profound implications for academic mothers; it was, "You can never show weakness in higher education" or the wolves will circle.

How sad. Because, as an organizational scholar and consultant, this I do know: While changing culture can be difficult, doing so is entirely in our hands. Institutional culture is a collective of decisions and rules that are continuously created (or re-created) and maintained by the people who are *present*. Edgar Schein, an author of seminal work on culture, defines culture as a product of "shared learning." Behavioral regularities; group norms, values and philosophies; rules of the game; climate or the "feeling" of the culture; embedded skills; habits of thinking and mental models; and shared meanings and symbols—combined with our human desire for consistency and meaning—form deeply held, shared assumptions. Arlie Russell Hochschild notes these are enduringly gendered. Assumptions that undergird cultural practices become unconscious and, as a result of deeply ingrained habits of thinking and behaving, culture accrues substance and power. As Schein argues:

> *Once formed and taken for granted, [cultural assumptions] become a defining property of the group that permits the group to differentiate itself from other groups, and in that process, value is attached to such assumptions. They are not only "our" assumptions, but by virtue of our history of success, they must be right and good. In fact ... we take culture so much for granted and put so much value on our assumptions that we find it awkward and inappropriate even to discuss our assumptions or ask others about their assumptions.* (373)

Culture becomes a part of our individual, professional identities. In other words, the strength of the masculine assumptions underlying long-established and accepted cultural practices allows a faculty member, a member of the culture, to observe that in higher education "*we* shoot our wounded." It's who *we* are.

Perhaps *we* should revisit this. In any given institution, our culture is *us*. Despite its exclusionary origins, contemporary academic culture is comprised of diverse embodied beings, including women whose bodies and lives continue to bear much of the responsibility for social reproduction. And when the complexity of their mothering lives can no longer be easily molded to the norms of professionalism, as my circumstances illustrate, mothering academics can become increasingly vulnerable. As Richard Wisniewski argues, "what most academics do was learned from their elders in the academy. Spending more time than most in school in order to attain a doctorate inevitably increases the likelihood of being like one's elders" (12). This statement is critical to understanding the reproduction of academic culture. It suggests that despite the appearance of new faces in academia, of new bodies and new needs, we may continue to reinvent the same culture again and again and then accept it as "ours"— the game pieces change but the rules of the game live on.[6]

T – 10 MONTHS TO TENURE: STRONG ENOUGH

The following year I openly worked as a woman of strength, rather than as a woman conditioned to carefully and appropriately cloak my femininity to accommodate established academic norms. Some of the most personal things a woman can experience—childbirth and post-partum depression, which led to a quite literal battle for my life—taught me that being wholly female doesn't make me second class; it doesn't make me weak. Indeed, my standpoint from my unique experiences have starkly illuminated for me, in productive and empowering ways, gendered patterns in academic culture that feminist scholarship has traced for decades. But I make no claims of having found a true balance between empowered contemporary mothering ("women who have benefited from feminist gains") and the socially "'proper'" ideology of intensive mothering" (O'Brien Hallstein 116). Identifying how to achieve this balance, while pursuing meaningful academic work, is perhaps the greatest challenge of my coming years.

However, given the significance of the PPD that previously erased emotion from my life, I consider the ability to connect with my *feelings*, a feminine construct, as a profound gift—a reminder of my humanity. I have accepted that organizational events can occur in which tears are an *appropriate* response and the willingness to show them a sign of great *strength,* in part because they are at odds with unspoken but normative organizational mandates. In my still ongoing redefinition of my beliefs about gender and organizational culture, I suggest that emotions and other aspects of my femininity I once shunned at work are quite literally the *lifeblood* of our institutions; for without feelings, there is no passion toward the shared cause. To deny spaces in our organizational environments for embodiment and emotion considered intrusive and inappropriate is to deny passion and the collective effort that is so often needed to achieve greatness.

I have continued to consider many questions in the wake of my experiences: Would events have differed if I was a mother employed in another type of organization? Were the seemingly universal organizational silences and responses to my gendered illness really about my untenured status—an inherently vulnerable and thus feminine position anyway? Why were the voices of other academic mothers muted or missing during my experiences? Was much of the organizational fallout really about bringing me to heel because I thought and acted differently? Was it about discomfort with the vulnerabilities of the human body and their intrusion into professional academic space ostensibly dedicated to the life of the mind? Or was it for, at least a few, simply that they were scurrying along in their daily lives and didn't notice, didn't know what to say, didn't want to intrude on my business, or were also untenured (and thus somewhat silenced lest they be associated with my perceived differences)? These are all legitimate questions and I see no clear-cut answers (see Wisniewski).

I am also left with broader questions to consider as, after that rebuilding year, I chose to stay at the university and am in the midst of tenure review as this narrative is completed. But I continue to reflect on my experiences and choose words over silence (Lorde). I am a part of the academic culture that I critique, a stance that feminist Patti Lather calls working both within and against (cited in St. Pierre and Pillow). And I have developed deep and abiding relationships that demonstrate the enduring possibilities for connection within any organization. In her writings about motherhood and academia, Andrea O'Reilly says of her own journey,

> I realized that feminism was to be about changing the system, not about securing a niche in it. Getting some of us in, I understood, would not set us free (76) … Looking back, I realize that, despite my insistent affirmations of my maternal self, my motherhood had not in any substantial way challenged the way the university worked: I seldom missed class, I was never late, I always had my readings done, and my course papers, though handed in late, were of the highest caliber. I was behaving, for the most part, as the good graduate student I was expected to be. (2006: 77)

However, in other space in the same writings, O'Reilly notes that "Mothers cannot effect changes … in an institution in which they have no power" (2006: 184). These statements capture the continuing and seemingly unrelenting maelstrom in which we, as mothering academics, remain. Does the system require that we first successfully transverse it in order to earn a voice for changing it? And is successfully navigating it simply "buying in" and perpetuating that which we so desperately long to change? When will all of the components of maternity and mothering become a visible, acceptable part of professional culture rather than an aberration, a distraction? I don't pretend to have these answers.

Women and mothers still struggle to claim equal professional space in the academy, and any progress toward an improved culture is not without cost. I have ceased to be as willing to accept that we must live compliantly in our established culture or that we must continue to do things in the traditional academic fashion. And as I pushed back in recent days, I was told that "it was much easier for all of us when you were sick," a statement that shocked and angered me because I know exactly how difficult and dangerous my fight back to full health really was. And, in that moment, I embraced my own truth and peace with being a visibly strong and outwardly comfortable *woman,* a *mother,* in a culture that provides little space for those aspects of my identity. But, as Saundra Stroope and Bonnie Hagemann have also stated, *I hold great hope.*

> Just as water seeks its own level, women will eventually … arrive at their own form of leadership … When water is seeking its own level, resisting forces can keep it tilted for awhile, but no amount of resistance will keep the level at bay forever. (53)

Many of the events I experienced, from pregnancy and PPD through my return to full health, offer powerful evidence that few, if any of us, have the skills to create the necessary institutional space to discuss and negotiate in productive ways the emotional and corporeal vulnerabilities that mark our lives. These conversations can be messy, and awkward, and they seem primarily reserved for stolen moments with confidants rather than organizational space. Those who violate cultural norms may navigate feelings of failure and shame as they confront the gap between their own needs and those of their institutions. "While organizations may be socially constructed realities, these constructions are often attributed a life and power of their own that allow them to exercise a measure of control over their creators" (Morgan 207). So we often remain silent on things that really matter, and in so doing perpetuate a culture that can be a psychic prison of assumptions, beliefs and practices that restrict our actions, our thinking, and our abilities to consider realities outside of our self-constructed world (Morgan)—all while we claim to be the last bastion of academic freedom.

POSTSCRIPT

As I read the final copy of this autoethnographic narrative, I acknowledge that the story is woefully incomplete. While it paints an accurate (but inevitably partial) picture of the impact of PPD on my professional life, it only hints at, and then leaves unwritten, other more personal elements of my story—elements that reach beyond my purpose here. And I am left to question the implications for others of telling only part of the story.

While there are many people to acknowledge for their positive roles in my own recovery from PPD, my thoughts now are mostly with my sister Kristi (1964-1997), who I hope would be fiercely proud of this piece, and with my beloved children, whose presence powered my very survival. In my darkest of days, stripped of any sense of myself and my feelings, it ceased to be a question of whose needs were privileged over whose. It was only for them that I continued to fight, until the time that I could reclaim the pieces of myself. It was said best by others well before I ever put pen to paper:

> The most notable facts that culture imprints on women is a sense of our limits. The most important thing one woman can do for another is to illuminate and expand her sense of actual possibilities ... it means the mother herself is trying to expand the limits of her life. To refuse to be a victim: and then to go on from there. (Rich 246)

For my three little loves—if ever you realize that the people around you don't appreciate the unique value that is truly you, it is time to change things. But always, always, you must stay in the fight.

[1]We discovered that Verta Taylor appropriately uses this lullaby to frame her study on women's experiences with PPD.
[2]Intensive mothering within the United States "rests on at least three core beliefs: 1) children need and require constant and ongoing nurturing by their biological mothers who are single-handedly responsible for meeting those needs; 2) in meeting those needs, mothers must rely on experts to guide them; and 3) mothers must lavish enormous amounts of time and energy on their children." See O'Brien Hallstein (107). For other discussions of intensive mothering, see Hayes as well as Douglas and Michaels.
[3]My interest is not in mother or father blaming; all parenting decisions are bound by time and context and can be judged in various ways through

the convenient lens of retrospect. Likewise I am not at all convinced that my mother's portrayal of intensive mothering was in lieu of empowered mothering ("the power to define and determine [her] own experiences of mothering," O'Brien Hallstein107) – instead I suspect these were her choices, influenced by both her family and her generation; but this is a question she would need to answer for herself.

[4]Shortly before publication of this chapter, I learned that the medical community also recognizes postpartum obsessive compulsive disorder (PPOCD), a condition believed to have almost no chance of causing a mother to harm her children. Given the common public perception that all post-partum illness is dangerous to children, and the implications of this belief in a culture of intensive mothering, it seems important to reference the increasing layering of understanding of illness related to the post-partum time period. For more information, please see the International OCD Foundation articles by Abramowitz and Penzel.

[5]For more on this phenomenon, see Thomas Benton's series of critiques of higher education culture and processes in the *Chronicle of Higher Education*.

[6]See Wisniewski for reflections on why scholars sometimes "avert their gaze" from interrogating their own institutional practices.

WORKS CITED

Abramowitz, Jonathan. *Beyond the Blues: Postpartum* OCD. International OCD Foundation, 2010. Web. 25 January 2011. <http://www.ocfoundation.org/EO_Postpartum.aspx>.

Benton, Thomas H. "Is Graduate School a Cult?" *Chronicle of Higher Education,* 28 June 2004: n.p. Web. 11 Jan 2011. <http://chronicle.com/article/Is-Graduate-School-a-Cult-/44676/>.

Dickens, Cynthia Sullivan, and Mary Ann D. Sagaria. "Feminists at Work: Collaborative Relationships Among Women Faculty." *The Review of Higher Education* 21.1 (1997): 79-101.

Douglas, Susan, and Meredith Michaels. *The Mommy Myth: The Idealization of Motherhood and How It Has Undermined All Women.* New York: Free Press, 2004.

Ellis, Carolyn and Arthur P. Bochner. "Autoethnography, Personal Narrative, Reflexivity: Researcher as Subject." *Handbook of Qualitative*

Research. 2nd ed. Ed. Norman K. Denzin and Yvonna S. Lincoln. Thousand Oaks, CA: Sage, 2000. 733-68.

Goodall, Harold Lloyd, Jr. *Writing the New Ethnography*. Walnut Creek, CA: AltaMira, 2000.

Grosz, Elizabeth. *Volatile Bodies: Toward a Corporeal Feminism*. Bloomington: Indiana University Press, 1994.

Hayano, David M. "Autoethnography: Paradigms, Problems, and Prospects." *Human Organization* 38 (1979): 113-20.

Hayes, Sharon. *The Cultural Contradictions of Motherhood*. New Haven, CT: Yale University, 1996.

Hewlin, Patricia F. "And the Award for Best Actor Goes To ... : Facades of Conformity in Organizational Settings." *Academy of Management Review* 28.4 (2003): 633-642.

Hochschild, Arlie Russell. "Inside the Clockwork of Male Careers." *Gender and the Academic Experience: Berkeley Women Sociologists*. Eds. Kathryn P. Meadow Orlans and Ruth A. Wallace. Lincoln: University of Nebraska Press, (1975): 125-140.

Johnson, Allan G. *Privilege, Power and Difference*. Mountain View, CA: Mayfield, 2001.

Kochan, Frances K., and Carol A. Mullen. "Collaborative Authorship: Reflections on a Briar Patch of Twisted Brambles." *Teachers College Record* 12 Feb 2001. Web. 30 January 2011. <http://www.tcrecord.org>

Lorde, Audre. "The Transformation of Silence into Language and Action." *Sister Outsider*. New York: Crossing (1984): 40-44.

Morgan, Gareth. *Images of Organization*. Newbury Park, CA: Sage, 2006.

"Mothering in the Academy." *Journal of the Association of Research on Mothering* 5.2 (2003).

Murray, Lee. "Secrets of an 'Illegitimate Mom'." *Journal of the Motherhood Initiative* 1.2 (2010): 126-136.

O'Brien Hallstein, D. Lynn. "Second Wave Silences and Third Wave Intensive Mothering." *Mothering in the Third Wave*. Ed. Amber E. Kinser. Toronto: Demeter, 2008: 107-118.

O'Reilly, Andrea. *Mother Outlaws: Theories and Practices of Empowered Mothering*. Toronto: Women's Press, 2004.

O'Reilly, Andrea. *Rocking the Cradle: Thoughts on Motherhood, Feminism and the Possibility of Empowered Mothering*. Toronto: Demeter, 2006.

Patton, Michael. *Qualitative Research & Evaluation Methods (third edition)*. Thousand Oaks CA: Sage, 2002.

Penzel, Fred. *"But I love My Kids…": Parents Who Think About Harming Their Children*. International OCD Foundation, 2010. Web. 25 January 2011. <http://www.ocfoundation.org/EO_IntrusiveKids.aspx>.

Pillow, Wanda S. *Unfit Subjects: Educational Policy and the Teen Mother*. New York: Routledge, 2004.

Raspin, Sally. "Memories of Post Natal Depression." *Journal of Motherhood Initiative* 1.2 (2010): 121-125.

Rich, Adrienne. *Of Woman Born: Motherhood as Experience and Institution*. New York: Norton, 1976.

Schein, Edgar. "Defining Organizational Culture." *Classics of Organization Theory*. 6th ed. Ed. Jay M. Shafritz, Steven Ott, and Yong Suk Jang. Orlando: Harcourt College, 2001. 369-376.

St. Pierre, Elizabeth and Wanda Pillow, eds. *Working the Ruins: Feminist Poststructuralist Theory and Methods in Education*. New York: Routledge, 2000.

Stroope, Saundra, and Bonnie K. Hagemann. "Women, Water and Leadership." *T&D Magazine* 65.3 (2011): 50-53.

Taylor, Verta. *Rock-a-By Baby: Feminism, Self-Help and Post-Partum Depression*. New York: Routledge, 1996.

Ward, Kelly Anne, and Lisa Wolf-Wendel. "Academic Motherhood: Managing Complex Roles in Research Universities." *The Review of Higher Education* 27.1 (2004): 233-257.

Wisniewski, Richard. "The Averted Gaze." *Anthropology & Education Quarterly* 31.1 (2000): 5-23.

3.

"You Can Slip One in Between Your Thesis and Comps"

Unanticipated Consequences of Having a Baby in Graduate School

SERENA PATTERSON

I ALWAYS WANTED TO BE A MOTHER. And, a scientist. And a writer. I would set up rows of Coke bottles in my garage: test tubes filled with rotting mixtures of lilacs, dandelions, clover, and water. If I could recruit my little brother and his friends, I would keep them busy hunting for specimens, and I would show them where violets grew in the shade and how to pull the golden yellow portion out of a blade of grass. My mother said, "You'll be a great teacher," but I would record the day in my diary; "I'm going to be a great scientist."

In college, I would put Barbra Streisand on the stereo and belt out, "Ask what I want, and I will sing: I want everything, everything!" My head swam in the world of ideas like a newly hatched minnow in the pond. Once I discovered my savant-like talent for writing papers and passing exams, I set my sights on an academic career in Psychology. I had played "other mother" to children, who provided me with endless motivation to work out how they learned, how they felt, what they needed, and how they could flourish. Whatever I couldn't learn, well, I'd discover and write about. And, like Jean Piaget, I would have my own children to observe and to wonder in.

So, at 23 years old I packed a bag, got on a plane in Chicago, bound for Vancouver. In a six-hour flight, I went from the rural Midwest to Vancouver, British Columbia, and Simon Fraser University of the 1980s. I could hardly wait to immerse myself in the upper levels of academia, to discover a community of real-live feminist scholars, to experience urban life, and to see the ocean.

I didn't have a clue about what I was in for. I had come from a small, liberal arts college, where we were nurtured as scholars within a benevolent institution. I still believed that the growth of knowledge would be steeped in wonder, as it had been the day I first saw individual cells under the microscope, or when I saw that dendrites mirrored the limbs of trees, reaching outward. I was not prepared for indifference to my well being, disdain for the human subject of study, or seminars as the arena for debate as a blood sport. I had not yet separated nurturance from learning, feeling from knowing, or creation from writing. I didn't want to split the world of ideas from the world of growing things, but it seemed a requirement that I must do so.

A small department, Simon Fraser University's Clinical Psychology program had few bragging rights at that time other than brute performance pressure; faculty members expressed open pride in low acceptance and high attrition rates. My life narrowed; I was making no music, writing no diary, creating no puppets. I was so starved for creativity that I made miniature poems out of the names of variables that I would print, like haiku, across the tables of my statistics assignments. But the most passionately inspired of these were clichés of desperation, like "Get Me Out Of Here," or "Eat Shit And Die." I blamed the limits of the genre. I missed family, cornfields, woodlands, and growing things. Even when I found a community of feminists, I felt like a creature from another planet, and I was not at all inclined to accept an urban disdain for the place I came from as inferior. Only the lack of funds for a plane ticket, and a certain amount of stubborn pride that would not give up, kept me from returning "home" to my Midwest small town roots.

This loneliness may explain, if it needs explaining, the bass track to all of my other mind-work: a deep, low voice chanting, "Baby ... Baby ... Baby." By the time I was 26, I had latched on to a likely-looking husband, and was actively trying to get pregnant. I had read enough Anthropology and Labour History to know that the stay-at-home ideal of middle-class motherhood was an anomaly. Women had babies with them while they gathered and worked the fields, organized general strikes, protested nuclear armaments, and, yes, wrote articles and dissertations. I planned it on the advice of my office-mate, who genuinely encouraged me to "slip one in between your thesis and your comps." I could study for comprehensive exams during the baby's first year, then enroll her in free childcare on campus. I'd always been a straight-A student; how hard could this baby thing be?

Again, I didn't have a clue what I was in for. I had come from the land of extended families, church potlucks, and really small town neighbors—the kind that know everybody's business but will pitch in with things like babies. But here, daycare was not free, and the paternal grandparents did not baby-sit. My beautiful daughter did not play at my feet, but seemed to come with a book-detection alarm that went off in a squall every time I tried to read. There it was again, that split between the world of growing things and the world of ideas. The demand that one be put aside for the other was like a wedge through the live center of my being.

I certainly tried to accomplish the split. I put Laura in daycare at four months old, but my breasts still sprung to life like geysers at the sight of her photograph on my bulletin board. I became adept at capturing the flow into Playtex Nurser bags. I brought these to the daycare at noon and at 4:30, when I and the other mommies in bean-bag chairs breast-fed happy, sleepy children before the commute home. Even as my body ached for her presence, I counted every child-free hour as gold. On the day Laura turned six months old, I failed my Comprehensive Exams and lost my milk. The latter was restored within the week; the Exams would not come around again for an entire year.

Given the situation, reading psychodynamic theory on infant attach-ment and object relations felt akin to poking hot needles into my eyes,[1] so I changed my dissertation topic to Maternal Adjustment. A little easier on my maternal guilt, this literature was still pretty much limited to treatises on a) Post-partum Depression, and b) how depressed mothers compromised child development. Just asking mothers about their own needs and experiences appeared to be a radical act; hardly anybody was doing that. So I started observing life from the maternal side. With a wonderfully supportive supervisor, I began a project that saw nearly 80 new mothers interviewed about their changing and connected sense of identity, and about the languages of morality that they used to navigate the return-to-work vs. stay-at-home dilemma (Patterson 1992).

That's what I did during daycare hours. Meanwhile, as our third-floor walk-up was demolished for urban renewal, we moved into a student apartment on campus: one bedroom, 400 square feet, with the fire alarm next to our front door. Laura slept in three-hour shifts. At the age of eighteen months, she would sing out, "I want a nice, warm, bottle, please!" several times a night with perfect articulation. I could handle the bottle requests with my eyes closed. But nighttime fire alarms left us both in an adrenalin state that lasted until the daycare opened, and my precious study hours would be passed in semi-somnolence. I stuffed the fire alarm with the cloth diapers that I had abandoned for disposables, and became both an environmental disaster and a building code outlaw at the same time.

I should have shed my loneliness; the building was full of young children. But their fathers, not their mothers, were the students. I had lunch weekly with Alison, a graduate student in education whose first pregnancy corresponded with mine and whose robust little daughter led Laura around enthralled. But, when her second child was born, Alison and her family left us behind for a Gulf Island and "Attachment Mothering": family bed, breast-feeding on demand, home-schooling, the works. Such were the polarized options that we could see: 24-7 parenting or daycare at four months; stay in the academic race encumbered, or wait on the side for the next two decades. These became the breaking points for friendships; if we could not validate one another, we also could not bear to watch what we might be missing. The mothers that I interviewed mirrored this split. I would wince inwardly when an at-home mother would refer to those who "dumped" or "parked" children in daycare, and I wondered how objective I could be in assessing the compromises made by those who returned to employment or schooling. I envied those with eager grandparents, career-established husbands, and houses with grass around them.

I did not lack for even extraordinary gestures of kindness or pieces of luck. During my internship in a strange city, the Neuropsychologist that I worked with lent me a car, with the insurance paid, for over six months. I house-sat, rent free, from February through August, and my portion of a clinic coffee fund was mysteriously marked "paid," saving me $60: the cost of my pride. Laura loved cabbage; the one fresh vegetable that you can buy all winter, cheap. One of my supervisors volunteered to take Laura for nearly a week while I presented my very first conference paper in 1990, on "Autonomy and Connection: New mothers' sense of self and the return-to-work dilemma" (Patterson 1990).

Still, my most precious adult company during those years was from writers: Adrienne Rich,[2] Tillie Olsen,[3] Jane Lazarre,[4] Grace Paley[5] and Sara Ruddick[6] formed a circle of imaginary confidants. When I read Tillie Olsen's view that mothers, even working class mothers, must write,[7] I heard her whispering to me, personally. Sara Ruddick's *Maternal Thinking* convinced me that I wasn't stalled out at all, but gaining some kind of wisdom and knowledge that the academic world was so blind to that it didn't even know how to name what was missing. Jane Lazarre's painful ambivalence toward a child that demanded and interfered, and her found camaraderie with feminist mothers in consciousness-raising groups, and Rich's powerful treatise on the warping of mothering-as-experience into Motherhood-as-institution moved me to tears. Like me, they had lived out on the margins of Academia; that privileged place where no babies cried, no toddlers refused to get dressed, no elementary school teachers criticized, and clothes remained clean and dry all day. They understood that mothering was not just a stumbling block, but also a muse; a voice of wholeness that might point the way forward out of amoral, sterile Sciences and starved Humanities and into the kind of excitement that I had felt as an undergraduate, or, even earlier, as a child with pop bottle "test tubes" full of rotting goo in the family garage. "I will get back to it," I promised myself, "and I will have so much more to say than I would have if I had missed this part."

Meanwhile, I was nearly too busy living my dissertation to write it. Although I did eventually finish and defend it, the version for publication remains, like Tillie Olsen's "Yonondio,"[8] an unfinished work nearly two decades later. The child, Laura, is now 20 and has sworn to a life of neither motherhood nor academia. Instead, she records her journeys in brilliantly funny and poignant drawings. They are the antithesis of what my graduate supervisor called "the highly stylized literary genre" of research reports, and much of her material comes from her tumultuous childhood.

As for my academic life, eventually one finishes the dissertation (or not) and has to seek a real job. With my marriage and graduate school behind me, I took my newly-minted Ph.D. to the first job that offered a benefits plan. My graduate-school supporters had warned me that community college teaching was a road to nowhere, in terms of scholarly contribution. "If you take a college teaching position", they said, "you will never publish again." And maybe they are right; I've been teaching in that community college for 16 years. I have a small private practice in Clinical Psychology, and it competes with the teaching job, the union activism, the garden, the three dogs, the loving partner, and the twenty-year-old daughter, for my attention. I don't get much writing done.

Yet whenever I am free from intensely observing, correcting, planning for, cooking for, or reacting to those in my care, I am trying out the words to express what it has learned. In the car and in the shower, I hold forth as an eloquent, life-affirming, anguished scholar. The split between scholarship and motherhood has never been complete, and I have come to re-embrace the vision of nurturance and knowledge being intertwined and inseparable.

My teaching still provides me with a place to play with ideas. One day last fall, I sat with six students in a seminar called, "Feminist Perspectives on the Helping Professions," and it hit us: we seven were the only apparent living things in the room. How strange: the contrast between the fluid, living nature of our thoughts and stories (rooted in mother-work), and the solid, formaldehyde-infused pressboard of industrial-quality classroom furniture. Even the language that we had inherited was hostile: analyses were "penetrating," key ideas were "seminal," superior science was "hard," and its material was the "object" of study. One of my students (who goes by the lovely writing name "Treegirl") said of schooling: "It's not that it's such a bad system; it's just that if I were designing it, I would started from somewhere else, entirely."

As a maternal scholar, I do keep starting from somewhere else, entirely. I want to create a "wet," not a "hard" science. I hold "ovulars," not seminars. I want to be a midwife, a doula, a mother of humans and of beautiful, useful, ideas. I want to write the products of a loving relationship with the world.

An academic environment that is hostile to mothers is also necessarily one that is silent about love. All silences must erase their own roots; the injustices and the fears that underlie their practiced conformity. This silence obscures the difficulties that mothers have getting to the halls of Academia at all, the barriers to access that my current students fight, even harder than I did, to overcome. It is rooted in the tradition of misogyny itself in the Ivory Tower, and that, in turn, is rooted in the fear of our own organic, imperfect bodies.

And when the silence is broken? Imagine what a toddler's anguished wail will add to the discourses of Psychology, Philosophy, Literature, Theoretical Physics; how the smell of bodily secretions will inform to Sociology, Medicine, Engineering, and Law; What a mother's worry and fatigue will say to graduate students of Education, Nursing, Criminology, Women's Studies. How can anything remain the same—clean, simple, sterile—when we remember the lives that are birthed, not springing from the head of Zeus or any other creator/creatrix in the realms of beautiful abstractions, but in spurts of blood and amniotic fluid, ripe with the smells of iron, milk and shit, from between a woman's legs? This echoes with what Mary Belenky and her colleagues call "Connected Knowing,"[9] Carol Gilligan calls "A Different Voice,"[10] and Sandra Harding calls "Standpoint,"[11] but it goes further. It is not just a subjective or a connected epistemology; it is also an organic, messy, chaotic, morally challenged and uncertain one. This, to put it mildly, changes everything.

When I think back to where I started, with Coke bottles in the garage, the smell of rotting lilacs and a cadre of smaller children around me, I think that motherhood is not the problem. It is the hostility of academia toward motherhood and toward all that mothers know that is the problem. The very language of academia limits what questions it can ask, and what answers it can create; it does not lend itself easily to what mothers know or want to know. [12] The structural barriers, too, both practical and economic, are too pervasive to be dismissed as trivial or entirely accidental. Where can a nursing mother express and store breast milk on campus? How many graduate seminars are accessible from home, should a child fall ill and need us there? Because of all that, Academia holds up a mirror of life that is more than impoverished; it is distorted. It is un-whole. It is, too often, hostile to life itself.

It is my mothering self that knows that we can't afford to keep turning our backs on wonder, appreciation, and the protective impulse while we go about creating systems of knowledge and understanding. Yet, how do we bring about this change? Scholarship that is grounded in maternal realities and maternal ethics may be necessary, but it is also nearly impossible for mere mortals to achieve.

The main consequence, for me, of becoming a mother in graduate school is that what is not rooted in the need to nurture living things is no longer interesting to me, and I will not perpetuate models of human experience that deny the inequalities and inter-dependencies of family and community life.

Yet right behind this inspiration come the consequences of a dependant creature who needed my total support. Because I needed the money, I took up teaching, another kind of mother-work, rather than research and writing. Thus, I have almost no publications. Thus, the work of re-creating my field through a lens of love keeps getting put off for the everyday practice of nurturing work. And my male or childless colleagues, who do have time and free space to write, keep missing the big picture.

This I know: I am a mother. And a scientist. And a writer. They aren't as separate as all that. So, if I am at the margins, I will look both ways: to the world of the women with strollers, and to the world of ideas and thought. I will figure it out, yet. If I don't get it written down, I will tell it to my students. It will be part of the oral tradition, perhaps, of wet science: flowing, mixing it up in the currents, forgetting which drop came from where, who said what, where the socks went in the laundry, and what it was that moved us to change the way we practiced knowledge. Perhaps I will live long enough to become a sharp-eyed, clear-tongued crone who can still write of it when I finally have plenty of time without children coming to me hungry. Or perhaps I will slip envelopes of money into the bags of young single mothers who are struggling to remain in academia. Or, when I can't manage that, take them for lunch and tell them about the pearls of great price that they carry for a world in need of reality checks.

And what do I tell those young women, with their books and their babies and their love of both written in their faces? I'm afraid my advice won't be very practical. Oh, I can cook up a mean split-pea soup on a dime, and I know how to express breast milk and store it in the department refrigerator. I can advise on choosing a daycare, but not on how to finance it. I still don't know how to deal with children when they miss you at the school concert but it's final exam time, or when they have the stomach flu and you have a graduate seminar. I have few gems on how to do better time management, or how to present as competent to people who consider competence to be antithetical to the fact of your mothering. Fitting into such a world is destructive in itself; what we need is a less managerial approach to time and more, not less visibility for the unpaid work that we do.

Instead, I will tell them that to be a maternal scholar requires great faith and optimism for times that we, ourselves, may not see. It's like parenting that way: it's an act of hope. Some of these women will break through the silences, the way that my own literary mentors did, and this chain of knowing will continue. Maybe this is just its time to gestate, like a seed in the ground or a babe in the belly, but one day its time will come and it will change everything. Our job is to keep it alive, nurture and treasure it and believe in it the way we do our children, even in the hardest of times.

[1]My training at this point was mainly Psychodynamic, and the emphasis in infancy was on "Attachment," in John Bowlby's terms, or "Basic Trust" in Erik Erikson's, and the "Object Relations" of the infant toward the mother setting the stage for virtually all that was to come in the personality, cognitive and spiritual development of the infant. Donald Winnicott, Heinz Kohut, and Melanie Klein each write with rich detail about how the infant perceives and perhaps comes to love the omnipotent Mothering person.

[2]Rich's 1986 classic, *Of Woman Born* is required reading for maternal scholars and for scholars of maternity.

[3]In particular, the short story "I Stand Here Ironing," from her 1961 collection, *Tell Me a Riddle*.

[4]*The Mother Knot*, first published in 1976, was available in reprint from Duke University Press in 1997.

[5]The character of Faith, to whom Paley turns many times in her writing for a clear, strong voice of a mother in spirit and in practice, first appears the short story collection *The Little Disturbances of Man*, published in 1956, within the selections "Two Short Sad Stories from a Long and Happy Life."

[6]*Maternal Thinking; Toward a Politics of Peace* first appeared in 1986, and continues to provide a structure and tone for describing the cognitive, philosophical and moral practice of thinking like a mother that underlies the work of taking care.

[7]See her book, *Silences*.

[8]*Yonondio, From the Thirties* was published in 1974, having been pieced together by Tillie's life partner, Jack Olsen, from fragments in papers and on envelopes.

[9]First appearing in *Women's Ways of Knowing*, published in 1986 (Belenky, Clinchy, Goldberger, and Tarule), this theme is more richly explored among mothers in the chapter, "A Tradition That Has No Name: Public Homeplaces and the Development of People, Families and Communities," in *Knowledge, Difference and Power* (Belenky).

[10]In her book by the same name, 1982.

[11]See Sandra Harding's *Whose Science, Whose Knowledge?*

[12]For a wonderfully descriptive analysis of how this came to be, see Evelyn Fox Keller's *Reflections on Gender and Science.*

WORKS CITED

Belenky, M., B. Clinchy, N. Goldberger, and J. Tarule. *Women's Ways of Knowing.* New York: Basic Books, 1986.

Belenky, M. "Public Homeplaces: Nurturing the Development of People, Families and Communities." *Knowledge, Difference and Power: Essays Inspired by Women's Ways of Knowing.* Eds. Nancy Goldberger, Jill Tarule, Blythe Clinchy and Mary Belenky. New York: Basic Books, 1996. 393-431

Bowlby, J. *Attachment and Loss: Vol. 1 Attachment.* 1969. New York: Basic Books, 1982.

Bowlby, J. *A Secure Base.* New York: Basic Books, 1988.

Erikson, E. *Childhood and Society.* New York: W.W. Norton, 1951.

Gilligan, C. *In A Different Voice: Psychological Theory and Women's Development.* Cambridge, MA: Harvard University Press, 1982.

Harding, S. *Whose Science, Whose Knowledge?* Ithaca, NY: Cornell University Press, 1991.

Keller, E. F. *Reflections of Gender and Science.* New Haven: Yale University Press.

Klein, M. *The Writings of Melanie Klein, Vol 1, 2 & 3.* London: Hogarth, 1975.

Kohut, H. *The Restoration of the Self.* New York: International Universities Press, 1977.

Lazarre, J. *The Mother Knot.* Duke University Press, 1997.

Olsen, T. "I Stand Here Ironing." *Tell Me a Riddle.* 1951. New Haven, CN: Yale University Press, 1985.

Olsen, T. *Silences.* 1974. New York: Dell, 1989. Reprinted 2003, New York: The Feminist Press (CUNY).

Olsen, T. *Yonondio: From the Thirties.* 1974. New York: Dell, 1989.

Paley, G. "Two Short Sad Stories from a Long and Happy Life." 1959. *The Collected Short Stories, Grace Paley.* New York: Farrar, Straus and Giroux, 2007.

Patterson, S. *Autonomy and Connection: Identity, Moral Reasoning and Coping Among New Mothers.* Unpublished Dissertation, Simon Fraser University, British Columbia, 1992.

Patterson, Serena J. "Autonomy and Connection: New Mothers' Sense of Self and the Return-to-Work Dilemma." Unpublished paper presented at the Canadian Psychological Association annual conference, Halifax, Nova Scotia, 1990

Patterson, S. *Two Part Inventions, What New Mothers Tell Us About Selfhood, Identity and Love.* Unpublished work in progress.

Rich, A. *Of Woman Born: Motherhood as Experience and Institution.* New York: Norton, 1986.

Ruddick, S. *Maternal Thinking.* 1989. Boston: Beacon Press, 1995.

Winnicott, D. W. *The Maturational Processes and the Facilitating Environment,* London: Hogarth, 1982.

4.

Balancing Work and Family in Higher Education

Best Practices and Barriers

HEATHER WYATT-NICHOL, MARGARITA M. CARDONA AND
KAREN SKIVERS DRAKE

MANY WOMEN HAVE BEEN ATTRACTED to the teaching profession over the years. Teaching in the higher education environment may, on face, have great appeal as an opportunity in which faculty enjoy a high degree of autonomy in their work and scheduling flexibility.

Those outside the faculty (e.g., students, citizens, even university administrators that have never worked in a tenure-track position) may perceive faculty positions to be an ideal career path for those who seek to balance work and family. It is not always evident that the research and service demands of faculty positions coupled with teaching impose a work week requiring well beyond a 40 hours. Indeed, writing is often reserved for evenings or weekends at home. As a result, the advantages of autonomy and flexibility that appear inherent in the position have the potential to turn into disadvantages as the boundaries between work and home blur, increasing the likelihood of work-family conflict. Compared to faculty members who are either single or married with a stay-at-home wife, women with young children are more likely to experience obstacles to maintaining productive time for research and publication.

This chapter examines the tenure rate among women with young children and considers explanations for the disparities. Our intention is to raise awareness of inequality, to advocate for broader implementation of family friendly policies in higher education, and to promote supportive organizational cultures. We consider explanations for the "mommy penalty" in academia including: structural inequalities, stereotypes, and attribution theory. We also integrate a best practices approach with results of a recent quality of life in academia survey conducted by the authors through the University of Baltimore Work/Life Balance Initiative, funded by a grant from the ACE/Alfred P. Sloan Foundation (hereinafter referred to as the UB Sloan Survey). The best practices approach examines family friendly policies among a variety of U.S. colleges and universities that have been recognized for family friendly policies, specifically parental leave, child-care, tenure-clock stop, and active service-modified duties. The UB Sloan Survey was administered during the spring semester of 2010 to examine policies and perceptions of barriers that discourage the utilization of family friendly policies. The results of the study represent 247 respondents from four public universities in the United States. Respondents represented a variety of academic fields across ranks: 39 percent were tenured, 24 percent were tenure-track, 24 percent were full-time non-tenure track, and 14 percent were part-time adjuncts. Through the examination of best practices combined with the results of the UB Sloan Survey we contend that policies designed to eliminate or minimize structural inequality will only be effective through supportive organizational cultures.

THE STATUS OF WOMEN IN HIGHER EDUCATION

The number of women pursuing advanced degrees has increased over the past couple of decades. In 2005, 60 percent of graduate students were women (Sotirin). Using data from the 1993 National Study of Postsecondary Faculty, Martin Finkelstein, Robert Seal, and Jack Schuster found that women have made substantial gains in acquiring faculty positions across institutional types and program areas. Representing 41 percent of the total new faculty cohort, women accounted for 47.9 percent of new entries into research universities (an area of previous under-representation) while the new entries of women in liberal arts colleges have gained statistical parity with their male counterparts. Nevertheless, 70 percent of professors are male at the most prestigious universities (Wilson 2004). Similarly, male professors outnumber female professors by two to one at doctoral institutions and female professors are more likely to represent full-time faculty positions at two-year institutions (AAUP). In addition, underrepresentation persists in the fields of science, technology, engineering, and mathematics (STEM). The Committee of the National Academy of Sciences examined the problem of the small portion of female faculty in STEM at research universities. They concluded that women are being or opt out at every educational transition. Most notably, while women made over 30 percent of the doctorates in social and behavioral sciences and 20 percent of the life sciences in the last 30 years, they only make 15.4 and 14.8 percent of the full professors in these areas—and the picture only gets worse for the "hard sciences" and engineering. The committee determined that women face discrimination and biases in STEM fields. Specifically, academic organizational structures and promotion/tenure evaluation criteria contain arbitrary and subjective components that disadvantage women. This is not too surprising given that the fields being male dominated is composed primarily of male evaluators. The report has specific recommendations for universities, higher education organizations, scientific and professional societies, honorary societies, journals, federal funding agencies and foundations, federal enforcement agencies and Congress. Among these, the most notable is for universities to "develop and implement hiring, tenure and promotion policies that take into account the flexibility that faculty need across the life course, allowing the integration of family, work, and community responsibilities" (8).

While women in graduate programs and the labor force have increased in recent years, the number entering full-time tenure-track positions and promoting through the ranks is much smaller and women are also more likely to work in contingent positions. A review of the entrance into full-time faculty positions reveals that women represented 39 percent of full-time faculty positions and 48 percent of the part-time positions in 2003 (Euben). In addition, newly minted male Ph.D.s with children under six year of age were twice as likely as female Ph.D.s with young children to enter a tenure-track position (Frasch et al.). When one considers occupational rank, women are more likely to occupy the lower ranks of instructor, lecturer, or assistant professor (Jacobs and Winslow; Mason and Goulden 2004b). According to *The Chronicle of Higher Education* (2008a), women only accounted for 25 percent of the professors and 38.8 percent of the associate professors in U.S. academe in the fall of 2005. On the other hand, more than half of the instructor, lecturer or otherwise non-tenured positions (often referred to as the "second tier") are occupied by women. A recent survey by the American Association of University Professors (AAUP) reported that within the rank of full professor women represented only 26 percent compared to men who represented 74 percent. When we consider the proportion of faculty with tenure, we find that only 35.5 percent of female faculty at private institutions and 43.3 percent of those at public institutions are tenured, while their male counterparts achieve tenure at a rate of 51.1 percent and 57.1 percent, respectively (*Chronicle of Higher Education* 2008b). There is also concern that in recent years some universities have experienced a decline in tenure offers to women. For example, at Harvard University tenure offers to women have declined since 2001 (Wilson 2004).

The problem is that when academic mothers accept work in contingent positions, community colleges, or at "less demanding" four-year institutions it is often framed as a voluntary choice in order to balance the demands of work and family. This dichotomy between work and family establishes the perception that motherhood is incompatible with tenure-track positions. It is possible to assume that some might consider the demands of parenthood so pressing that there is a de facto non-negotiable priority assigned to the family responsibilities in comparison to the work. John Curtis asserts: "A part-time or non-tenure track position may allow some individual women to give more priority to their families, but their having to make that choice is an indication of continuing structural inequity in faculty careers" (22).

Establishing work in a way that positions men's lives as normal and women's as problematic places working mothers at a disadvantage. Joan Williams (2000) uses the term "ideal worker norm" to refer to jobs structured around traditional family patterns in which men were breadwinners with stay-at-home wives. The ideal worker norm has also dominated academia. According to the American Association of University Professors (AAUP), tenure was based on the premise of a male faculty member with a stay-at-home wife (Sotirin). Although teaching and service requirements are typically completed on campus (even though many committee reports and grading takes place at home), research is often reserved for "spare time" in the evenings and on weekends at home. Such arrangements are likely to disadvantage academic mothers who lose the "productive time" for research and publication available to women without children or men with stay at home wives (Allison; Fothergill and Feltey). A study by Ramona Gunter and Amy Stambach (based on interviews with 22 male and 22 female faculty members at a public research institution) found that faculty work under the perception that in order to succeed in academe one must spend as many hours as one can afford advancing the research work and drafting publications. Given the level of domestic responsibilities still resting on women today, even when they are the principal breadwinner in the household, the process places women (particularly those married with children) at a disadvantage. The men interviewed in this study tend to characterize the pursuit of tenure as a "game" to be played and won, while women perceive it as a "balancing act" whereby they must sacrifice elements of their personal life in order to ensure career success. These perceptions are also evident in recent empirical studies. Using data from the 1998 National Study of Post-secondary Faculty (NSOPF), Jerry Jacobs and Sarah Winslow found significant positive correlations between working 60 hours or more per week and publication rate. Unfortunately, the study also revealed that married fathers were more likely to work more than 60 hours per week than married mothers. Similarly, a study by Steven Stack demonstrated a statistically significant negative relationship between publication rates and women with preschool age children. Particularly disheartening is a study by Mary Ann Mason and Marc Goulden (2004a) that found that having "early babies"—children less than six years of age within five years of receiving a doctoral degree—had a negative impact on tenure rates for women but not men. Men with early babies were 38 percent more likely to receive tenure than women with early babies. Similarly, women who either waited five years after the Ph.D. or did not have children at all were more likely than women with early babies to receive tenure.

THE STATUS OF FAMILY FRIENDLY POLICIES IN HIGHER EDUCATION

Family-friendly policies are organizational initiatives that have been established to assist employees in achieving work-life balance. One study by Cathy Trower and Jared Bleak of tenure-track faculty at six research universities found that among the junior faculty 46 percent were dissatisfied with the balance between personal and professional time, 68 percent stated that tenure-clock stops would be helpful while 64 percent stated that childcare would be helpful. Similarly, the UB Sloan Survey found that 46 percent of respondents were neither satisfied nor dissatisfied with family friendly policies at their universities, 13 percent reported dissatisfaction, and four percent reported strong dissatisfaction. One respondent commented on the competing demands of motherhood and academia, as well as the different levels of support (or lack of) within the university:

*I feel that balancing the responsibilities as a new professor and
mother of three young children is almost impossible at times. I
know there are moments when one or both suffer. I don't know
if there is an answer to this dilemma. My division chair and the
dean of the college of education are both incredibly supportive
and that helps so much—I feel that the system wide support of
maternity leave, family leaves, etc. are not well supported.*

As early as 1974, the AAUP issued a statement "Leaves of Absence
for Child-Bearing, Child-Rearing, and Family Emergencies" (cited in the
"Statement of Principles") that called for flexibility in meeting career
and family obligations through reductions in workload or longer leaves
of absence without loss of professional status. Nevertheless, in 2001 the
AAUP found itself restating the importance of work-life balance through a
"Statement of Principles on Family Responsibilities and Academic Work"
through its Committee on the Status of Women in the Academic Profession and its Subcommittee on Academic Work and Family. Included in
the principles are parental leave, tenure-clock stop, active service-modified
duties, and childcare.

Parental leave in the United States is typically interpreted under the
Family Medical Leave Act of 1993 (FMLA) that requires up to twelve
weeks of unpaid leave for an employee to care for his or herself or an
immediate family member. The legislation is limited to organizations with
fifty or more employees and only covers full-time employees who have
worked 1,250 hours the year prior. While this does provide job protection for women who have recently given birth, it does not benefit those
who cannot afford to take unpaid leave. In some cases, women are not
faced with the single of option of unpaid leave as the policies and administration of this law varies somewhat in that some organizations provide
paid leave. Nevertheless, many organizations interpret adherence to the
law (FMLA) as a family friendly policy, which absent federal legislation,
might never have been implemented within those organizations. It is for
this reason we examine parental leave beyond FMLA. Not surprisingly,
parental leave beyond FMLA varies among institutions of higher education. One study of 84 colleges and universities by Charmaine Yoest and
Steve Rhoads found that 82 percent failed to offer paid parental leave.
At many colleges and universities an absence of formal policy results
in many faculty members negotiating their leave on an individual basis

(Gilbert). A study by the Center for the Education of Women (CEW) at the University of Michigan at Ann Arbor (2008) found that unpaid leave beyond FMLA was provided by 44 percent of the institutions within their sample. The study also revealed that leave applied to men as well as women if they were able to demonstrate the status of primary caregiver. Similarly, a study of 255 institutions of higher education found that 25 percent offered paid maternity leave (Sullivan, Hollenshead, and Smith). Once again, however, many employers might include paid sick leave under FMLA in their interpretation of paid maternity leave. Most universities combine sick leave or short-term disability to account for paid leave. In contrast, some universities offer full pay or partial pay for one semester. For example, upon the birth or adoption of a child, primary caregivers are offered one semester of paid leave at Duke University and The Massachusetts Institute of Technology.

Tenure clock stop is also included in the *AAUP Statement of Principles on Family Responsibilities and Academic Work*.[1] The recommendations include stopping the tenure clock without taking a full leave of absence during the stop. This allows parents to adjust to their new role as caregivers, including those first months of sleep deprivation as well as transitioning to a new balance between work and family. Universities that offer tenure clock stops typically offer one to two year exclusion off of the tenure clock. While many universities directly tie tenure extensions to leave, it is important to point out that true tenure clock stops do not require a leave of absence.[2] In 1970, Princeton was one of the first institutions of higher education to implement a one-year tenure extension to female faculty members who gave birth while on the tenure clock. In 1991, the policy was amended to include adoptions and extended to male faculty members who were able to demonstrate the role of primary caregiver (Valdata). Research universities are also twice as likely to offer tenure clock extensions. According to one survey by the Center for the Education of Women (CEW) at the University of Michigan at Ann Arbor (2008), 92 percent of research universities provided a tenure clock stop compared to only half of the liberal arts colleges. The paradox is that tenured and tenure-track women were less likely to be employed at research universities. One explanation for this paradox is found in the previous discussion on the underrepresentation of women in STEM fields. Another explanation is the leaky pipeline of female Ph.D.s—some women are "voluntarily"[3] avoiding positions at such institutions in order to meet the demands of work and family.

Active service-modified duties (ASMD) represent the third principle in the *AAUP Statement of Principles on Family Responsibilities and Academic Work*. In comparison to a tenure clock stop, ASMD provides reduced teaching loads with minimal to no pay cuts for faculty members who are primary caregivers for newborns or adopted children. According to the CEW study (2008), 21 percent of the institutions within their sample offered ASMD without a reduction in pay. Duke University has one of the most generous policies by offering flexible arrangements for up to three years. The University of California Berkeley offers ASMD three months prior and one year following birth or adoption.

Childcare is the final principle in the *AAUP Statement of Principles on Family Responsibilities and Academic Work*. Some universities offer a wide variety of support to defray cost and/or provide greater access to meet child care needs. Campus based child care centers provide various care services to students, faculty, and staff. The National Coalition for Campus Children's Centers reported that in 2001 there were 2,500 campus based child care centers.

Center services range from child care only, laboratory schools, or a combination of both. Funding is typically provided directly through parent fees, however, subsidies and in-kind donations may also be available. Stanford University offers one of the most generous child care benefits by hosting on-site childcare through six programs and providing childcare grants ranging from $5,000-$20,000 for junior faculty members (Jaschik 2007). Nevertheless, the challenge for any employer that offers on-site child care is the long waiting lists. It is not that unusual for a faculty member to be on a waiting list for two years in some universities. As a result, many universities partner with external service providers. For example, Harvard offers childcare through affiliated centers that are independently owned and operated ("Report of the Taskforce"). Similarly, Duke University has partnered with 33 child care centers in the university region.

BARRIERS TO EFFECTIVE FAMILY FRIENDLY POLICIES

In order for family friendly policies to be effective at minimizing or eliminating structural inequality of the academe, they must be utilized by faculty members. Barriers preventing the full utilization of family friendly policies include procedural barriers, discriminatory stereotypes,

Table 1- Best Practices Family Friendly Policies Comparisons

	Tenure Clock Stop	Parental Leave beyond FMLA	ASMD	On-site childcare
Duke	X(A)	X($)	X	X
Harvard	X (A)	X ($)		X
New Jersey Institute of Technology	X	X		X
Northwestern	X(A)		X	
Pennsylvania State University	X	X		X
Princeton	X(A)		X	X
Stanford University	X(A)			X
University of California at Berkeley	X(A)	X	X	X
University of Delaware	X			X
University of Maryland, College Park	X		X	
University of Michigan, Ann Arbor	X(A)		X	X
University of Pennsylvania	X	X($)	X	X
University of Wisconsin at Madison	X(A)			X

and negative organizational cultures. Procedural obstacles often have a negative impact on the use of family friendly policies. For example, the more burdensome the procedure for requesting a tenure clock stop, the less likely a faculty member will invoke the request. In addition, as more decision-makers are involved in the process the likelihood for denying a request increases. One respondent to the UB Sloan Survey stated:

> Informal adjustments are sometimes made but it depends on the good will of the administrator entrusted with a particular case. Tenure clock stops, parental leave beyond FMLA, or the provision of active-service modified duties granted on an individual basis in closed meetings has the potential to result in arbitrary decisions and increases the risk of lawsuits by faculty members who believe that they have not only been treated unfairly, but also discriminated against on the basis of sex and/or familial responsibilities.

The process for granting tenure clock stops varies among universities with formal policies in place, however, most universities require a written request by the faculty member or department chair to move through the organizational hierarchy. For example, some universities require approval from a promotion and tenure committee, the dean, and the provost. Others (e.g. University of California) allow the request to move directly to the Provost or Chancellor. The reluctance to use tenure clock stops will persist as along as approval is required from chairs, deans, and provosts. One solution is to adopt automatic tenure clock stops that do not require written approval unless a faculty member chooses not to use the policy. Recognizing the problem of procedural barriers a few universities have moved toward automatic stops that do not require approval from one or more superiors. For example, a one year tenure clock stop is automatically granted to faculty members who make a request due to pregnancy or childbirth at the University of Michigan. Regardless of whether tenure extensions must be requested or are automatic, a few universities have included language in their tenure-clock stop policies to reinforce the position that faculty members who use such policies should not be subjected to heightened scrutiny or standards that otherwise would not be applied had they not invoked the tenure-clock stop.

The *1997–2000 Master Agreement* between Northern Michigan University and the university's AAUP chapter provides that "the taking of [family] leave shall not otherwise prejudice future tenure or promotion consideration." Similarly, Pennsylvania State University's policy provides that a "staying of the provisional tenure period should not penalize or adversely affect the faculty member in the tenure review." In addition, the University of Wisconsin policy provides that if "the faculty member has been in probationary status for more than seven years, the faculty member shall be evaluated as if he or she had been in probationary status for seven years, not longer." (AAUP)

Discriminatory stereotypes are also a barrier to the utilization of family friendly policies. Women in the academe continue to be plagued by ascribed reasons for success. The success of men is often perceived to be the result of knowledge, skills, and ability while the success of women is perceived to be the result of external factors such as "being in the right place at the right time" or as recipients of preferential hiring policies. Men are often extended opportunities in admissions, hiring, and promotions based on their potential rather than past performance or experience while women with comparable credentials tend to be judged more harshly. Bernice Sandler points out, "A man with two articles in press might be seen as 'showing great promise'. A woman in the same situation might be seen as seriously delayed and the articles not seen as either scholarly achievements or a sign of potential" (7). In an experimental study comparing paired vitae of male and female applicants, department chairs were more likely to recommend males to the rank of associate professor while females with the exact vitae were assigned the rank of assistant (Fidell). In addition, female scholars whose work is published in women's studies journals are more likely to be discredited by tenure review committees (Kritek).

Mothers are also more likely to experience discriminatory stereotypes than non-mothers. One experimental study demonstrated that mothers were perceived as less competent and committed, held to higher performance standards, less likely to be hired, and if hired, offered much lower starting salaries than non-mothers or male applicants (Correll, Benard and Paik). Some faculty members have also reported lower performance ratings after the birth of a child despite increased research activities and improved teaching evaluations (Toepell). In addition, when male faculty members or female faculty members without children work from home there is an assumption that he or she is working or researching or doing other work-related activities. In contrast, academic mothers have noted a difference in perception among their colleagues when working from home prior to having children compared to working from home after the birth or adoption of a child—there is an assumption that she is now engaged in childcare rather than work (Allison; Fothergill and Feltey).

Bias avoidance behavior typically results from discriminatory stereotypes and may be reinforced through organizational culture. Women often assume that having a child while on the tenure track will decrease their chances of tenure and promotion. Many women are reluctant to use family friendly policies available to them, particularly the tenure clock stop, out of fear of reprimand—that some tenured professors will hold them to a higher standard due to a perception that the new mothers had more time, rather than less, to conduct research (Ward and Wolf-Wendel). The majority (64 percent) of 247 respondents to the UB Sloan Survey reported fear that they would be held to a higher standard during tenure review if they took extended leave or invoked a tenure clock stop. This is consistent with the study by Yoest and Rhoads that found that utilization of family friendly policies drops when women perceive a lack of support of such policies within their departments. Others may be reluctant to take advantage of the policies available to them out of fear of resentment—that colleagues will view the faculty member as not carrying her weight in the department. Then there are the faculty members who fear that they will be perceived as less capable if they utilize family friendly policies. One study by Alice Fothergill and Kathryn Feltey found that less than ten percent of the new mothers in their sample requested a tenure clock stop and 87 percent did not request parental leave or ASMD. Similarly, a University of California survey on work-life balance found that 51 percent of female faculty respondents were reluctant to use ASMD for fear of negative tenure decisions (Frasch et al.).

UB SLOAN SURVEY

Bias avoidance is reinforced when faculty mothers bear witness to nega-

Table 2: Reasons For Not Utilizing Extended Leave and Tenure Clock Stop

	Extended Parental Leave	Tenure-Clock Stop
This option did not exist when I needed it	85%	55%
I earned tenure prior to starting a family	75%	75%
I could not afford it financially	96%	13%
Fear that I would be perceived by others in my department as not "carrying my weight"	58%	42%
Fear that I would be held to higher standards for research productivity during tenure review	64%	64%

tive tenure decisions of women who used family friendly policies. At the University of California at Santa Barbara, a female faculty member had taken leave twice for childbirth through the policies available at the university. She had received excellent reviews until she had taken leave and had been a productive scholar even when compared to colleagues who had not taken leave, however, tenure was denied. After filing a sex discrimination complaint, the Equal Employment Opportunity Commission investigation reported in her favor and she was eventually granted tenure (Jaschik 2005). In a separate example, a female faculty member at the University of Oregon was denied tenure but later received a monetary settlement when an internal memo issued by the Provost stated that her duties as a mother were incompatible with her duties as a professor and that her tenure clock stop was a red flag (Williams 2004).

RECOMMENDATIONS AND CONCLUSION

While we are limited in our ability to generalize the findings of the UB Sloan Survey, the results do lend support to previous research on family friendly policies. Combined the studies provide evidence of a need for formal work-life balance policies to reduce discrimination in academia, procedural fairness in the application of those policies, and an organizational culture that supports faculty members who choose to utilize such policies. Academic mothers at institutions without formal family friendly policies should work to form coalitions of support through faculty governing structures (e.g., faculty-senate, special committees) and professional networks (e.g., American Association of University Women, Motherhood Initiative for Research and Community Involvement) to raise awareness and eliminate practices that discriminate against academic mothers. Academic mothers at institutions in the nascent stages of policy development should also raise awareness about discriminatory stereotypes and structural inequality by sharing existing research and expanding their own research agenda to promote equality. In addition, they should assess the rank and status of academic mothers within their own institution. Academic mothers at institutions with formal family friendly policies should hold leadership accountable for the utilization and effectiveness of the policies in place. This includes requiring the administration to implement formal training programs that inform faculty members, department chairs, deans, the Provost, and the University President on the procedures for faculty members to utilize the various policies. Promotion and tenure committee members should also be trained on the proper interpretation of family friendly policies, particularly tenure clock stop and ASMD, when making tenure and promotion decisions. University leadership should also be held accountable through performance measures. At a minimum, performance measures should include: assessing the utilization rates of family friendly policies by faculty members who qualified in the past five years; developing annual policy performance measures that track qualification and utilization; and tracking the career progress of faculty members who have utilized family friendly policies. Ultimately, support from leadership is necessary with an understanding that faculty engagement is mission critical to attract, retain and encourage the best work from the faculty. Family friendly policies are essential to academic mothers in terms of loyalty, desire to participate, productivity, ability to be effective ambassadors of the institutions to colleagues, students, and the outside world in general.

[1] The AAUP language for the tenure clock stop is available at: <http://www.aaup.org/AAUP/pubsres/policydocs/contents/workfam-stmt.htm>.
[2] Model policies for tenure clock stop are available at the University of California at Berkeley, Duke, Harvard, Northwestern, Princeton, and Stanford.
[3] "Voluntarily" is in quotes because the reluctance to apply for such positions in the first place as a result of competing demands represents the problem of structural inequality addressed in previous pages.

WORKS CITED

Allison, J. E. "Composing a Life in Twenty-First Century Academe: Reflections on a Mother's Challenge." *NWSA Journal* 19.3 (2008): 23-46.

American Association of University Professors (AAUP). "Statement of Principles on Family Responsibilities and Academic Work." May 2001. Retrieved September 15, 2006 from: <http://www.aaup.org/AAUP/pubsres/ policydocs/contents/workfam-stmt.htm>.

An Agenda for Excellence: Creating Flexibility in Tenure-Track Faculty Careers. American Council on Education, Office of Women in Higher Education, 2005.

Aubrey, J., M. Click, D. S. Dougherty, M. A. Fine, M.W. Kramer, R. J. Meisenbach, L. N. Olson and M. J. Smythe. "We Do Babies: The Trials, Tribulations, and Triumphs of Pregnancy and Parenting in the Academy." *Women's Studies in Communication* 31.2 (2008): 186- 195.

Bridges, J. S. and A. M. Orza. "The Effects of Employment Role and Motive for Employment on the Perceptions of Mothers." *Sex Roles* 27.7/8 (1992): 331-343.

Center for the Education of Women (CEW). *Family Friendly Policies in Higher Education: Where Do We Stand?* University of Michigan,

2005. Retrieved December 1, 2008 from: <http://www.cew.umich.edu/PDFs/pubs/wherestand.pdf>.

Center for the Education of Women (CEW). *Family Friendly Policies in Higher Education: A Five-Year Report, 2005 and 2008.* University of Michigan, 2008. Retrieved January 18, 2009 from: <http://www.cew.umich.edu/PDFs/Redux%20Brief%20Final%205-1.pdf>.

Chronicle of Higher Education Almanac, 2008-09. "Number of Full-Time Faculty Members by Sex, Rank and Racial and Ethnic Group, Fall 2005." 55.1 (2008a): 24. Retrieved October 12, 2008 from <http://chronicle.com/weekly/almanac/2008/nation/0102402.htm>.

Chronicle of Higher Education Almanac, 2008-09. "Tenure Status of Full-Time Faculty Members by Type of Institution, 2005-6." 55.1 (2008b): 25. Retrieved October 12, 2008 from <http://chronicle.com/weekly/almanac/2008/nation/0102502.htm>.

Committee on Maximizing the Potential of Women in Academic Science and Engineering, National Academy of Sciences, National Academy of Engineering, and Institute of Medicine. *Beyond Bias and Barriers: Fulfilling the Potential of Women in Academic Science And Engineering* [Free Executive Summary]. 2006. Retrieved February 16, 2009 from <http://www.nap.edu/catalog.php?record_id=11741>.

Correll, S. J., S. Benard and I. Paik. "Getting a Job: Is There a Motherhood Penalty?" *American Journal of Sociology* 112 (2007): 1297-1338.

Curtis, J. W. "Balancing Work and Family for Faculty." *Academe* (Nov/Dec. 2004): 21-23.

Dow, B. J. "Does it Take a Department to Raise a Child?" *Women's Studies in Communication*, 31.2 (2008): 158-165.

Euben, D. "Win Some, Lose Some." *Chronicle of Higher Education* 52.41 (2006, June 16): B8.

Fidell, L. S. "Empirical Verification of Sex Discrimination in Hiring Practices in Psychology." *Women: Dependent or Independent Variable.* Eds. R. K. Unger and F. L. Denmark. New York: Psychological Dimensions, 1975. 773-785.

Finkelstein, M.J., R. K. Seal and J. H. Schuster. *Academic Generation: A Profession in Transformation.* Baltimore: The Johns Hopkins University Press, 1998.

Fothergill, A. and K. Feltey. "'I've Worked Very Hard and Slept Very Little': Mothers on the Tenure Track in Academia." *Journal of the Association for Research on Mothering* 5.2 (2003): 7-19.

Frasch, K., M. A. Mason, A. Stacy, M. Goulden and C. Hoffman. "Creating a Family Friendly Department: Chairs and Deans Toolkit." 2007. Retrieved December 15, 2008 from *University of California Faculty Family Friendly Edge* at <http://ucfamilyedge.berkeley.edu>.

Gilbert, J. "Why I Feel Guilty All the Time: Performing Academic Motherhood." *Women's Studies in Communication.* 31.2 (2008): 203-208.

Gunter, R. and A. Stambach. "As Balancing Act and as Game: How Women and Men Science Faculty Experience the Promotion Process." *Gender Issues* 21.1 (2003): 24-42

"Inequities Persist for Women and Non-tenure track Faculty." *Academe* (Mar./Apr. 2005): 2130.

Jacobs, J. A. and S. E. Winslow. "Overworked Faculty: Job Stresses and Family Demands." *Annals, American Academy of Political and Social Science* (2004, November): 104-129.

Jaschick, S. "Faux Family Friendly?" *Inside Higher Ed.* September 15, 2005. Retrieved 10 December 2008 from: <http://www.insidehighered.com/layout/set/print/news/2005/09/15ucsb>.

Jaschick, S. "The Family Friendly Competition." *Inside Higher Ed.* April 25, 2007. Retrieved February 16, 2009 from: <http://www.insidehighered.com/layout/set/print/news/ 2007/04/25/family>.

June, A. W. "Grad Students Think Twice About Jobs in Academe." *The Chronicle of Higher Education* 55.20 (2009, January 23): A1.

Kritek, P. B. "Women's Work and Academic Sexism." *Educational Record*, 65.3 (1984): 56-57.

Mason, M. A. and M. Goulden. "Do Babies Matter (Part II)? Closing the Baby Gap." *Academe* (Nov/Dec. 2004a): 11-15.

Mason, M. A. and M. Goulden. "Marriage and Baby Blues: Redefining Gender Equity in the Academy." *Annals, American Academy of Political and Social Science* (2004b): 86-103.

McCurdy, A. H., M. A. Newman and N. P. Lovrich. "Family-Friendly Workplace Policy Adoption in General and Special Purpose Local Governments." *Review of Public Personnel Administration* 22.1 (2002): 27-51.

Newman, M. and K. Mathews. "Federal Family-Friendly Workplace Policies." *Review of Public Personnel Administration* 19 (1999): 34-48.

Parsad, B. and D. Glover. *Tenure Status of Postsecondary Instructional Faculty and Staff: 1992-1998.* National Center for Education Statistics (NCES), National Study of Postsecondary Faculty, 2002.

"Report of the Task Force on Women Faculty." Harvard University, May 2005. Retrieved December 10, 2008 from: <http://www.news.harvard.edu/gazette/daily/2005/05/women-faculty.pdf>.

Sandler, B. R. "The Campus Climate Revisited: Chilly for Women Faculty, Administrators, and Graduate Students." *Project on the Status and Education of Women,* Association of American Colleges, Washington, DC, 1986.

Sotirin, P. "Academic Motherhood: In for the Long Haul." *Women's Studies Quarterly* 31.2 (2008): 258-267.

Stack, S. "Gender, Children, and Research Productivity." *Research in Higher Education* 45.8 (2004): 891-920.

Steinpreis, R. E., K. A. Anders and D. Ritzke. "The Impact of Gender on the Review of the Curricula Vitae of Job Applicants and Tenure Candidates: A National Empirical Study." *Sex Roles* 41.7/8 (1999): 509-528.

Sullivan, B., C. Hollenshead and G. Smith. "Developing And Implementing Work-Family Policies for Faculty." *Academe* (Nov/Dec. 2004): 24-27.

Tenure Denied: Cases of Sex Discrimination in Academia. American Association of University Women Educational Foundation and Legal Advocacy Fund, Washington, DC, 2004.

Toepell, A. "Academic Mothers and Their Experiences Navigating the Academy." *Journal of the Association for Research on Mothering* 5.2 (2003): 93-102.

Trower, C. A. and J. D. Bleak. *The Study of New Scholars: Gender Statistical Report.* Cambridge: Harvard Graduate School of Education, 2004.

Untener, J. "Giving Birth to a Good Policy." *The Chronicle of Higher Education* 54.45 (2008, July 18): B30.

U.S. Bureau of Labor Statistics. *Women in the Labor Force: A Databook.* September 2007. Retrieved March 15, 2008 from: <http://www.bls.gov/cps/wlf-databook-2007.pdf>.

Valdata, P. "The Ticking of the Biological and Tenure Clocks." *Diverse Online.* November 17, 2005. Retrieved August 31, 2006 from: <http://www.diverseeducation.com/artman/publish/ printer_5087.shtml>.

Ward, K. and L. Wolf-Wendel. "Fear Factor: How Safe Is It to Make Time for Family?" *Academe* (Nov./Dec. 2004): 28-31.

Williams, J. C. *Unbending Gender: Why Family and Work Conflict and*

What to Do About It. Oxford: Oxford University Press, 2000.

Williams, J. C. "Hitting the Maternal Wall." *Academe* (Nov/Dec 2004): 16-20.

Williams, J. C. "The Glass Ceiling and the Maternal Wall in Academia." *New Directions for Higher Education* (Summer 2005): 91-105.

Wilson, R. "Where the Elite Teach, It's Still a Man's World." *The Chronicle of Higher Education* (2004, December 3): A8-A14.

Wilson, R. "More Colleges are Adding Family-Friendly Benefits." *The Chronicle of Higher Education* 54.45 (2008, July 18): B22.

Wolf-Wendel, L. E. and K. Ward. "Academic Life and Motherhood: Variations by Institutional Type." *Higher Education* 52 (2006): 487-521.

Yoest, C. and S. E. Rhoads. *Parental Leave in Academia.* The Family, Gender and Tenure Project. University of Virginia, 2004. Retrieved January 15, 2009 from: <http://www.faculty.virginia.edu/familyandtenure/institutional%20report.pdf>.

5.

Solving the N Puzzle

Memoir of a Mother-Scholar

CAROLYN BARBER

THREE AND ONE-HALF YEARS into my doctoral program I "opted out" (Stone). It was during the final moments of an ethnographic methods seminar, in the midst of receiving feedback about my field notes from one of the co-professors, when the choice became crystal clear. The course required eight to ten hours of fieldwork per week on top of the weekly three hour seminar meeting and seminar prep. She was especially disappointed with the lack of immediacy of my nocturnal field notes and insisted that I have a tape recorder with me to synchronously capture my thoughts and feelings whenever I tended to my toddler son during the night. This is what it would take to truthfully capture these moments. As she delivered each phrase of feedback with a chopping motion to the seminar table, I choked back a volcano of tears and silently protested. *But, with whom would I be present while I captured those moments? And do I simply retire to the living room—after changing his sweat-soaked bed sheets, or, cleaning up his vomit from a coughing spell, or, calming his flailing, disoriented body after a nightmare—and spend time recounting the experience further depriving myself of more precious sleep?* Buried in this silent protest was the kernel question that twigs on so many mother-scholars—to whom and what am I more committed? Academia or my family? My overheated emotions melted into equanimity. I could no longer withstand the "omnivorous" demands of two very "greedy institutions" (Coser)—motherhood and academia. Nor could I ever simultaneously perform the roles of mother and academic to ideal lengths (Williams). Doing so would deplete every dimension of my being.

My departure came at the tail end of a brief media flurry regarding the unique struggles of mothers in academia. I am sure the other authors in this anthology remember it well. Staggering statistics projected an exodus of women from the academy, in particular research institutions (Mason, Goulden and Frasch). Countless personal narratives—blogs, anthologies, auto-ethnography, memoir—began washing up on the pristine shores of academia.

I was not aware of these voices when I composed my brief, excessively obedient response to an annual departmental evaluation I received in November 2008. The annual evaluation process requires graduate students to submit a progress report to the graduate faculty who meet to review student's progress. The graduate chair then refracts the views of the faculty into a composite evaluation.

This chapter is a retrospective response to the composite narrative evaluation, this time stripped of any "bias avoidance" strategies frequently employed by faculty and graduate students to minimize the impact of family interference on academic performance (Drago and Colbeck). I use the auto-ethnographic practice of "emotional recall" (Ellis) in coordination with the department's narrative evaluation letter (partitioned, yet left in its original sequence). To scholars who hold themselves accountable to a more formal and systematic approach to data collection and analysis, I confess that this is a "messy vulnerable" (Denzin) account, which crosses genres into narrative non-fiction. My intention is not to turn every stone over. Rather, I want to show readers how structural pressures can compress a particular point in a structure to the point of breaking. My aim is to bring readers into the very moment when the structure cracks.

* * *

November 4, 2008

> *Dear Carolyn,*
> *Last week the graduate faculty of the Department of Sociology asked me to review your academic progress since last spring....*

March 12, 2008. I'm sitting at my desk at home. I open the urgent memo from the Department Chair, also my advisor. Department leadership's "probabilistic estimates" were off. They had "overcommitted" teaching assistantships. The "budget crisis" precludes appealing to higher levels at the university and therefore one or two students are being defunded, and three others are being sent warning letters simultaneously along with this memo. The decision-making criteria includes the following "objective measures": poor grades, incompletes, slow pace of completion of coursework, lack of progress toward developing qualifying papers, and not meeting deadlines set in previous annual review letters. I think of the four incompletes on my plate—one current, two of them over a year old, one from one term ago. My body tenses as I open the SOC-GRAD-DIR folder and see "Important Note from Graduate Director." The warning letter isn't a surprise. I know I haven't met anyone's expectations, certainly not my own. I compose an extremely appropriate response, one that masks my anger over not being able to take this term off to get used to motherhood and get back on my feet intellectually.

*

Amidst outrage at the way in which the defunding episode is handled, the two defunded students are reinstated. The graduate chair broadcasts a message regarding the reinstatement of one of the defunded students. The student, named in the email, is being reinstated despite his unsatisfactory academic progress. I'm confused and disappointed that the student is named in the email. This type of public shaming is unheard of in the corporate banking world I came from. I am even more disappointed that a public apology does not follow, ever. It gives the appearance that department leadership is allowed to expose students this way with impunity. Power relations within the department, within the university and beyond start to crystallize for me. An ombudsman position is created to ease tensions between the graduate faculty and students.

* * *

We are terribly upset that you have not cleared your two remaining incompletes. Last March you wrote me that you intend to complete the work for "Classical Sociological Theory" (from two years ago!) by the end of the month and for "Time, History, and Memory" (from three semesters ago) by July 15. It is now November and neither has been completed yet....

September 2006. I'm here. What an accomplishment! This is the right choice for me. I knew shortly into my Masters that I wanted to continue on in academia. I never dreamed I would ever get funding to do the things I love to do most—read, write and reflect. I want total immersion and am convinced I can handle it. I decide with my advisor to take four courses the first term with the knowledge that I will be taking an incomplete. When I discuss my schedule with upper years, they nod with great concern and tell stories of students who have regretted this decision. I ignore this. Faculty knows best.

*

I'm just about to hit cruising altitude when turbulence strikes. For Andrew, autumn represents the anniversary of a profound sudden loss. It seems making ourselves vulnerable to new love opens up other pathways of vulnerability. For the second time in his life he is experiencing a major depression. Andrew and I commit to seeing one another every third weekend. Unsure whom to share this new development with, I drop into the counseling center to find a much needed confidante.

*

October 2006. Our engagement emerges out of a conversation about whether we'd like to be parents one day. Despite my advisor's encouragement and support for my long-distance relationship, I don't tell him of my new "engaged" status. I also feel a strange discomfort my new commitment will be met with disapproval. Choosing to commit to someone instantly brings existing commitments into sharper focus.

*

New career. New home. New relationship. I'm trying to process it all on top of digesting the x's and y's of causal thinking and the magisterial language of eminent classical sociologists. I think back to the advice of a retired professor friend. "Whatever you do, don't get into a relationship during doctoral work, the two don't mix." And then, in a research methods class we examine how men and women fare in graduate school fare when they become parents. The professor shakes her head, "I honestly don't know how women have kids before tenure." I am 34, one of the oldest members of my cohort. When would tenure come around for me? If I'm extremely lucky, 40, 41, 42? It is possible to have children at this age. Hell, didn't a 70-year-old Italian woman just give birth?

*

Christmas 2006. Cape Breton is everything it's cracked up to be, even in the dead of winter. Andrew wrote the GRE and submitted his applications to graduate school during our week in Halifax. I'm excited and nervous to meet my in-laws-in-waiting. We've only ever spoken on the phone. I wonder what they all think of such a speedy engagement. I've heard stories about the children and the constant struggles the family has had trying to live off the land. Being around kids and dogs brings out the inner parents in both Andrew and me.

*

January 26, 2007. With home pregnancy test in hand, I skype Andrew. "Do you have three minutes?" The next five months are marked with stress of the best and worst kind. I have finally made some lasting friends in Highland Park. They listen and sympathize as I navigate a deliberately confusing health insurance system. Keeping on top of bills becomes a part-time job in itself. Most of my peers are covered under the state health plan but as a non-unionized Fellow I am allowed the less desirable plan. I voice my concern to the department that the hours I am spending dealing with health insurance fatigue is getting out of hand but I have no time to follow through on the complaints. I also need to look for a new apartment for June. Mid-pregnancy the university switches insurance carriers for Fellows, adding to my growing confusion. When I express my concerns with the staff at the health insurance office, I am told that my stress will upset the baby.

*

At five months pregnant, I return to Canada. At six months, Andrew and I move back down to New Jersey. Finally, we're together. We spend the summer adjusting to one another's constant company. I am adjusting daily to my growing body and to the idea of making two lifetime commitments: one to my child and one to Andrew on August 4th.

*

We plan an environmentally friendly wedding at the family cottage in Maine. Flatware from Goodwill, locally bought lobster and mussels, produce from a local farm. Planning the wedding around these values brings us closer together, as does shielding our wedding vision from the unyielding expectations of family members.

*

My body is changing every day. The promised second trimester energy boost never arrives and I am planning a wedding and finishing a long overdue incomplete while struggling with pregnancy-induced carpal tunnel syndrome, severe coccyx pain, and unexpectedly high weight gain. I angrily muse at how many of my aches and pains are dismissed as simply being "part of some women's pregnancy process."

*

August 4, 2007. The bride wore a lovely hemp gown and a gerber daisy in her hair; the groom wore a white linen shirt, khaki pants, and flip-flops. The ceremony was officiated by a member of the notary public, using Unitarian Universalist scripture. In lieu of wedding bands, the couple chose a water ceremony, combining waters from the streams and rivers of their childhoods.

*

September 2007. My advisor suggests I take the current comparative-historical methods course even though I have elected to take two seminar courses and an independent study. This was the best full-time arrangement I could come up with given that I will be giving birth during the term. He persists with high praise for the course and suggests I take it and take an incomplete in it at the end of the term. I remind him of my current incompletes. He backs down, reminding me that to succeed I should work some "wiggle room" into my schedule. I note the irony of him mentioning this while in transit between his two offices in the department, one in which he functions as graduate chair and the other where he focuses on his teaching and research obligations.

*

October 12, 2007. It's 10:05 pm. Amon releases his first cry. I only hear him and see a flash of him as he is handed over to the team of nurses who perform all the necessary APGAR tests. He scores 9.9. Andrew moves back and forth between Amon and me making sure his two loves are okay. Amon's nose is so defined and his eyes glisten from eye drops. He wrestles a little within the swaddling blanket but is very quiet and relaxed as he hangs beside me, cradled along Andrew's forearms. He senses me but is trapped by his limited motor skills. My arms are stretched out and strapped down. It will be six hours before I can hold him. A tug at my torso brings me back to what is happening to me. A surgical veil hangs down separating my head from the rest of my body. The surgeons are suturing my abdomen. I am parched, unable to summon a drop of saliva. My requests for water are denied. I will have to wait for ice chips in the recovery room.

*

My gestating body is gone. The current one feels like a city in ruins, its hormone inhabitants racing around in chaos looking for a new project. A few evenings later, they commit to bringing my milk in for the first time. I wake on the fourth morning in hospital and bring my hands to my chest. I think it's my chest. Either another woman's breasts have been sewn on to my chest or my breasts suffered a bee attack during the night. I gingerly get out of bed and walk directly to the bathroom mirror. I pause, afraid at what I am about to see. I lift my shirt. This happened overnight? I now regret eschewing so many of those pregnancy books.

*

I miss two full weeks of classes. Returning is surreal. Pads absorb the heavy vaginal bleeding. Nursing pads absorb the leaking breasts. I suck up the pain of a healing abdomen and fight like hell to maintain some semblance of focus during my classes. Adrenaline is keeping me going, but I wonder how long it will last.

*

My nipples are cracked and bleeding from breastfeeding; I tell Andrew I want to stop. Can we switch him to formula? How am I supposed to sustain this pace? My body feels wrecked. Does anybody hear me! My body feels wrecked! But, "breast is best." Breast is cheaper. I commit to six months of breastfeeding, and then we'll see. I finally have to confront the one thing that has always made me recoil in disgust, the blessed piece of technology that enables women to combine wage labor and breast-feeding—the breast pump.

*

December 14, 2007. Andrew is worried about me. Two weeks off after a c-section was ridiculous. I'm coming apart at the seams. I meet with my advisor/graduate program director to discuss taking the following semester off to regroup, expressing my concern to him that it may be the only way toward completing a Ph.D. At the meeting he says with certainty that I will not come back if I take a semester off—the pull of motherhood will be too strong. I half-heartedly concur, balancing the need for a mental and physical break with the need for stability and security. I have not yet adapted to all the changes in my life but not going full steam ahead would result in even greater change. I need full-time status to maintain health insurance for my family. Amon's eczema is terrible. Andrew's back is a mess from having to do all household lifting for six weeks following my c-section. Going off the anti-anxiety meds that I've been on since November 2007 doesn't appear to be an option for me at this point. At least keeping with the program will ease my growing sense of isolation. Full speed ahead, then. I take the offer of prematurely using up three research credits to lighten my load. Perhaps taking "Sociology of the Family" would be a safe space for me at the moment. Cognitive sociology—practically the entire reason for my being here—is also being offered, perhaps for the last time.

*

Spring 2008. Andrew and I have been splitting the childcare as best we can. It is highly advised that parents should try to sleep when the baby is sleeping, but there is so much to do: weekly readings, research for course papers, housekeeping, dealing with health insurance companies. There is little time to rest during the day and I am up a few times a night to feed Amon. Andrew and I make a deal. Whoever does not have to be "on the ball" the following day does nightly feedings. Most nights I have to either pump or feed, so I may as well just breastfeed Amon. No use in both of us being up. I'm grateful for the breast pump. No more cracks, no more bleeding. But my breasts respond better to breastfeeding; suckling acts as a strange form of communication between Amon and my milk supply. Pumping routinizes my milk production but causes painful engorgement. I am frequently massaging out blockages to prevent mastitis.

*

I am so proud of myself—I did it! I am at the campus library for the first time in ages. It's my first outing aside from class time. I have pumped enough milk to be able to leave some with Andrew for feedings and have my breast pump, two empty bottles to ease the inevitable engorgement. I approach the information desk attendant. He must be a sophomore or junior. I lean in and ask if there is a room in the library where I can use my breast pump; I have to pump breast milk for my baby. He looks perplexed and then shakes his head. With a laugh he informs me there's no such thing, he's never heard of such a room. No matter, this type of thing is outside his experience. I ask his older female colleague at the reference desk. Once again, no luck. I will have to use the public washroom. Deflated, I settle into a cubby hole in the graduate reading room. The university no longer feels like a place I belong. This sudden estrangement occupies my mind as I try to read. I absorb part of an article but only the sentences that aren't too taxing or long-winded. Another hour passes, I will need to pump soon. Thankfully the restroom is empty but the library is relatively full so I doubt I have the 15 or 20 minutes of privacy I would like to pump both breasts. I try a stall but feel immediately uncomfortable. I need space to do this. I deserve a space. I return to the sink area and I unpack the equipment. A student bursts in chatting on her cell phone and continues to chat in the restroom stall. I tell myself that I can do this. I have to be able to pump in a restroom. I wipe the wet counter off and place the bottles and caps on clean paper towels. With everything screwed into place, I plug the adapter into the socket. I start the pump. Nothing. No power. I try the other outlet. Nothing. The restroom outlets on the floor below do not work either. Defeated, I head home.

*

I have checked with the women I share an office with. Both support my need to pump at school and even offer to give me some privacy if need be. I decide to pump during class break. I have ten, maybe 15 minutes. I rush to my office in the opposite wing of the building. In the midst of pumping, the department's computer lab manager quickly knocks and enters. He looks to the pump and then to me then covers his eyes as he ducks out, apologizing repeatedly. My embarrassment is somehow lessened knowing that he is a father and has seen all of this.

*

I'm thoroughly enjoying my Sociology of the Family class. The readings are so timely for me and class discussions have a nice ebb and flow. One class discussion brings up the issues of combining work and motherhood. I tell the class breast pumps are integral to managing the all-consuming and dueling identities of motherhood and graduate work. In a misguided attempt to merge theory with practice I reach down offering to quickly show the class what one looks like. You would have thought I was reaching for an angry skunk. The class squirms, recoils and shakes their heads.

The professor is a mother. She and the other gradmother ask about our family's ongoing battle with Amon's eczema. It goes from mild to severe, and requires antibiotics to prevent infection. I wish I could just sit in a warm oatmeal bath with him all day. To see him so uncomfortable frequently brings Andrew and me to tears. The guilt of being away from him and the frustration of not being able to cure the eczema devours my attention most of my waking hours.

*

Andrew calls as I am leaving class. "Can you come home? I'm losing my mind, I don't know how to stop the itching." An hour later, I walk through the front door. Andrew is seated on the coffee table behind the stack on reusable diapers he's folding—unshaven and wearing that all to familiar look of defeat we exchange on a daily basis. "I wasn't sure what to do. I couldn't stand watching him scratch anymore." he says. I look down at the floor at our happy, chortling son, swaddled in a towel and duct-taped to a change table mattress completely absorbed in the film, *A Bug's Life*.

* * *

Last March I also wrote to you that sometime over the summer you and I should meet and work out a detailed plan to bring you back to a steady pace of progress. As you know that has not happened either....

September 2008. A detailed plan would give us time for our own work and time for ourselves, family time and a "date night" once in a while. All our anxieties are relieved when the daycare up the road accepts Amon. This will give us the luxury of full weekdays to fulfill academic commitments. Our teaching assistantships don't quite cover daycare expenses—$1020 per month—but I secure a part-time lecturing job to cover the costs. I teach Monday and Wednesday evenings, 7:40-9:00pm with an additional recitation hour after Wednesday's class. Andrew's stipend from CUNY requires him to take three graduate seminars and teach two sections of the same course. He teaches the same evenings in New York. Luckily, a former student of mine emails offering to babysit.

We create a Google Calendar showing all known commitments for the term: who is daily responsible for cooking dinner, making lunches, dropping off and picking up Amon, bathing Amon, reading to Amon; who is weekly responsible for vacuuming, dusting, doing laundry, paying the bills, cleaning the bathroom, tidying; seminar schedules; teaching schedules.

This term will be better, we tell ourselves. I divide myself into three tidy folders on my desktop: "PTL Carolyn," "TA Carolyn," and "Grad Student Carolyn."

Amon starts spiking fevers in October. Cancer strikes my only family living close by. The professor for whom I am a teaching assistant falls ill leaving me to take up the slack.

*

December 2008. In the last three months Amon has been on five rounds of antibiotics; the last of which are a three-day regime of injections, with the last one injected intravenously in the ER after a chest x-ray to diagnose the "crackling" in his chest. Placing Amon in daycare has turned my family into a vector for every pathogen known to man. During the semester the bug presents as pink eye, stomach flu, and strep throat in Andrew; strep throat, pink-eye, and a sinus infection in me. Every single day of the term at least one family member is depleted.

In my desperate search for an analogy to express what all of this feels like, I think back to the little square-shaped sliding puzzles I played with as a child, the ones with one piece purposely removed. The objective is to move the numbered pieces into numeric order. Depending on the particular arrangement of the puzzle in its initial state, the puzzle may never be solved. On a good day, Andrew and I feel we have that one opening, just enough space to shuffle obligations around slightly, if necessary. When Amon gets sick, the flexibility dissolves completely. If anything else goes wrong, the puzzle pieces buckle under stress and our immaculate, detailed plans crumble before our eyes.

* * *

Most of your professors keep believing that you have the ability to produce excellent work. At the same time, however, they all note that they have yet to see you following through and working toward realizing your potential. While we keep noting your highly promising ideas for projects (for example, your paper on the social roots of post-partum depression, which we were glad to see you present at the SSSP), we are somewhat unsure as to your ability to complete such projects....

October 2008. I run into the graduate chair who is still serving as my advisor. I keep pushing the deadlines on papers I owe him. We greet one another. I tell him I wake up every morning wondering whether or not I can sustain both motherhood and a Ph.D.

"It can be done," he reassures.
"Some people can do it," I reply.
"It can be done," he repeats.

If "it" can be done, then surely there is something wrong with me.

*

A gradmother in the department confides in me that it takes tons of therapy just to hold it together long enough. Even in the dissertating stage, she considers giving it up. Another gradmother, living down the street from me, recalls the sinking feeling moments after her dissertation proposal was accepted, when the chair of her department advised, "Now if you can just avoid having any children, you should be able to complete your Ph.D."

*

Anecdotal evidence builds and builds. The experiences of managing their limited physical, mental, emotional, temporal, spatial and financial resources triggered sadness, laughter and a new clarity. Shortly thereafter I send an email to every graduate program assistant I could find searching for other gradparents with dreams of organizing for change.

* * *

Furthermore, a number of your professors have deep concerns about your disciplinary fit with our program, not having seen your full commitment to thinking sociologically. I should also note that you have yet to have a formally approved proposal for your first qualifier, which we expected you to do by October 15....

I wonder more and more about the mental and emotional costs of trying to fit in.

* * *

In my annual review letter to you last March I also suggested that you consider switching academic advisors and that perhaps someone else can offer you better help than I have. [name omitted] is willing to serve as your advisor and, given your current interests, you might want to also consider either [name omitted] or [name omitted]. Anyway, you should definitely have an advisor with whom you maintain regular contact....

Please let me know soon how you intend to take care of all the problematic matters I have outlined above.

Director of Graduate Program

December 21, 2008. We made it to the Christmas tree lot 15 minutes before closing. Despite the rush, not being too late filled my husband and me with a triumphant feeling and the satisfaction that we were going to have our real Christmas tree. Amon had fallen asleep in his car seat. His head was drooping forward. Lifting it up I paused and took in his peaceful sleep, the moisture above his brow and the current perfection of his plump skin. Moments like this I have hope that he's licked eczema and ear infections and is finally putting on some weight. The phone rings. It is my professor calling to talk about the incomplete draft submission of my final course paper. She's trying to figure out what grade to assign such questionable performance. I don't know what to say. We agree that I will hand in a new paper at the beginning of the spring term.

A few hours later, I am cc'd on a third-person narrative evaluation of my performance in the course. Its conclusion suggests we meet for a serious conversation about what I hope to accomplish in my graduate studies. Coming on the tail of my most recent annual evaluation, this third-person narrative evaluation hits a raw nerve. I call her and when she picks up I pour my anger into the mouthpiece.

I run to the back porch and punch the screen door open, feeling the burn of the ice-cold aluminum on my bare hands. It slams against the icy railing, bouncing back. There is still more anger to discharge. I snatch the plastic cooler off the porch floor and throwing it across the lawn with a scream. I buckle over letting out another scream, only this one is silent, because the last one winded me. I collapse to my knees and lie over a plastic storage bin, punching the top of it. Finally I bury my head into my arms and breathe. I soon feel the warm weight of the blanket Andrew is wrapping around me. I hear Amon crying from his crib and I mouth the words that I am sorry to wake him. Andrew reassures me it's just his normal late evening cry of discomfort. Probably molars coming in.

CONCLUSION

In their 2009 article, Kristen Springer et al. provided academia with a veritable white paper on reducing work-family conflict for graduate student parents. Their survey of 60 chairs of sociology departments revealed that, in addition to the indisputable lack of institutional support for graduate student parents, department chairs themselves knew little about the existing formal supports. Support tends to be extended informally on a case-by-case basis.

Springer et al. provide precise solutions, on both institutional and departmental levels, to challenge and combat the persistent message that children are unwelcome at universities. Parent-friendly university infrastructure would include comfortable and accessible lactation rooms, change tables in campus washrooms and stroller-friendly entries/exits and walkways. Formal university policy would include paid or unpaid parental leave, part-time graduate training, academic deadline extensions, affordable health insurance for dependents and, most importantly, affordable, quality, routine child care with needs-based subsidies.

In my estimation, all of these recommendations are reasonable and attainable. The required real estate for a more inclusive infrastructure exists as do the funds to carry forth a plan to ensure that the graduate training experience is "family-friendly." We need to go further with these excellent and create objective assessment tools for evaluating the family-friendliness of academic departments. Universities owe it to women to provide an accurate assessment of available and projected institutional and departmental support for parent students. I would be weary of academic departments that self-label as "family-friendly" as it is most likely based on informal and inconsistent departmental policies.

EPILOGUE

When I peered into my academic future in December 2009 I saw mostly exhaustion, bitterness and burnout. I was not merely looking into my own crystal ball. I saw it all around me in the experiences of tenured and tenure-track moms at my university. I read it in, and between, the lines of "grad-mothering" blogs. I heard it in the voices of stressed-out graduate student parents.

The months that followed my departure were challenging. The sudden loss of structure and linearity was both liberating and disorienting. Time spent with my family was now joyfully unfettered by the omnipresence of academic work yet I was completely unsure about what my next steps should be. The healing and renewal process was slow because my social network was (and still is) mostly comprised of graduate students all of whom were intensely curious about my decision. When people asked how I made the decision I told them it came down to one question: If I spend another three to four years finishing a Ph.D. and land a fabulous tenure-track position in the location of my choice, will all of this have been worth it? Will the end forgive the means?

There have been difficult moments watching Andrew proceed with his Ph.D. This was once a dream of mine and now much of my energy is devoted to helping him get through the process. An internal tension emerges at times as I observe my feminist sensibilities admonishing my current devotions as wife and mother. The tension never lasts long, though. I soon remind myself that I have simply internalized the choices thrust upon women in academia.

When I stroll through the university campus with Amon, now four and one-half years old, quizzical glances from students, faculty and staff remind me that motherhood and academia are not even close to being at ease with one another. As we walk hand in hand, I am satisfied with my decision to leave a culture that would have demanded all of my attention, all of the time.

WORKS CITED

Coser, L. *Greedy Institutions: Patterns of Undivided Commitment.* New York: The Free Press, 1974.

Denzin, N. K. "Analytic Autoethnography, or Déjà Vu all Over Again." *Journal of Contemporary Ethnography* (2006): 419-428.

Drago, R. "Challenges of Raising a Family in Academia." Paper presented at the 2006 Work and Family Conference at Rutgers, New Brunswick, NJ, 2006.

Drago, R. and C. Colbeck. *The Mapping Project: Exploring the Terrain of U.S. Colleges and Universities for Faculty and Families.* University of Pennsylvania, 2003.

Drago, R., C. Colbeck, K. D. Stauffer, A. Pirretti, K. Burkum, J. Fazioli, et al. The Avoidance of Bias Against Caregiving: The Case of Academic Faculty. *The American Behavioral Scientist* (2006): 1222-1249.

Ellis, C. *The Ethnographic I: A Methodological Novel about Autoethnography.* Lanham, MD: Altamira Press, 2004.

Mason, M. A. *Why So Few Doctoral Students Parents?* (2009, October 21). Retrieved October 21, 2009, from *The Chronicle of Higher Education* <http://chronicle.com/article/Why-So-Few-Doctoral-Student/48872>.

Mason, M. A., M. Goulden and K. Frasch. *Why Graduate Students*

Reject the Fast Track. Retrieved November 29, 2009, from *Academe* (2009). Online: <http://www.aaup.org/AAUP/pubsres/academe/2009/JF/Feat/maso.htm?PF=1>.

Mykhalovskiy, E. "Reconsidering Table Talk: Critical Thoughts on the Relationship Between Sociology, Autobiography and Self-Indulgence." *Qualitative Sociology* (1996): 131-151.

Springer, K. W., B. K. Parker and C. Leviten-Reid. *Journal of Family Issues* 30.4 (April 2009): 435-457

Stone, P. *Opting Out? Why Women Really Quit Careers and Head Home.* Berkeley: University of California Press, 2008.

Williams, J. *Unbending Gender: Why Work and Family Conflict and What to Do About It.* New York: Oxford University Press, 2001.

6.

"Which June?" What Baby?

The Continued Invisibility of Maternity in Academia

LAURA J. BEARD

I CAN TRACE AN INTEREST IN MOTHERS AND DAUGHTERS throughout my academic career, from my undergraduate thesis as an English major on the development of the maternal role in the novels of Jane Austen to a later dissertation proposal on mothers and daughters in the novels of contemporary Latin American, African American, and Native American women writers. (Immediately after the proposal defense, I jettisoned that dissertation as too broad and wrote on another, more focused topic). As a professor, I presented papers on female sexuality from adolescence to maternity, citing such texts as Marianne Hirsch's *The Mother/Daughter Plot: Narrative, Psychoanalysis, Feminism*, E. Ann Kaplan's *Motherhood and Representation: The Mother in Popular Culture and Melodrama*, Nancy Chodorov's *The Reproduction of Mothering: Psychoanalysis and the Sociology of Gender*, or *The (M)other Tongue: Essays in Feminist Psychoanalytic Interpretation*, edited by Shirley Nelson Garner, Claire Kahane, and Madelon Sprengnether. I wrote on all of these topics as a feminist scholar and as a daughter, but not as mother. Then, after tenure, I got pregnant.

I teach at a large, state university that does not grant paid maternity leave. My university does comply with the federal *Family Medical Leave Act,* which states that "Covered employers must grant an eligible employee up to a total of twelve work weeks of unpaid leave during any twelve-month period" for a variety of reasons, including "for the birth and care of the newborn child of the employee." As it happened, my baby was due in mid-June, so I figured that, if all went well, I could teach both semesters and stay home with the newborn in the summer, then return to teach in the fall, without needing to take the unpaid leave. It was when asking for a very minor accommodation for the spring semester prior to the birth that I first realized how invisible and incomprehensible maternity still is in academia.

Because I was scheduled to teach classes that required the regular use of films in a building in which most classrooms were not appropriately equipped, I had to push a cart with a TV and VCR/DVD equipment to class. Hoping to avoid that in the latter months of pregnancy, I spoke to my associate chair to request a classroom with video equipment "for medical reasons." He approved it immediately, but for some reason I then had to repeat the request to the department chair, who wanted to know the medical reasons. When I informed him I was pregnant, he wanted to know when the baby was due; when I said, "June," he asked, "which June?"

The department chair's seemingly impossible (or perhaps impossibly hostile) question—how could anyone ask which June? Doesn't everyone know how long the gestation period is for humans?—made it clear to me that maternity remains invisible and incomprehensible in academia. That invisibility was reinforced at the end of that school year when, after classes had ended, I ran into an undergraduate student who had studied with me in both the fall and spring semesters. He asked me what I was going to do in the summer. I said, "Have a baby." Shocked, he immediately looked down at my stomach. This student had been in my classroom three times a week all year, as an active, engaged participant, but he had never noticed that I was pregnant, even at eight months. From these experiences I draw my title: "Which June, what baby?"

While feminist scholars are beginning to focus on the ways in which academia—its structures, its policies, and its insidious assumptions—are built for and by male professors,[2] the topic of academic mothers too often remains both silent and invisible. But that invisibility may not be so surprising, when we consider that at many universities, all members of the upper administration are male and if there are any females, they most likely are childless. This academic scenario mirrors that of other segments of society. As I finish this article in late spring 2010, there exists the possibility that there could be, for the first time in history, three women on the Supreme Court of the United States. If that does become the case, two of the three will be childless women, reminding us all that it is easier to reach the top if you do so without children (see Ashburn).

But for those of us who have chosen to have children, and who have chosen to do so within the realm of academia, we often find that the path is trickier than expected. Certainly, universities and departments are not allowed to discriminate openly against women who are pregnant, who are nursing, or who have children; but, as in so many areas, it is the subtle discrimination that remains a powerful barrier, as Mary P. Rowe argues in her article "Barriers to Equality: The Power of Subtle Discrimination to Maintain Unequal Opportunity." Rowe focuses on what she calls "discriminatory microinequities," which she defines as

> tiny, damaging characteristics of an environment … distinguished by the fact that for all practical purposes one cannot do anything about them, one cannot take them to court or file a grievance. They are actions which are unjust toward individuals, when reasonable people would agree the particular treatment of the individual occurs only because of a group characteristic unrelated to creativity and work performance (for example, sex, race, religion, age, or country of origin). (155)

These inequities are, as Rowe notes, "fiendishly efficient in perpetuating unequal opportunity, because they are in the air we breathe, in the books we read, in the television we all watch, and because we cannot change the personal characteristic that leads to the inequity" (155). They are "woven into the threads of our work life and of U.S. education" (155). She calls them micro not because they are trivial but because they are miniature (155). Rowe focuses on discriminatory microinequities around race and gender, but which are the discriminatory microinequities that make the career path more difficult for academic mothers? And what can we do to eliminate them from our career paths? This article begins to address those questions, proposing that to eliminate the microinequities, maternity cannot remain invisible and incomprehensible in academia. Academic mothers need to be visible and recognized as important members of the academy. Making the experiences of academic mothers more visible and recognizable in the academy will make the academy a better workplace for us all.

In exploring these microinequities, I speak in part from my own experiences as an academic mother, in part from the experiences of colleagues, particularly at my own university,[3] and also from the experiences reported in published articles and documents, including the reports from the

Modern Languages Association's Committee on the Status of Women in the Profession. I am interested in exploring the inequities that exist within our academic culture, the ways in which we as women sometimes participate (willingly or unwillingly) in perpetuating those inequities, and the ways in which we might all work to change the academic systems to eliminate those discriminatory inequities.

STANDING STILL

In 2009, the Modern Languages Association published "Standing Still: The Associate Professor Survey," a report from their Committee on the Status of Women in the Profession. In English and the foreign languages, men disproportionately hold positions of higher rank and move through the ranks more rapidly than women do. Such is the case even though more women earn Ph.D.s and get hired as Assistant Professors in these fields. The Committee on the Status of Women in the Profession (CSWP) did a study to understand the causes of this lack of parity at the rank of professor, via an online survey questionnaire developed to provide both quantitative and qualitative information that might help explain the substantial differences in time between men and women in attaining the rank of professor. While the committee members concluded that "no one cause can explain women's status in the profession" (2), one of the many items noted in their report was that "women report they devote a significantly greater amount of time to childcare than do men" (2).[4] In the responses to open-ended questions in the CSWP survey, the time spent on child-rearing and other family obligations was mentioned as a roadblock to career progress.

Correspondingly, the lack of family obligations was cited by both men and women as something that helped them moved forward in their careers:

> As one man put it, "Being single and having time to devote myself obsessively to my writing, teaching and service" was the key to success; another person reported that "living alone and throwing myself into my work after a divorce helped meet requirements for promotion." A woman who is an associate professor at a doctoral institution explained, "The cost of getting ahead professionally has been almost entirely personal. I'm single with no kids; I've

worked more or less unremittingly for the past six years and my family and friends have not gotten the love and attention from me that they deserve. I'm hoping now that I have the book done I'll be able to spend more time with them...." (13)

Those faculty members who spend all their time working on their research and writing are following the academic path we are all socialized to follow. Deviation from that path is difficult. As Gail M. Simmons wryly notes in "Reproductive Success for Working Scientists," looking back on her experiences of being on the job market in the sciences while pregnant (she got no job offers), "as a society, we have far to go in rethinking how careers for gravid and postpartum academic mammals should proceed. Up to now, all we have really done is modify the protocol followed for decades by the sperm donors" (Simmons).

In following that protocol, in doing our best to minimize the interruptions of our maternity in our academic careers, are we contributing to the invisibility of motherhood in the profession? Are we just accepting (and perhaps internalizing) the microinequities? Planning a due date to coincide with the academic calendar (all those babies born at the end of May!) or returning to work as soon as possible after the birth of a child (a colleague who gave birth to twins in her first year in a tenure-track job at a major state university and returned to work after just a couple weeks, because she didn't know how many days she could take and was afraid to ask in her new job) are examples of how we help to perpetuate the invisibility of maternity by the employment of what are called "bias avoidance strategies" (Colbeck and Drago). As Kelly Ward and Lisa Wolf-Wendel note, this bias avoidance is rooted in fear: "Faculty members, women in particular, are fearful that if they use policies they will face negative repercussions" (2008: 264). This fear can come from the dominant discourses associated with tenure and academic culture but also from the women's need to be seen as legitimate faculty members. Even when departments or colleges have policies that allow women to stop the tenure clock for the birth or adoption of a child or to take time off from work, some faculty mothers are afraid to utilize the policies as they fear that doing so may put their legitimacy as scholars into question.

Other times, the faculty member may not utilize an informal policy within a department, one in which a department chair may offer a professor who has just given birth some time off, because the burden for arranging for that leave falls entirely on the person who has just given birth. As one untenured assistant professor noted in an exit interview conducted when she left my university:

> With the first chair I had, he said I could take six weeks off but I would have to get someone to cover all of my courses and make sure it was all covered. At the time I was so overwhelmed that I thought I didn't have the energy to orchestrate that. With the second child, there was this kind of mixed message of 'Are you taking maternity leave?'[5] And I'd say I didn't see how I could with this graduate class and this undergraduate class because I didn't see how I could coordinate all of that. The chair said I could take one if I wanted to but I didn't see how it was possible. So it was really difficult. (WS exit interview, August 2006)

Her description of the way in which the situation was handled in her department reveals a number of microinequities. Again, these were "tiny, damaging characteristics of an environment," actions which were unjust toward her, but which were also "distinguished by the fact that for all practical purposes one cannot do anything about them, one cannot take them to court or file a grievance" (Rowe, 155). In cases like this one, to put the responsibility onto the pregnant woman, who in many instances may be new to the university, to find other people to cover all her classes, may not be the best policy for a department to follow. In other instances as well, the lack of a formal policy and the lack of understanding on the part of department chairs and administrators can make it impossible for academic mothers to take advantage of what few policies exist at their universities.

In some cases, women may choose not to look for a job at a research university, or not to stay in a position at a research university, if they wish to have a family, as they perceive that the goals of having a family and achieving tenure within a research university system are incompatible.[6] One woman, who had been three years in a tenure-track position at my university, left for a job at another institution when she became pregnant. She noted that the decision was made "based on lifestyle and personal issues.... I really like the environment at this other school. I'm having a baby in the Spring and I know it would be very difficult …

here with a two or three month old baby and to be able to work at the level that I would need to work" (WS exit interview, Spring 2001). When she shared her reasons with colleagues in the position she was leaving, she was told, "Well, I guess you're not a serious researcher" (WS exit interview, Spring 2001). Making a choice that allows her to keep time for her family puts her identity as a scholar into question. Do women have to choose whether to be serious researchers or to be mothers? Or can we change the structure and the climate at universities, including top research universities, to make it possible for women to be academic mothers, excelling at various facets of their lives?

Many academic mothers have chosen to have successful careers and raise happy, healthy children. But it is hard to make that choice. We all know the guilt that comes when you are trying to be both the successful academic and the good mother. When you are at the office, chatting with someone in the hall who talks about what they did the previous weekend, you feel guilty because you didn't spend your entire weekend working on your research and writing. Talking with other mothers inspires just as much guilt. Two conversations from when my son was younger stick out vividly in my mind. Both were with mothers who had daughters the same age as my son. One was telling me about her daughter's baby teeth. She could name each tooth and knew the date when it came in. I just stared at her as she talked. Was I supposed to know that about my child? Wasn't it enough that he had teeth and could eat? Another summer, a few years later, a different mother told me that her daughter was in a summer program, and that each day, when they got home, they were scrapbooking pages about what they had done. I experienced more instant pangs of maternal guilt. I was not creating a scrapbook with a page for every day of our summer, but I was getting my own book done, the one being published with a university press that would contribute to my promotion to full professor.

MOVING FORWARD

So what can we do, as academic mothers, not just to deal with our own maternal guilt, but more importantly to reduce the invisibility and incomprehensibility of maternity in academia? What changes can we make in our own lives and careers as academic mothers and what changes can we advocate in our institutions to make those institutions more welcoming places for all those who are working in them, including the academic mothers? What can we do to combat the microinequities? In this section, I make suggestions of changes we might make, depending on our own institutions and our own places in those institutions. Those of us who are tenured, who may be full professors, who may be department chairs, deans or associate deans, or occupy some other position in a college or university administration may have the opportunity to exercise stronger voices than those who are not; but all of us can look to this list and to our own individual lists of what we might do to impact change. Departments need to look at their own policies to see how they impact academic mothers (and parents) across the board. First off, are there policies? Are they clear? Do all members of the faculty and administration understand them properly (not just those who might take advantage of the policies, but also those who might be voting—in tenure and promotion cases—on those who have taken advantage of these policies)? When someone has the tenure clock stopped, her senior faculty colleagues need to understand what that means and cast their next votes accordingly. If external letters are requested for third year reviews or tenure and promotion decisions, then those outside reviewers would need to know that a person has received a year (or more) off the clock as well and be asked to evaluate the dossier accordingly.

A tenure-track assistant professor in the humanities at my university, in her exit interview, wrote that she received a negative annual peer review after her year off the tenure clock (having had a very good review the year previously), because her colleagues thought she had not done enough research: "as if they expected me to do a year or more of research while my clock was stopped.... The comments showed that the faculty members really didn't take that into consideration" (WS exit interview 2001). While this particular faculty member left for a job at another college prior to going up for tenure, she feared that had she remained at the institution where she stopped the tenure clock, having stopped the clock would have hurt her in the long run.

In addition, if a department, college or university has a stop the clock policy for tenure, is it one in which the faculty member has to make the request or is it automatic (one in which the faculty member would have to opt out)? The latter can be the better option, taking the heat off the untenured faculty members who may feel that a department discourages them from utilizing the policy.

Not only do department chairs, deans, and provosts need to have clear policies regarding maternity leaves, the stopping of the tenure clock, the adjustment of workloads, etc. , and ensure that those policies are clearly understood, but they need to be sure they are applied equitably across departments and faculties. When a faculty member in English finds out that faculty members in History get reduced teaching loads but no such accommodations are made available to her in English, the college will have unhappy faculty members.

Other policies should be examined as well to see if they are impacting academic parents. Are faculty meetings held at times that are difficult for faculty members with children? In my department, for many years, faculty meetings have been held Mondays at 3:00 pm; the time when parents have to pick up children from school. In such a case, is it possible to reschedule the meetings for another time that would be more convenient to all the parents of young children in the department yet not inconvenient for faculty members in general? If so, a simple change in meeting time can make a big difference to the academic parents. In the case of my department, the change also benefits the department members who serve on a college committee that meets every other Monday at 3:00 pm. Other faculty members may also be happier with an earlier meeting time, as it allows them to end their day earlier.

Gail Simmons, in her article on "Reproductive Success for Working Scientists," gives advice to department heads and deans about many things they can do to make prospective female faculty members feel welcome as well as to encourage current faculty members who have or are about to have children. Her suggestions include introducing job seekers to faculty members with children so that the ones already on campus can share information about their arrangements; "offer information about family policies to all job candidates. Discuss child-care options, health insurance, leave policies, tenure-clock modifications, part-time possibilities, flexible teaching schedules. Don't wait to be asked, and don't ask whether the candidate intends to take advantage of those options. Just put the information out there" (Simmons); sharing your own experience if you are an academic mother and have been through it yourself; looking for informal solutions to problems; and providing parenting space in your building. Simmons recalls that "one of the simplest accommodations I ever received was from the scheduling officer in my department. She knew that two of us in the department had small children and lived near each other. So she arranged our teaching schedules so that we taught on different days of the week. That way I could baby-sit her kids if they were ill and could not go to day-care, and she could baby-sit mine. It worked very well" (Simmons).

The options for combining parenting and academia need to be a safe topic of discussion for graduate students who wonder if they really can have children and pursue a job in the academic field. If they look around the department and see no women, or no mothers, or only people working 60-80 hour weeks, they may decide they don't want to go into the fields we have chosen to pursue. Having academic mothers who are department chairs or deans is important, especially if those academic mothers are open to talking about how younger parents or would-be parents might combine careers and families. Some universities have websites or forums to promote these discussions, like the Berkeley Parents Network site, with a section entitled "Is an Academic Career Compatible with Being a Mom?"

We need to think about all the mothers working in our academic departments, not just the faculty members and the graduate students, but also the staff members. Are there ways we can make working in the academic environment more accommodating for the mothers in staff positions? If our office jobs are 8:00–5:00 pm, but we have mothers who need to drop kids at school or daycare, might a flex-time arrangement where someone can get there at 8:15 or 8:30 and take a shorter lunch hour work better for that working mother?

One colleague who is a department chair at another university spoke of a limited time period when one of her staff members brought children to work. The staff person was going to have them in a daycare situation after school and the department chair told her that if they came to office and did homework quietly, then, they could come to work. It worked out; the working mother saved money and was very grateful for the accommodation.

Having more academic mothers in the positions of department chair, dean, provost or university president will help both to address the invisibility and incomprehensibility of maternity in academia and to create and implement better policies and more welcoming environments for academic mothers. It is my hope that with more academic mothers in leadership roles, no other faculty member will be faced with such questions "Which June?"

[1]The university also has, on an informal basis which varies by department and college, other work and family policies that may apply. For example, in many cases, the tenure clock may be stopped for a year after the birth or adoption of a child by an untenured faculty member, in recognition of the time that must be devoted to a new child. This policy recognizes that having a young child may have a negative impact on work productivity during the crucial and finite probationary period of the tenure process. Some department chairs may choose to modify teaching or service duties in response to the birth or adoption of a child, but such modifications are not a university policy and therefore cannot be counted on by the faculty parent.

[2]See Bracken, Allen and Dean; Lester and Sallee for a variety of examples.

[3]In this chapter, I make use of exit interviews that were done with female faculty members who left my university between the years 2000-2006. These interviews were done through the auspices of the Women's Studies Program, and the faculty members interviewed chose to allow their interviews to be made available to researchers, sometimes immediately, sometimes after a period of a year or three years. They could choose to make their interviews available with their names or anonymously; I do not use the names of any individuals in this article.

[4]Women report, on an average and across the different types of institutions included in the MLA report, that they devote 31.6 hours a week to child care, while men report that they devote 14.2 hours per week (12). As pointed out in the survey, that difference alone cannot account for the slower pace for women in attaining the rank of full professor, as only 38.1 percent of the women who responded to the survey had children at home.

[5]There is no paid maternity leave at the university, but faculty members can take up to 12 weeks of unpaid leave.

[6]See Lisa Wolf-Wendel and Kelly Ward's article "Faculty Work and Family Life: Policy Perspectives from Different Institutional Types," particularly pp. 55-57.

WORKS CITED

Ashburn, Lauren. "Childless: How the Most Ambitious Women Choose Not to Be Sidetracked by Family." Online: <http://www.huffington

post.com/lauren-ashburn/childless-how-the-most-am_b_574249. htm>.

Bracken, Susan J., Jeanie K. Allen, and Diane R. Dean, eds. *The Balancing Act: Gendered Perspectives in Faculty Roles and Work Lives*. Sterling, Virginia: Stylus Press, 2006.

Chodorov, Nancy. *The Reproduction of Mothering: Psychoanalysis and the Sociology of Gender*. Berkeley: University of California Press, 1978.

Colbeck, C. L. and R. Drago. "Accept, Avoid, Resist: Faculty Members' Responses to Bias Against Caregiving ... And How Departments Can Help." *Change* 37.6 (2005): 10-17.

Exit interviews with women faculty. Texas Tech University Women's Studies Office.

Family Medical Leave Act. Online: <http://www.dol.gov/esa/whd/ fmla/>.

Hirsch, Marianne. *The Mother/Daughter Plot: Narrative, Psychoanalysis, Feminism*. Bloomington: Indiana University Press, 1989.

"Is an Academic Career Compatible with Being a Mom?" Berkeley Parents Network. Online: <http://parents.berkeley.edu/advice/allkinds/compatible.html#ray>.

Kaplan, E. Ann. *Motherhood and Representation: The Mother in Popular Culture and Melodrama*. London: Routledge, 1992.

Lester, Jaime and Margaret Sallee, eds. *Establishing the Family-Friendly Campus: Models for Effective Practice*. Sterling, Virginia: Stylus Press, 2009.

Modern Language Association. *Standing Still: The Associate Professor Survey*. Report of the Committee on the Status of Women in the Profession, Modern Language Association of America, 27 April 2009. Web: <www.mla.org/cswp_report09>.

Nelson Garner, Shirley, Claire Kahane, and Madelon Sprengnether, eds. *The (M)other Tongue: Essays in Feminist Psychoanalytic Interpretation*. Ithaca, NY: Cornell University Press, 1985.

Rowe, Mary P. "Barriers to Equality: The Power of Subtle Discrimination to Maintain Unequal Opportunity." *Employee Responsibilities and Rights Journal* 3.2 (1990): 153-63.

Simmons, Gail M. "Reproductive Success for Working Scientists." *The Chronicle of Higher Education* April 26, 2005. Online: <http://chronicle.com/article/Reproductiv-Success-for/44907>.

Ward, K. and L. Wolf-Wendel. "Choice and Discourse in Faculty Careers:

Feminist Perspectives on Work and Family." *Unfinished Agendas: New and Continuing Gender Challenges in Higher Education*. Ed. by Judith Glazer-Raymo. Baltimore: The Johns Hopkins University Press, 2008. 252-272.

Ward, K. and L. Wolf-Wendel. "Faculty Work and Family Life: Perspectives from Different Institution Types." *The Balancing Act: Gendered Perspectives in Faculty Roles and Work Lives*. Ed. by Susan J. Bracken, Jeanie K. Allen, and Diane R. Dean. Sterling, Virginia: Stylus Press, 2006. 51-72.

7.

Academic Mothers Climb the Ladder of Promotion and Tenure

One Rung at a Time

MICHELE L. VANCOUR

WOMEN TAKE THE LEAD in earned doctorates in the U.S. with the most recent data showing that women receive 50.4 percent of doctoral degrees, which is up from 44 percent in 2000. This places women in the lead for degrees at all levels (Jaschik). However, if post-doc women are able to find a tenure-track position in this abysmal economy, they can expect to be outnumbered by men in tenure and at the highest rank[1] (deVise). Their presence, regardless of rank, supports the 50 percent increase of full-time female faculty members in the U.S. between 1984 and 2008, which translates to approximately "31 percent holding non-tenure track positions, 25 percent on the tenure track, and 43 percent tenured" (Auriemma and Klein 1).

Despite women's success in nearing equity in academe, it is well documented that there is a leak in the pipeline resulting in some women's lack of advancement to "professor" and their untimely departures while on the tenure track (Mason and Goulden 11; Vancour and Sherman 235). Danielle Auriemma and Tovah Klein suggest that timing is the main culprit. Women typically receive their doctorates around age 34, and receive a tenure decision approximately seven years later. Further, the potential collision of the tenure clock and the biological clock, leads some women to postpone children, if not entirely put them off. This reality, coupled with women citing work-family balance as one of their main reasons for leaving higher education, suggests that combining motherhood and an academic career is insurmountable challenge for some.

Women are lured to academia under the impression that they will have summers off and flexibility (deVise). What they soon realize is that summer is likely the only time they will be able to progress in their research, and that the flexibility comes at a cost often detracting from their ability to meet their scholarly demands. In addition, the playing field recently has changed as a result of the external pressures regarding teaching and research. Over 30 percent of women faculty work over 60 hours a week and between 60 and 75 percent of women work over fifty hours a week, regardless of rank (full, associate and assistant) and institution type, potentially establishing a new norm for overwork. The effect of technology increases the amount of time faculty work, and the prevalent use of email increases the hours faculty can work at home (Jacobs 9), further blurring the lines of flexibility and adding to the never-ending job.

The disproportionate responsibilities inherent in housekeeping and care of young children, may additionally overload some women (Dominici, Fried and Zeger 25). The requisite time invested in completing these tasks has been estimated to be 40 hours a week for academic mothers, bringing their total hours worked a week up around 100. This is in contrast to the 80 total hours academic fathers' work, with about 25 hours dedicated to domestic and family responsibilities (Mason 1). However, in stark contrast, parenthood positively affects men's progression through the tenure and promotion process (deVise). The literature suggests that fathers are rewarded for their family commitments, while mothers are viewed as neglecting their work responsibilities. Further, faculty fathers are less likely than faculty mothers to have full-time employed partners (56.2 percent compared to 88.5 percent respectively) (Jacobs and Winslow 155), suggesting that fathers' have more support at home with regard to childcare and housekeeping.

I agree with Auriemma and Klein (1), but I believe that timing is only part of the equation resulting in women's struggle in academia. The other portions of the equation are time pressures, as previously demonstrated, and support, or lack thereof. Regardless of the extensive education academic mothers achieve, they likely are no different from the rest of the population in terms of their plight. Childrearing is still primarily considered women's responsibility, and they are expected to advance in their positions despite support from their partners, employers, or society. This is evidenced in Ann Crittenden's sentiment, "Nowhere is it more dramatically illustrated [that mothers adjust their lives to accommodate the needs of their children, including forgoing status, income, advancement, and independence] than in the experience of the nation's most educated women—the ones who had the best shot at having it all" (27). Further evidence is provided in that many mothers arrange for childcare; transport their children to and from childcare; pay for childcare out of their paychecks (Hattery 158); take time off from paid labor; decline promotions; and inevitably increase their total workload (Crittenden 28).

Statistics provide evidence that the timing of children coupled with time pressures and lack of support negatively affect women's progress in academia, but narrative is needed to more fully examine this reality in higher education. In an effort to better understand the timing of children to women's pursuit of tenure and promotion and their support at home and at work, I interviewed women with children under five years of age.[2] This chapter tells their stories and provides depth for understanding their plight. The following broad questions guided my exploration of academic women's experiences:

•How did they define being a good academic mother?
•How did they meet the demands of being a mother and a faculty member?
•Where and in what form did they receive support to help them balance their multiple roles?

This essay suggests that the answers to these questions are complex. In fact, I will argue that a combination of culture and the absence of workplace supports attempt to sabotage women's efforts to have it all. To do so, this essay first details the method, followed by women's narratives supported by the literature. The results suggest that faculty mothers of preschool children suffer at the expense of workplaces that don't provide adequate supports for work-family balance.

METHOD

Women with preschool children were recruited from an earlier, larger survey study (n=69) of academic mothers with children up to age four-teen. As part of that study's protocol, women were able to volunteer to be contacted for participation in this follow-up study. Of the original 69 survey study participants, 31 women or 45 percent (44.9 percent) had children under five. I emailed all volunteering survey participants and seventeen women with preschool children meeting the study criteria agreed to be interviewed.

My interviewees were primarily Caucasian (70.6 percent), which was representative of the universities at which they worked. Almost eighteen percent (17.6 percent) identified themselves as Asian and approximately twelve percent (11.8 percent) as African American. Women were between twenty-nine and forty-five years of age. Almost seventy-one percent (69.5 percent) were tenured. Forty-one percent (41.2 percent) were assistant professors, fifty-three percent (52.9 percent) were associate professors, and one (or 5.9 percent) was a full professor. Women represented various disciplines, including English, Nursing, Psychology, Chemistry, Mathematics, and Computer Technology. All of the women interviewed were partnered at the time of the study, and all except one of their partners were employed full-time. Two of their partners also held faculty positions within higher education (i.e., dual-career couples). More than half of the women (56.3 percent) had two children, and the majority of the remaining women (37.5 percent) had one child. And two women had three children (1.25 percent).

Data collection took place at four comprehensive public universities in New England. Combined, these four-year universities educate approximately 36,000 students annually in over 160 subject areas. These universities were classified as Master's Universities and Colleges I, and their tenure-track faculty were required to maintain a twelve-credit teaching load each semester (fall and spring), and maintain five office hours over at least three days. In addition, they were held to slightly ambiguous requirements for earning promotion and tenure, and there were very few, if any, formalized family-friendly policies, such as stopping the tenure clock or paid maternity leave, available. Faculty were evaluated on their teaching, creative activity, which includes research, presentations, and publications, as well as artistic expressions in related disciplines, along with service to their department and university, and professional development.

One-on-one interviews were conducted with seventeen women (54.8 percent of those previously eligible from survey study) in their on-campus offices to provide comfort and convenience. Consent forms were reviewed and signed before beginning the study protocol. Once the consent was secured, women completed a brief demographic questionnaire containing 25 items. Then, they were given a $25 gift certificate to a bookstore for their time. Interviews followed and averaged an hour. They were audio-taped and transcribed verbatim. The semi-structured, open-ended interview covered several areas, including: motherhood, motherhood in the academia, role balance, health practices, and work-life balance support. Transcripts were analyzed using grounded theory (Strauss and Corbin) analysis where themes emerge from participants' narratives. Themes were based on a thorough review of transcripts and comparisons between two coders.

RESULTS AND INTERPRETATIONS

Timing of Children on the Tenure-Track

> "...babies do matter for men and women Ph.D.s working in academia. They matter a great deal, especially their timing." (Mason and Goulden 11)

Research suggests that having children while on tenure-track may be counter-productive for women expecting to expeditiously summit the ladder of the promotion and tenure. With the exception of one, the women interviewed were raising preschool children while preparing for tenure and/or promotion. Considering that "academic jobs demand far more time and energy than is reasonable," and that mothering norms stress impossible standards, it is likely that mothers' opportunities for success are limited as a result of combining these two challenging roles (Jacobs 21). Tenure-track and tenured faculty build their portfolios toward tenure and promotion respectively, which necessitates quality in teaching, creative activities, service, and professional development, while simultaneously providing care for their young families.

Considering the average age for receiving doctoral degrees is 34 and tenure is 41, it appears that some of the women interviewed may have had "early" babies[3] (Mason and Goulden 11), while other mothers, like Sue and Laurie, said they delayed children until they felt they were more established on the tenure-track. Delaying children has been cited as a reason some women leave academia (Mason and Goulden 13) and may serve as a possible explanation why mothers expend so much time and energy into their children's care. I believe the latter was evidenced in several mothers' responses, and may result as a potential precursor to the former. For example, Tina, a mother of two, said, "At this point in my life, family is much more important than my academic career. I would rather have it be said 'what a good mother'. It is definitely more important to me that I am there for my kids. I am not going to win teacher of the year or publish a book right now."

Since women may delay motherhood until they are established in their first tenure-track position, the multiple competing demands associated with mothering their first child may derail their attempts to secure tenure (O'Laughlin and Bischoff 85). Although Laurie had achieved tenure and promotion to associate professor prior to her son's birth, she reflected that she was not convinced she would have been able to perform as well if she did things in reverse. Laurie had her son after being in academia for several years, and he was about two and a half at the time of the interview. She described the transition:

I was so immersed in my academic role and my professional career that it's been such a shift for me trying to balance. The last 24 months for me have been like academically on survival mode. Where I am just trying to survive in terms of teaching my courses, attending to students the way I feel I need to, and engaging in some research. I am doing just what I need to survive. Not really what my professional goals are, but really just what I need to survive.

Laurie concluded by saying, "I am at the treading water adequately stage."

Another potential consequence of delaying children until landing tenure-track positions is related to the lack of accumulated leave time and the perception that taking time off from a newly attained, and often highly competitive, position may result in their encountering the "maternal wall" or "caregiver bias."[4] Two mothers interviewed, Cindy and Betsy, returned to work after two weeks and one day respectively after the birth of their children. Typical unpaid sick leave for having a child at these four institutions is six weeks, although many women take more time off, and a few, like Cindy and Betsy, take less. However, six weeks minimally is preferred for developing breastfeeding, bonding, and healing. In 2000, the World Health Organization made a statement to the

International Labor Conference advocating for a minimum of 16 weeks leave after childbirth to improve maternal and child health outcomes (World Health Organization). Further, maternity leave of less than 12 weeks has been associated with mothers' higher rates of postpartum depression, more detachment from the infant, less knowledge of infant development, and more negative impact of birth on her marriage (Feldman, Sussman and Zigler).

According to Jerry Jacobs, the demands of academic positions require unreasonable time and energy, which likely places inordinate stress on mothers in the professoriate, especially as mothering similarly requires a serious investment time and energy (21). Further, uncertainty about evaluation criteria requisite for tenure and promotion and the absence of support may derail their best effort for success.

Ambiguity Enhances Women's Time Pressures

> Individuals facing tenure review must demonstrate high levels of competence and research productivity in the earliest years of their academic career to avoid losing their jobs ... thus the risk of being denied tenure is likely a very significant factor in the work/family stress of pretenured academicians. (O'Laughlin and Bischoff 83)

Ambiguous guidelines for tenure and promotion may lead women to exceed the expectations resulting in greater time spent than necessary. Each of the five untenured faculty mothers described the criteria for promotion and tenure as vague, which led to women feeling as if they spent more time than ultimately would be necessary building their portfolios. I reviewed the guidelines that were provided by several different groups, including the union, faculty senate, and promotion and tenure committees at the universities studied. The guidelines presented an all-inclusive list of options for each category (i.e., teaching, creative activities, service and professional development) in which faculty were rated in their evaluations. This approach seemed to promulgate the idea that files should contain a limitless amount and type of information to validate women's academic efforts and pursuits. Ellen said, "It's ridiculous that you never know if you are on the right track. There is no way to really judge where you are in terms of how likely you are to get the tenure. So, I think that causes a person to work harder than they need to meet this imagined standard." Now that Jane had tenure, she reflected:

The biggest stressors are the pieces around tenure and never knowing if enough is enough. Not having clear guidelines and being pulled into so many different directions because of work and family, makes me feel like I am at a disadvantage. I have family commitments, and so I can't work twenty four hours a day. But, there is always that stress of "oh, I should be doing this—."

Sue felt this was the case because older faculty had different expectations on their time when they went up for tenure and promotion. She believed that the expectations changed and older faculty didn't create criteria to fully explain what faculty needed to accomplish to be recommended for tenure and promotion. She recalled her pre-tenure anxiety, and explained, "Faculty that were hired in the last eight years were told something different. There weren't fewer classes expected to be taught. Nothing changed except the rhetoric which was that now we were expected to also do research and publish." She agreed with Ellen in that "some of the stuff is inflicted and is controllable." She said, "It's my definition of how much research I should be doing, and if I can get that manuscript to the publisher by the end of the month." Ellen similarly wondered "How many publications? What type of publications? Is a book review going to count or not? Does it have to be peer reviewed?" These unanswered questions added to the ambiguity surrounding their readiness for tenure and promotion.

However, ambiguity was not the only barrier to tenure and promotion. Discussing how having a preschool child impacted her career, Tina said, "I would be eligible to apply for full professor next year, but I am not ready to apply. I probably won't be, in my mind anyway since I haven't done enough publishing, ready to apply for maybe five more years." In response to the same question asked, Kim replied, "I think it has definitely impacted my career, I tend to be putting a lot of things on hold. I am not getting the research done that I would like to do or going the extra effort to make a class period." In reply to the time pressures, Kim admitted, "Now I pretty much go to class, come to my office, get things done as fast as I can, because I know my time is so limited." Similarly, Cindy, a mom of two children added, "I would say that being the mom of a preschooler definitely impacts my productivity, especially research and scholarship. I can't find the time to conduct research at a pace that I would like and be able to sit down hours on end to write a manuscript."

Mothers did not want to work harder than they needed to meet an imagined standard, especially as it related to research and publications, since this would translate to their "being pulled into so many different directions because of work and family" and being able to give less time and other resources to their families. My interviewees' comments suggested their role conflict, or incompatibility between two roles (Erdwins, Buffardi, Casper, and O'Brien 230). Jane described the balance between work and family as "a tug of war." She said, "I actually try to be proactive and set boundaries and make decisions to make things balance out. I mean you can't do it all and if that means that I can't be a stellar scholar, then I wouldn't even want that. I am much more interested in having quality time with my family than I am having thousands of articles published." Tina added, "People talk a lot about being the "super mom" and being really successful at work and really successful as a mother; I don't think it can be done. Work-family balance means doing a good enough job at work so that I can still be a great mom."

It is possible that women felt forced to make choices between work and family. In these instances, evidence suggests that women likely choose family, although this does not minimize the associated role conflict, guilt and angst. Kim, a tenure-track mother of a four year old, described her first two years in academia as "very fulfilling, but very exhausting." She said, "Being a mother really informed the type of projects I have chosen because I haven't wanted to travel." Maggie, a tenure-track mother of two, said she's restricted her conference attendance to in-state one-day events, so she can be back to put her boys to bed. It's quite possible that these mothers fear that others will not care as well for their children as they could. This is a symptom of separation anxiety as well as intensive mothering, and it is often accompanied by guilt and predominantly effects working mothers with young children (Erdwins et al. 230). Intensive mothering describes a woman's exhaustive commitment to and primary responsibility for her child's care and this is a prevalent ideology to which many mothers subscribe.

Additionally, time pressures from a never-ending workload at home and at work, resulted in role overload and led four of the mothers to feel unable to perform their multiple roles adequately (Erdwins et al. 231). Natalie said, "I feel like I always have a foot in the work world and a foot in the home world, and sometimes it's very hard to manage." She added, "I feel like I am never doing anything that well. I feel like I am never as good in my job as I was before my daughter was born and I feel like I am never as good a parent because of my job, and I feel like I'm never as good a wife, because I'm always making a sacrifice." Lily confessed, "Before having kids I was on every committee imaginable. Now I pretty much go to class, come to my office, get things done as fast as I can, because I know my time is so limited."

As these academic mothers are spinning their wheels trying to do all that they can accomplish in order to earn the coveted tenure and promotion without clear guidelines, support mechanisms would offset their inordinate efforts. Unambiguous guidelines for tenure and promotion, social support, and family-friendly workplace policies would enhance women's progression up their career ladders.

Lack of Support Leads to Feelings of Overwhelm

> Giving and receiving social support often has been viewed as women's core or major strategy for coping with stress. (Erdwins et al. 230)

There are various supports that lessen the effects related to the demands and pressures inherent in being an academic mother in today's challenging society. Social support at home and at work, chairperson support, and organizational support in the form of programs and policies have been shown to be effective in helping academic mothers better balance work and family responsibilities.

Social support was the mediating influence that seemed to help restore women's equilibrium. Social support was recognized as the strongest indicator of success for women in this study. Despite the unsupported tasks women must complete daily, being able to juggle the demands of career and family was possible due to social support. Support was identified as residing primarily with partners and parents. Some women relied on neighbors and their children's school teachers. However, the women predominantly were responsible for children.

While some women seemed to have made strides in equity at home, others, like Monica and Cindy, were doing the lion's share of childcare and housework. Monica said, "I can sit down five minutes and that's all. I spend my Sundays cooking, doing the laundry, baking, playing a game with my son or going for a walk with him outside. When I ask my husband to step in, he gives me an hour." Monica's husband was a professor at a different university and she said that they follow a more traditional division of labor. She said that she takes care of her son, her husband, and her work, and that she seldom has time for herself. Cindy often found herself in the same predicament:

> Work-family balance means being able to juggle the demands of career and the demands of the family alone. Ultimately the responsibility falls on the mother, at least in my case. I am responsible for drop offs and pickups five days a week unless there is some special thing I have to be at. I make the lunches. I plan the dinners. I do the grocery shopping, so it means juggling...who has activities or a school play or whatever. It means juggling all of the priorities and demands of work at the same time and being able to fit it all into a day. At the days' end, I am thinking, did I accomplish something or did I check off anything on my list.

Even among the mothers I spoke with who felt that they had good support at home, they described scenarios in which they were left asking for assistance, suggesting that the primary responsibility of childcare ultimately was theirs. Laurie's husband just started a business and was working at home. When her work took priority, because she had certain commitments or she had conferences, she said she would ask her husband to alter his schedule to do the things she normally did, like drop off and pick up their son from daycare. She said:

> It makes it a lot easier to balance when I know it's not a problem for him to take a vacation day. Then, I have the whole day and I don't have to worry about dropping our son off or having somebody come in, like my mom. If my mom is watching him, I am rushing to get home, but if my husband has him I know I have time and it's not as stressful and I am not as rushed thinking about it.

Workplace support comes in many forms. Studies have focused on support from supervisors, coworkers, and the organization. According to Erdwins et al., research findings link a non-supportive workplace, coworkers, and supervisors with increased work-family conflict (231). All of my interviewees felt that their chairpersons were supportive as they considered their needs in scheduling their course times and university commitments, like committee assignments. However, only half of the women felt that their universities were supportive in terms of family-friendly initiatives. Women shared tales of limited and informal flexibility, modified duties/reduced schedules, sabbaticals, maternity leaves, and lactation support available.

Although women acknowledged that the flexibility inherent in academic career made a huge difference, they admitted feeling like they were always being pulled in different directions, and that that was often very hard to manage. Women acknowledged that there was always more that could be done, but struggled with the nagging feeling that they were doing an inadequate job because they were not getting it all done. Flexibility was described as a system of paybacks. If flexibility is accessed one day, the next day is spent catching up. In response, Yvonne, a mother of two tweens and a toddler, said she is "constantly running out of time." She explained that self-motivation is requisite to avoid falling behind.

Only one mother, Tina, said that she received modified duties upon her return six weeks after her first child was born. She met with administrators and negotiated a 50 percent reduction in her workload and responsibilities for three years. The reduction lasted this long because she had a second child during this period. She said, "It would be so nice if part-time were offered as a standard option for new mothers. We lived on one and a half salaries for three years. We could have managed it for a few more years if I had the option to stay home with my daughter until she entered full time kindergarten." Kim agreed that a course reduction would have been helpful, especially since she was teaching two brand new courses. She said, "I don't know what the policy is for new parents and being able to getting any kind of reduction, but that would be helpful. I don't know in academia what the norm is, but the fact that it wouldn't even occur to people to ask says a lot. You don't want to be perceived as shaking your responsibilities." Being stigmatized or mommy-tracked because they had children was on women's minds. Mothers were resourceful but most supports they found were due to their diligence and initiative. There were no role-model mothers for moving through the ranks.

None of the mothers planned their sabbatical around their children's birth, but Lily found herself dealing with her mother's life-threatening illness, her father-in-law's recent death, and news of a third, unplanned pregnancy while she was on sabbatical. She said she felt fortunate that she was on sabbatical, so she didn't have to worry about her classes and students during this challenging semester. However, despite her break from her usual academic routine, she felt she was "losing" herself as she added the new role of elder caregiver to child caregiver and professor. She described the imbalance:

> *If the scale was tilted, it was always the work stuff and now I am finding it tipping the other way because of this additional responsibility. Even if it is not an issue with my mother, but my daughter comes down with a fever at night, I am not able to get everything done that I need to get done. Then, my family becomes a priority, but it's only in these emergency situations.*

In terms of maternity leave, the only options these women had were to use accrued sick time, disability insurance, or unpaid Family Medical Leave,[5] and mothers' leave ranged from one day to nine months.[6] Since Cindy had not accrued much sick time since starting her tenure-track job, she only took one week off after the birth of her first child (now 6 years old) and two weeks off with her second child. With the semester starting the Monday after her baby was born, Betsy returned to work after taking only one day off. It is not surprising that both of these women supported paid family leave. Cindy said, "With my first child, I think even if it was a paid leave I probably wouldn't have taken it because I needed to prove that I could do the job that they hired me to do. With my second child I think 100 percent I would have taken it. I had two weeks off with her rather than five days. Initially, I was tempted to go in but I said screw it, my family is priority at this point." If there was a paid maternity or family leave option, entitlement may replace women's fear that they will be penalized for taking leave, which may result in their encountering caregiver bias or the maternal wall. Both types of stereotyping and bias have resulted in women being passed over for scholarly opportunities, funding, and promotion and tenure, and many mothers fear this nature of consequences.

At the time of the interviews, none of the universities had lactation rooms or support programs. For Sue, being a public health professor meant to her that she had to breastfeed her child despite all odds and inconveniences. As Sue put it, "If I didn't breastfed my kid it would be equivalent to smoking three packs a day in terms of colleagues. Reflecting back on it, I should have just used a combination of formula and breast milk and made it easier on myself," she said. She and other women reported encountering nuisances associated with breastfeeding compliance that ranged from pumping in unsanitary and noisy toilet stalls to leaking milk while teaching, because there was not time in their busy schedule or adequate, private spaces to pump. Sue even confessed that she pumped while she drove to and from work because her time was so limited.

No matter what level of success these women achieved at the time of their interview, it seemed that their experiences were similar in their sacrifices, choices, and struggles. These seventeen academic mothers were working hard building their portfolios and raising their young families. They often perceived their efforts as insufficient, although it is likely that this was a result of being overworked. They were creative in their approach to manage their responsibilities. For example, Tina took the initiative and negotiated a reduced work schedule after her children were born. However, being resourceful seems to add another burden on these already overburdened women. Universities need to facilitate a culture and model of family-friendliness that supports parents to "have it all"—success at home and in the workplace.

Family-responsive workplaces, those that formally introduce programs, policies, and practices to enhance employees' work-family balancing acts, can prevent bias, support working mothers, and establish an encouraging organizational culture. For universities, being a family-responsive workplace may save money resulting from fewer employee absences, less recruitment, and an increase in productivity.

CONCLUSION

Timing, time pressures, and lack of support at home and at work fuel the inequities many mothers experience in academia. The women I interviewed reinforced existing themes in the literature. Being an academic mother presents specific challenges to women's views on and practice of their work. It appears that women suffer from the strain of the fast pace due in part to technology (Jacobs 9) and reinforced by societal expectations toward perfection (Douglas and Michaels 4). Academic mothers are susceptible to "new momism," and the accompanying pressure to "devote her entire physical, psychological, emotional, and intellectual being, 24/7, to her children" (Douglas and Michaels 4). Maintaining this rigorous weekly schedule of childcare, combined with housework and working 50 or more hours is likely to affect women's health while consequently taking them away from their work and families. Previous research shows that women who perceive inequity in housework typically feel less successful in their work-life balance. Future research needs to examine the potential relationship among academic mothers' health and wellbeing and the timing of their children to tenure and promotion, as well as their time pressures and social support at work and at home.

Social support has been cited as one of women's main health protective strategies for coping with stress, so it seems that this variable should be explored further. Although it may be challenging for workplaces to affect support at home, universities need to offer academic mothers more support in the form of policies, programs, and practices that facilitate the combination of two (or more) demanding and often competing roles. The business case for implementing family-friendly campuses is well documented (Van Deusen, Ladge, James and Harrington). Women's interviews appear to be a cry for attention and unsolicited support.

The complexity of challenges the academic mothers interviewed encountered likely result from the age of their children. Having preschool-aged children has been identified in other studies as particularly difficult for parents' work-family balance (Milkie and Peltola). It is possible that the challenges academic mothers' encounter may become easier as their children age and become more independent. However, technology may inhibit any reprieve. Although technological advances have made it more possible to work from home while maintaining around-the-clock contact with students and colleagues, technology consumes a great majority of time (Jacobs). Technology facilitates communication and instruction, but requires a large investment in terms of time and learning since it changes so frequently. Additionally, it requires time and energy in its preparation, upgrade, and maintenance, as well as the demands it enables for real-time responses and its occasional unpredictability. Further, the combined impact of new momism and technology presents challenges for mothering as well as teaching.

Other challenges exist in regard to the scarcity of family-friendly programs, policies, and practices available on university campuses across the United States. There is a need for new workplace norms that establish the needs of mothers as a priority. According to the business case, family-friendly initiatives will increase employee retention reducing recruitment needs, increase productivity, morale and satisfaction, decrease absenteeism, and lower employer health insurance costs (Van Deusen, Ladge, James and Harrington). Although the mothers I interviewed primarily emphasized a need for institutionalized family-friendly programs, policies, and practices around breastfeeding, paid maternity leave, and consistency in treatment as women return to work after having their children, the American Association for University Professors (AAUP) recommends that universities develop policies and practices regarding family care leaves, support for family responsibilities including childcare and eldercare modified teaching schedules, and opportunities for stopping the tenure clock. Initiatives like these will facilitate healthy work-family integrations in higher education.

Thanks to the nineteen women whose stories make up the data for this chapter.

[1]This underrepresentation at the higher ranks is likely due to the disparities in the responsibilities faculty men and women occupy. For example, women tend to do more service work, while men in engage in more scholarly research-based activities.

[2]Preschool years are documented as particularly challenging (Milkie and Peltola) and result in the highest levels of work-family stress (O'Laughlin and Bischoff).

[3]Faculty with "early" babies had "a child entering their household within five years of receiving their Ph.D." (Mason and Goulden 11).

[4]Caregiving bias is experienced by employees once their caregiving responsibilities are known at work while the maternal wall may be encounter during pregnancy, before, during, or after maternity leave, and when they want to use a family-friendly policy (Pitts-Catsouphes).

[5]Covered employers must grant an eligible employee up to a total of 12

Mother ID	Age of Mother	Age of Preschool Child 1	Time Off Child 1	Timing of Child 1*	Age of Preschool Child 2	Time Off Child 2	Timing of Child 2	Tenure & Promotion Status
Monica	35	2.5 years	3 months	DAC				Tenured Associate
Laurie	42	2 years	9 months	DAC				Tenured Assistant
Ellen	41	10 months	3 months	P2AC	3 years	3 months	P2AC	Tenure-track Assistant
Wanda	40	4 years	3 months	DAC				Tenured Associate
Natalie	36	4.5 years	6 weeks	DAC				Tenured Associate
Betsy	33	14 months	1 day	DAC	2 years	N/A	P2AC	Tenure-track Assistant
Sue	42	18 months	6 weeks	DAC				Tenured Associate
Yvonne	45	2.5 years	16 weeks	DAC				Tenured Associate

Tina	40	3 years	6 weeks	DAC				Tenured Associate
Mary	42	4 years	N/A	P2AC				Tenured Full
Maggie	36	2 years	N/A	DAC				Tenure-track Assistant
Abbie	38	3 years	3 months	DAC				Tenured Associate
Brett	29	4 years	P2AC		Pregnant			Tenure-track Assistant
Jane	45	3 years	6 months	DAC				Tenured Assistant
Lily	40	3.5 years	1.5 months	DAC	4.5	3.5 months	DAC	Tenured Associate
Kim	40	4 years	3 months	P2AC				Tenure-track Assistant
Cindy	J36	20 months	2 weeks	DAC				Tenured Associate

*DAC = During Academic Career, P2AC = Prior To Academic Career workweeks of unpaid leave during any 12-month period for one or more of the following reasons: for the birth and care of the newborn child of the employee; for placement with the employee of a son or daughter for adoption or foster care; to care for an immediate family member (spouse, child, or parent) with a serious health condition; or to take medical leave when the employee is unable to work because of a serious health condition (U.S. Department of Labor).

[6]Women's timing and time off taken with preschool children

WORKS CITED

Association of American University Professors (AAUP). *Statement of Principles on Family Responsibilities and Academic Work*. Washington, AAUP, 2001.

Auriemma, Danielle L. and Tovah P. Klein. "Experiences and Challenges of Women Combining Academic Careers and Motherhood." Lecture. Association of American University Professors Conference, Washington, DC, 11 June 2010.

Ann Crittenden. *The Price of Motherhood: Why The Most Important Job in the World is Still the Least Valued*. New York: Metropolitan Books, 2001. Print.

deVise, Daniel. "For Working Mothers in Academia, Tenure Track is Often a Tough Balancing Act." *Washington Post*. 11 July 2010. Web. 14 September 2010.

Dominici, Francesca, Linda P. Fried, and Scott L. Zeger. "So Few Women Leaders." *Academe* 95.4 (2009, July/August): 25-27. Print.

Douglas, Susan J. and Meredith W. Michaels. *The Idealization of Motherhood and How it Has Undermined Women: The Myth of Motherhood*. New York: Free Press, 2004. Print.

Erdwins, Carol J., Louis C. Buffardi, Wendy J. Casper, and Alison S. O'Brien. "The Relationship of Women's Role Strain to Social Support, Role Satisfaction, and Self-efficacy." *Family Relations* 50 (2001): 230-238.

Feldman, Ruth, Amy Sussman, and Edward Zigler. "Parental Leave and Work Adaptation at The Transition to Parenthood: Individual, Marital, and Social Correlates." *Journal of Applied Developmental Psychology* 25.4 (2004, July): 459-479. Print.

Garey, Anita. *Weaving Work and Motherhood*. Philadelphia, PA: Temple

University Press, 1999. Print.

Hattery, Angela. *Women, Work, and Family: Balancing and Weaving*. Thousand Oaks, CA: Sage Publications, 2000. Print.

Jacobs, Jerry. "The Faculty Time Divide." *Sociological Forum* 19 (2004, March): 3-27. Print.

Jacobs, Jerry, and Sarah E. Winslow. "The Academic Life Course, Time Pressures and Gender Inequality." *Community, Work & Family* 7.2 (2004, August): 143-161. Print.

Jaschik, Scott. "Women Lead in Doctorates." *Inside Higher Education*. 2010, September 14. Online: http://www.insidehighered.com/layout/set/print/news/2010/09/14/doctorates.

Mason, Mary Ann. "Men and Mothering." *The Chronicle of Higher Education*. 24 Feb. 2009. Web. 9 March 2009.

Mason, Mary Ann, and Mark Goulden. "Do Babies Matter (Part II)? Closing the Baby Gap." *Academe* 90.6 (Nov./Dec. 2004): 10-15. Print.

Milkie, Melissa and Pia Peltola. "Playing All The Roles: Gender and the Work-Family Balancing Act." *Journal of Marriage and the Family* 61 (1999): 476-490.

O'Laughlin, Elizabeth, M. and Lisa G. Bischoff. "Balancing Parenthood and Academia: Work/Family Stress As Influenced By Gender and Tenure Status." *Journal of Family Issues* 26.1 (2005, January): 79-106.

Pitts-Catsouphes, Marcy. "Conversations With The Experts. Caregiver Bias: Work/Life Issues as Diversity Concerns." *The Network News*. 2005, April. Online: <http://wfnetwork.bc.edu/The_Network_News/10/newsletter.shtml>.

Strauss, Anslem and Juliet Corbin. *Basics of Qualitative Research: Techniques and Procedures for Developing Grounded Theory*. Thousand Oaks, CA: Sage Publications, 1998. Print.

U.S. Department of Labor. *Family Medical Leave Act*. N.d. Web. 30 September 2010.

U.S. Equal Employment Opportunity Commission. "Employer Best Practices for Workers with Caregiving Responsibilities." 2009, May 22. Washington, DC: Author. Retrieved from: <http://www.eeoc.gov/policy/docs/caregiver-best-practices.html>.

Vancour, Michele L. and William M. Sherman. "Academic Life Balance: Pipeline or Pipe Dream." *Mothering at the 21st Century: Identity, Policy, Experience and Agency*. Ed. Andrea O'Reilly. New York: Columbia University Press, 2000. Print.

Van Deusen, Fred, Jamie Ladge, Jacquelyn James, and Brad Harrington. *Building the Business Case for Work-Life Programs*. Boston College Center for Work & Family, Executive Briefing Series, 2008. Online: http://www.bc.edu/centers/cwf/research/meta-elements/pdf/BCCWF_Business_Case_EBS.pdf.

World Health Organization (WHO). *Health Aspects of Maternity Leave and Maternity Protection*. 2000. Online: http://www.who.int/reproductive-health/publications/maternal_mortality_2000/ Health_aspects_of_maternity_leave.en.html.

8.
Contract-Faculty Mothers

On The Track to Nowhere

LINDA ENNIS

I REMEMBER THE DAY, VIVIDLY, when I entered the world of the invisible in academia at a Canadian university. When I arrived at my office, to be shared with other part-time lecturers, there were none to be found. There were no pictures to be taken with other contract faculty, no phone extensions, no value placed on those who worked so hard to take their place in the world of academia. The justification for my choice to be contract-faculty was that it felt as if it was an effective balance for me to combine motherhood with employment. At the time, it seemed as if I would have a flexible schedule, so that I would be available to my young children. In addition, I believed that a contract-faculty position would enable me to work part-time, thereby providing me the opportunity to spend more time with my family. However, I began to notice that this position felt rather oppressive. Why was it so hard to leave? Would it ever be possible to switch tracks, from the mommy contract-faculty track to the tenured one? Why is the contract-faculty mother's efforts being sabotaged and by whom? Is the reason for the failure to proceed onto the tenure track due to motherhood or because of factors beyond their control?

Contract-faculty mothers once had Ph.D.s that mattered. The possibilities seemed endless and academia appeared to be all embracing. I thought that choosing the contract-faculty road was similar to part-time teaching, which could be easily adjusted to full-time, as desired, which I did when I worked as a primary school teacher in the past. Unlike the teaching profession, I didn't realize that it would be close to impossible to get back on track since there is no permanent part-time track that encourages research and the other components involved in being a respected faculty member in a Canadian university. In addition, I sincerely believed that my skills at effectively balancing motherhood with teaching would be respected as an important contribution to the work milieu. I soon discovered that when graduates became mothers, a detour was taken onto the second-tier or mommy track, which ultimately took them further away from the ultimate destination, to be on the tenured track. The roads do not intersect. On this road to nowhere, contract-faculty mothers meet men and women without children, as well. Even though the experience of others on this road is similar, the reasons for taking this detour differ. Women with Ph.D.s with children are twice as likely than men with children to fall into the second tier (Mason and Ekman 85). It is motherhood that defines this choice, albeit some other component keeps them there. What needs to be explored further is why some mothers choose the tenured track, while others end up on the contract-faculty track.

Work-family conflict in academia represents discrimination against mothers, leaving women with children in academia over-represented among the second-tier of faculty, the adjunct faculty (Wolfinger, Mason, Goulden). This second-tier track is seen as a viable alternative and usually the only one for mothers, who hope to have a second chance down the road because it keeps them in academia (Mason and Ekman). The term "Contract-faculty Academics" has been used synonymously with the terms "adjunct," "the untenurables" and "non-tenure-track faculty." Even though there is a distinct difference between non-tenure faculty and contract-faculty in that the non-tenure faculty is full-time faculty with respectable pay, the misinformed implication is that adjuncts are "unqualified" teachers, waiting to get tenure-track positions. Additionally, there are works that speak of the erosion of tenured tracks by hiring contract labourers, the untenurables, which lowers universities' national ranking. (Hile Bassett 103). The association has been made that women who are unable, or unwilling, to stay in the mother closet, often find themselves marginalized in part-time and non-tenure-track positions. Another term equated with "contract-faculty" mothers is "second-tier," a default mommy track, which is over-represented and does not lead to the tenure-track. It has been noted that university women make up disproportionately large numbers of temporary (adjunct and non-tenure-track) faculty, while the majority of permanent, tenure-track positions are given to men (Evans and Grant xix). Academia encourages women to delay having children, and discourages them from attempting to balance motherhood with academia by penalizing them for having "a break" when they stray off the track. Young children under the age of six push women off the tenure track and keep them off. Although the intent of mothers is to keep in the game by being on the second tier, it is very difficult to switch tracks, taking into account that the likelihood of a tenure- track position plummets after three years. (Wolfinger, Mason and Goulden 1607). As Michael Dubson concludes: "Again and again, these adjuncts are passed over when permanent or tenure-track positions do open up; they are seldom regarded as colleagues by permanent faculty" (1).

In a recent Canadian study, a contract-faculty mother, who ultimately switched tracks, discussed the contract-faculty, the "hidden academics," in Canadian universities. This work spoke of the faulty hiring process that favored candidates from highly reputed universities; the lack of appreciation for the type of publications delivered by contract-faculty; the discrimination against contract-faculty, who were deemed less productive because of their age and years since graduation; the prejudice against academics, who were female with children; the marginalization of part-time faculty in academic decision-making; the departments' overloading of part-timers with teaching and not supporting their desire to be involved in research outside of the departments' interests; and the power that full-timers hold over part-timers in the way of hiring, firing, and rehiring (Rajagopal 121).

What remains underdeveloped is an understanding as to why contract-faculty choose this designation and often remain in it; why, from the contract-faculty mother's perspective, tenured faculty reinforce this inequity in their "colleagues" within the department; why mothers believe that balancing motherhood with academia is impossible and not desirable; and why, generally speaking, from the contract-faculty mother's perspective, there is such misunderstanding by universities and the public as to who contract-faculty are because they are treated as outsiders by the mainstream. Most importantly, what is lacking is the voice that contract-faculty can't seem to find because there hasn't been a place for it to exist due to the nature of their invisibility.

This chapter qualitatively examines the experience of mothers, who are contract-faculty, their reasons for choosing to be contract-faculty, what keeps them in this category of academia, the challenges and rewards, and the impact of this situation on their sense of well being. The research questions may be formulated as follows: What is the contract-faculty mother's experience, from her perspective? How can we further understand the dynamics of this phenomenon and the underlying reasons that inform this choice? How do relationships with significant others and colleagues enter into this experience? Why are contract-faculty mothers often viewed as less scholarly than their colleagues, who are tenured and full-time academics? In this chapter, I explore how a group of contract-faculty mothers view this experience, why they chose to be contract-faculty, how they deal with being on the second tier and all the conflict that it entails. It will focus on their lived experience of being a contract-faculty mother and how this career path leads to the loss of their academic self. The only way to reclaim their voice is to understand their experience and to talk and write about it, as difficult as that may be.

METHOD

The aim of this qualitative exploratory study is to give voice and credibility to mothers, who are contract-faculty, and to tap the lived experience of these mothers, identifying both similarities and differences among these women. Previous studies have explored the early careers of Ph.D. recipients by examining large numbers of Ph.D. recipients through administered questionnaires and a selected small percentage of that group for ongoing biennial interviews (Wolfinger, Mason and Goulden; Mason and Goulden; Mason and Ekman). This exploratory study examined, in greater depth, a smaller number of participants' lived experience of being a contract-faculty mother.

Interviewees were obtained through my posting requests for contract-faculty mothers on the union site of a Canadian university, which targeted specifically course directors, who were contract faculty. The criteria for participant selection was "purposeful sampling," which chooses participants for the purpose of understanding the phenomenon, contract-faculty mothers. Fifteen participants were chosen from respondents, who responded to an online message to all contract-faculty union members. All participants were mothers working at a Canadian university as a contract-faculty. My interviewees were mothers, who came from diversified backgrounds, which included French and Asian but predominantly Caucasian. Their ages ran between 32 and 55. The majority was married with two being single mothers and two divorced.

Interviews took place face- to-face at the university where they worked and over the phone. All interviews were tape-recorded, transcribed and analyzed for general clusters or themes. Interviews were open-ended and lasted for approximately one and one half hours. The participants signed consent forms and confidentiality was respected, through the use of participant pseudonyms, throughout the process. The analysis was carried out according to the Grounded Theory Approach in order to derive clusters of similar ideas or themes that were prevalent throughout (Strauss and Corbin).

RESULTS AND INTERPRETATIONS

From the interviews, each individual's voice and story was heard in its uniqueness, while they also served to demonstrate that there were similarities throughout. As a result, five views of contract-faculty mothers were derived from the data: the almost finished contract-faculty mother; the retired-professional contract–faculty mother; the teacher-on-leave contract-faculty mother; the balancing contract-faculty mother; and the transitional-contract-faculty mother. The almost-finished contract-faculty mother is a graduate student, who has not finished her Ph.D. because of teaching load and financial constraints, and wishes to remain in the system, leaving her options open as to whether to complete the degree or not. The retired-professional contract-faculty mother is a retired teacher, who is usually on pension, and wants to remain in the educational system for educational stimulation. The teacher-on-leave contract-faculty mother is a teacher on leave, who is seconded to teach and run programs in the Education Department of the university for a limited period of time. The balancing contract-faculty mother is balancing another job commitment with teaching in the university, while the transitional contract-faculty mother views teaching as contract-faculty as a stepping-stone to becoming full-time and tenured. The higher percentage of contract-faculty mothers fall within the two categories: the almost- finished and the transitionals, and both are in states of transition. This is where the focus of this study will lie.

Contract-faculty mothers' descriptions of their lived experience resulted in the identification of the following five themes: feeling second rate; juggling too much; stuck on the mommy track; the need for reliable support systems; and valued from the inside but not from the outside.

FEELING SECOND-RATE

The majority of the respondents experienced a general sense of feeling second-rate to the tenured-faculty. As this contract-faculty mother explained:

> *I don't ever see them (other members in the department), and you also feel like your work is not valued. I just feel like there was a whole, like, hierarchy that was I think unfair. Here, I am trying to be helpful and collegial and collaborative and hope this is how the game works. Full-time faculty use contract-faculty's lesson plans. At that time, I was still only teaching part-time, so you know, you sort of like don't know how much of a stink you want to make.*

As indicated by this interviewee's comment, she is expressing her feelings of not being good-enough, partly because her preparatory work is being used by full-time people, without their consent. Oftentimes, contract faculty are also, asked by the department to train new full-time faculty, who have just arrived, fresh from school, with or without their Ph.D.s. The above comment also speaks to the lack of a relationship between contract-faculty and full-time faculty unless it is of an oppressive nature. This was verified by another participant who stated, "Now that I'm thinking about it, I think we are all contract-faculty at the meetings. I get the feeling, sometimes, it's a hierarchy. I get the feeling that we're at the bottom of the totem pole."

Further to this issue of a hierarchy, a contract-faculty mother adds that contract-faculty are exploited labour and that full-time faculty are dismissive of part-time faculty and communicate to them by this behaviour that they have no right to full-time status; "They (full-time faculty) could decide to teach my course, if they wanted to. Even though I have seniority, they have priority."

It would appear that full-time faculty choose the courses they want to teach, even if they have never taught it before, while contract-faculty wait until a few weeks before the class begins to find out whether they will be teaching the course they may have taught for years.

These experiences were also noted by Wendell Fountain when he noted:

We wandered into this thing called adjunct teaching, liked it too much to quit when we should have, and allowed ourselves to be used and abused by the powerful and the petty. I have no regrets. I have enjoyed my teaching experiences in spite of the power hungry, cost cutting administrators, annoying underlings, jealous full-time faculty, and policy wonks that make you as miserable as they can, when they can, because they can. (46).

With regards to how the contract-faculty is identified in the course calendar and feeling second-rate, the following participant said:

I got special permission this year from the chair of the department to have my picture taken and my name put with the picture on the website with the other professors because I have students, who want to take courses with me and they cannot find any trace of who I am, where I am. I'm a TBA: to be announced. Here, only full-time people have extensions and their profiles are listed. Part-time doesn't, other than if you search them on your own. They're not featured on anything. So, there's a real sense of a divide, you know, and a real or unreal perception of who's more valued.

The above comment clearly illustrates the feelings that many contract-faculty have, of being an impostor. If no one can find you and you don't have a name, perhaps you do not exist or are a fraud and shouldn't be teaching a course at all. This affects one's sense of an authentic academic identity, which is critical to one's sense of well-being. Participants speak of having a travelling office in their backpacks and feel like a homeless person with no fixed address, not having an office they can call their own. There is no permanency or security.

The following contract-faculty mothers expressed feelings of financial and emotional insecurity, as a result of being treated as second-rate in these ways:

At the psychological level, it's the stress of the insecurity, the uncertainty, a problem of purpose. Will I remain contract-faculty forever? Is this what I want? I would like to become a full-time professor, feeling a sense as an invisible wall, so psychologically, it's difficult. Financially, it has been a disaster. Each time I had a baby it's been difficult, financially. I'm teaching four courses and I earn half of what colleagues earn with just two courses or one and a half. I'm behaving and working exactly like a full-time professor without the pay, without the pension and the health care.

Full-time people have maternity leaves. They have a level of income that they can foresee what their needs will be, financially. They know what to expect, when they return. I have no stability. I don't know if I'm going to have a course, two courses or nothing. So, that makes me come back earlier with a three month old baby. I cannot take one year off. I didn't have the luxury.

A small number of participants suggested that they could counter-act feelings of being second-rate to tenured- faculty by rationalizing their experience in the following way: "The only advantage of being contract-faculty is that there's a certain amount of prestige when people think you teach at a university." As a result, there is a disconnect between the way others think of the contract faculty and reality, a form of cognitive dissonance, in that one feels proud to be associated with academia, si-multaneously with being ashamed and devalued.

Some of the contract-faculty mothers observed that, initially, they were under the misconception that part-time would offer them flexibility but soon discovered that this was a myth that led to feelings of being second-rate. One such participant said, "I didn't want to be full-time faculty. I wanted the freedom to be who I am, raising my kids on my own. I regret that decision now."

There seems to be confusion between freedom and flexibility. Where initially, the choice was made to be contract faculty because of flexible hours, it was discovered that there was no flexibility, only less and more inconvenient hours. Another mother conferred that this myth of flexibility was, indeed, just that when she said:

Even though from the outside, one would think, oh, I have this flexibility, you don't have the flexibility because it is what you are given and you cannot say, you know, can I have a different time frame or can I have a different day of the week. The best hours of teaching, in the middle of the day, are given to full-time professors and we teach odd hours like nine in the morning with children to take to school and it isn't easy.

Contract-faculty mothers begin to feel the nagging self-doubt and truly feel second-rate when they know that they have been trained as researchers and designated as incompetent to do so. One contract-faculty mother said of this discrimination against contract faculty as researchers:

There is no career path for contract-faculty. They are perceived as hanging around, not aspiring towards something. It doesn't mean if the chair approves of a contract-faculty that it would lead to tenure. Contract-faculty are not involved in research in my department. They become trapped and have no moral support. Contract-faculty want to do much valuable research but lack the opportunity to do so. Teaching is devalued in the university.

The obvious point where contract-faculty mothers feel as if they are not good enough is related to tenured-faculty's perception of their inability to conduct effective research. Contract-faculty mothers explained that having a research career is not possible if you are teaching excessive amounts of hours in order to financially survive:

I think, personally, that you can have a better research career as contract-faculty because no one else is going to tell what to do. You have this wide-open freedom, the risk is all yours but the reward is too but if you're teaching five courses, chances are you just don't have time.

The majority of contract-faculty participants realized that they would always remain second-rate and would never progress from this status to a tenure-track faculty. This was expressed in the following way by one respondent; "It's a bit of a road to somewhere but it's also a bit of something in itself. The disadvantages are sometimes feeling disconnected because you are sort of the peripheral piece of the faculty." Another contract-faculty mother expanded upon this by saying:

There's a misconception that some people that teach in Unit 2

just teach and aren't interested in research and just keep do-
ing that. So that would certainly be hard to transition into the
full-time track but that's a misconception that doesn't apply to
everybody. I was doing tons of research and I was publishing
through different kinds of channels, through government pub-
lications and I was commissioned to write all sorts of papers
and documents and I was keeping that active. The transition
is as difficult as your ability to maintain an active research
portfolio.

Contract-faculty mothers differ, depending on whether they are in a transitional phase, leading to something else in their careers or whether they have accepted their situation as something in itself. For those academic mothers, who choose work outside of academia, they are even less likely to get tenure (McElrath). If the contract-faculty mother is financially secure, has a pension from another career that has ended, is augmenting another career, or juggling contract-faculty teaching with another career for the pure joy of teaching, the degree of satisfaction is greater. If, however, like the majority of contract-faculty mothers, the aim is to bridge the second tier with the tenured track, then clearly, there is enormous disappointment and a feeling of being misled and let down. Many contract-faculty mothers stayed within the academic environment to continue their research, to be visible, and to gain experience and ultimately enter the ivory tower, which has, for them, turned toxic because they, ultimately, could never make the leap from one track to the other.

JUGGLING

In their attempt to balance or juggle motherhood with academic employment, most contract-faculty mothers have a particular challenge. They, as mothers, are trying to find their own unique way "to balance togetherness and separateness, and the feelings of love and loss that go along with them, in their own life and with their children" (de Marneffe). One contract-faculty mother said of this difficulty:

It's very challenging, uncertainty, lack of money, lack of support,
too. You're not understood by your colleagues in the department.

They don't understand what it means to juggle like this with two precarious situations and you go back and forth between trying to be a mother at home and give as much time as you can and care and attention to your children and at the same time, come to the department and also being very present at your job. The employer should have a system that would help mothers. There is a misunderstanding of what a contract-faculty is and being a mother is a contribution to society. It's not a selfish activity, something we do just for pleasure.

In an attempt to explain how to effectively balance motherhood with employment, my research in this area has shown that there are three types of working mothers: the splitting-working mother, the integrating- working mother, and the transitional-working mother (Ennis 1997). At times, work is in the forefront and motherhood in the background; at other times, the reverse is true. Still, at other points, a fine balance is struck and both motherhood and work co-exist harmoniously. The working mother feels in equilibrium when she can operate in a comfortable place between work and motherhood in an intermediate or transitional space between the two.

In balancing work with motherhood, some working mothers are able to combine both, such as the tenured-track mothers, while others give up some activities temporarily, such as the contract-faculty mother. When working mothers feel a sense of powerlessness, the results are a sense of feeling frazzled, torn, tired, anxious, depressed and guilty. The same is true with contract-faculty mothers as to how and where it all breaks down, as explained by the following:

I feel, as a person, that I have energy stores for different roles that I play, the mom role, the teacher role and I'm only tired in those little compartments or sometimes, there's overlap. I kind of compartmentalize and in my own sort of psychological way, manage it and of course. There are times when that whole thing clashes and it all leaves a mess and it's very stressful and I don't know what to do at sick or peak periods of marking students' papers.

From the above, it is clear that an effective balance is particularly difficult to strike when there is uncertainty, financial instability, and emotional insecurity, resulting in feelings of feeling torn, frazzled and tired. While tenure-track mothers likely feel this way, as well, they do not have to contend with the additional burden of uncertainty and financial insecurity, that the contract-faculty mothers experience.

STUCK ON THE MOMMY TRACK

Most of the contract-faculty mothers that I interviewed felt stuck on the mommy track, which is actually equivalent to the contract-faculty track. They spoke of the reasons why they feel stuck, such as their inability to move cities, and dedicating themselves fully, sometimes excessively, to motherhood in this manner:

> *Women are disproportionately contract-faculty. So, it's not a stretch to call contract-faculty the "mommy track" for women. Once you've stepped out, it's really hard to step back on. If you've got a kid, it means you're not as mobile so you can't go to post-docs all over North America or the world. Being a part-time faculty member can facilitate having a child, but at the same time, having a child means you're probably going to end up part-time faculty if you are a woman because chances are you are going to bear the primary burden of caring, having a kid makes you more likely to be a part-time faculty member anyway because it arrests your progress, it puts a break on any writing, publishing.*

The geographic unavailability of contract-faculty mothers was also discussed by Nicholas H. Wolfinger, Mary Ann Mason and Marc Goulden when they noted that adjunct professorships are readily available and therefore may be sought out by married women, whose geographic mobility is frequently constrained by their husbands' careers, who are also in academia.

For most contract-faculty mothers, there is a choice to get on the mommy track but not their choice to stay on it. Women are situated into contract faculty, not of their own choice. The departments are not hiring women full-time, who are having babies. If a woman has a baby too early, the perception is that she is not dedicated enough and she, subsequently, is devalued. As a result, contract-faculty mothers report how they do not talk about their children in the department. What has become clear in these interviews is that there needs to be a choice as to which track to take, as the following contract-faculty explains; "I don't feel the invisibility of motherhood because I've chosen to do this and maybe if I didn't choose to do that, that'd be a different story."

THE NEED FOR RELIABLE SUPPORT SYSTEMS

Support systems ease the dual commitment of working and mothering and helps effectively balance the two. There is an intricate, developmental interaction between states of independence and dependence that becomes apparent in combining motherhood with employment (Ennis 2010). The new wave of feminism encourages mothers to work with both models, one of dependence and one of an independent being with individual choices. An example drawn from the interviews, which was a commonly held opinion among many of the others, expands upon the contract-faculty mother's need for effective support systems:

Take it for what it's worth. If you don't have time to network and hang out with other colleagues because you feel like you're a little bit of an island, make your own social network elsewhere, have your like-minded mommy colleagues. You know, make life for yourself in other ways. The other thing, too, is I've had to really re-negotiate or negotiate my partner. I consider myself a feminist but I was still doing the majority of household duties and more childcare responsibilities and because I had done that for years, because he worked evening and weekend jobs. And I had to say, you know what? Buddy, you're in a new job now, you get home at four every day, you get summers off, hello? And, also, my son, I mean, he's been raised to do more chores and so you know we've sort of worked it out as a family.

VALUED FROM THE INSIDE BUT NOT FROM THE OUTSIDE

It is critical to feel adequately reflected as a human being in our environment. The contract-faculty mothers that I interviewed talked about feeling valuable, from their perspective, but devalued by others from the outside, thereby resulting in self-devaluation. One contract-faculty mother, echoing the sentiments of many of the others, explained it in this way:

> *I did some research on part-time faculty and it was called "second class scholars academic entrepreneurs" because there's a psychological sense that many contract-faculty that we will say, "I'm just a sessional." There's always a sense that we are lesser than being tenured. We are a necessary evil. Never say you're just a contract-faculty. List all the things you do so the university knows the kind of value you add that's not just teaching.*

Contract-faculty mothers are striving to simultaneously maintain an academic and motherhood identity and are struggling how to manage such a balance, especially with the disconnect from the outside, namely the department, their tenure-track colleagues and the administration.

CONCLUSIONS

This research set out to examine the qualitative experience of contract-faculty mothers, their reasons for becoming and remaining contract-faculty, the challenges and rewards and the impact of this experience on their sense of well-being. The aim was to give voice and credibility to contract-faculty mothers for the purpose of bringing authenticity and recognition to these women, who need to be fully integrated into academia.

The results of this study supported the work on "hidden academics," with regards to the marginalization of contract-faculty mothers, especially by full-time tenured faculty; the lack of appreciation for research by contract-faculty; the over-loading of contract-faculty with teaching rather than research despite their qualifications to do so; and the prejudice against mothers with young children.

What emerged, in addition to the above, was that contract-faculty mothers are not encouraged to do independent research unless it complements tenured faculty's research; that there is an enormous discrepancy between the contract-faculty and tenured faculty mothers' financial status; that contract-faculty mothers may choose to work part-time initially but are forced to stay on the "mommy track," with no alternative options; that full-time tenured faculty are sabotaging part-time contract-faculty mothers' efforts; and that it is excessively difficult to leave the contract-faculty status for emotional and financial reasons.

The question arises, continually, as to why contract-faculty do not leave this wretched arrangement. Getting out of this designation is emotionally difficult work. It requires mourning the loss of who you were suppose to be, and accepting that this was not achieved. To work as a contract-faculty implies that one can rationalize to herself that she is still working in a university setting. The contract-faculty mother has a "false self" that is accepted as her "true self" by carrying on this façade. The outside world, which cannot differentiate between full-time and part-time faculty, reinforces the belief that they are the same. Consequently, the contract-faculty mother feels a sense of prestige when others are impressed that she teaches at a university and she doesn't have to deal with facing the fallacy of it all. In addition, she is respected by her students, while simultaneously being devalued by her "so-called colleagues," resulting in a solution of falsely reconciling the dual experience of being a contract-faculty mother. Something, however, is being achieved in contract-faculty mothers assuming the role of contract faculty, primarily having the intrinsic satisfaction of a job well done.

What is left to explore, I feel, is what differentiates contract-faculty from tenured-faculty mothers. What experiences would lend themselves to each group's part in choosing their fate and resigning themselves to it? Perhaps the choices are different for each group because the tenured-faculty may be adopting a splitting mode of mothering and treating their experiences quite separately, while the contract-faculty might be adopting a transitional one, in their attempt to balance motherhood with employment. In addition, it is necessary to further understand why many tenured faculty devalue contract-faculty mothers, as indicated by many of the participants in this and other studies. Perhaps the answer lies in the discomfort that tenured-faculty feel about motherhood, manifesting itself in a projection of these feelings onto the contract-faculty mother. As for the contract-faculty mothers, there is a need to do further analysis as to why these academic mothers believe that in order to mother effectively, one has to leave the tenure track rather than being a good-enough mother on the tenure-track. Much of this behaviour is learned by one's parents and internalized. Even though notions around working and motherhood are socially driven, we need to consider how early experiences have had an impact on this choice to view motherhood as "all or nothing" in order to change this internal working model to a "both and" one. In addition, we need to better understand why there is denial by contract-faculty mothers, whereby they do not realize nor accept that usually there is no way back onto the tenure-track, once one steps off. Perhaps there is an element of learned helplessness at play here whereby the contract-faculty mother has lost confidence in her own abilities to potentially switch tracks because of all the projections, that she is not sufficiently competent, from tenured faculty. Additionally, there are real barriers to contract-faculty getting on the tenure-track since there are no standards in place, set up by the university administration, for them to do so. Since tenure-faculty are left with the responsibility to hire faculty within the department and recommend changes in the programming, more constructive involvement, in including contract-faculty as respected members of their departments, is highly recommended. Perhaps then, it will carry over to the senior administration's perception of contract-faculty and result in change. For this to happen, however, tenure-faculty need to be reflective and deal with their fear of somehow being usurped by contract-faculty, should this happen.

Contract-faculty mothers differ from each other, depending on whether they are in a transitional phase, leading to something else in their careers or whether they have accepted their situation as something in itself. If the contract-faculty mother is financially secure, has a pension from another career that has ended, is augmenting another career, or juggling contract faculty teaching with another career for the pure joy of teaching, the degree of satisfaction is greater. There are contract-faculty, who can afford not to pursue tenure or do not want to engage in research, which suits them quite nicely. However, if, however, like the majority of contract-faculty mothers, the aim is to lead to a higher ground, tenure, and the feeling is one of failure and discontent, then clearly, there is enormous disappointment and a feeling of being misled and let down. Many contract-faculty mothers stay within the academic environment to continue their research, to be visible, and to gain experience and ultimately enter the ivory tower, which, for them, turns toxic. Contract-faculty mothers are on the road to nowhere with unfulfilled dreams. As for me, I stay because I believe that academia should be as much about teaching as research. Even though contract-faculty are shut out of research, I remain because of a commitment to teaching, as other contract-faculty mothers have concurred.

RECOMMENDATIONS

In order to help to ease the pressure that contract faculty feel, as indicated above, and to educate all parties involved, there needs to be an appreciation of the expertise of contract-faculty mothers. To help alleviate contract-faculty mothers' feelings of being second-rate, research opportunities should be offered to contract-faculty mothers and independent research should be encouraged. Contract-faculty mothers should be offered the same courtesies as the tenured faculty such as their own offices, extension numbers, and pictures of themselves included with the others.

Because contract-faculty mothers feel as if they are juggling too much, they should not be overloaded with teaching to discourage them from engaging in research. They should be offered courses to teach, in their areas of expertise, rather than being given courses to teach that full-time faculty are not interested in teaching at the last moment. Contract-faculty mothers should be encouraged to be involved in policy and curriculum changes, which should reflect both tenured and contract-faculty's interests and expertise.

Financial discrepancy between full-time tenured and contract-faculty should be modified. Since many contract-faculty feel as if they are stuck on the mommy track, tenured- faculty members should help mentor them to move towards becoming tenured faculty, if they so desire, rather than perpetuating the myth that they are not qualified enough to teach or do research, as tenured faculty do. Tenure-track faculty need to be more introspective as to why there is discrimination against contract-faculty mothers.

It is recommended that there be more reliable support systems offered by tenured faculty mothers to encourage contract-faculty mothers in their transition from being contract-faculty to tenured faculty. Contract-faculty mothers need to examine whether they are engaging in excessive, rather than good-enough, mothering, at the expense of their career. Finally, workshops should be conducted to help support contract-faculty mothers and to offer strategies as to how to effectively manage the stress of being one. Perhaps, if these recommendations were implemented, contract-faculty mothers would feel both valued from the inside, as well as from the outside.

WORKS CITED

de Marneffe, Daphne. *Maternal Desire*. New York: Back Bay Books, 2004.

Dubson, M. *Ghosts in the Classroom: Stories of College Adjunct Faculty and the Price We All Pay*. Boston: Camel's Back Books, 2003.

Ennis, Linda. "Motherhood and Employment." *Encyclopedia of Motherhood. Vol. I*. Ed. A. O'Reilly. Toronto: Sage, 2010. 343-346.

Ennis, Lina. *On Combining Motherhood With Employment: An Exploratory Study*. Toronto: University of Toronto Press, 1997.

Evans, Elrena and Caroline Grant. *Mama PhD: Women Write About Motherhood and Academic Life*. New Brunswick, NJ: Rutgers University Press, 2008.

Fountain, W. *Academic Sharecroppers*. Bloomington, IN: AuthorHouse, 2005.

Hile Bassett, Rachel. *Parenting and Professing: Balancing Family Work with an Academic Career*. Nashville: Vanderbilt University Press, 2005.

Mason, M. A. and E. M. Ekman. *Mothers on the Fast Track*. New York: Oxford University Press, 2007.

Mason, Mary Ann and Marc Goulden. "Do Babies Matter? The Effect of Family Formation on the Lifelong Careers of Academic Men and Women." *Academe* 88.6 November/December 2002): 21-27.

McElrath, Karen. "Gender, Career Disruption and Academic Rewards." The Journal of Higher Education 63.3 (1992): 269-81.

Rajagopal, I. *Hidden Academics: Contract Faculty in Canadian Universities*. Toronto: University of Toronto Press, 2002.

Strauss, A. and J. Corbin. *Basics of Qualitative Research*. Thousand Oaks, CA: Sage, 1998

Wolfinger, N., M. Mason and M. Goulden. "Stay in the Game: Gender, Family Formation and Alternative Trajectories in the Academic Life Course." *Social Forces* 87.3 (March 2009): 1591-1621.

2. Strategies

9.

I Should Have Married Another Man; I Couldn't Do What I Do Without Him

Intimate Heterosexual Partnerships and their Impact on Mothers' Success in Academe

ANDREA O'REILLY

IN MY MANY YEARS OF WRITING I have found that the beginning of a writing project is often marked by an uncanny event in my life, one that resonates as I put pen to paper, or in today's world, fingers to keyboard. I have been reflecting on this chapter for a couple years, as it comes out of my three-year research project, "Being a Mother in Academe" 2006-2009),[1] for which I interviewed 60-plus academic mothers from across Canada and the U.S. The transcribed and analyzed interviews have been sitting on my desk gathering dust for far too long, as one and then yet another urgent task jumped queue on my ever growing "to do list." While the above research project explores many and diverse issues of academic motherhood (and will someday—sooner than later I hope—be published in a monograph), in this chapter I will explore one particular theme that, while central to my completed interviews, has not been considered in the scholarship on academic motherhood thus far: what role do intimate relationships play in determining women's success as academic mothers? As evidenced in the introduction and the chapters of this collection, the work and public context of mothers' lives as academics and how factors such as mentoring, childcare, institutional and governmental policy, and workplace practices and attitudes determine women's ability to successfully combine motherhood with an academic career have been well examined by the scholarship on academic motherhood. However, there has been little said on what impact the private and intimate life of women as partners has on women's academic careers.

This paper will consider women's partnered heterosexual relationships and the role they play in determining mothers' success as academic workers. While women's mother work and identity will be considered in this chapter, it will be looked at specifically in the context of women's partnered relationships. I have chosen this focus not because I view the partnership relationship as more important than that of motherhood in relation to women's work identity—my completed interviews suggest that both are equally significant—but because partnerships have been even less considered than motherhood in the scholarship on academic motherhood and because, if the findings of my interviews are any indication, the type of relationship a woman has with her life partner is a crucial, though largely overlooked, variable, that hugely determines, arguably more so than workplace policies or practices, women's ability to successfully combine an academic career with motherhood.

The literature on academic motherhood has rightly identified the need to counter and change the normative discourse of the ideal worker and, to a lesser degree, that of the ideal mother, in order for women to achieve academic success. This chapter will argue that women must likewise defy and deconstruct traditional partnered relationships particularly as they are manifested in the normative ideology of the ideal wife in both identity and practice. The normative wife role assumes and expects that 1) the family will be organized around the career of the husband 2) that the career of the wife, should she have one, will be necessarily secondary to that of her husband 3) that the wife is to support her husband's career and its advancement 4) that the woman is responsible for and performs the many and varied tasks of maintaining the household and home making. The normative wife role is particularly detrimental to an academic career due to the length and intensity of training required for such and because a career in academe, more so than most, necessitates frequent moving for training and employment (academics often relocate four to five times before they secure a tenured position) and extensive travel for research and conferences. It is difficult, if not impossible, for a woman to live up to these career obligations if her career is secondary to that of her husband, and if she is solely responsible for the care and running of the home and household. As discussed in the introduction and seen in the chapters of this collection, it is essential that mother academics have support and validation from their families so that they have the ability—and authority—to confront and survive academe's particularly masculine culture, a feat which is especially difficult to do within the ideal wife role. Indeed, what the findings of my research show is that the merging the excessive gender scripts of academe (masculinity) and conventional marriages (femininity) creates a perfect storm situation for academic mothers, making it impossible for them to achieve academic success. So much so that traditional gendered partnerships become more of a deterrent to academic success than single motherhood.

This chapter will argue that the highly gendered scripts of the normative wife and husband role serve to hinder women's employment success. In particular, it will argue that in order to make successful academic careers possible for mothers, it is just as critical to challenge patriarchal marriage as it is the masculinist culture of academe; likewise, it will propose that women must secure gender equity in the home as well as in the workplace. Sharing stories of four academic mothers—Julie, Leanne, Pamela and Sally—this paper will examine how and why traditionally gendered partnerships, particularly as they are manifested in the normative wife role, hinder a mother's success in academe. Conversely, it will show how and why domestic relationships modeled on gender equity work to enhance such.

As noted above, the start of my writing this chapter was paralleled by two significant events in my life that were thematically linked to this chapter's subject matter in a most uncanny way. Last week, after two long years of my file working its way through the labyrinth of my university's bureaucracy, I learned that my promotion to Full Professor was final and complete. While the official letter from the president on my promotion was certainly a cause for celebration, what was equally important to me, and of particular relevance to this chapter, was a Facebook post from my eldest daughter, age 25, after she received the news of my promotion. She wrote:

> congratulations to the world-renowned mama scholar and my own mom (yes, i'm a lucky grrrl!) Andrea O'Reilly for her accomplishment of promotion to full professor! so proud of you mom! to all those who say women can't achieve success in both their careers and as mothers, you need to take a look at my mom, her long list of publications, her adoring students and her even more adoring children. she's done it all and then some. way to go mom ♥.

Even though my daughter uses the word "mother"—as my daughter she views my identity in this context rather than in the context of me being her father's partner (I consciously choose to use the term partner over wife because I am in a common-law relationship of soon-to-be 30 years and to signify my resistance to the normative wife role)— I would suggest that her comment signifies the larger argument of this chapter; namely, that only by refusing the normative wife role both in name and, more importantly, in practice, have I "done it all and then some." In reading my daughter's post in the context of writing this chapter, I realized that my success as an academic was indeed largely attributable to my own lived resistance (never easy, never fully achieved) to the gendered expectations of the normative wife role, that which dictates that my identity should be derived more from my role of homemaker than that of worker, and that my career should be viewed as secondary to that of my partner's.

Twenty-five years ago my partner and I realized that, being broke and with three children under the age of five, it would be impossible for us to both continue in graduate school. It was he who made the difficult decision to leave his program and work as contract faculty, while I would be the one to finish grad school and secure the tenure track job needed for our family's financial stability. Undoubtedly, traditional gendered scripts would have dictated otherwise: my partner, eight years older, much further along in his degree than me, and the man in the relationship, should have been the one to continue his career in academe, and I as a "good" woman and mother should have accommodated such by giving up my own career to be a devoted wife who would support his. The aim of this chapter is not tell this story—that is for another time and place. What deserves emphasis and is of relevance to this chapter is that it was precisely this so-called "unconventionality'" of my private life—our family being organized around my career—that made possible the peculiarity of my professional accomplishment: achieving Full Professor at a research university at the relatively young age of 50 and most significantly as a first generation university student, woman, feminist, motherhood scholar, "leftie," activist (or as I am oft-told, a troublemaker), mother of three (who had her children young and close together), and with (until recently) little money or financial support from family.

The second event, though not as momentous as receiving a promotion, was reading *Professor Mommy: Finding Work-Family Balance in Academia* by Rachel Connelly and Kristen Ghodsee, a book I only recently discovered and read the night before I began writing this chapter. A brilliant must-read book, it "provides practical suggestions gleaned from the experiences of the authors, together with other women who have successfully combined parenting with professorship." Indeed, both authors have secured academic success: both are, as they note, colleagues at a prestigious Liberal Arts college and "internationally recognized scholars with five kids, five books, and more than forty-five journal articles between [them]" (9). Connelly, a married mother of four, was the first woman to receive tenure in the economics department at her college, the first to be named Full Professor, and the first to be named to a Chaired Professor. Ghodsee, a junior scholar, earned her Ph.D. when her daughter was seven months old and became a single mother three years later in the critical years of her tenure clock. She has been awarded numerous prestigious fellowships and grants and received tenure and promotion in 2008 (9-10). Though they do not specifically take up the argument of this chapter, I would suggest that their lived experiences illustrate such; that is, they demonstrate that traditionally gendered partnerships, particularly as they are enacted in the normative wife role, are as much a barrier to academic success as that of the ideal worker and ideal mother. Ghodsee achieves academic success as a single mother and Connelly, while married, is the sole breadwinner of her family; her husband is at home full-time with no paid employment. At the conclusion of Ghodsee's biography she writes: "She is well aware that her situation was easier than many since she has a supportive spouse who celebrates what she does and who stays home with the children. Since she had someone else at home, snow days, and ear infections were much easier to cope with than they were for most of her women colleagues" (20).

In keeping with the argument of this chapter, I would suggest that it was precisely this challenge to normative gender roles and, in this case, a complete reversal of them—woman as breadwinner, man as homemaker—that contributed largely to Connelly's success as an academic mother. Given this, I believe that such warrants more than a passing mention at the end of her biography. Specifically, though such is not detailed in the book, I would argue that it is precisely because Connelly is not viewed or positioned as "wife" or solely responsible for the work of such, that she was afforded the time, space and, of equal importance, the validation and legitimacy to make her career central to her life and that of her family. In this, both Connelly's biographical reference, as well as my daughter's Facebook post, are able to aptly illustrate the argument of this chapter and provide an appropriate backdrop for its telling.

Moreover, by implicitly referencing the significance of private gender roles in determining academic success, they also reveal how gender roles tend to be obscured from our understanding of how academic success for mothers is or is not achieved.

"I SHOULD HAVE MARRIED A DIFFERENT MAN": WIVES, HUSBANDS AND CONVENTIONAL MARRIAGES

My interview with Julie, an Anglo-American woman, took place in a busy and crowded restaurant in New York City on a wet and windy December evening in 2006. At the time of the interview Julie was in her late forties and a mother of two children ages sixteen and eleven. She holds a Ph.D. in political science from a tier one university and currently is an untenured adjunct faculty member at state college. The research for her Ph.D. required lengthy stays in a foreign country, which she visited regularly. After completing her comprehensive exams she was awarded a prestigious fellowship at an ivy-league university, a position normally reserved for post-docs. She held the fellowship for a term, married a man she had met overseas, and then returned to that country with her husband for additional research. They then asked her to return to continue her fellowship for a second term, which she did. However, her husband remained in the other country and she felt compelled to return there because, as she explained, "It would be really nice to spend some time with my husband because he is completely freaking out—he's going to have a heart attack." She returned to be with her husband, secured a good (non-academic) job in her area of research, and had her first baby in 1990.

When the baby was still very young they returned to the States and they settled in a suburb outside of New York. Her husband landed a job in the city, which, in her words, "has him out the door at 5:30 am and not home till 10:00 pm," and she commuted daily for the fellowship. She explains, "I was doing this hellish commute: 5:00 am start to get the 7:00 am train in New York, pumping in the toilet so I could get to a seminar at the university by noon." She goes on to explain, "I had never lived in the suburbs. I didn't know a soul. We didn't have a washing machine or a broom. I mean it was the whole buy a house, fill a house, have a baby plus commute. Needless to say I didn't get to write anything (for her dissertation)." Later in the interview she elaborated:

"The suburban homes were nicely decorated because their wives were not working and he is wondering when we are going to get curtains. There was frankly a lot of pressure you know from him to kind of get the house together." She commented further, "The days I was home I was trying to be Mom and get the house together and maybe vaguely recalling that I had some research to do somewhere. I was getting nothing done. So you know they (the university) were bending over backwards. They did offer me this other position but I figured it was just going to be more of the same."

When she was offered this other position she declined explaining, "My marriage is going to collapse or I am going to drop my child on the toilet or I am going to have a nervous breakdown because I am not getting anything done on any dimension, wife, mother or researcher." When they learned of her decision she was told, "You can't do that. This will be the end of your career. No one will ever take you seriously again if you just go home." Julie suggested a compromise solution: a position at a state university near her home. Their response was anything but encouraging: "If anyone hears that you are considering this you are dead in the water." Reflecting on this part of her story, Julie commented: "During all those years I was one of those star candidates. I was getting jobs that, you know, offers for jobs when I never finished my dissertation. People were throwing money at me and giving me positions so here I was just saying I am not doing anything. So I went home."

Julia had a second baby a few years later, finished her dissertation and graduated in 1997. Around that time she was interviewed for another fellowship. It was made clear to her that "she needed to move up there and have her husband commute." She attempted to clarify her predicament in response to this possibility: "I tried to explain that we can't really do that because he works so late." Julie later commented to me, "My husband has one of those not very flexible jobs and he also comes from a very traditional family and it wasn't so much I want you home to do the diapers but it is definitely you know basically he makes a decent salary, a very nice salary and I am like on the temporary position. It means nothing in terms of income … he can't just abandon his career so that I can have two years at an ivy-league university." A few years later, she was encouraged to apply for a job at a R1 university but she did not apply as she said to me, "I can't do the super mommy.[2] I tried that. I cannot do it." She explained later in the interview that she "kept pushing my husband to take parental leave and he would say he can't do that in my field." Julie ended up taking a position at a local state college which, as she explained, "works her like a dog; she has no money and gets no research done." She remains at the college, currently untenured. Near the end of the interview I asked, "What could have been done to make it easier?" Her response: "A different husband."

From her story, it is clear that academia could have done more to support and advance the career of this "superstar" scholar: maternity leave, on site-childcare, flex-time, and mentoring, to name but a few. However, as her story suggests and her comments confirm, it was largely the demands and expectations of the normative wife role, rather than those of the ideal worker of academic culture, that were the greatest obstacle to Julie achieving academic success. In particular, her husband's excessively long work days (usually seven days a week), his refusal to relocate or take parental leave, and his expectation that she be the traditional stay-at-home wife in suburbia. Given the intractable gender roles of their partnered relationship, Julie, in my view, was left with two choices: give up her academic career or give up her marriage. Choosing the latter, Julie found herself mommy-tracked, or more accurately, wife-tracked and working in an untenured position at a state college. I believe that if their partnership had been less scripted by traditional gender roles, and her husband had supported and validated her career, Julie would have had a far greater chance of becoming the superstar scholar she was destined to be.

Six months later while attending a conference in Manitoba, Canada, I interviewed Pamela, an Anglo-Canadian woman, who was in her late fifties at the time of the interview. The married mother of three children ages 30, 27 and 26, Pamela holds a Masters degree in science and is currently a tenured instructor at a Canadian university. During her Masters degree she held a TA position and supported the family as her husband was unable to secure a TA position through his department. She had her first child, a planned baby, at the age of 32 just after completing her Masters Degree. After her Masters degree they moved to Ontario for her husband's work; during this time she had her second and third child, a year apart. They moved, she explained, because "it was really hard for him to get jobs in what he wanted to do; because he could get one there I went with him." At the time she said she felt no resentment, she explained that she "felt okay about it cause I felt then we'd come back in two or three years and I'd start my Ph.D." She explained that initially her husband "was very supportive (of her plans) but became less supportive and less supportive." With the unplanned pregnancy of her third child, she comments, "he really wanted me to have an abortion; he did not want another child…but you know after our son was born it was fine but it was never quite the same I think between the two of us. He told me that I would never do my Ph.D. and he was quite adamant about that." She goes on to say that she told her husband and her former supervisor "that I would [complete her Ph.D.] but as it turns out I put it off."

Later, when I asked why she never did the Ph.D. that she longed to do, she explained that there were only two cities in Canada where she could do her planned program of study; she said to her husband at the time "that he could find something" to which he responded, "well there might be not be anything." She described how he reacted to the possibility of this prospective change: "If I wanted to do that fine I should just go and do it and he would take the kids and if I was not, you know if that was more important to me than the kids…." Pamela reflected upon her eventual decision: "Looking back on it if I just would have left and said I am taking the kids come or not, he would have come … but I went with him because the kids were little, really little and I didn't want to be without them and I didn't think you know … I said we can make this work, it's going be tough but I could maybe get some funding." Reflecting further, she comments: "he felt that I had my chance. He was really upset. I think that with the third child, that I wanted it; that it was my choice." They eventually moved to another city for his employment where she secured work as an instructor, a position she has held for 17 years. She thought about finally doing her Ph.D. but, as she explains, "we never had the money and I always felt that to do it I would have to go away." Fortunately a few years ago she was able to secure tenure as a long-service adjunct faculty (though she will never be able to receive promotion as an instructor). Although Pamela is very happy in her position doing research as well as teaching, as she emphasized throughout the interview, she "really wanted that Ph.D.: to me it was kind of a beacon and it is really a sore spot all those years that I don't have it."

In my view Pamela's career aspirations, like Julie's, were thwarted less by the demands of the ideal worker of academe than they were by the demands of the ideal wife in a normative marriage; as a wife in a traditionally gendered partnership, it was expected and required that Pamela follow her husband and relocate twice for the advancement of his career. Both she and her husband recognized that, in order for her to fulfill her dream of completing a Ph.D., the family would be required to move or, at the very least, achieve such through a commuter relationship. Nonetheless, the husband was unwilling to do so as his employment assurance took precedence; Pamela was unable to insist upon such changes given that he was the primary breadwinner and she the primary homemaker. While these traditionally gendered partnerships impeded the academic careers of these two women, they also significantly and ironically enabled Pamela and Julie to leave or "opt out" of such careers. With husbands earning an income they were not required to secure a career and bring in money to support their families, particularly in Julie's case. Here is where we see traditionally gendered partnerships, more so than single motherhood, working against the career advancement of academic mothers. As evidenced in many of my interviews, single mothers have no choice but to stay with and in their academic careers, despite the many challenges they face; as the sole breadwinner, they are responsible for the family's financial stability and well-being. As single mothers, they must have paid employment, and ideally in a career such as academe that is relatively well-paid, secure, and with the required benefits for the family (particularly health care benefits for mothers in the United States). Therefore, "opting out" is simply less of an option for single mothers than it is for married mothers, as the latter have their husband's income to rely upon should their career in academe falter or fail. One of my single mother interviewees attests to this dilemma: "You know it is only going to be me looking out after me, and it's only me who's creating the financial stability for my children ... I have no choice [but to remain in academe]." Traditionally gendered relationships thus hinder an academic career both by making it difficult to achieve such as a wife, and easier to leave with a husband. Significantly, while Julie and Pamela's stories were not unique among the sixty plus mothers interviewed, I speculate that such stories are more common than my study would suggest, as I interviewed only mothers who are still in academe. Had my project included mothers who have left the profession, I suspect that traditionally gendered partnerships would emerge as an even more decisive factor in determining mothers' achievement in academe. Indeed, as the two stories that follow reveal, gender equity in intimate partnerships play a central, if not constitutive, role in the success of academic mothers.

"I COULDN'T DO WHAT I DO WITHOUT HIM": PARTNERS IN PARTNERSHIPS

Leanne is a 42-year-old African American woman, mother of two children, ages three and seven. She is currently tenure track at a university in the South-West: she holds a bachelors degree in physics from a prestigious university or, as she called it, an "all white boys school," a Masters in a science field from a State School—the first African American to graduate with such a degree—and a Ph.D. in an area of science, which she completed in four years time. Between her Masters and Ph.D. she spent four years working with the Peace Corps overseas. Racism was rampant throughout her Ph.D. years; Leanne recalls the experience: "They treated me like rubbish: I was living in a war zone." Also, on two occasions she was accused of stealing computers from the computer lab room. At the age of 32 she was offered a tenure track position immediately following her Ph.D., but at that point she switched the focus of her research from pure science to an interdisciplinary field and held a post-doc for several years. She was married during the first years of her post doc. Leanne comments on her marriage: "My husband proposed to me while I was in graduate school. But I thought, you know, he was living in another city, we are having booty calls and all that, and I feel like I don't know if we're going to get married or not. But he wanted to marry me so I, we went ahead and married. And it is not that I don't love my husband but I was at the point where I don't believe, if he leaves that's fine, I'd get another one. You know, there is something particular to women at my university; there are so many men. You know what: you're going to give me some trouble: there are five others waiting for me."

Leanne had her first baby in the first years of her post doc and was back to work at her field research soon after the birth. She describes her reasoning for this decision: "I'm a workaholic and control freak. And I'm not saying that is a bad thing. I wouldn't be a professor without it." Leanne elaborates further "I admit: I love my work. I was doing exactly what I wanted to do. I was transcribing the notes from the fieldwork. Hold the baby and dictate. There was no reason for me not to keep working and, you know, I only can read so many novels before I get bored." When the baby was still a young infant, Leanne did a four-month post-doc in Africa, with her sister joining her as her nanny and translator. Shortly after she and her husband moved to her current city, when the baby was eight months old, she applied for and received another post-doc and her child began daycare. Her husband was in Europe working on his post-doc and she joined him a year later for a fourth month post doc, her sister joining her again to serve as a nanny for the baby. Leanne and her husband went out into the job market at the same time seeking a joint hire; they were unsuccessful so she accepted a tenure track position at the university where I interviewed her (her husband accepted another post-doc and was hired at the university a year later). She had her second baby four years after her first, two years after receiving a tenure track position. Leanne had wanted another baby but her husband was not so keen: he said "no, no, no, no, no ... and finally I said okay, my husband clearly can't handle one more child ... it would have ruined my marriage because he couldn't handle any more work because I wasn't doing any ... for the first two years they were attached to my boob and then they're his."

Midway through the interview Leanne recalled a comment made by her husband's supervisor when they were both in graduate school: "You know your wife is going to be more famous than you in five years." When I asked what her husband felt about her successes, she replied, "You know what he says: I don't care if you're more famous. Bring home the bacon sweetheart. Whatever it is, bring home the money. Actually he's paid more than me because he's in the Sciences. And I am in the Social Sciences." Elaborating more on their partnership she explains, "He does most everything. He does because I just like, you know, of the six hundred things I'd rather be doing, washing dishes is not one of them. If I could live in a hotel I would. I get up. I leave, I come back, and everything's clean. That is my fantasy." She goes on to say, "I said at the start, my husband and I have the same degrees. I haven't been training to be a housewife. I've been training to be a professor the whole time." Reflecting on the larger issue of gender roles and marriage, Leanne commented: "We need a wife, I need a wife. I don't need a husband." She explains further: "It must be very clear that there's a division of power. You know in a way that the whole thing is balanced.... And so that balanced power happened before we even got married. I just had to do less and less until I felt like things were equal. And the only way I feel like things are equal is if he does more. Right? And so he does his part of the chores, I hire somebody to do my part of my chores. And I'm willing to pay for somebody to come in and clean the house. Right? But he is really, pretty much the primary caregiver for our girls."

Four months after this interview, I interviewed 33-year-old Sally, an Anglo-American woman who is the mother of three children ages ten, eight and six. She is a tenured faculty member in the department of psychology at a liberal arts college in the mid-west; she was the first woman to be hired and tenured in her department. Like Leanne above, Sally describes herself as a "workaholic." Sally married at the age of 21, just after completing her Bachelors degree, and had her first child two months before completing her Master Degree at the age of 23. Her second child was born just after her Ph.D. preliminary exams, and her third child was born immediately following the completion of her dissertation. She finished her Ph.D. degree in four years, taking no maternity leave for any of her children. A week after the birth of her third child she moved to her current city where she had been offered a tenure track position. Early on in the interview I asked her about the challenges of working in a male-dominated field as a mother of three children, and she responded before I could even complete my question: "I couldn't do what I do without my husband."

She then proceeded to explain that she and her husband have moved four times throughout their marriage and he was the "trailing spouse" in each instance. Shortly after they married they moved for her Masters degree, then again for her Ph.D., and yet again for her current position, all across state lines. As well, a few years earlier, while still tenure track, she accepted a position at another university. The husband and children moved to the new city so the children could start school there while she stayed behind to complete the fall semester. For five months he was a single father, and she commuted on weekends until she joined the family in December. She was very unhappy in this new position and soon returned to her original university; again her husband and children followed her. On all four occasions, as she explains, he moved "without a promise of a job." With each move, he was unemployed temporarily until he found employment in his area of work (a non-academic position). When I inquired on his willingness to accommodate the frequent relocations, she explained that "We've always known that my job is, this is terrible to say because academics don't make much, is probably going be the primary source of income and also that I have less flexibility in where I can go, and so he's always said you know what? We'll follow;

we'll follow your position." Their last move—when they temporarily moved for her new position—was a difficult one, as she explained, "It was tough on him because he was happy in his position here." However, he did relocate with the children and without Sally so she could finish the semester at that university.

When I asked Sally to describe their relationship she remarked, "We are partners; I can't claim 60/40 even. I mean he is there in the trenches as much as I'm in the trenches." Sally described an average working day in their household: "He gets up before I do, he is usually the one getting the kids up and ready for breakfast while I'm getting ready for work. He allows me the extra time; it's purposeful in that he gives me my time in the morning to do my thing." Her husband is also the one the school or daycare calls if they children become ill and he is the one who stays home with them when they are sick. On this topic she shared a humorous story: "It's funny ... the other day I got a call from my kids school—they had forgotten something—and they called me, and I think it surprised the secretary that I had answered the phone. She goes 'Oh, I think I dialed the wrong number.'" Sally's husband is also the one responsible for picking the children up from school and getting dinner started. At the time of the interview she was having a particularly challenging semester, as she was covering courses for a colleague who had left the department. Given this situation, she told her husband, "I will not be a great wife this semester, I am not going be a great mother this semester," and so, as she explained to me, "often there are evenings where he's fully responsible from getting them home to putting them to bed."

Later in the interview when I asked her how she copes with stress, particularly on those days when the challenges seem insurmountable, Sally remarked: "Well you know a lot of it is seeking comfort from my spouse. He knows me better than I know myself often and you know we were just talking last night that I'm at the moment of oh my god what have I taken on, and he says you know what? You have to sit down; you know he recognizes that better than I do." She shared a particular touching story: "A couple weeks he called and scheduled a massage for me. He says you know you have to start caring for yourself. I think if I didn't have him, if I didn't have some kind of the sanity in this insane house I don't know what I would do. I would probably just continue to work and work and work and work and work and work and neglect that part of me." Throughout the interview, Sally emphasized that she needs to find a "healthy-balance" in her life, but says that such is prob-ably unlikely, even with tenure, given her "self-driven personality." Speaking of this in relationship to her partner, Sally shared her opinion: "He knows me well enough to know that I'm never going slow down. I think the moment I slow down is the moment I die. But he's kind of got that sense out. I think he's been more forceful in saying to me: you know you don't have to. They're not going to fire you, your job is secure, and you know you can let some things go." At the conclusion of the interview when I asked Sally what she attributed her academic success to, she responded without hesitation: "I would say first off my spouse. I joke with my sisters only half-heartedly that if I were married to any of their husbands I would not be doing what I'm doing because their husbands are very traditional: the woman is the one who does this; they're involved in that."

Because their partners validated, supported and accommodated their academic careers, both Sally and Leanne were able to achieve academic success despite the many challenges they faced as mothers in male domi-nated fields and within the larger masculine culture of academe; Leanne having also experienced racial discrimination as she navigated her career. By following their wives as they relocated for study and employment, and by living apart from their wives as such was required for the wives' research or work, these husbands played a valuable role in their wives' academic accomplishments, something Pamela and Julie's husbands were unwilling to do. Moreover, while Sally and Leanne were not the primary breadwinners, and in Leanne's case she made less than her professor husband, their careers and the income they generated were essential for the family's financial well-being; thus, "opting out" of their academic careers was not an option for either woman. As well, the husbands of Sally and Leanne were not only true partners in the relationship, participating equally in the rearing of the children and the running of the household, but often assumed the role of primary caregiver and household manager when the wives' careers required it. Notably, both Sally and Leanne had husbands who valued the work they did as academics; they sincerely and actively encouraged their wives' careers and gave both practical and emotional support to their wives freely and often, something seldom observed in Julie and Pamela's stories. Finally and most significantly, Sally and Leanne attributed their academic success not to support given in the academic workplace—there was, in fact, little of this—but to the support provided by their husbands and to the larger gender equity or, in Leanne's words, the "balanced power" of their households.

CONCLUSION: "PICK YOUR PARTNERS CAREFULLY"

A career in academe requires long and intensive years of training, travel for conferences and research, and repeated relocations, all of which are integral to the profession and necessary for advancement in it. Too frequently motherhood is given as the reason why women leave academe or fail to succeed within it, but I would suggest that if we look more closely at such stories, tease out the details, we see that traditionally gendered partnerships are often the real reason why mothers 'opt out' of careers in academe. Traditionally gendered partnerships, organized as they are around the husband's career, make it difficult if not impossible for the wife to attain the very things required for a successful academic career: the ability to travel, move, or secure the needed time and focus for her scholarship (and the authority to demand such). As seen above with Professor Connelly, it is often assumed that such support can only be achieved through a complete reversal of gender roles whereby the man becomes the wife (he is the primary at-home parent), while the woman becomes the husband (she is the primary breadwinner). However, given that such a solution is available only to a select few who have the financial means to support a family on one income, gender reversal is not possible for most families and, as importantly, such does not address the larger problem of gender inequity within households. With Sally and Leanne we see that gender equity is possible without a complete reversal of gender roles, as both women are not wives to their husbands but rather true partners. They, along with their partners, are responsible for and perform what needs to be done to create a home and family: childrearing, housework and paid employment. In this, their relationships do not merely reverse gender roles but, more importantly, eliminate them all together.

In the introduction we discussed the split subjectivity of contemporary mother professors. As they seek success in the masculine culture of academe, they are still restrained by their identification with normative understandings of good motherhood. I would suggest that much of this tension and conflict, as illustrated in the above stories, is more often derived from the normative wife role than the actual work of mothering. However, as a society we are reluctant to acknowledge, let alone analyze, how our intimate partnerships shape and influence the public lives we lead and the work we do: after all we partner for love not for career success. But I would argue, as I conclude this chapter appropriately enough on Valentine's Day, that if mothers hope to secure success in academe, they must be as attentive to the discriminatory gendered politics and patterns of love as well as work, or as one of my interview respondents astutely advised, "women need to pick their partners carefully."

[1]In 2006 I was awarded a three-year Social Science Humanities Research Council of Canada grant for my research project "Being a Mother in the Academe." I interviewed 60-plus mothers from across Canada and the United States. Mothers from more than 25 states were interviewed as well as women from all ten provinces in Canada. Mothers from the level of Masters Students to that of Full Professor were interviewed from a wide range of colleges and universities. A wide and diverse group mothers were interviewed to include: Aboriginal, African American/Canadian, South and East Asian, Latina/Chicana, Lesbian as well single, adoptive mothers and mothers who self-identified as having a disability. The interviews lasted between one and three hours.

[2]It is interesting that Julie describes herself as "super mommy" rather than a super wife when the oppression she experiences and describes is caused more by wife work than that of mothering. Such misidentification underscores the larger argument of this article; namely that as motherhood is given as the reason why women leave academe or fail to succeed within it, it is actually the role of wife that prevents women from securing academic success. However, unable or unwilling to identify the oppression of the normative wife role, we attribute such to the ideology and practice of normative motherhood. It would seem that women are more willing and able to acknowledge and analyze the oppression in motherhood than that caused by their intimate partnerships. Certainly a revealing and compelling insight and one deserving of further reflection and research.

WORK CITED

Connelly, Rachel and Kristen Ghodse. *Professor Mommy: Finding Work-Family Balance in Academia*. New York: Rowman & Littlefield, 2011.

10.

From Motherhood, Through Widowhood

The Path to Receiving the Academic Hood

YVONNE REDMOND-BROWN BANKS

T
HE FRAMING PROCESS FOR MY ROLE as an academic mother
came upon me within fourteen months of starting my doctoral
program. I became a widow with a two-and-a-half-year-old
daughter and a six-and-a-half-year-old son. Lesson number one came in
the form of overwhelming grief and loneliness stemming from the loss
of my husband of less than eight years. In his death I lost more than a
primary source of income. I lost support, companionship, and was literally living a "dissertation widow" life, a common phrase to those going
through the dissertation process. I lost a loving and comforting ear; I lost
my soul mate. Before applying to start my doctorate, we formulated a plan
that would allow me to graduate debt free, utilizing the "pay-as-you-go
plan." With his unexpected death, I was left with puzzle pieces of how to
meet our day-to-day needs as well as struggling to find resources to pay
for my degree. Covering the cost of daycare for my toddler and paying
the before and after-school fees for my second grader left me with very
little in terms of paying my college tuition.

In facing the loss of my husband I faced a loss that loomed larger than
any daycare or tuition bill: I lost confidence in myself. I lost confidence in
believing I could parent my children alone. I had so many instant decisions
to make that I began to question my ability to be a "good mom." I faced
questions of survival, not only for myself, but for my children. Riding on
the plane with my husband's coffin in the cargo bay, I held on tightly to
my children and prayed. I prayed that I would receive clear direction for
how to proceed because I had no experience in the role of solo parenting. Every decision was mine alone to make. With his unexpected death,
I found myself mothering through the loss with much confusion, fear,

and despair as to what I would do from day to day. To say that it was a difficult time is simply an understatement. I was in the midst of despair and it was clear that I needed to recalculate my plan. I needed to know exactly what my next steps would be as I assessed the loss at this point in my life for not only me, but for my children. I felt as though an adze had been swung into my chest. The loss of my husband hurt on more levels than I can put words to even today, sixteen years later.

As a full-time working widow with two small children, I was bombarded with questions related to my survival. *Could I endure keeping my job as a mid-level district administrator as I pursued my degree and still parent effectively? Could I do this without damaging my children?* I needed to calculate the loss to my children as I redesigned my plan to finish my degree, as a widow, in the original timeframe of three years. Acknowledging that there would be losses if I continued on the path to securing my degree, I had to decide how to minimize the casualties as I moved forward.

In this chapter I discuss the impact of that decision and the experiences that ensued in my life and in the lives of my children. Moms who are widows with children in higher education are a rare, unexpected breed, and our stories matter. Our stories matter to the point that authors such as Martha Chen capture the voices of women to outline the many phases of widowhood in *Why Widowhood Matters*. We know that working moms face barriers associated with an uneven playing field, as outlined in "Gender Matters," an article provided by insidehighered.com that outlines the multiple barriers of academic moms. When you add young children, and widowhood into the mix of the dissertation process, the barriers are almost insurmountable. Exploring the journey of what it meant for me to continue to seek the academic hood through motherhood and widowhood combined is what my conversation is about in this chapter. I provide voice to the many dilemmas I faced and offer my experiences to other moms on a similar journey through the writing of this paper. As a family, we were lonely, isolated, and vulnerable during this initial stage, and sharing that story sixteen years later is, in some ways, a part of the journey.

MOTHERING THROUGH DISTANCE: THE LACK OF RESEARCH

The day-to-day stressors of being an academic mom were compounded by the fact that I was a solo parent. I did not have Grandma or Grandpa in arms reach, and no aunts or uncles to give weekend relief. They were all five hundred miles away, in one direction. The direction of the research on this topic was even further away as I searched for it sixteen years ago. The lack of research on widows with children pursing academic degrees was disappointing. I went searching for answers in the literature and found none worth noting. The reality I faced at the time is that there were few, if any researched notations on the combined topics of working, widowed moms with small children. I found little research to guide me in answering questions that would help me prepare for how to be a mom under the circumstances I faced. I had many questions about how to parent my children in their loss, socially and emotionally. What would happen to them if I continued to pursue my academic hood as a widow? The number of widows with children reported by Michelle Vasquez was calculated to be around 554,000 in the U.S from 2004-2005. Therefore, the topic of widowhood combined with seeking an academic pursuit is a topic of relevancy for moms seeking answers for support. How do we face the feelings of helplessness and loneliness?

Revisiting now what Barry Wellman outlined as "the realm of my reality" (Wellman and Tindall), brings me back to the thoughts and fears that filled my day. I was consumed with the awareness of what I had lost in the death of my husband. It was clear that I needed answers and I needed help, but as I searched for advice on how to be a widow-mom pursuing an academic hood, the answers were short to none. The search for answers left me frustrated. I found solace in learning how to listen to other moms' stories. This practice became essential to my survival as a mom during this chapter of the ever-unfolding story of my new status in widowhood. I located a weekly grief support group that offered classes for both me and my two kids on the same evening and it even offered an evening meal. From my first meeting I knew that I would survive and my children would survive this loss, even if I knew nothing else. When fear entered my thinking about the distance between my family and me, I learned to put it aside. When I dwelled too long on my frustration about the lack of research, I moved on. In the reality of my life, I was a dissertation widow literally, and I was challenged to face this fact head-on. Katherine Norris, in her book *Dakota: A Spiritual Journey*, makes reference to "one who keeps death before his [her] eyes conquers despair" (190). I entered the next chapter of widowhood and bereavement embracing survival skills that would allow me to strengthen my resolve as a mom, and as an academic scholar. Facing the day-to-day doubts successfully would help me conquer and survive the more distant fears that came in the form of "*What if?*" questions.

MOTHERING THROUGH DOUBT: FACING INTERLOCKING REALITIES

Survive may appear to be a strong word, but it was clear that I needed strategies to survive the day-to-day realities of raising my grieving children. My children's pain was presented daily: as I prepared them for school, fixed their favorite pasta dinners and read to them each evening. During the initial stage of my loss, I held on to the joy my kids found in Dad reading to them each night by trying to continue the pattern Dad had set. But, as a full-time working mom, I had my own work to prepare for as a professional. I questioned the reality of this path and questions of doubt continued in my head. *Was I willing to face the emotional difficulties of carrying the title "widow-mom?"* Deeply intertwined with the steps needed for my survival as a widowed mom were the steps needed to guide me in my research as I worked a full-time job and parented. I found this reality interesting as I sat with my head in my hand one evening, struggling to get my daughter to stop crying and go to sleep as she insisted that I "just go and get Daddy, Mommy—now!"

Vividly, sixteen years after the loss of my husband, I can recall how I desperately looked forward to our Monday night grief support group as a family. In my small group of four widows and one widower, we offered each other unconditional support and opportunities to share stories from the week without judgment. Two hours of freedom from being in the mom-on-duty role is what I gained on Monday nights. As I worked, mothered, and attended to my academic obligations, I believe the support group is what saved me. The association with individuals outside the grief group who could identify with my realities was not available to me. Even today it is rare that I meet a woman with the mixture of challenges that I faced during that time. Few people can understand the emotional intrusions that widow moms face. As a widow mom, I struggled with on-going and nagging questions about death, faith, or a matrix of thoughts about "*Why me?*" Moms parenting alone face resurfacing doubts about the quality of their parenting skills. Gregory Patterson captured well our doubts about our ability to manage it all in higher education in his article, "Scholar, Teacher, and Mother: Managing Motherhood and Tenure." My doubts came upon me unexpectedly'—in meetings, on the way to Boy Scouts, during the father/daughter dances for Girl Scouts, or during any event where it was clear that I was both Mommy and Daddy. Sometimes it was as simple as seeing couples holding hands. My reality was clear: I had no mate, but I had his two children.

The demon of defeat would enter my thoughts most often at night when I was tired and worn down from the day. This was often my reality; the only time I found to work on my doctoral requirements without interruptions or have the chance to prepare for the next day's requirements of my job were in the moments carved out of the stillness of the night. Because of this, I would caution academic moms with young kids, through widowhood or otherwise, about staying up too late; late nights were difficult times for me. A tip to combat those times that I would like to pass on is one that worked for me: the radio. My radio time, as I worked late into the early mornings, got me through many tired nights. I found a station that had soothing music and a commentator with a soothing voice. I did not listen to anything that was stressful, noisy, or distracting. In my work space, as I recall, I surrounded myself with words, phrases, and pictures of affirmations! I offer this as another tip for academic moms. I celebrated the good times I had with my husband by putting up funny pictures. I allowed myself to cry as I listened to the radio and typed away on my dissertation project. I listened to the stories of the many people who called in and I allowed myself to cry. My workspace was a place where I allowed my emotions the space to run freely and breathe.

It was during this period of time that I learned to cry for myself. I had cried for my children, I had cried for my husband and his loss, but I had never really cried for myself. It was during this time that I embraced the grieving process, and started to understand that allowing myself to cry did not mean defeat. How wrong I was during the first chapter of entering my widowhood experience! Once I faced the reality that he was gone, I became more effective in settling my kids down in their deep moments of grief. Accepting the interlocking realities that I was a solo parent hit me the hardest when I realized that no grandparents, aunts, or uncles who could offer weekend relief, shared rides, or help with the afterschool pick-ups from day care, or school projects, or even be the extra helping hand with the required Mom duties on the Butterfly dance team would be available for me. I was *it* for my kids—in every area of their lives! My experiences were very much unlike that of a single parent or a divorced parent. I resented being referred to as a single parent; my experiences were similar, yet different, but no one seemed to acknowledge the differences, not even family members.

On the job, after the respected acknowledgement of my widowhood state, I was expected to be there as usual and perform. As mentioned previously, academic Moms have an uneven playing field to combat in the workplace, and that theme forces many academic moms to put in lots of extra time to avoid being stereotyped. I made no requests for extensions on my graduate course work. I met every deadline and ignored the wide-eye surprises that lingered at my back when I handed in papers and projects on time. I learned to celebrate what I had with my husband before his death, and so did my children. As I met deadlines for classes, I put up gold stars for myself on a chart as an affirmation. I borrowed ideas from what I saw teachers doing with my kids. Charts and stars are great ways to celebrate doing coursework. Academic moms can use what they know best to survive. In the case of my family, we celebrated Dad's Saturday burnt pancakes and laughed and cried together. During this stage of loss, I encouraged my kids to put pictures up of Dad everywhere. We had pictures of Dad on roller skates, wearing silly birthday hats, fishing outings, tents in the backyard and the special events of births and christenings. We all have stories that interlock, and I learned not only from my grief support group, but from the caller on the radio station that faced loss. Little in the formal binding of the research world on academic-widow-moms existed to help me, but I found a lot of antedoctal data about how to survive the unexpected blows of life.

Widows with young children should take up this practice of show-and-tell and celebrating Dad's contributions. Tell his story and let the kids add to it as they can. As I learned to interlock my research with my family's journey, the pinned up pictures of my husband often overlapped with clippings from the professional journals that guided my research. As I made collages of my research findings, my children made collages of their adventures with Dad. I was never more grateful for Polaroid pictures and all the silly trinkets from vacations and other family events than in this stage of widowhood. Their collages told their stories and kept Dad's love fresh for them. My academic collages shaped my research as I smiled at my discoveries. Learning to associate the steps of grief from death with the steps of grief found in the lives of families raising a special needs child was a great revelation for me. Realizing that concepts from my training and professional life had interlocking themes that became a life jacket for framing my dissertation work and pointed me towards steps of reality I could manage.

My journey as a widow-mom, combined with my experience from the field of special education allowed me to articulate the process of embracing grief and overcoming experiences of loss. Parents lose and grieve daily their ideal child when raising a child identified with a special need. This reality made telling my story and writing my project epic because there was no separation of truth for me with this discovery. Loss is Loss! As widow-moms, our stories are worthwhile topics, and our voices need to be included in the data. Sharing the reality of being thrust into a struggle beyond my control became my anchor, as I faced the realities of writing with young children. How could I separate being a working mom, being a widow, and being on the academic path? I could not and would not for any reason separate the three realities of my life. My experiences co-existed and the experiences left strong impressions upon me. When I see young academic moms up and down the halls of my institution with their children in tow, I smile because that was me sixteen years ago, but with one difference: I was a widow. Academic moms work late and juggle many tasks while striving after safety and success for their families. They hold onto the hope of finishing well, as they face the realities of their day and persevere. I hold the lessons I learned during this phase close to my heart.

The truth is some people simply don't know the world of academic moms, just like they don't know the challenges of the field of special education. So, remarks about professors as academic moms not giving enough or being on the wrong committee are addressed directly by me. I steer the conversations to a reality point that many are unaware of for academic moms. At times, I actually laugh inside and think to myself, *she is on the right committee because she is on the mom's macaroni and cheese committee or the costume-making committee, but you just did not get the memo on her life. Is she experiencing the loss of a mate or the isolation of parenting alone or do you know how often in the day she feels guilty? Is she running late to appointments, and how is she feeling about keeping her full-time job?* Reflecting on such questions reminds me of my journey through widowhood as I pursued the academic hood. I can recall how running late to my children's activities brought forth moments of shame and guilt, and when I relied too much on quick stops for food on the way home brought about feelings of incompetence. The feelings that came with being the last parent to get my children from daycare smothered me in clouds of defeat at times. Each experience I faced, each question I asked myself, or questions asked of me by others, helped me formulate and heighten my awareness of the deeper goal I held of completing my degree. I challenge academic moms to do the same. Use the experiences to gain strength, a theme reflected in Elisabeth Kübler-Ross' five stages of grief. I would say this confronting is necessary for academic moms because grief intrudes upon every part of our lives unexpectedly.

MOTHERING THROUGH LOSSES: IDENTIFYING THE GAINS

As I turn the clock back sixteen years and review the beginning of my journey, it is clear that on the front end of losing my husband, I did not know how to confront the unexpected. I did not know how it would play out for me as a widow-mom with two children. Death had the upper hand at that time. *Did I know how to survive with two small children?* It was an unclear process, but it turned into a process of determination. Above all I knew that I needed to love my children to the best of my ability as I moved through the process of loss with no road map. I did not know how deciding to continue to pursue my degree would impact my children, but I knew that I needed to stay on the path of degree completion. Proverbs 22:1 in the Bible tells us to listen to the words of the wise, and I offer that saying to widow moms seeking degrees or work opportunities. It is the strength that is needed to confront death. Others have gone before you, so seek out their stories and celebrate the skills and discoveries you and your children make daily.

Looking back on the two emotionally frazzled children under my wings sixteen years ago, they learned early the importance of being organized. There was no one at home to bring a left behind backpack or pair of sneakers. The calendar was king and each Sunday as part of our ritual, we color coded and doubled check all events. The rule was, "If it is not on the calendar, it was not happening." The children learned to put directly on Mom's spot at the table notices from teachers and coaches, invitations to parties or sleepovers, otherwise "No Go!" An excellent source for understanding what children gain from being raised by moms doing it on their own is found in the works of Roshan D. Ahuja and Kandi M. Stinson. The authors highlighted the decision making skills learned by children raised in a female-headed single parent home. Like the children in that study, my children gained early opportunities to be involved in the decision making process within the home; ranging from menu selection for the week, buying groceries, and helping select our vacation activities. We faced as a family similar challenges as the ones associated with a single female headed household. My children did not have the luxury of hearing another authority's voice and they had no one to go tell on Mom. They were stuck with me, and I believe working through our grief under such conditions gained us the needed skills for being a strong family unit as we faced our loss together.

As I mothered through the process, I accepted a few losses as widow-mom in my career in order to have some gains that anchored us as a family. For example, I grasped a few facts about what my career would look like early on as a widow-mom in academia. I embraced a selective process by accepting that I would not publish as often as others at my institution, but that I would celebrate whenever I did publish; I would not attend all the big conferences in my field of study, but I would strategically plan how to travel internationally every two years, with my children in tow. I would avoid certain committee assignments in order to avoid late evening meetings that required a babysitter. What did I gain by giving up some things as widow-mom in academia? I gained two children who have tons of stories of Mom-the-hockey-driver, Mom-the troop-leader, Mom-the-sleepover-queen, Mom-the-grilled-cheese-maker, and Mom-the-sausage-biscuit-expert. I gained what could not be measured in a bound dissertation. Sixteen years later, I measure my gains by the smile I quietly hold in my heart every time I overhear my children engaging in conversations about the wacky Halloween costumes I sewed, the matching hats we wore to events, and Mom getting lost because MapQuest was not invented. They talk about Mom being directionally challenged, so in order to be involved in activities, we had to always give ourselves an extra hour or two to get to unknown places, even in the city. They talk eloquently about the countries they have visited because they had to help Mom present her papers and they always talk in terms of being international travelers. Above all, I love when they refer to me as the tag-team Mom because of all the cool things we did together. I would say "not bad" for a measure of how the gains stack up against the perceived losses related to career options—we need to affirm, as working moms, that we are on the right committees and reading the right memos when our children are happy and secure.

We have gains and losses as academic moms in both arenas, and that is the plain truth of the matter. Do I have two young adults involved in higher education with a passion for traveling the world? Yes I do. Do we still on occasion face the residue of losing dad too early? Yes we do. On the other hand, my children have embraced foreign languages, they have had numerous international experiences with and without me, both love study abroad programs, they can pack and get themselves to the airport in an hour, and they understand the importance of keeping their passports renewed. One widow-mom moment that I celebrate is the time when my children demonstrated that they could travel internationally without me, getting through customs all on their own. They will tell you that PowerPoint is their friend and they are comfortable in discussions on how best to present a paper at a conference, poster session, or discussion forum. Did I give up some things as an academic-mom? Of course I did. Did my kids? Oh yes, but was it worth it? Looking back from then to now, I would say yes. My son is an Eagle Boy Scout and my daughter is a Girl Scout Gold, which speaks to their leadership skills and sense of community. Focusing on what I could do and do well early on in the process of becoming a widow-mom seeking an academic hood proved to be an invaluable mindset that my children benefited from greatly. If asked today, sixteen years later, I would say that our gains during this process outweighed what I gave up as an academic mom.

MOTHERING THROUGH INNOCENCE: LEARNING FROM MY CHILDREN

Two important events marked a memorable turning point for me as a working widow trying to finish her degree. We all have heard the phrase "out of the mouths of babes," meaning honest and innocent truths are spoken by children. I have my daughter to thank for my reality check in this area. Her boldness during this phase of the process clearly reflected who I had become for her during my time of working, writing, and mothering. The most vivid memories I have are associated with her red crayons and the little tote bag she carried around constantly. As I learned later, she was pretending to be me. The first event that brought this truth to my attention happened at church one Sunday when my daughter sashayed down the corridor with her pretend briefcase and was asked, "What are you carrying?" She turned, smiled, held up her pretend briefcase, pulled out her red crayon, and said, "My Chapter Four," in a tone that said, "What else?" I was startled because I would have expected her to say her Bible, her doll, or her picture books. At that moment that I knew I needed to do something else with my time to remove this image of me from her mind. My view of how well I was balancing all of my roles received a blow from her innocent response. I left church knowing that I needed to complete my program as soon as possible.

One evening after midnight, in my office, my emotions collided with the events of my daughter's statement from church and sent me to a place I didn't want to go. My kids were on the floor of my office surrounded by McDonald's bags and it hit me that they actually had school the next day. I had picked them up at the appointed deadline of 6:00 p.m., got them to McDonald's, and came back to the office to edit and it was now past midnight. I recall, in my frustration, throwing the two hundred pages of my rough draft against the wall and weeping. The desire to quit and maybe find a husband was overwhelming. So many of my problems would be resolved. I found myself listing them as I pondered what to do about the editing of my dissertation. I resolved that I would either find a more efficient way to edit or I would quit. I was learning truth from my children.

This was an important junction for me because I had to acknowledge that maybe I had taken on too much as I continued to move through the grieving process. It is important for academic moms to know when they are done and to know when they have taken on too much. As moms we often take on too much and attempt to jump through too many hoops, both at home and on the job, a state of mothers that is outlined by Lucy B. Mallan in "Young Widows and Their Children: A Comparative Report." Our children have the gift of showing us truth in ways that can't be ignored. My daughter did that for me with her statement and demeanor on that particular Sunday. To this day I am grateful for her reflection of how my desire to achieve the academic hood had crossed over a limit. We all have limitations and the limitation of time is often the reality check we need as moms to step back and assess what is important. Trying to complete the weekly revisions on my dissertation immediately was not a realistic approach and caused me to impose long evenings upon my young children. In their innocence they rebelled, and I am thankful for that—it helped me learn from them both. The intensity of pain was raw and inflicting, but clearly it was what I needed to grow.

The five stages of grief, denial, anger, bargaining, depression, and acceptance can be generalized in other areas of our lives. I believe that I was in the denial stage of realistically assessing how much I could do with my kids in tow. I would offer to widow-moms in the academic world to listen closely to their children as they face similar bouts of despair that come from an overwhelming reality that there are limitations to what they can do during this stage of grief. Our status as moms, especially single, solo, or widow moms, places us in positions that we are not always content to face. Working, mothering, and doing school work to earn a degree add calamity to our lives. It put me in a position of facing unreasonable and unexpected challenges that I imposed on myself. I saw truth in the dissertation scattered on my office floor, I heard truth in my daughter's confident response. Truth in that it was hard, that I was lonely, that at times I was tired, in the fact that I feared that I may not make it over this last hurdle of editing in order to be done with my degree. Another truth that many working moms rarely talk about is that at times, we are resentful of our situation. So many emotions are tied to the truths we face as academic moms or solo parent moms, and often we don't speak of them for fear of being judged as bad or unfit mothers, or even worse, mothers who want professional success over our families. It took me a while to even admit this to my therapist for fear of being judged or having my children taken away if I shared at the deepest level. During this phase I learned a lot from my children and it revealed the systemic impact of a mom's heart engulfed in fear and pain.

Reliving the history of that moment defines me even today, because I have an established commitment to always check in and put family first. I can be a workaholic and I still count on my children to hold me accountable. I would recommend working moms find a way to have balance. I see now how overhearing my daughter's comment was a blessing and how it guided me to find ways to include my children in healthy ways while earning a degree. The two events outlined gave me courage to allow my children to see me cry, courage to let them to know that Mom gets tired and that Mom's project was hard school work. I told them directly that it was not fun, but necessary, that I missed Dad too, and that I was sorry that we could not go visit Grandma and Grand-daddy more often. Allowing my children to see me vulnerable took a long time.

As I thought about how to include my children, the idea came to me that I could include them by giving my son and daughter old revisions of my chapter reviews. I encouraged them to use their red crayons to creatively edit Mom's work. I set specific times when they could help and when Mom would grade her paper. When that time was up, it was up, and Mom would not work on her paper any more that day. I saw in my children's behavior that they needed to see the truth of my life in a healthy way and by allowing them to grade my paper, we had additional time together. After taking a new approach to my editing, I found joy because my babies always returned the pages to me with loving comments, creatively spelled, indicating that Mom had done a good job. Sharing the editing experience of my dissertation work allowed me to experience two realities and create harmony in the pit of despair and depression. I did not have to be the Rock of Gibraltar for everyone and I offer this awareness to academic moms sixteen years after my journey with a footnote of thanks for the truth that came through the innocence in the words from my daughter that Sunday in church.

CONCLUSION: MOTHERING THROUGH CHAOS: A STRONG FINISH

Compartmentalized boxes cannot contain the experiences of widow-moms in academia. The field of grief and loss is a step in the direction for offering others a picture of our experiences. During the chaos of the first season of my husband's death, a friend gave my children a book titled *The Fall of Freddie the Leaf* (Buscaglia). In this book Freddie, as a leaf, tells about the seasons of our lives, as we experience and discover death. Needless to say, Freddie was read often to my children. In Freddie's realization that he is one of the last leafs on the branch of an Oak tree, he ponders why the season of his happy life—of sunshine and joy—changes to a life of brisk winds and sadness. As Freddie experiences the season of change that he faced as a leaf, his story became a favorite for us as a family especially in moments of needed quiet. I used the book to put order to the chaos that we faced in many stages of our lives as a family. Annually, on Dad's anniversary, we read *Freddie the Leaf*.

At the center of the chaos that comes with the unexpected death of a parent and a spouse are the puzzle pieces that come together and fit into our lives. We can't always explain why sometimes we are fearless as moms in the midst of a loss, and other times we simply collapse from the weight of the moment. As mothers, we have the ability to rearrange agendas to meet the needed objectives. This ability to adjust is what can help in the face of the chaos that occurs for our families as we seek academic degrees. The story of *Freddie the Leaf* was an example of that for me. What my family and I went through, Margaret Wheatley wrote about—as order at the center of chaos. As academic moms we can find that order, even in a children's book.

Completing my dissertation as a widow with two young children was a feat I could not have done without experiencing support and direction along the way. I did not see a strong finish as part of my story after losing my husband, but my children's voices through this journey were a source of strength. In small ways, our children can be that strength, such as when I went to get my son from school on the day I had of my dissertation defense. He had told his teacher, "My mom has a big test today; I want to call and check on her." He was only in third grade at the time, but by including him in my journey he could reach out in his own way to support me. When I got to his school to pick him up, his teacher had allowed him to make me a card, saying "Mom, I hoped you pass[ed]!" After I read his card, I said, "yes," and he said, "good job, Mom, love you." His teacher asked about my "big test" and she was the second person outside of my committee to know that I passed. It was a special moment because my son obviously had been thinking about me during the day, and that is the kind of support that will get widow-moms seeking academic degrees through the chaos.

Accepting that I did not have access to weekend relief given by grandparents, aunts, or uncles helped me put my energy into what I could do and could change. I did experience many of the sacrifices that Jody Jessup-Anger reviewed, involving the research on the challenges faculty women faced on the way to success. I could not change what I did not have available. Mothers entering academia should know that the path to an academic hood takes many twists and turns. Terry Muller's work on the persistence of women outlines how we will experience many joyful, as well as painful, lessons along the way to degree completion. For me, however, those were the bookends of remembrances that I honor as my story. My summary does not center on how I was at a total loss regarding how to keep up with the mortgage, private tuition, daycare, babysitter's fees, or general household expenses. My story centers on how I figured out how to move through the challenges of widowhood, as an academic mom. My story centers on the events during this time that moved me to a higher ground with a strong finish.

Today, I am the parent of two college students who have skills that grant them a unique voice to talk about affirming victories in difficult times. My son is an Eagle Scout. His Eagle Scout's project focused on grief and loss for youth. He donated the final project to our church in a ceremony that allowed his entire troop and friendship circle to witness his journey. Even today, he demonstrates a heart for those with special needs and I am sure this passion comes out of my dissertation work and his witnessing over the years of my advocacy work for those labeled with special needs. Coming right up behind her brother, my daughter has received the highest Girl Scout Award, the Girl Scout's Gold Award. Her project focused on building self-esteem in girls through sports. At her final project presentation, held in her middle school, all her teachers from first grade through eighth came to honor her accomplishment. She is a social justice advocate and to this day she is still involved in Big Brother/Big Sister, giving to and sharing with youngsters who have experienced challenges beyond their control. I want widows to be encouraged and know that there will be time when it looks like your efforts will not bear fruit. For me, being able to look back now and see the fruits of the experiences and then have the opportunity to share those experiences with other academic moms adds to my confirmation of a strong finish.

The affirmation of my journey is seen in my children's lives and how we weathered the chaos. Their stories are beginning and erase many of the leftover scares from my academic pursuit as a widow. Standing on the platform of the stage, prepared to received my Ed.D. in Educational Policy and Administration, I wondered in the those final moments if I had done the right thing for my family by pursuing this academic path as a widowed-mom. Needless to say, the answer came upon me quickly as I looked out at the faces of my two children—beaming, waving and giving me the thumbs up! The answer was clearly a "Yes!" We had conquered the hurdle of grief and loss together, so being on the platform was a victory for all of us. As I walked across the stage and shook the respected hand of each committee member, and acknowledged the smiles and head nods, I was able to look into the eyes of widowhood as Dr. Mom because I had not been defeated during the chaos.

I believe my experiences of being a mother and widow while pursuing an academic hood encapsulate the experiences of many women like myself. So, I leave the conversation of widows in pursuit of the academic hood as mothers with these thoughts: *Was it rough? Yes! Did I learn?*

Yes! Can others benefit from my story? I hope so. In the career I have today as a professor and administrator, I mentor young women. Some are non-traditional students who are moms, some are single. Many come to my office facing defeat or feeling defeat of some sort, and being academic moms, we share stories. I know to wait, listen, and then share my journey in short. Usually, by the end of our talk the response is: "I have no excuse not to do it," or "You are my inspiration," or "How did you manage?" Women as moms in academia must support each other, and one way is to tell our stories. I always encourage them to bring their child(ren) to my office, if they wish. As moms, we need to know that our children are welcome in the academic world. This act alone changes the dynamics of our relationships and it builds trust for us along the way.

My dissertation is dedicated to my children for the simple fact that they are my story and they shared it with me. My children still show an interest in my scholarship and I am often asked about the when and where of my next presentation. It is a simple way of asking me where we are traveling next on this journey that started sixteen years ago. Since finishing my degree and entering higher education, I have traveled to eleven major countries and continue to present my research—amazing, given that at one point I felt that it was worthless. I am grateful for the strength I have today because it did not come from the papers thrown on the floor or the tears shed over the death of my husband. My strength to finish came from the clarity of my children's role in my life. What academic moms can accomplish can be summarized in the final words of one committee member to me on the day I receive the needed five committee members' signatures that would grant me my degree. Dr. Bill Ammentorp's kind words came with a wink that guided me to go forth and make a difference: "Do well because that's what Dr. Moms do!"

WORKS CITED

Ahuja, Roshan D. and Kandi M. Stinson. "Female Headed Single Parent Families: An Exploratory Study of Children's Influences in Family Decision Making." *Advances in Consumer Research* 20 (1993): 469-74. Web. 30 July 2010.

Buscaglia, Leo. *The Fall of Freddie the Leaf: A Story of Life for All Ages.* Thorofare, NJ: Slack Incorporated, 1982. Print.

Chen, Martha Alter. *Why Widowhood Matters*. 04 June 2010. Web. 30 July 2010. <http://www.un.org/esa/gopherdata/conf/fwcw/pim/feature/2WIDOWS.TXT>.

"Gender Matters." Inside Higher Education. 16 December 2009. Web. 30 July 2010. http://www.insidehighered.com/news/2009/12/16/gender>.

Jessup-Anger, Jody E. *"Challenges of the Faculty Career for Women: Success and Sacrifice, A Book Review."* Sept 2008.Web. 30 July 2010. http://www.aaup.org/AAUP/pubsres/academe/2008/SO/br/brjess.htm>.

Kreider, Rose M. *Living Arrangements of Children: 2004*. Feb. 2008. Web. 30 July 2010. <http://www.census.gov/prod/2008pubs/p70-114>.

Kübler-Ross, Elisabeth. "Five Stages of Grief: Model for Death and Bereavement Counseling, Personal Change and Trauma." 1969. Web. <http://www.businessballs.com/elisabeth_kublerross_five_stages_of_grief.htm>.

Mallan, Lucy B. *Young Widows and Their Children: A Comparative Report*. 2004. Web. 30 July 2010. <http://www.socialsecurity.gov/policy/docs/ssb/v38n5/v38n5p3.pdf>.

Muller, Terry. "Persistence of Women in Online Degree-Completion Programs." *International Review of Research in Open and Distance Learning* 9.2 (June 2008). Web. <http://www.irrodl.org/index.php/irrodl/article/view/455/1042>.

National Center for Education Statistics. *"Educational Attainment: Better Than Meets the Eye, But Large Challenges Remain."* U.S. Department of Education, Pew Hispanic Center: Fact Sheet: University of California, 2002. Print.

Norris, Katherine. *Dakota: A Spiritual Journey*. New York: Houghton Mifflin Co, 1993. Print.

Vasquez, Michelle E. *Young Widowhood. Grieving Challenges*. 2005 Web. 30 July 2010. <http://ezinearticles.com/?Young-Widowhood---Grieving-Challenges&id=4208670>.

Wellman, Barry, and D. B. Tindall. "Social Network Analysis and Canadian Sociology." *The Canadian Journal of Sociology / Cahiers Canadiens de Sociologie* 26.3 (2001): 265-308. Web. 30 July 2010.

Wheatley, Margaret, J. *Leadership and the New Science: Learning About Order in a Chaotic World*. San Francisco: Berrett-Koehler, 1992. Print.

11.

Non-Tenure-Track Academic Work

The "Mommy Track" or a Strategy for Resistance?

JILL M. WOOD

MY ACADEMIC WORK is filled with contradictions, as is the case for many women in so-called "second tier" academic jobs. I earned my Ph.D. at a research one university, and as a result I am a very capable and skilled researcher specializing in women's health and sexuality. In the middle of my graduate career with a cushy research assistantship, I left this position in order to find meaning in academia, through teaching. Teaching satisfies something deep and primal in me; indeed, its rewards are much like mothering for me. Seeing students have "ah ha" moments, giving them the tools to discover their own power and to see their value in the world, helping them to unlearn assumptions that maintain their apathy as social citizens—these are gifts that feed my soul. I found my home in academia in a women's studies department, allowing me to produce meaningful scholarship about women's bodies and health, and most importantly for me, a space in which teaching had some value.

After a brief visiting assistant professor position at another university, I returned to the institution where I earned my degree to teach full time as a non-tenure-track faculty member in women's studies; I am still there. On purpose. I have a "good job" in terms of being a non-tenure-track faculty member. I am not an adjunct; I have a multiyear contract, my teaching load is reasonable, and I teach primarily 400-level courses in my area of expertise. I truly love the work that I do in my current position, but I'm also aware that my publications, like this one on non-tenure-track work as a mother in academia, don't "count" for me in terms of my evaluation. None of my scholarship has any promise of eventual monetary rewards for me, and actually if I factor in the cost of paying for childcare as I write, I actually lose money on scholarship. As is true for all non-tenure-track faculty, I am significantly underpaid and have poor job security, and have no further opportunity for advancement. I have been urged repeatedly to apply for tenure-track positions at my University as they become available; administrators and colleagues assure me that I am "good enough," suggesting to me that my colleagues imagine that I'm in this job as a last resort. In fact, I'm quite sure I am "good enough" for the tenure-track, but for me, a tenure-track job, with its seemingly unreasonable demands, just isn't worth it. I have two children, with a third due soon, and I am an unapologetically emotionally and physically present mother. You see, for me, my mothering is a beautiful part of me, and when I'm able to access the space of mothering outside the institution of motherhood,[1] this mothering place nurtures deep parts of my being, helping me to feel connected to myself, my children, and my community. Like Adrienne Rich describes in *Of Woman Born*, there are places in mothering that are so pleasurable and so meaningful that the joy seems endless. The opportunity to spend as much time as I can with my young children seems fleeting to me, and I don't want to pass it up, especially not for just, well, a "better" job.

My commitment to raising my children as I do wasn't always so clear cut to me; I felt a lot of pressure to get a "good" job upon completing my Ph.D., especially because I had won numerous research and teaching awards, indicating that I'm good at this academic thing. I interviewed for a tenure-track position in a women's studies department soon after having my first child. I brought my daughter (a nursing infant) and my husband with me to the out of town interview (he cared for her during the interview process). Well in advance of the interview, I requested breaks to pump breast milk, and I was told this request could be easily accommodated. Yet, after hours of meetings, guest teaching a class, and my job talk (read: very sore breasts), I asked for a few minutes to pump when an opportunity arose. The department head was scornful, and told me where the nearest bathroom was, which I indicated in an as nice as possible way, wasn't an ideal place to produce food (would you make food in a bathroom?!). At this point, I realized that I had "lost" the job, and then happily realized I didn't want the job (the job opening was for a women's health position in a women's studies department!). Yet, as a radical (cultural) feminist, I also realized this was a teachable and actionable moment, so I asked again where I could pump (notably there were several empty offices in the department wing). I was told again that I could use the bathroom down the hall, or pump where we were sitting—in a large conference room filled with members of the search committee. I got out my pump, took a deep breath, unbuttoned my shirt, attached the pump, and imagined being with my baby—my milk flowed. If you've ever pumped, you know that in order to do so you need to relax and B-R-E-A-T-H-E. For me to do so in the environment I was in, I needed to re-imagine my situation, to re-member being with my child, to convince my body that I was safe, even though, I clearly wasn't. In the midst of my meditative breast-pumping session in this large institutional conference room filled with women disdainful of me and my exposed breasts, I realized that I will never be comfortable hiding my commitment to mothering, and that it's not reasonable to expect a mother to give up what may very well be the most important and empowering moments of her life.

I finished the interview, and walked, sobbing, into the hotel room where my husband and daughter waited; sobbing at my naïveté that I could "have it all," and mourning the tenure-track path not taken. Yet thankfully, I knew that the contradictions in a system that enables a women's health expert to interview for a job in a women's studies department and shames her for breast-feeding her baby were not mine to claim; I felt no remorse and no embarrassment for choosing my family as more important than my academic career. Indeed, my metamorphosis during that weekend was so powerful that my husband too chose to prioritize our family over his career. Certainly, as a white heterosexual married woman, my privilege has enabled me to choose to prioritize my mothering practice over my paid work; yet other barriers to my working outside of the home in academia (as discussed later in the chapter) helped me to feel that my choice was legitimate, if not simply financially smart once I had calculated the cost of childcare in relation to my salary.

Fast forward five years; this morning on the phone, a friend of mine, a woman who is older than my mother and considers herself a second wave liberal feminist, explained to me, "It wasn't supposed to be like this for you, for women of your generation." We talked about the impossibility of "choosing" between a tenure-track job and a genuine commitment to caring for one's own children, and how this is so problematic for women. For women like me, I have "chosen" to remain in a poorly paid job with no opportunity for advancement; other women have "chosen" to hire replacement caregivers for the children in order to meet the unreasonable demands of their academic jobs. Yet it is the dichotomy between work in the university and work at home (which is still not considered as such) that serves to maintain this false sense of "choice" that academic mothers juggle. In our phone call, my friend asked me how I manage to not feel like I am being taken advantage of by the university in my current, non-tenure-track position. I explained, as I will detail in this chapter, how I came to believe that my current role as a non-tenure-track mother in academia is my empowered claim on my agency as a both a mother and an academic; I have consciously sought out a path that has enabled me to make personal choices about how I live my live within a system that offers little choice to mothers as a result of institutional and structural barriers. I argue here, as others have, that a sense of personal agency is still possible within the confines of institutional patriarchal limits on personal choice (see, for instance, Hayden and O'Brien Hallstein). My resistance to this culture in which academic mothers are encouraged to be ashamed of their mothering, or at the least to distance themselves from the realities of mothering, is my non-tenure-track job.

I view myself as having agency and choices within the academic system because I am the one who has chosen to prioritize my family; it's not the case that I have simply ended up in this job, I have pursued this career path in order to be able to mother in the way that is important to me. Daphne de Marneffe describes my interest in mothering my children in a full and present way as maternal desire. She explains, "The desire to mother is not only the desire to have children, but also the desire to care for them. It is not the duty to mother, or the compulsion to mother, or the concession to mothering when other options are not available. It is not the acquiescence to prescribed roles or the result of brainwashing. It is the longing felt by a mother to nurture her children; the wish to participate in their mutual relationship; and the choice, insofar as it is possible, to put her desire into practice (3). de Marneffe describes maternal desire in terms of women's agency, and I too experience my mothering as a form of empowerment and agency. For me, my mothering practice is rooted in my conceptualization of mothering as real work that is valuable, necessary, and vital. As a radical feminist,[2] my mothering work is even more important to me than my paid, academic work; it is from this perspective that I am able to make choices about my mothering practices even within an institution like the academy that is inherently oppressive for mothers. My maternal desire and my feminism enable me to claim my mothering practice as an active, empowering, radical feminist form of resistance to the prescribed notions of how academic mothers should behave.

The nature of tenure-track work is such that often the entire focus of an academic's being becomes their intellectual capacity and the products of this very narrow part of them. Tenured or tenure-track mothers are expected to prioritize the academy, often to the exclusion of other life interests and needs, such as family. In fact, structural and institutional barriers exist in the academy that serve to disconnect academic mothers from their families, in order to serve the needs of the academy. In this chapter, I argue that these institutional and structural barriers in the academy prevent mothers from realizing their maternal desire, and prevent these mothers from creating real change in the academy (after all, these barriers keep them too tired, far too overextended, etc.). To this end, I first review these barriers, explaining how such barriers create impossibility for mothers who wish to enact maternal desire, while simultaneously being successful in academia. A systematic review of these barriers reveals that such institutional barriers create an impossibly complex situation for academic mothers in which women are required to prioritize either their careers or families. Finally, the chapter will conclude with a reflexive narrative in which I offer my own strategy for making sense of my academic position in the context of my commitment to my mothering practice.

ACADEMIC MOTHERHOOD: WE'VE COME A LONG WAY BABY … MAYBE?

Feminist researchers and scholars have argued that academic mothers face a vast array of barriers and obstacles in their career pursuits (e.g. Drago et al. 2005; Swanson and Johnston; Williams). Some of these mothers, many of whom have left academia, have shared their personal stories through narrative writing, detailing their experiences of their constant struggles and chronic exhaustion related to issues such as the elusive work/life balance, "opting" out, the timing of children, maternity leave, overt discrimination at work, and oftentimes incapacitating stress from life on the tenure-track with (often young) children (e.g. Evans and Grant; Hile Basset).

Despite decades of women's efforts to work in the ivory tower in an egalitarian fashion, researchers have conclusively demonstrated that academia is rife with gender discrimination (e.g. AAUP, Drago et al. 2005; Mason and Goulden 2004a, 2004b; Williams). For instance, the American Association of University Professors (AAUP) 2001 Annual Report on the Economic Status of the Profession (commonly referred to as the "salary survey") found that women are underrepresented in tenured and tenure-track jobs in the academy. Yet, more than 57 percent of all instructors, lecturers and non-tenure-track jobs in the academy are held by women, while only 26 percent of full professors are women. Only 48 percent of women faculty are tenured, compared to 68 percent of male faculty who have tenure. Women still work predominately at non-research institutions, and men make more money than women do at all ranks and at all types of academic institutions. For instance, at the rank of full professor, women make only 88 percent of their male colleagues' salary. At Berkeley, only 25 percent of tenure-track faculty are women (Mason and Goulden 2003: 2). The situation for academic mothers is often so unbearable that 59 percent of married women with children considered leaving academic (Mason and Goulden, 2003, 8), and graduate students often reconsider academic careers if they intend to have children based on their observations of the seemingly irreconcilable differences between work and family life for tenure-track mothers (Masson and Goulden 2003: 7). Similarly, narratives from academic mothers in volumes like, *Mama, PhD* (Evans and Grant) and *Parenting and Professing* (Hile Basset) share women's lived experiences of the contradictions and impossibilities of life in academia for mothers. For many women, mothers especially, the institutional forms of oppression in the academy are simply unbearable, and as such increasing numbers of mothers are working in non-tenure-track jobs.

THE GYPSY SCHOLARS

Compared to tenured and tenure-track faculty, non-tenure-track faculty have been the focus of little research; the available research on non-tenure-track faculty typically focuses on the proportion of such faculty in an institution. For instance, various studies have found that the number of non-tenure-track faculty members have increased quite dramatically over the past decades, with researchers reporting that non-tenure-track faculty compose anywhere from 27 percent (Harper, Baldwin, Gansneder, and Chronister 238) to 43 percent of all faculty in U.S. colleges and universities ("Trends in Faculty Employment"). Researchers have also focused on the nature of non-tenure-track employment, including salary, job security, and prestige. The AAUP's report on the status on non-tenure-track faculty illustrates that non-tenure-track faculty are the lowest paid group of all faculty members (n.p.) and this has been corroborated by other researchers as well (e.g. Harper et al.). For instance, James Monks found that full time non-tenure-track faculty are paid nearly 30 percent less than tenure-track faculty, and part time non-tenure-track faculty are paid nearly 65 percent less than comparable full time tenure-track assistant professors (499). Elizabeth Harper and colleagues found that non-tenure-track faculty describe feeling marginalized and "ghettoized" (239), and that non-tenure-track faculty are especially concerned with lack of job security, an inability to advance in their positions, and concerns with compensation packages (253-256).

More recently, researchers have examined how women have come to make up the majority of non-tenure-track academics. Nicholas Wolfinger, Mary Anne Mason and Marc Goulden report that women are almost 50 percent more likely than men to hold non-tenure-track jobs, and that mothers are disproportionately represented in such jobs. An academic mother with a young child is 132 percent more likely to work in an adjunct position than a father with a similarly aged child. These researchers conclude that, "Young children not only push women off the tenure-track, they keep them off. Women with children under six are disproportionately likely to remain off the tenure-track" (1612). Yet, these researchers simultaneously acknowledge that non-tenure-track work is beneficial for mothers. Perhaps because of the benefits such jobs offer mothers, non-tenure-track work has become so feminized, especially by mothers and particularly in female dominated fields such as English, that women teaching introductory composition courses in academia is a field now referred to as "the kitchen" (Toth 53).

While non-tenure-track jobs are paid less, have less job security, little opportunity for advancement, and often have higher teaching loads compared to tenure-track jobs, perhaps the worst aspect of these jobs is their characterization as being second tier, gypsy work (e.g. Mason and Goulden 2004). Terms like, "gypsy scholar" illustrate the derogatory manner in which such non-tenure-track work is viewed. Indeed, even among researchers who seek to understand the realities of women and mothers in these non-tenure-track jobs, the language used to describe such work frames non-tenure-track work as less than ideal at best, and at worst, a mere consolation prize on the way to a "real" (tenure-track) job. For instance, Wolfinger, Mason, and Goulden say, "For many aspiring scholars, adjunct professorships are the academic graveyard, the place to go when all dreams of a tenure-track position has been extinguished" (1592).

In reading the scholarship on academic mothers in non-tenure-track jobs, it is clear that non-tenure-track work is viewed as conciliatory (e.g. Cross and Goldenberg 145). This assumes that women should be and want to be tenure-track academics, thereby preventing women from making the legitimate choice to work in academia in a non-tenure-track job. For me, the fact that I have been deemed "good enough" for the tenure-track only complicates my choice to remain off the tenure-track. Tenure track work is characterized by a set of unspoken and often unrecognized patriarchal standards; this male paragon of work expectations requires tenure-track academics to adopt a specific set of values in order to be successful. These ambiguous standards and expectations require an academic to irrevocably and constantly change one's life. As will be discussed later, men are better able to meet such demands because the male academic standards are based on men and therefore better mirror men's values and life experience, whether or not they are fathers. For women, mothers especially, these standards create an unshakable pressure in which tenure-track mothers feel (correctly so) that their work is never enough. These expectations also serve to shame "good enough" non-tenure-track mothers for their choice to operate outside the tenure-track system, or they shame non-tenure-track mothers into feeling not good enough because of the nature of these jobs. Either way, women are shamed for non-tenure-track work, even if it is an ideal situation for them, as it often is for mothers. This position privileges the importance of academic work over caretaking work, reinforcing the dichotomy between academic work and mothering.

While a majority of research on non-tenure-track employment assumes that this work is less than ideal, some researchers have begun to examine the benefits afforded to mothers through non-tenure-track work. In a study designed to understand how academic mothers' conceptualization of motherhood shapes women's academic selves, Debra Swanson and Deirdre Johnston found that part-time academic mothers are more able to separate their work lives from their home lives in ways that are not possible for full time academic mothers. One interviewee explains how avoiding full time work in the academy has benefited her as a mother: "I'm glad that I have that flexibility that I don't have such a big deadline hanging over my head that I can't stop to enjoy my kids and just go at a slower pace that I think it's a little bit more moderate and healthy" (7). Harper and colleagues found that non-tenure-track faculty were generally happy in their jobs, and often enjoyed their ability to focus on teaching without the pressures of publishing (242). Similarly, Daniel Feldman and William Turnley found that some academics prefer non-tenure-track positions which offered more flexibility as well as the ability to focus more on teaching (285). Non-tenure-track academic positions offer many advantages to mothers, namely flexibility, the option of part time employment, and a more reasonable work load (Wolfinger, Mason, and Goulden 1595), yet non-tenure-track work is not viewed as a legitimate avenue for mothers to simultaneously pursue caretaking and academic work. Recently, Cross and Goldenberg have called for a new conceptualization of non-tenure-track work (one free of judgment), extolling the virtues and possibilities of this work for many academics (144). Clearly, non-tenure-track work is not viewed as a legitimate career choice for academics, yet the barriers to achieving tenure for academic mothers are often insurmountable, as discussed in this next section.

IT'S NEVER ENOUGH: LIFE FOR MOTHERS ON THE TENURE-TRACK

As discussed earlier, academics are expected to adopt a set of male values that guide their work expectations and standards. Women, mothers especially, are disadvantaged by virtue of their gender and their caretaking work. While tenure-track mothers may not be able to elucidate how they fall short of these expectations (after all, they are indiscernible), they are nevertheless made to feel that their work is never enough; research on tenure-track mothers' career success confirms this assertion. For instance, Joan Williams reviews over 100 studies to document gender biased discrimination against women in academia, particularly against mothers. Gendered stereotypes, in a variety of forms, explain how women and men can be similarly qualified and even achieve requirements for tenure at equivalent rates yet men are judged as more competent and are therefore more successful. Similarly, Mason and Goulden examine gender bias in the academy noting that increased numbers of women in academia has not resulted in women's equality, due in large part to what the researchers term "leaks in the academic pipeline for women," which explains how and why women faculty leave academia at various points in their career for family-related issues. Alice Fothergill and Kathryn Feltey describe the paradoxical flexibility of tenure-track jobs for mothers, describing how on the one hand, academia offers mothers flexibility. Yet, conversely, academia adheres to a male work model including 60 hour work weeks, travel, relocation for work, and that academic culture makes it quite difficult for women to attend to family responsibilities. Similarly, Mason and Goulden examine how academic women juggle various competing demands in their 2002 study, "Do Babies Matter?," and found that babies do matter, not just for women but also for men in the academy. The timing of having children is especially important in how tenure-track faculty proceed in their careers; men who become fathers within five years of completing their Ph.D., are 38 percent more likely to earn tenure than women who become mothers in this same time period. In a later study, Mason and Goulden again ask, "Do babies matter?", yet this time in the context of how faculty make decisions about having children based on their career. The researchers found that men who marry and have children are more successful in academia, while the opposite is true for women. The researchers found that women frequently delay and/or put off having a baby in lieu of their career; among women who secure a tenure-track job before having any children, only one in three will ever have a baby. The researchers also found that women who earn tenure are more than twice as likely as tenured men to never marry, and that women who are married before starting a tenure-track job are 50 percent more likely to divorce or separate than their male counterparts. Moreover, Robert Drago and colleagues (2005) studied tenure-track and tenured faculty's engagement in bias avoidance behaviors, which are ways in which faculty alter their behavior in order to avoid bias from colleagues related to their responsibilities as parents. For instance, a faculty member who does not stop their tenure clock, take family leave after the birth or adoption of a child, or use other family leave policies in order to avoid seeming less invested in their academic lives engages in bias avoidance. The researchers found that women engage in more bias avoidance than do men; 18.9 percent of men and 32.8 percent of women performed their normal teaching load without asking for a reduced load even with they needed it for family responsibilities, and 51.1 percent of academic mothers returned to their academic responsibilities sooner than they were ready to do so. Almost half of faculty mothers reported missing out on important events for their child so that they would be taken seriously in their career. Notably, the researchers report that such bias avoiding behaviors work! Women who engage in such behaviors earn tenure earlier in their careers and at an earlier age than women who do not report such behavior.

These institutional barriers for academic mothers serve several functions, and notably these barriers most severely penalize tenure-track mothers. First, these barriers disconnect women from their ability to experience maternal desire because as de Marneffe explains, maternal desire involves a woman's interest, ability, and her experience of caring for her children in a way that holds deep meaning for her. The academic culture for mothers is such that in order to earn tenure, women must distance themselves from their children, sacrifice caring for their own needs, or a combination of both of these strategies. Secondly, these barriers enable the male academic standards and values (discussed earlier) to exist; in order to meet academic standards women must adopt these male values. Women who choose not to participate in this academic culture are either not tenured or are shamed for not working on the tenure-track. This explains mothers' experience of feeling that "it's never enough" on the tenure-track, or the shame for being "good enough" to be tenure-track but not choosing the "right" academic path. If academic mothers are shamed, either by virtue of their non-tenure-track status or by attempting to combine the tenure-track with children, why work on the tenure-track given all its costs? In addition to these institutional barriers that disadvantage academic mothers, nonexistent family leave policies further complicate the ability of academic mothers to make legitimate choices about how to work in academia and authentically care for their children.

FAMILY LEAVE POLICIES

Kelly Ward and Lisa Wolf-Wendel (2004) address work and family policies in the academy, asking what policies exist and how faculty use them. The researchers note that family leave policies are markedly disjointed among U.S. colleges and universities. They describe three types of policy environments: institutions with no policies (or policies that were completely unusable), institutions that had policies, but faculty were too afraid to use them, and institutions that had newer more family-friendly policies, but faculty still rarely used them. Of course, family leave policies are useless if faculty are afraid to take advantage of them, which Ward and Wolf-Wendel term "the fear factor." Other researchers have also found evidence of the fear factor. For instance, researchers on the Faculty and Families Project at Penn State report that between 1992 and 1999, only 4 of 257 tenure-track parents took any formal family leave (Drago, Crouter, Wardell, and Willits). Ward and Wolf-Wendel explain that at the root of the fear factor is the assumption by many academics that a woman can choose to plan her pregnancy and the birth of a baby at times that are convenient and conducive to her career, ignoring the fact that many women do not have ideal pregnancies, problem-free deliveries, and that women can and do get pregnant at less than ideal times. In addition to such problematic assumptions, Ward and Wolf-Wendel explain how such thinking damages the academy:

> [Women] Feeling obligated to plan in this way puts work and family in opposition to one another. Failure to help faculty integrate work and family smoothly could compromise higher education's ability to recruit and retain quality faculty members. … Conceptions of the academic career that see work and family as "either-or" propositions—that is, that faculty can have a career or a family, but not both—do not bode well for the future of the academic profession (4, online view).

Indeed other researchers have found that graduate students are concerned with their future inability to combine their careers with their interest in having a family, especially for graduate students who are at research universities who have experienced firsthand the culture in which women are forced to "choose" between a career and children (Golde and Dore; Mason, Goulden and Frasch).

In an effort to improve the academic climate for women surrounding the balance between academic work and family, the AAUP has developed guidelines for academic administrators in an effort to change policies and academic culture. The guidelines make specific suggestions about instituting new policies, as well as changing the culture of academia. The AAUP statement explains that the pervasive nature of academic work has been at the detriment to the family, noting that academic culture and policies are based both theoretically and historically on a male model. Other institutions and scholars have also made recommendations for offsetting the disproportionate demands on women faculty, many of them mothers. For instance, Drago and colleagues (2001) advise implementing a part-time tenure-track (3, online view). Mason and Goulden share the University of California's new family friendly policies, designed to be competitive in recruiting and retaining faculty who have family responsibilities, especially women. The package includes options for part-time tenure-track options, child care solutions, and ways to help faculty re-enter the academic world following a leave for family care (2003: 13-14).

In addition to changing the culture of academic motherhood through institutional policies, Anne Stockdell-Giesler and Rebecca Ingalls seek to rewrite the rhetoric of academic motherhood in which women are forced to "choose" between having children and earning tenure, noting that this false dichotomy between work and family does not exist in women's real lives. The authors note that despite some improvements in parental leave policies, it is the rhetoric of academic motherhood that reinforces the notion that women's work as mothers is completely separate from their work as academics. The authors explain, "As teachers and scholars, we nurture ideas and minds in our classrooms and scholarship. The metaphors of birthing and parenting are present in both of these areas of faculty work" (1, online view). The authors seek to use these metaphors to rewrite the rhetoric of family life in academia. Indeed, feminist pedagogue bell hooks has noted in her book, *Teaching to Transgress*, that teaching emerges from bodies, yet women's bodies especially are invisible in the academy. Academic mothers produce work via their bodies in a context in which the maternal body is largely ignored (see, for example, Kimberly Wallace-Sanders, "A Vessel of Possibilities: Teaching Through the Expectant Body").

EMBODIMENT OF MATERNAL DESIRE: TAKING UP MATERNAL SPACE

This chapter proposes a rewriting of one type of academic motherhood, rooted in the freeing possibilities of non-tenure-track academic work as a form of resistance to the unreasonable demands and requirements of tenure-track academic positions. The pitfalls of what have been termed "second tier" faculty positions have been well noted, most importantly that the "gypsy scholars" of academia are primarily women, many times mothers (Mason and Goulden 2003: 6). Yet, these positions offer academic mothers the possibility of different life choices than what oftentimes exists for most mothers on the tenure-track. While the oppressive nature of these non-tenure-track "mommy track" jobs has been well documented, the freeing possibilities, the subversive and empowering nature of refusing to capitulate to the grueling nature of motherhood on the tenure-track has not yet been well established. Using my perspective as a radical (cultural) feminist, I suggest that academic mothers who value caretaking work can use non-tenure-track positions to subvert current discourses that dictate what it currently means to be a mother in the academy. In this way, non-tenure-track mothers can rewrite academic motherhood through their maternal desire.

In the beginning of the chapter, I share my experiences on a job interview for a tenure-track job in women's health, and how this was a pivotal experience for me in terms of feeling pulled between being a mother and an academic. My journey to resistance of a life on the tenure-track grew, in large part, out of my understanding of the many barriers and forms of discrimination that academic mothers face, as described earlier in the chapter. My metamorphosis from a promising new Ph.D., fresh out of a research one university to where I am now, ever more confidant in my refusal of tenure-track work in order to nurture my maternal desire, has been a six year journey on a path which I have actively built.

This final section of the chapter consists of a reflexive narrative in which I offer my own strategy for making sense of my academic position in the context of my commitment to my mothering practice. Researchers and scholars explain that the value in reflexive narrative is that it is both a methodological tool for critically examining one's own experience (Webster and Mertova), and an approach to offer others the opportunity to make meaning of their own experi ences from an alternative perspective (Lyle 294). Bloom describes the ebb and flow of meaning making that results from reflexive narrative, describing a "journey of becoming" through reflecting on past experiences, allowing an individual to move forward in an experience with a new, altered (possibly enlightened) perspective (162). In this way, I offer my own reflexive narrative on my experience as a non-tenure-track academic mother seeking to resist the negative implications associated with life on the "mommy track," in part as an effort to reconceptualize the notion that non-tenure-track work can be a viable and even desired life and career path.

From my perspective, the nature of academic tenure-track work is such that the entire focus of a person's being becomes their intellectual capacity and the products of this very narrow part of themselves. Tenured or tenure-track mothers are expected and required to prioritize the academy, often to the exclusion of other life interests and needs, such as family. As discussed earlier, structural and institutional barriers exist in the academy that serve to disconnect academic mothers from their families in order to better serve the needs of the academy. In fact, these institutional and structural barriers in the academy prevent mothers from realizing their maternal desire, and serve to keep mothers constantly struggling with time, energy, and the elusive balance between their academic career and family. For instance, the lack of formal family-leave policies in the academy create a difficult situation for academic mothers in which they are often individually responsible for creating maternity leave policies for themselves. For tenure-track mothers, the very perception by colleagues and administrators that they need time off to care for themselves and/ or an infant can damage, and often ruin, their careers. Lack of family leave policies, coupled with the various other forms of discrimination that academic mothers face, creates a culture in which academic mothers are pushed and pulled in all directions. Mothers on the tenure-track must devise strategies to maintain their careers, like the impossibility of creating an optimal time to have a baby that coincides with their work schedules and biological clocks (which are likely ticking away). Similarly, mothers must implement ingenious and creative strategies to arrange for childcare, which is difficult under normal circumstance, but outrageously complicated in terms of travel to conferences, attendance at evening events, and other socially oriented activities that may be critical to how women are perceived by colleagues and administrators.

My decision to forgo tenure-track work is due, in part, to observing my friends who are tenure-track mothers. All have gone to extreme lengths to arrange for childcare; one had to fly grandparents across the country for extended childcare in order to travel out of the country for a conference. Another friend needed to coordinate how to arrange to freeze and transport breast milk to her infant while she was abroad for a conference. Yet another friend regularly checks in to a hotel for the weekend (at least once a month) to "catch up on work" so that her irregular sleeping and waking hours don't disrupt her children. She explains that it's easier for her children, who look forward to seeing her on weekends since she's so busy during the week, to not even see her in the house when she has an important deadline. She feels too guilty, she says, to repeatedly explain to them throughout the weekend that she needs to prioritize her work over spending time with them. And yet another friend found the only way to combine her new out-of-town tenure-track job was to live apart from her young children three days a week. Actually, I have three friends, all tenured or tenure-track mothers, who live separately from their families almost half-time.

Still, many of my other women friends in academia have told me that having children seems impossible to them while they are working on tenure, to the extent that some have been forced to end relationships over the contentious issue of whether or not to have children, and others are horribly grief stricken as they struggle with fertility issues in their late thirties and early forties. For women on the tenure-track who want to parent, the situation seems crazy making. Indeed, by making motherhood on the tenure-track so impossible, the academy requires women to often forgo having children in order to succeed in their academic career; yet academic men are not required to make similar choices between their desire for children and their desire for a successful career. Women without children, like men, serve the interests of the academy quite well, and indeed these women are often the most successful and highest ranking women in the academy. Alternatively, women who attempt to combine life on the tenure-track with motherhood are often so overwhelmed, so under-supported, and have frequently internalized the lunacy that the patriarchal academy has created, that they are simply too busy to create change within the system. These women often can't change the academy; they are quite simply too overwhelmed, overtired, and too overworked. Finally, there are mothers like me—who have for whatever reason circumvented the tenure-track, and I propose that it is this group of women who are best able to resist the institutional barriers that the academy has created.

I do not intend to be disdainful or judgmental of tenure-track or tenured mothers, but in all honesty, prioritizing anything before my children and perhaps most importantly, my experience with being my children in terms of what it means for me, is simply inconceivable. It pains me, literally, to watch my friends have to check in to a hotel to meet a grant deadline or pass off a brand new baby to attend a conference in another country. These mothers, my friends, have performed herculean feats to mother their children in the best possible way they can while on the tenure-track (the hours of breast milk pumping in bathrooms alone deems them saints, I think). What is missing, for them, I believe is their ability to embody their maternal desire if they so desire, because in the academy maternal desire is incompatible with success on the tenure-track. My embodiment of maternal desire is the form my resistance takes, and it's empowering and freeing for me. Sonja Foss and Kare Foss suggest that the act of claiming taboo choices is, in itself, a form of revolution, and for an academic woman claiming the work of motherhood as a deeply moving and meaningful experience is certainly taboo.

I am currently pregnant, and I have just recently begun to appear pregnant now with my round belly poking out through my clothes, bumping into things because I'm not quite used to it yet. My protruding belly seems out of place in the academy, perhaps because academic women often hide their pregnancies, as a way to seem more professional or more committed to their careers. Other scholars have written about the taboo nature of pregnant professors, noting that the visible nature of pregnancy often clashes with others expectations of what an academic woman should look like (for example, see Wallace-Sanders). Colleagues have looked at me quizzically as I proudly display my newly rounded belly (no blousy shirts to disguise my pregnancy here!) and even other academic mothers I know can barely hide their disbelief as I explain, "Yes, this will be number three"; "Yes, this pregnancy was planned," or if I'm feeling somewhat less generous, "Yes, I know how 'it' happened." I refuse to hide the manifestation of my maternal desire that is my pregnant belly, yet this notion is so foreign to academics, even to academic mothers. My pregnancy pride feels liberating because I am taking up space in the academy (literally and figuratively), claiming a space for mothers who are connected to their maternal desire; my resistance to the academic culture that seeks to distance women from their pregnancies, from their families, creates a space in which other mothers can refuse to be overly modest about their growing bellies, too.

My resistance to tenure-track work is most pleasurable to claim when I am able to remind colleagues that my non-tenure-track status is my choice; I have not just ended up in this position. For instance, last year my teaching and scholarship was highlighted by three awards, all of which were presented at ceremonies attended by colleagues and administrators. Because I was chosen to represent our faculty at our college's commencement ceremony (a very prestigious honor), I was invited to a lunch with our Board of Trustees and our University President. I was asked at all three award ceremonies if I'd be interested for applying to a tenure-track position at our University. Each time I graciously but firmly answered "no" to the astonishment and bewilderment of colleagues and administrators. As kindly as possible, I explained my maternal desire, and that my academic life is actually a very small part of myself, that I have other interests that I enjoy in my life. I'm never sure if my refusal to even apply for a tenure-track job is written off as naïve or just plain obstinate, but I do know that the fact that I am desired as a tenure-track faculty member fuels the power of my resistance. The fact that I am actively resisting the tenure-track is very freeing for me; I have wonderfully meaningful interactions with students, am lauded for my academic accomplishments, and yet my academic work is on my own terms in a way that is consistent with my values and priorities as a mother. I am honest about my maternal desire in other ways, too. I never hide that I have family commitments that often conflict with meetings that run into dinner time, and when invited to a department party, I always bring my children. I make point of being clear that my attachment to my children isn't out of duty, but out of my desire to spend time with them. I've noticed that other women in the department have started bringing their children to events too.

For me, non-tenure-track work is part of my path to mothering but I resist the categorization of being on the "mommy track." My ability to be true to my maternal desire would not be possible in a tenure-track job, as I believe the institutional barriers for academic mothers serve to keep mothers in these jobs too busy to take up (maternal) space. In resisting tenure-track work, I have created a space in which both forms of my work can co-exist. At the end of the day, I have scholarship that I am proud of, moments spent witnessing students' embrace of true learning, and genuine interactions with my children that feed my soul. I am openly proud of my mothering practice in my department, my classroom, and my community. My resistance to enter tenure-track work is the best choice I've ever made; resistance for me is creating a space in which my "second tier" job is something other than a consolation prize. Foss and Foss explain, "resistance is to deliberately choose what we want for our world instead of resisting what we do not want, moving toward rather than away from something. We focus on or pay attention to those things we choose for our world, and we ignore what we do not like" (50). The possibility exists for non-tenure-track jobs to help move academic mothers towards their embodiment of maternal desire in a way that is empowering; academic mothers in non-tenure-track jobs can enact agency, both as women and as mothers, by claiming their (maternal) space.

The author would like to thank Helen Kollar McArthur-Eastman and Rino Sato for their help with library research on this chapter, and the editors for their support and insightful suggestions.

[1]As other scholars (e.g. O'Reilly; O'Brien Hallstein) who draw on Rich's work suggest, there is a significant distinction between patriarchal institutional motherhood and mothering as practice, which has the potential to be deeply pleasurable, rewarding, and empowering to women.

[2]To be more specific, I describe myself as a radical cultural feminist, and this feminist perspective locates women's source of power within the potentially transformative work of reproduction and mothering. As such, this feminism enables me to privilege my maternal desire because mothering is valued as real and essential work based, in part, on women's ability to transform future generations. Rosemary Tong provides a thorough overview of radical cultural feminism as distinct from other types of feminism.

WORKS CITED

American Association of University Professors (AAUP). "Academe Online: Balancing Faculty Careers and Family Work, 90.6" November-December 2004. AAUP March 2010<http://www.aaup.org/ AAUP /pubsres/academe/2004/ND/>.

American Association of University Professors (AAUP). "Statement of Principles on Family Responsibilities and Academic Work." November 2001. AAUP. February 2010 <http://www.aaup.org/AAUP/pubsres/policydocs/contents/workfam-stmt.htm>.

American Association of University Professors (AAUP). "The Status of Non-Tenure-Track Faculty." June 1993. AAUP. February 2010 <http:// www.aaup.org/AAUP/comm/rep/nontenuretrack.htm>.

Cross, John G. and Edie N. Goldenberg. "Off-Track Vetting." *The Aca-*

demics Handbook. Third ed. Ed. A. Leigh Deneef and Craufurd D. Goodwin. Durham: Duke University Press, 2007. 143-154.

de Marneffe, Daphne. *Maternal Desire: On Children, Love, and the Inner Life.* New York: Little, Brown, and Company. 2004.

Drago, Robert et al. "Bias Against Caregiving." *Academe* 91.5 (2005): 22-25.

Drago, Robert, A. C. Crouter, M. Wardell, and B. S. Willits. "Final Report for The Faculty and Families Project." *The Pennsylvania State University Work/ Family Working Papers* 01-02. University Park, 2001.

Evans, Elrena and Caroline Grant, eds. *Mama PhD: Women Write about Motherhood and Academic Life.* New Brunswick, NJ: Rutgers University Press, 2008.

Feldman, Daniel C. and William H Turnley. "Contingent Employment in Academic Careers: Relative Deprivation among Adjunct Faculty." *Journal of Vocational Behavior* 64 (2004): 284-307

Foss, Sonja K. and Karen A. Foss. "Our Journey to Repowered Feminism: Expanding the Feminist Toolbox." *Women's Studies in Communication* 32.1 (2009): 36-62.

Fothergill, Alice and Kathryn Feltey. "'I've Worked Very Hard and Slept Very Little': Mothers on the Tenure-track in Academia." *Journal of the Association for Research on Mothering* 5.2 (2003): 7-19.

Golde, C. M. and T. M. Dore. "At Cross Purposes: What the Experiences of Doctoral Students Reveal About Doctoral Education." A Report Prepared for the Pew Charitable Trust. Philadelphia, 2001. <www.PhD-survey.org>

Harper, Elizabeth P., Roger G. Baldwin, Bruce G. Gansneder and Jay L. Chronister. "Full-time Women Faculty Off the Tenure-track: Profile and Practice." *The Review of Higher Education* 24.3 (2001): 237-257.

Hayden, Sara and D. Lynn O'Brien Hallstein, eds. *Contemporary Maternity in an Era of Choice: Explorations into Discourses of Reproduction.* New York: Lexington Books, 2010.

Hile Bassett, Rachel, ed. *Parenting and Professing.* Nashville: Vanderbilt University Press, 2005.

hooks, bell. *Teaching to Transgress: Education as the Practice of Freedom.* New York: Routledge. 1994.

Lyle, E. "A Process of Becoming: In Favour of a Reflexive Narrative Approach." *The Qualitative Report* 14.2 (2009) 293-298.

Mason, Mary Ann and Marc Goulden. "Do Babies Matter (Part II):

Closing the Baby Gap." *Academe* 90.6 (2004a): 10-15.

Mason, Mary Ann and Marc Goulden. "Marriage and Baby Blues: Re-defining Gender Equity in the Academy." *Annals of the American Academy of Political and Social Science* 596 (2004b): 86-103.

Mason, Mary Ann, Marc Goulden and Karie Frasch. "Why Graduate Students Reject the Fast Track." *Academe* 95.1 (2009): 11-16.

Monks, James. "The Relative Earnings of Contingent Faculty in Higher Education." *Journal of Labor Research* 28 (2007): 481-501.

O'Brien Hallstein, Lynn D. "Conceiving Intensive Mothering: The Mommy Myth, Maternal Desire and the Lingering Vestiges of Feminist Matrophobia." *Journal of the Association for Research on Mothering* 8.1,2 (2006): 96-108.

O'Reilly, Andrea. *The Encyclopedia of Motherhood*. Thousand Oaks, CA: Sage Publications. 2010.

Rich, Adrienne. *Of Woman Born: Motherhood as Experience and Institution*. New York: W.W. Norton and Company, 1986.

Stockdell-Giesler, Anne and Rebecca Ingalls. "Faculty Mothers." *Academe* 93.4 (2007): 38-40.

Swanson, Debra H. and Deirdre D. Johnston. "Mothering in the Ivy Tower: Interviews with Academic Mothers." *Journal of the Association for Research on Mothering* 5.2 (2003): 62-73.

Tong, Rosemarie. *Feminist Thought: A More Comprehensive Introduction*. Third ed. Boulder: Westview Press, 2009.

Toth, Emily. "Women in Academia (With updated afterword)." *The Academics Handbook*. Third ed. Ed. A. Leigh Deneef and Craufurd D. Goodwin. Durham: Duke University Press, 2007. 47-61.

"Trends in Faculty Employment." *Chronicle of Higher Education Almanac* (2000): 34-41.

Wallace-Sanders, Kimberly. "Vessel of Possibilities: Teaching Through the Expectant Body." *Teacher's Body: Embodiment, Authority, and Identity in the Academy*. Ed. Diane P. Freedman. New York: Albany State University of New York Press, 2003. 187-197.

Ward, Kelly and Lisa Wolf-Wendel. "Fear Factor: How Safe Is It to Make Time for Family?" *Academe* 90.6 (2004): 28-31.

Webster, Leonard and Patricie Mertova. *Using Narrative Inquiry as a Research Method*. London: Routledge, 2007.

Williams, Joan C. "Hitting the Maternal Wall." *Academe* 90.6 (2009): 16-20.

Wolfinger, Nicholas H., Mary Ann Mason and Marc Goulden. "Stay in the Game: Gender, Family Formation and Alternative Trajectories in the Academic Life Course." *Social Forces* 87.3 (2009): 1591-1621.

12.
Demeter on Strike

Fierce Motherhood on the Picket Line and the Playground

LAURIE J. C. CELLA

I N HER ESSAY, "THE FACTS, THE STORIES," Leah Bradshaw argues that it is impossible to ask an academic mother to choose which identity, mother or scholar, is more important to her:

> Fierce loves compete for one's loyalty, and I see no way out of the tension that characterizes the life of a woman who feels these twin passions. We are, as Aristotle says, a combination of what we are given by nature, the way in which we are habituated, and what we choose.... My life is messy and highly unprofessional, and I am a scholar. If someone were to ask me point blank who I am, I would have to say all these things. I am a woman. I am a mother. I am a scholar. (122)

These twin passions shape my life, and so I have learned to craft a maternal vision that allows for loss, for growth, and for continual reminders that that fierce love I feel for my children can exist in tandem with the fierce love I have for my academic identity. Bradshaw's description of love as "fierce" is one that resonates for me because I didn't always understand fierceness as a key element of mothering. As a girl and young woman, I had been encouraged to take myself seriously as an individual, to strive for the highest degree possible, and to make my own dreams come true. I had worked with a single-minded focus on these goals, and foolishly believed that this focus would take me through having children as well. I didn't realize that my ambitions had a masculine focus, or that having Cody would challenge my ideas about achievement or academic success. I imagined that the academic life would simply accommodate children, and now I see that as a naïve view. I know that these twin passions will never rest easy in my heart—at some points, taking Cody to his friend's birthday party will be the high point of my day; at others, with an article finished, a class complete and grades in, my academic self will rest easy. I have learned that these two fierce loves are simply a part of my identity, and my struggle lessened once I understood three key aspects of academic mothering: that time becomes more complicated because it is so valuable, that mother-mentors, those who have juggled these demands most recently, provide the most practical, and often the most life-saving support, and finally, that the bonds between academic mothers, once strengthened into a visible and productive community, translate into a powerful community of support and encouragement. I have learned that without this community, the struggle is long, and often too hard to bear alone.

ACADEMIC BLINDERS: THE COST OF THE INDIVIDUAL QUEST

When I began graduate school and before I had children, I had internalized a "quest" mentality; in other words, I believed that staying late at the library, spending all my weekends on research, giving all of myself to my work—that was the test of the true academic. In "Ideal Mama, Ideal Worker," Jean-Anne Sutherland writes about the definition of the "good" graduate student: "We know that, in most cases, the graduate student who plows through at breakneck speed, puts in those long hours, and produces the most is the most valued and revered" (216). My first graduate level oral presentation is a painful example of my endless devotion to this masculine ideal. It was a Chaucer class, and I was assigned *Triolus and Cressida*—a work I knew nothing about. I spent my life in the dusty stacks, coming out only to eat, and even then, I would snack over photocopied articles. The stacks of books and articles eventually threatened to take over my tiny graduate dorm room. I constructed a ten page, double-sided handout, and while my peers groaned at the "bar" I had set as the first presenter, my professor smiled at my "determination," and awarded me a higher grade in the class. However, by the end of that first semester, I had worked myself so hard that my physical health suffered; my back began to spasm, and I woke up one morning unable to move without excruciating pain. My friend Joanne clucked at my stupidity, but still she brought me soup, magazines and support. Unfortunately, this physical sign that my priorities were out of balance did not sway me from my single-minded drive; I began reading my Chaucer text during prescribed massages; clearly missing the most relaxing aspects of a massage. I soldiered on, eventually presenting my Chaucer essay at a graduate level conference, and chastising myself for losing any time to ill health.

Then, in the summer of 2004, as I began searching for a dissertation topic, I came across the heroic working women of the Gastonia strike, and I was instantly attracted to their tenacity and fierceness. Like me, they fought for what they wanted in a masculine arena, though they went even further to attract the national media, and change perception of what working women could achieve. Strikers like a woman named "Texas Bill" wore men's clothing in order to establish her strength and independence; another, "Trixie Perry," became known for her "wandering eye," and became a symbol of what historian Jacquelyn Dowd Hall, in her article "Disorderly Women: Gender and Militancy in the Appalachian South," called the "erotic undercurrent" of the strike.[1]

At the same time, the difficult challenges of mothering and working quickly became a central element of the Gastonia strike. Ella May Wiggins, a 29-year-old mother of five, led rallies by singing "Mill Mother's Lament" and organized across racial divides. When she was murdered by management thugs on the way to a rally, she instantly became a symbol of the strike, and for working-class mothers across the country. However, at the time point in my graduate career, I wasn't ready to view mothers as "heroic," and so I ignored any evidence that these striking women used their maternity as part of their motivation for a better life. Even as my husband Matthew and I decided we were ready to have a baby and become parents, I wasn't willing to bring mothering into my research. I wanted the women I wrote about to be fiercely independent, troublemakers with no ties to anyone else, rule-breakers who would grab a rifle out of a soldier's hand, but definitely not mothers.

In the summer of 2005, I was entering my second trimester, and still living the life of an unfettered, single-minded researcher. I spent a few hours every day in my cramped research carrel, searching for more evidence that these women were interested in romance, freedom, independence, but certainly not anything so domestic and boring as motherhood. I would sneak granola bars, apples, and crackers into my study space to keep hunger away as I wrote. Paging through Dowd Hall's book, *Like a Family: The Making of a Southern Cotton Mill World*, I pounced on anything that would paint a wider picture of the women's social lives; I wanted to know as much as I could about women like Trixie Perry and Texas Bill, the real strikers, so I could trace the way that the six Gastonia novelists had altered their stories, and I kept coming back to Ella May Wiggins, the working mother who had become a symbol of the strike itself. I was fascinated by her leadership ability—she organized many of the African Americans who also worked at the factory, but she was also known for her wild ways; she seemed to embody that erotic undercurrent that Dowd Hall describes in "Disorderly Women"; she was exactly the kind of "disorderly woman" that functioned as a leader for these striking women.

According to Gastonia labor historians, Ella May's life experiences and her singular efforts as a union leader led her to become the most recognizable heroine of the Gastonia labor struggle. Ella May married John Wiggins while still in her teens, took a job at the American Mill in Bessemer City, and had borne nine children by the age of twenty-nine. By that time, her husband had deserted her, and she began to search for night work so that she could be home with her children by day. When the strike broke out in Gastonia, Ella May became a regular at union meetings, and often led rallies with renditions of "Mill Mother's Lament" and a variety of other songs. Ella May's identity as a single mother of five (four of her children had died of malnutrition and poor health care) made her extremely useful as a recognizable icon for the radical media. When she was murdered, pictures of her five orphaned children mourning at her funeral appeared in *Working Woman, The Labor Defender, The Daily Worker*, and local newspapers. Many of the stories describing her murder highlight her role as mother as the primary reason she became involved in the union. For example, the editor of *The Working Woman*, a Communist periodical focused on the plight of working women, argued that sympathies should lie with this woman primarily as a fallen mother: "Ella May wrote the brief story of her life, *first as mother of a mountaineer's family of five*, and later as an impassioned pleader in action and in writings for the organization of the textile mill 'hands'" (my emphasis December 1929).

As I pored over these photos of Ella May, I was disturbed by the way that the media, and even scholarly work, seemed to elide her "disorderly" behavior in order to highlight her status as mother. It was true that she owned her role as mother; she authored the song, "Mill Mother's

Lament" and used her children in her speeches and negotiations with management. However, I was not willing to view Ella May as only or primarily a mother; to me, her strength came from her ability to work and to lead her fellow workers, and what made even more interesting to me was that Ella May had a "bad reputation" whose "character was not above complaint" (Salmond 51). In her article "Radical Mothers: Maternal Testimony and Metaphor in Four Novels of the Gastonia Strike," Lisa Schreibersdorf points out that Ella May's identity as a mother has provided the dramatic contours of the literary representations of her life and death: "Although she had walked the picket line and served the union in other roles, the roles of mother and singer-songwriter of the often reprinted "Mill Mother's Lament" (or, "How it Grieves the Heart of a Mother") consistently describe this "martyr" who became a defining character of the strike" (307). In her analysis of the Gastonia novels written by women, Schreibersdorf argues that each author capitalized on this fascination with the image of a "militant mother" in order to secure a place for the working woman within the highly masculinized world of labor agitation. Schreibersdorf writes:

> Vorse, Lumpkin, Page and Burke all use maternal figures to testify to the relevance and specificity of women's experience as workers and as union members. Their radicalism is ultimately motivated by their maternity; characters in all four novels repeatedly state that they fight, not for themselves, but for their children. (308)

When I read this, I wanted to spit fire; there was no way MY disorderly women were motivated only by their motherhood—they were transgressive radicals who fought for the rights of working women, not just their children! How could Schreibersdorf miss the excitement of the picketline as a mixture of fierceness and flirtation? Yes, these women were heroic mothers, but at that point in my life, I wanted something more from my heroic women than nurturing support, I wanted independence, freedom, and choice. I still saw these as separate; mothering would teach me that nurture and support could exist in tandem with fierce independence.

Thus, I chose to focus my research on Ishma Waycaster, Olive Tilford Dargan's protagonist in *Call Home the Heart*. She was the only character in the Gastonia novels whose maternal identity was not central to her activism, and I wanted to shine a stage light on Ishma's transgressive behavior. Moreover, her name was such an obvious allusion to Melville's hero, Ishmael, and she was such a strong-minded character, who (I thought) had an admirably masculine vision for activism. Ishma did have a son, Ned, but he seemed almost an afterthought; she left him pretty quickly in order to explore the world, away from her mountain home, and at the time, before my son Cody arrived, I was proud of Ishma for having (what I thought was) the strength of mind to leave personal worries, like children, behind in order to focus on the common good.

In 2005, as I waited for my own belly to grow, I began my dissertation chapter on Ishma, and here is what I wrote in my dissertation chapter, in response to Schreibersdorf: "Although my focus is not primarily on Ishma's role as mother, I believe that her motivation cannot be reduced to a maternal instinct. Rather, I see Ishma's commitment to the strike as a quest impulse that must be balanced against, and within, her participation in an unconventional romance" (Cella). This was my academically appropriate way of negating Ishma's—and all the fictional characters'—motherhood, and putting their activism ahead of their role as mothers. Moreover, I defined Ishma's quest in masculine terms—like Melville's quest—because I believed that highlighting her motherhood would weaken her power as heroine, diminish what she accomplished by muddying her motivation.

In my original chapter, I echo Melville and construct Ishma's romance as a masculine quest, one that had no room for children or mothering: "In effect, I intend to argue that Dargan manipulates both the standard proletarian conversion narrative and the conventional romance plot in order to create a fuller representation of women's lives as lovers, leaders, and activists in the labor movement." In my assessment, Ishma's life is full without any ties to her son. From my perspective at the time, a true heroine embarks on a quest and follows in the footsteps of her male predecessors; I continue with a number of references to Ishmael: "In the first novel, Ishma falls in love with the farmer Britt Hensley, but, true to her literary heritage, Ishma was 'tormented with an everlasting itch for things remote' (Melville 5). Thus, despite her intense passion for her husband Britt, Ishma leaves Britt and her small son Ned for another man, Rad Bailey, in order to find out what lies beneath the mountain and fulfill her destiny as heroine on a quest." When I wrote this bit, I was more horrified that Ishma left the love of her life, and not all that interested in Ned as a character or as a potentially meaningful aspect of Ishma's commitment to the cause.

My continued emphasis on the individual achievement is reflected in my analysis of Ishma's romance: "It is Ishma who has a 'man's heart,' embodied in the need to embark on her own quest for knowledge and adventure. Indeed, [this story] pits the domestic cost of infidelity against the desire to embark on a quest, and Ishma is simultaneously the heroine with the 'red heart' and the hero who embarks on a search for answers to her own questions" (46). This emphasis on individual achievement still shapes the academy; collaborative essays are still worth less when it comes to tenure, and children are still are impediments to real "progress." Before we had Cody, I believed that we would simply add him to our lives, and I would continue with a single-minded focus toward a fast track graduation and a tenure track job. I didn't realize all the ways he would change our lives, and so in many important ways, Cody—and the many challenges and joys he brought—reframed my focus, reshaped my priorities, and brought the unspoken inequities of academic life into sharp focus.

As I finished out my analysis of Ishma's radical romance, one that brought her to the heart of the labor struggle in a fictionalized Gastonia, I was annoyed to see yet another reference to Ella May in Dargan's text; I had hoped to avoid any more discussion of this martyr-mother. Here is what I wrote at the time:

> When Ishma awakens, she realizes that she could easily die of her wounds if she is not rescued quickly. However, she makes peace with her death, imagining herself as a force more powerful after death, "Let her die then. She would go on helping after death, like Ella May, who still marched and sang" (411). It is significant that Ishma identifies herself with Ella May, one of the most prominent figures of the Gastonia strike, because this recognition suggests that Ishma has fulfilled her political and intellectual quest. She has given herself totally to the fight, and she is now willing to give her life for the workers' cause.

Rather than seeing this reference as a connection to Ishma's motherhood, I chose to view this reference as clear evidence that Ishma had "given herself totally to the fight," a quality I admired then because it reflected my desire to lose myself in my work. I gave myself totally to the academic struggle, and believed that my commitment would be rewarded.

TOWARD A NEW UNDERSTANDING OF "PROGRESS"

However, by the time I reached my third trimester, I began to feel the tension that would shape both my scholarly and mothering life after Cody was born. I had planned on going to the MLA that December, just six weeks after Cody was born. I wanted to defend my dissertation that spring, and follow the "get in, get done, get out," model that our new graduate director was pushing. I had always given everything I had to my graduate work, always pushed myself to achieve, be the best, and I wanted to finish that way. However, applying to jobs seemed to be monumental task, a task that would take me out of my body, and away from this experience. As the summer began to fade, I unpacked the bags of maternity sweaters. My belly began to swell even larger, and I began to feel as if I was holding Cody against me, my hand over a protruding elbow or knee. We sometimes played a game of tag, my hand tracing his body as he moved against me, turned against my touch, rolling and twisting at the sound of my voice. Sitting at my desk in my carrel, I would read about Ishma, about Ella May, but the words began to swim in front of me. I suddenly didn't care anymore why they went on strike, or how they fought; I wanted to hold my belly and feel Cody roll against my hand.

One afternoon in October, as I sat heavily down at my kitchen table, looking at my print out of the MLA job list, I decided to call my friend Jenny, a graduate school friend who had successfully managed to have a baby, finish her dissertation, and land a job soon after.

"Jenny, do you think I should wait, do I need to go now?"

"Laurie, your dissertation is only half done, you would have to write like a mad woman all spring, leave for interviews, and Cody would only be a month old at MLA."

"But we could do that. I could do that. He will sleep a lot, and I could ask my mom to come…."

"Just wait, you'll see. You can stay in Connecticut for another year, take the time to really finish your work, and enjoy this time with Cody."

As I pushed the "end" button on the phone, I let the tears come. I rocked, and wailed, and let go of the plan I had mapped out—a plan that had at first seemed fierce, and now seemed impossible.

Thus began a slow re-mapping of my academic life, a restructuring that happened in fits and starts. That moment was my first lesson in mothering time management, a concept in stark contrast with the efficiency model espoused by the ideal graduate student. I learned that it would be okay to move at a slower pace, and that time with Cody made me happy. However, having a new baby meant working when I could, how I could, where I could. I wasn't always able to get to a quiet office; instead, I graded in bed, on the couch, at the kitchen table.

Like the women of Gastonia, I relied on a strong network of female support in order to manage my family and my work, and their support gave me guidance, courage, and, most importantly, a plan for finishing my work. As I made plans to balance writing with family life that summer, I relied on Jenny for advice regarding the tricky issue of childcare: "Laurie, you can finish with fifteen hours of dedicated writing a week. As long as you have the plan in place, don't let anything interrupt those hours, and you will be done by Cody's first birthday." So, in May of 2006, I spoke to two women we befriended in the Master's program. Emily and Mary were both smart, kind, and willing to help. We set up schedule of Monday/Wednesday/Friday, 9:00-1:00, and my husband and I wrote at Starbucks while Emily and Mary watched Cody for us. While it was suddenly so freeing to have a grande coffee, a laptop, and stack of research in front of me, I could always hear the clock ticking as I wrote, the small bit of money we paid our sitters slipping away. Writing was now a race, and the key was to focus on the narrative and to shape the story, the pieces, as quickly, as efficiently as I could. I would return home exhausted, happy to hold Cody in my lap with my eyes closed for a moment, happy to be making slow, plodding progress toward a completed dissertation.

A NEW COLLABORATIVE QUEST

Early that summer, a long walk with a close friend helped, again, to bring my life back into focus. Joanne was my closest confidante in graduate school: she had brought me good food when I overworked myself into back spasms, she was the first I told that we were expecting a baby, and she offered me the support and kindnesses I needed as a new and struggling mother. We often walked in her neighborhood, but she encouraged me to bring Cody in the stroller, so I could use my afternoons to write when my husband watched Cody. It was hard to get myself moving to walk with Cody, but Joanne was both encouraging and patient.

"Joanne, I don't think I can walk today. I'm too tired, and Cody is too fussy—he won't sit still in the stroller long enough to get down the driveway."

"Ok, Laurie, let's just see what happens. You need to take care of yourself, and it's okay if he cries for a bit—he'll settle once we walk. You'll see."

She was right. Cody did settle, and with Joanne's encouragement, I created a schedule that included much needed exercise, and with that exercise, a full hour of sharing that helped me gather the strength to face the rest of the day. Walking with Joanne, discussing the competing desires of my heart—those moments helped me to understand my academic life more fully. My quest had been enriched by my mentor academic mothers in much the same way that Ella May's life was strengthened by her ties to the working mothers in Gastonia. My work could not continue in this solipsistic focus on individual achievement, nor could I continue to ignore the importance of an academic mothering community. I had followed Jenny's advice on pacing my work, and listened to Joanne's thoughts on the ways mothering influences our understanding of the world. I knew that these role models would help me forge my own identity as an academic mother.

I didn't let go of my "quest" vision of scholarly work immediately or even easily. What happened over that year was a slow process of making plans, losing control, and sometimes letting my love for Cody take center stage in my heart. In response, I began to work quickly, with a new, sharper focus. Since I set a goal to defend by Cody's first birthday, the next year was a balance of focus, vision, and loss. I began to respect the physicality and intensity of motherhood and slowly, I began to incorporate flexibility into my research. I began to see, without trying to force myself into an academic argument, how essential both selves are—the intellectual and the maternal—and that made me ashamed of my negation of motherhood in my work. After having and balancing my love for Cody against the pull of my work, I began to see and understand Ella May more fully. While I still thought the media worked too hard to create a martyr figure out of her, I began to see her mothering as an integral aspect of her identity.

A NEW VISION OF ISHMA

When I had started my research, I spent most of my energies reading Dowd Hall's "Disorderly Women," but she and her colleagues had worked tirelessly to create a fuller picture of life in Appalachia before and during the strike; their book, *Like a Family: The Making of a Southern Cotton Mill World*, captures women's social lives and the intricate networks they relied upon for childcare. They argue that Appalachian women "set up networks of assistance, childcare, information transference, and community policing" (qtd. in Squire 44). This heavy book had stayed in the higher reaches of my study as I wrote my radical romance chapters, but after Cody was born, and my chapters were written, the importance of the family structure started creeping back into my research. I started seeing events in Ella May's life from my new perspective as a mother, and her pain was no longer a slogan to me, it was real.

According to Dowd Hall's book, *Like A Family*, it was the complexity of support in the mill towns of southern Appalachia among women that made the strike itself possible. Women traded children or switched shifts in order to care for their children and take home a paycheck. Most of the best news about the strike activity was exchanged in the women's bathroom. But Ella May had made headlines too because she had close ties to the African American women living in Stumptown, the African American mill town that was her home. Her African American friends watched her children while she worked, and that exchange solidified their friendship.

My network of support consisted of academic mothers whose various styles of balance inspired me and I leaned on them at various points that last year. When should I aim to hand in chapters? How much should I work at nights and on the weekends? And, as the summer progressed, and I handed in chapter four with only one to go, I started answering questions myself. On the softball field during inter-mural games, in the hallways on campus, at parties, young female graduate students starting asking me, "How are you doing it? Aren't you tired?" It felt good to be a role model for them, even as I struggled with the answers myself.

That summer, I brought eight-month-old Cody to a professional conference in Chattanooga, TN, and while I used some of the time to meet with colleagues and present my essay, I carved out more time to spend with Matthew and Cody. We brought him to the cocktail hour and let him roam around beneath our feet; while a few attendees scowled at our lax parenting, most smiled warmly at Cody's investigations, and a few even played with him as we stood, chatting and entertaining our son. I hoped his physical presence would be a reminder that we were all more than academics, we were people with families. After spending time at the conference with my colleagues, I met up with Matthew to travel to Nashville, where we took Cody to the zoo and walked down Music Alley together. While my husband and I were spent by the end of the trip, I felt satisfied that we had made the conference part of our travel experience rather than simply adding a moment of fun into an academic trip.

I have since traveled by myself to academic conferences, and those trips certainly have their value. However, I felt proud to have integrated my lives so well in Chattanooga. In her essay, "That Mommy Thing," Alissa McElreath writes about her colleague's advice not to get too caught up in "that mommy thing" so that she could stay focused on her career. That advice and that attitude still permeates much of my academic experience—don't bring your children to school, to conferences, avoid telling stories about them at parties. Until academic mothers—and fathers—begin to make their children visible at these academic events, we will continue to perpetuate this stifling attitude toward academic parenting.

As I got tantalizingly close to my November defense date, I knew that I was sacrificing time with Cody to get my writing done. In order to make deadlines we set for ourselves, we would go to our home state of New York, and our parents watched Cody while we spent weekends at the library. Every hour counted to that next page, a finished footnote, and each morning away from Cody brought us closer to the finish line. But having a deadline, a goal we could taste, didn't make it less painful to lose those hours, that time with Cody. (Even now, as I write these words, my mother-in-law, Cheryl, watches Cody in the next room. He brings me the pictures he drew, and I hear his voice as he makes plans, plays games, and describes his drawings in more detail for Cheryl.) I've learned that every essay, every chapter, everything I write comes with a price tag more valuable to me than cash: time.

Ella May experienced that loss even more acutely than I do; she chose the night shift so that she could watch her children during the day, but even so, four of her nine children died of malnutrition by the time she reached twenty-nine, just one year younger than I was as I wrote the last pages of my dissertation. This loss is more than I will ever face, and her activism, while it certainly was only because of her mothering, gained a power, a resonance, and a courage that I understand more fully now that I am a mother. And loss, however small or mundane, has become a staple of my parenting: what will I lose if I stay at home in the mornings with Cody and neglect my own writing, my student essays, my email? More importantly, what do I lose when I travel to conferences by myself for an extended period of time? What do I lose on a daily basis when I leave Cody at daycare for eight hours at a time? Academic mothers do have much more flexibility than mothers facing dire or extreme poverty like Ella May did, but the pressure to produce, to write, to grade, to contribute never lets up at night, over the summer, or on the weekend. It is easy to listen to friends who say that Cody's life will be richer for the variety of his caretakers, that his education will begin earlier in day care, that his teachers are well-trained, generous, kind. And all of these things are true, though my heart still aches when I say goodbye in the morning to walk across campus toward my work as a teacher and scholar. These days, Cody attends a day care center three days a week, 9:00-5:00, and I am happily teaching a large, public institution in Pennsylvania. And despite my ability to relish my role as academic mother, leaving Cody brings that price tag of time into painfully high relief. We walk down the hallway together, lunchbox and "sharing item" in tow, Cody shyly nods to the little friends who crowd us when we enter, and, depending on the day, leaves willingly to share McQueen matchbox cars, build wooden houses, and draw with his friends at the miniature table. I walk out of the room quickly then, ready to capitalize on his social behavior, but also unwilling to face my feelings of loss at this moment; Cody will embark on a day without me, on activities that he will forget or be unable to describe, have exchanges that, for good or bad, will never reach our dinner table discussion. That is the bargain I've struck with myself: I will trade these days away for the ability to teach American literature and first year writing and, at five o'clock each day, I can walk down the same hallway, find my towhead in the bunch, and gather him up in my arms again to begin "that mommy thing" once again.

THE STRATEGIES I TAKE WITH ME

When I began my graduate school career, I didn't realize that my identity would divide upon itself when I had a child; no one prepared me for the difficulties of combining a single-minded quest for knowledge with the demands, challenges and joys of parenthood. My academic life is richer now for the struggle, and I see what I didn't before. Upon re-reading the end of *Call Home the Heart*, I see maternity even in Ishma's heroic quest. This time around, I recognize her emotional reaction to meeting her seven-year-old son, Ned, for the first time in years:

"You my mother?"
"Yes, Ned," she answered, doubting her own words, and pressing her heart to keep it in her throat. If he would only act like a child! Put his arms around her neck, and cry a little. But he'd never do that. And he was so beautiful that to look at him made her feel that she was melting away. (404-5)

How could I have missed Ishma's love for Ned on the first read? Was I so consumed with my argument that I could see how motherhood had, at least in part, reshaped Ishma's life? I don't want to wear these blinders anymore; I've had those moments looking at Cody—where his sweaty, wriggly self seems more miracle than reality—when I felt as I might melt myself. Allowing those moments into my academic self means acknowledging a different set of rules: a slower pace, but a richer, more meaningful integration of life and work, home and school. Now I can see that the web of connections in the Piedmont region was strong and deep. And my own connections—mentor mothers, supportive friends and family—made writing my dissertation possible.

The fierce twinned pull of mother love and academic work will never dissipate, but now I ready to accept these challenges and follow my quest as it happens: a life influenced by those academic mothers who have gone before me, and made choices that strengthened their ties to their children while building a vision of academic success that moves at a separate pace. I know that my choices will come with loss: I will not finish the essays waiting for revision this year, but I will the next; I will not travel to every conference I want to, but when I do, I will bring Cody, and we will go to the zoo after the panels are over. These fierce loves make life intense, and it takes confidence to make decisions not sanctioned by our institutions. However, we owe it to the young women just about to enter graduate school to make honest choices so that they will have the benefit of a confident community of academic mothers, willing and able to guide them toward the fierce loves of academic mothering.

[1]For labor historians and literary critics alike, the series of strikes that rocked the Piedmont region of the Southern United State in 1929 are central to critical discussions of women as participants in the labor movement. Just like the Shirtwaist strike in 1909 and the Lawrence strike in 1912, the Piedmont strikes were led by women who took center stage in the activism, leadership, and organization that propelled the strikes into the international media. The strike began on March 12, 1929, when Margaret Bowen, a supervisor in the Baldwin Mill, asked for a raise for herself and her section. When management said no, she led her section out on strike. Two weeks later, the workers at the Loray Mill in Gastonia, North Carolina, walked out.

WORK CITED

Bradshaw, Leah. "The Facts, The Stories." *Mama Ph.D.: Women Write about Motherhood and Academic Life*. Eds. Elrena Evans and Caroline Grant. New Brunswick, NJ: Rutgers University Press, 2008. 166-122.

Cella, Laurie J. C. *Radical Romance: The Intersection of the Conversion Narrative and the Romance Plot in Proletarian Novels, 1862-1939*. Unpublished Doctoral Dissertation. University of Connecticut, Storrs, 2007.

Dowd Hall, Jacquelyn. "Disorderly Women: Gender and Labor Militancy in the Appalachian South." *The Journal of American History*. 73 (1986): 354-382.

Dowd Hall, Jacquelyn. *Like a Family: The Making of a Southern Cotton Mill World*. Chapel Hill: North Carolina University Press, 2000.

McElreath, Alissa. "That Mommy Thing." *Mama Ph.D.: Women Write about Motherhood and Academic Life*. Eds. Elrena Evans and Caroline Grant. New Brunswick: Rutgers University Press, 2008.89-92.

Salmond, John. *Gastonia 1929: The Story of the Loray Mill Strike*. Chapel Hill: University of North Carolina Press, 2009.

Schreibersdorf, Lisa. "Radical Mothers: Maternal Testimony and Metaphor in Four Novels of the Gastonia Strike." *Journal of Narrative*

Theory 29 (Fall 1999): 303-322.

Squire, Walter. "Resisting Being Written Out of History: Women Activists and Recorders of the 1929 Gastonia Strike." *North Carolina Literary Review* 9 (2000): 43-57.

Sutherland, Jean-Anne. "Ideal Mama, Ideal Worker: Negotiating Guilt and Shame in Academe." *Mama PhD: Women Write About Motherhood and Academic Life*. Eds. Elrena Evans and Caroline Grant. New Brunswick, NJ: Rutgers University Press, 2008. 213-221.

Tilford Dargan, Olive. *Call Home the Heart*. New York: The Feminist Press, 2000.

13.
Re-Writing the Script

JENNIFER HAUVER JAMES

S HORTLY AFTER ACCEPTING my first academic job in the spring of 2006, my husband and I took an exploratory trip to our soon-to-be new hometown. In preparation for our visit, I had reached out to one of my new colleagues, Cole,[1] a third-year assistant professor at the university. He kindly welcomed us into town and invited us over for drinks after our first full day of house hunting. I was excited by the opportunity to get to know Cole, whose work I'd read as a doctoral student and for whom I already had tremendous respect. Though only a few short years ahead of me on the tenure clock, he had quickly managed to establish quite a presence in the field. I looked forward to getting to know him and talking about the intersections of our work.

Cole was a bachelor, and his apartment reflected the singular focus of his life: his job. As I entered his apartment, my eyes fell on the many books, papers, and journals that filled the space before me. Notes were scribbled on napkins and scraps of paper were scattered across floor, table and seating. Not a surface in the apartment was without its dose of academic paraphernalia. Cole noticed my interest and offered an apology for the mess. The scene before us, he explained, was evidence of just how absorbed he tends to be in his work. He spent most of his days buried in reading and writing, evenings grading and preparing for classes. He had a hard time escaping work because it called to him from every tabletop in the apartment.

Later that evening, as my husband and I walked back to our hotel, I reflected on the scene in Cole's apartment and what it represented for me. I was confronted by what I considered the quintessential image of a scholar like Cole who devotes his life to his work. I thought about Cole's long and growing list of publications and the race for tenure I would soon be engaging with him and others. Prevailing discourses about what constitutes success, of competition and achievement, informed as they are by this patriarchal model, flooded my mind, seemingly devaluing my own circumstances and limiting my possibilities. I bemoaned aloud the fact that I would never be able to keep up with someone who could so immerse himself in his work. Being the sage that he is, my husband pointed out how much poorer my life would be without all the wonderful distractions I have that keep me from writing all day long as Cole does—him, for instance, and our two beautiful children. He was right, of course. And yet, I couldn't get the image out of my head.

MOM'S KITCHEN TABLE

Two years later I sat at my mother's kitchen table during an extended visit home over the winter break. The honeymoon period of my first academic job had long been over. I was desperate for an intellectual community that had never materialized. I was emotionally exhausted by the drama-filled environment in which I worked. I was overworked (sometimes teaching as many as seven classes in a semester) and entirely underpaid and underappreciated. I felt consumed by the stress of my work with little else to give to the other parts of my life. I gave whatever emotional and physical energy I had left at the end of the day to my kids and still felt as if it wasn't enough. And the Jenn who liked to read, craft, see movies, go on long walks, dance, play games, keep up with friends—I could hardly remember her. My marriage, my friendships and my health were suffering. I was neither the scholar nor the mother (nor the wife, friend or woman) I wanted to be. I wished to reshape my experience in ways that involved more than a constant push and pull between work and mothering; in ways that allowed me to better attend to my whole self. I longed for a healthier work environment and a more flexible schedule. Working within the existing structures, however, made such a task seem impossible.

Against my better judgment (and for reasons only Freud himself knows for sure) I found myself pouring out these thoughts and more to my mother that December evening over a glass of wine. I say *against my better judgment* because I knew all too well how my mother's once persistent message of "you can do anything you want to do if you set your mind to it" was silenced once I made the decision to have children. No longer was my life my own. No longer was I allowed to be sick, or feel sorry for myself, or want—anything—for myself. Mothering is about sacrifice, after all. And so it was that as my soul-bearing went on, Mom's looks of disappointment increased in frequency, like little invisible guilt slaps from across the table. Until the moment came when she dropped the ultimate insult and told me that I was simply being selfish. The writing could wait. I'd have years to do that. The kids will only be young for a short while. She wasn't sure why I ever left teaching in the first place—I was a good teacher. When I was a school teacher I had done something that mattered. Now I was thinking about uprooting my family (again), moving them to a new place so that I could tend to my own personal needs. What kind of a mother would do such a thing, she seemed to be saying. What kind of mother indeed.

This moment in time reified for me powerful discourses of mothering that emphasize sacrifice. The contrast between this moment and the moment in Cole's apartment was sharp: to succeed in Cole's world, I needed to be entirely selfish; as a mother I needed to be entirely selfless. These competing discourses about who I ought to be—as an academic and a mother—seemed then, and many times since, irreconcilable. Sitting at their intersection I have felt utterly hopeless to do either scholarship or mothering well—as it seems that by the very nature of the reality created, doing one well meant failing at the other. Here, in the midst of trying to come to terms with who I might be as an academic and as a mother, I struggled to resist, to name myself, to challenge the discourses and structures that seemed to bound my experience. This essay is a reflection on that continuing struggle.

THE POWER OF MESSAGES

These two moments in time—my visit to Cole's apartment, the conversation with my mother at her kitchen table—and the images they project, stay with me. In order to understand how and why they stay with me, and to begin to dismantle them, I acknowledge the role I play in lending them credence. I sometimes imagine two alternate versions of myself sitting atop my shoulders, whispering in either ear competing messages about whom I ought to be—the perfect scholar who devotes herself to her work, the perfect mother who devotes herself to her children. I suspect that somewhere deep down I have bought into these images: the absent-minded, semi-obsessive scholar who lives rather like a hobbit, happier to be in the company of books than people. At times, I long for Cole's anonymity and freedom. The woman who serves as room mom at her daughter's school, meets her children at the bus, healthy snack in hand, ready to assist with homework. At times, I long for the joy she must feel in sharing so many precious moments with her children. I struggle with my desire to become either—the perfect scholar or the perfect mother—a useless pastime to be sure, because I know I could never abandon one in a quest to become the other. The costs are much too high.

Instead, I resist the either/or by striving to name for myself the academic mother I am becoming. Recognizing the power of the messages I carry with me is an important first step. The two images captured here are powerful not only because they are legitimized by people I hold in high regard, but because they are constantly reinforced by those around me. The teacher who holds all of her family events at ten in the morning on Thursdays and then gently reminds me on Fridays that I was the only mother unable to attend. The male colleague who tells me he knows how hard it is to be a parent (he is one, after all) … and who suggests that the key to success is locking yourself up in the office for days on end and leaving the children to your spouse (his spouse, a stay-at-home mom).

Not long ago, I attended a lifetime achievement award ceremony for two scholars at an annual meeting of the American Educational Research Association. The scholars, a man and a woman, were being recognized for their outstanding contributions to the field. As an introduction to the ceremony, the speaker read biographies for each, highlighting their total numbers of publications. The man had managed to write over 120 articles in his lifetime and 12 books. The woman had written 60-some articles and three books. Curious, I thought, that their respective contributions to the field were boiled down to mere numbers on a page. What is the message here, I wondered? Sixty articles are good—for a woman? This measure of success, like dominant constructs of motherhood, have been crafted outside of my experience, and yet influence my sense of self-worth. Discourses like this one about what constitutes "achievement" in the field of academia, like the one perpetuated by my children's teacher about what constitutes good mothering, legitimize and reproduce "regimes of truth" both about academic success and about motherhood. This "saturation of consciousness," is described by Kreisberg as "the process through which the dominant culture supplies the symbols, representations, morality, and customs that frame, form, and constrain what we do and say, the principles that underlie our thoughts and actions and the broader structures that shape our experiences" (15). It is so thorough and deep, he argues, that the realities of domination become "common sense." Hegemony as an ideology is powerful and all encompassing as it works on our body and mind on the level of our everyday experience. Similarly, Paolo Freire writes, "[The oppressed] are at one and the same time themselves and the oppressor whose consciousness they have internalized" (49).

The actualization of these regimes of truth, of course, takes place within the individual—me—through what Jennifer Gore calls "technologies of the self." My experience in Cole's apartment stays with me because it "rings true"—it calls up many other instances where this discourse has been present. The power of this discourse resides in me and is evidenced by the degree of guilt I feel at not living up to it. Our lived realities, then, are both socially-imposed and internally-constructed, as we continue to act upon and judge ourselves within the technologies of self we adopt. Despite the power of messages I have internalized, though, they are neither static nor unalterable. Rather, they are constantly being negotiated in light of my own experience and my conscious efforts to disrupt them.

RECOGNITION AND RESISTANCE

The struggle to resist being defined by discourses such as "the self-absorbed scholar" or "the selfless mother" is made easier by an understanding of the process of internalization of messages. Holding them up for examination, acknowledging that they are not "just the way it is" or "common sense" can make them easier to adapt, resist or restructure. The act of agency, of challenging dominant discourses in an effort to obtain freedom from them, begins with the discovery that we are "hosts" of the oppressor (Freire 49). Only by seeing what we typically take for granted can we begin to name ourselves as subjects of our own becoming—to perform our own imagined possibilities (Greene). Of course, our agency is constrained in that we cannot ever be completely free of the discourses that structure our lives. But we can fight against them in an effort to name ourselves.

These notions of agency and performativity are core to critical and post-structural feminist thought, which aims to recast gendered identities in more equitable, representative ways. Critical post-structural feminist thought resists traditional male-female binaries, constituted by relationships of power and given meaning through discursive practices, instead recognizing the fluidity of gender constructs, including those that are "misrecognized or unrecognizable precisely because they exist at the limits of established norms for thinking embodiment and even personhood" (Butler, ii). There are gender performances, which have yet to be named, or perhaps even imagined, because they exist outside of the discourses that make them possible. As I resist the existing discourses of success in academia and in motherhood, I step out on new ground—trying to name a performance that has yet to be named; one that so far lacks the language to describe it. Judith Butler explains,

> To say that gender is performative is to say that it is a certain kind of enactment; the "appearance" of gender is often mistaken as a sign of its internal or inherent truth; gender is prompted by obligatory norms to be one gender or the other (usually within a strictly binary frame), and the reproduction of gender is thus always a negotiation with power; and finally, there is no gender without this reproduction of norms that risks undoing or redoing the norm in unexpected ways, thus opening up the possibility of a remaking of gendered reality along new lines. (i)

When we choose to resist discourses that do not adequately capture our realities, we embark on a re-writing of the script that names our experience. Take, for example, the title of "academic mother." This title is inadequate as an articulation of my identity for a whole host of reasons. First, it reflects the very binary I am trying to resist—the academic on one hand, the mother on the other. This binary suggests a metaphor of balance—the scales of identity, if you will—in which doing too much of one (achieving success at work) necessarily results in my inability to do enough of the other (being a "good" mom). In this dichotomous framing, perfection (mastering the delicate balance) and failure (tipping the scales) are my only possible outcomes. Second, this title fails to recognize the multitude of identities I perform. I am more than an academic and a mother. I am an intellectual, spiritual, sexual, cultural being with desires, fears, and needs. The title "academic mother" neither acknowledges nor values my varied dimensions of self. Instead, it essentializes my being into two categories and limits possibilities for who I might become.

Finally, the title "academic mother" sets me apart from other academics by drawing attention to my role as a mother. Embedded in this label is the assumption that as a woman, my identity as a mother is paramount and, thus, the most threatened by my choice to become an academic. After all, who ever heard of the phrase "academic father"? Nobody seems to worry about the tension men feel as a result of their decision to pursue a career in academia. No one worries that men's ability to perform their fatherly duties will be jeopardized because they have made this choice. The very existence of the label "academic mother" suggests that women who choose such a path are no longer whole, but instead suffer from split personalities—having to attend to their primary and natural roles as mothers as well as the tensions caused by their choice to be something else as well.

The title is inadequate and limiting as a descriptor of my identity and experience. It is unable to represent who I am in so far as it is bound up in discourses of academic success and mothering that are at odds *and* in so far as it makes salient two of my many identities without my choosing. But once I have recognized the power of prevailing discourses and the inadequacy of labels generated from those discourses, then what? In the wake of this deconstruction, we create space for new, imagined possibilities that are more just in their representation. In the wake of this deconstruction, we may recreate, or rewrite the scripts for our lives.

REWRITING THE SCRIPT

In my experience, rewriting the script involves active and continued resistance. Such resistance involves a mindfulness about the discourses that shape my life and a conscious effort to disrupt them whenever I can. It involves engaging in projects such as this one—using my written voice to tell my story, a counter story to the prevailing narratives. This volume is a monument to such rewriting. Consisting of varied, evolving, and sometimes contradictory narratives, theorized through differing lenses, such a collection serves to open the door to newly imagined possibilities, to reorder realities and undo the messages that fail to do them justice. It is a testament to the many ways women negotiate and make meaning of their evolving identities as academics and as mothers. It celebrates women's voices and experiences as significant sources of knowledge. Collectively, it serves to disrupt the taken for granted.

My resistance also involves using my spoken voice to disrupt discourses that threaten to bound my experience or potential in unjust ways. And there are many! Just last semester a colleague, upon having spotting me at my daughters' elementary school earlier that morning, remarked, "When I saw you I just knew you were the kind of woman who had her priorities straight. You weren't going to let work get in the way of being a good mom." In this moment, I remember my initial reaction being one of both pride and anger. I *liked* being called a "good mom"—who wouldn't? And yet the compliment was all tied up in the very discourses I am trying to resist. After a brief pause, I replied, "Thanks. I do try to get here whenever I can and I'm lucky that my flexible schedule allows me to do that. There are many good moms, though, who can't get to school as often as I can." A small step, perhaps, in pointing out the limitations of the narratives that get perpetuated.

In another example, a male colleague once stated that he didn't know how I managed to get anything done with so many distractions (referring to my children). "How can you think sufficiently about work when you're always having to think about dance schedules, babysitters and naptime?" I wondered aloud whether he would ask the same question of a male colleague who was a father. For a few minutes, we chatted about whether it was necessarily true that women are distracted by family matters in ways that men aren't or whether such a "truth" is socially constructed. Though we resolved nothing, my colleague left our encounter saying, "Hmmm… hadn't really thought of that." I'm hopeful that these moments, if they are multiplied, might make a difference—both in shifting the discourses as they exist and in giving voice to my experience.

Another way I try to resist is to use my roles as mother and academic to raise a generation of children to might see things differently. Because I am a professor of education, I spend a great deal of time in the company of prospective and practicing teachers. I use these opportunities to talk about the many ways we can break down the barriers such discourses erect. We spend time talking about gendered discourses about play and ability, about hetero-normative discourses that inform thinking about gender roles and acceptable behavior. We practice finding and using resources to challenge these dominant discourses in classrooms. At home, I keep this conversation alive with my own family. I challenge my daughters to think about the limitations of the "truths" they encounter at school and in society. We practice ways to restate and question those truths in respectful but assertive ways. We talk—a lot—and this I think is incredibly powerful.

But probably the most powerful act in which I engage in an effort to resist and rewrite my script is connecting with other women (and men) who feel frustrated by the discourses that structure our lives. I am constantly struck by the feelings of isolation women in the academy share. In so many instances—at conferences, at work, among friends—I encounter others who feel like I do—bound by discourses that don't capture our experience and yet guilty for not living up to them. Our stories are unique and yet the struggle is shared. Connecting with others, giving voice to our shared experience, supporting one another, is, a source of strength and identity for me. Connecting with others means knowing that I am not alone. Collectively, through our use of voice and action, we can resist. Together we can resist binaries, challenge dominant notions, and articulate silences. We can acknowledge the powerful messages we encounter, our predispositions to accept them as judgment of our worth, and our struggle to rewrite them. We can celebrate the many dimensions of our identities, of which academic and mother are only two. We can rename ourselves in light of our experience, our hopes, our knowledge. We are, in fact, the only ones who can.

Cole and my mother have taught me valuable lessons—about who they are and what they strive to become. Though their stories stay with me, they are not the same as mine. In so far as I can recognize them for what they are, and then adapt them in light of my own experience, I have the power to rewrite my script.

MESSAGES

"I've been there—raised kids while trying to make tenure—nobody gave me any breaks."

"You might hold off on the R1 thing—lots of moms find teaching positions allow for better balance between home and work."

"Hey, I'm a dad. I get it."

"You're one of the most promising young scholars in the field."

"Don't you want to be with your kids? How can you let others raise them?"

"I don't know how you do it."

"We missed you at the play this morning. You were the only mom who wasn't here."

"You're excellent at what you do, and by the way, you've got a great ass."

"Mom, I missed you."

"It's pretty selfish to focus so much on work when your kids are so young, don't you think?"

"I admire you."

"Congratulations on your recent publication.... Brilliant work."

"Mommy, I love you the most."

"Imagine the scholars we could be if we didn't have kids."

"When I grow up, I want to be just like you."

"You're too good for this place."

I am ... becoming.

¹Pseudonym

WORKS CITED

Butler, Judith. "Performativity, Precarity and Sexual Politics." Lecture given at Universidad Complutense de Madrid, June 8, 2009.

Freire, Paolo. *Pedagogy of Freedom: Ethics, Democracy and Civic Courage*. Lanham, MD: Rowman & Littlefield Publishers, Inc., 1998.

Gore, Jennifer. *The Struggle for Pedagogies: Critical and Feminist Discourses as Regimes of Truth*. New York: Routledge, Inc., 1993.

Greene, Maxine. *A Light in Dark Times: Maxine Greene and the Unfinished Conversation*. New York: Teachers College Press, 1997.

Kreisberg, Seth. *Transforming Power: Domination, Empowerment and Education*. Albany, NY: SUNY Press, 1992.

14.

Being a Mother Academic

Or, I Didn't Get a Ph.D. to Become a Mom

JOANNE C. MINAKER

TWO THINGS WERE LATE THIS SUMMER—this paper and my daughter's birth. I have tried to begin this paper what feels like a thousand times. I am a mother and an academic, so it stands to reason that I would have much to write about both and perhaps even more to say about their relationship. However, each time I took the proverbial pen to page I found myself resistant, distracted, and unwilling to commit my thoughts to paper. I spent several months fighting this impasse; time and again I attempted to write something poignant and witty, with equal parts professorial expertise and practical "know how." Yet, quite simply, the paper eluded me.

It occurred to me recently with hackneyed accuracy that my problem was located in my own fear. This fear was of having to articulate specifically what *being* a mother meant for me and coming to some conclusion about how my academic life was inter-related to, or dis-connected from, motherhood. I was reticent to actually make claims about and give explicit meaning to these significant roles, responsibilities, and very real identities that consume who and what I am in the world. Finally, after much ado about nothing, I realized that being an academic and being a mother are in a constant state of flux and continually in process. Currently, my academic process is on hold: I am on maternity leave. My three children are my top priority. This is the most important role I will play—the most significant pupils to learn my lessons.

To pass as objective and scientific and be recognized as rigorous scholarship, academic writing is steeped in verbiage distanced from the ground level and filled with jargon that obscures the very reality it attempts to explain. Indoctrinated in the customs of my own discipline of sociology I also felt it at first problematic to depart from the usual literature search and write from the vantage point of personal experience rather than the findings of my research—or words of my research participants. Initially, I designed the paper around the narratives of five women I interviewed who were also mother academics. In reviewing the interview transcripts I realized that so many of the issues they struggled with resonated with my own experience of balancing work and mothering. I felt inauthentic, though, writing about their lives when I hadn't examined my own.

So, in the pages that follow you will read about me—the mother academic. Rather than accept my words as final or complete, the thoughts and feelings I express herein are those ideas and interpretations that resonate with who and what I am in this moment and where I am located presently.

To begin where I am requires some foray into where I have been. Therefore, the paper is organized sequentially following the fault lines upon which my life and work are traced. Motherhood has always shaped my academic life, in indirect and direct ways. The discussion begins with my reflections on the influence having children and being a mother has had on my academic trajectory. I explore how different periods of my mothering journey have altered the course of my work.

It is difficult to think about life before motherhood, yet there was a time when I responded, "I am an academic," when asked what I do. As I sit writing this paper my daughter is perched in my bosom asleep in her baby carrier. I can vaguely recall when my career goals were mine alone, when I thought of work as an end in itself, and when I figured my most worthwhile contributions would be listed on my CV. How much has changed seven years later!

Now my oldest son, Ayden, is entering grade two; Taryk, my youngest son, is starting kindergarten and my two-month-old daughter, Maylah, is struggling to break herself free of the carrier she was sleeping in on my chest only moments ago! I am 36 and a happily married mother of three beautiful young children. I am on maternity leave, but (as the present paper suggests) still attempting to remain engaged in research and writing. I have an ongoing research project called the Mothering Contexts Study, which explores the relationship between mothering and other areas in women's lives. I struggle daily to locate the intersection.

BECOMING A MOTHER

I vividly recall my first and only academic job interview (incidentally I was five months pregnant). I was nervous and excited. I was about to officially enter academia, and leave graduate school behind. It all seemed so important. And it still is—only not in the way I initially thought it might be. I was hired at the university where I still work. The position was to begin July 1st 2003. That little baby in my belly at my interview was due July 12th! Being new to both motherhood and the university, I humbly requested that my employment begin six months later in the winter semester. It was all set. I would have the baby, stay home for six months, then my husband would take the next four months leave and we would enjoy a summer together as a family. That way, the baby would not have to attend daycare until thirteen months of age. Wonderful! What I hadn't planned on was the mother guilt, and the incessant desire to be the perfect mother and have the perfect child. Perhaps I held to these illusions longer because I had a little boy who slept through the night (eight hours or more) by three months of age, walked at nine months, talked in complete sentences long before anyone expected, and was otherwise the "textbook child." There were so many moments where I marveled at how lucky we were, how awesome it was to have a great job, a loving husband and a healthy child; yet I have more vivid memories of the challenges. Honestly, the first six months of my son's life are a blur. Two key moments really stand out.

The fall after Ayden was born I flew from Edmonton, Alberta, to Kingston, Ontario, to defend my dissertation. As I look back on this trip where I had my own exclusively breast-fed newborn in one arm and my three-hundred-page dissertation in the other, I am amused at how people refer to their theses and dissertations as their "baby." The defense itself is a distant memory. I'm sure there were congratulations and hugs and words of encouragement, maybe some tears. But the ones that mattered more to me were those of my screaming infant, crying in desperation for his mom. I cannot forget the mad dash I made in the pouring rain to the car to nurse Ayden. While he sucked I cried, feeling like such a bad mother to have left him, even for a couple of hours with his grandparents. While I did not realize it back then, this would be the first of many moments that have revealed to me how my responsibilities as a mother have to take priority over my work life. I was still under the impression that having it all meant having it all at the same time—to extend the familiar analogy—to not only have my cake and eat it, but bake, decorate, and get told it was "the best cake" anyone has ever eaten too; all without so much as a speck of flour left on my sleeve.

I still have much regret about not staying at home with my son the first year of his life. Compared to the contexts in which many women mother (in poverty, as lone-parents, without community supports etc.) our situation many have seemed ideal. My husband, who is also an academic, took paid parental leave to care for our son. I remember leaving Ayden that first morning with his loving father, who was armed with baby bottles, an array of nipples, and infant formula. What happened during that period is their story, filled with Dad's own memories. I will never forget how upon my return my son clutched at my breast through my clothing in a desperate attempt to nurse. Mother guilt anyone? So there I was playing professor by day, mommy by night. I dressed the part and (by appearances anyway) acted it out well. When I was at work I was serious about my teaching and writing. When I was at home I was all about the baby. Somehow through it all I managed to excel at work and feel reasonably adequate at being a new mom. I had only been back to work about a year when we were pregnant with our second child. There was no doubt in my mind that I wanted to be at home with my baby a full year and have time with my toddler. I didn't want to put my academic life on hold, though. I continued to grapple with balancing, coordinating, and otherwise connecting being a mother and being an academic.

MOTHERING IN ACADEME

When our youngest son was born in October 2005 I was able to be the primary caregiver for our kids, and at the same time, write and attend conferences. Unfortunately, we suffered financially because my leave was unpaid. One of the hardest moments I have stained in my heart was when Ayden, then three, said: "I don't want you to be a professor, I just want you to be my Mommy!"

What I realized during that period was that I couldn't go back to work and leave my mothering behind. Being a mom didn't begin and end at our front door. I felt I needed to share more of my life as a mother with my colleagues and my students. A pivotal point in merging motherhood and my academic life was when I made the choice to teach an Advanced

Topics in Deviance course under the title, "Contesting Motherhood." Expecting discussions of serial killers and gang violence, two men scurried from the classroom. For the 18 students who remained (among them four males), our term was spent unpacking taken for granted assumptions about motherhood and challenging the cultural myths and social barriers mothers face. For the first time I read and engaged with the literature on motherhood, in and beyond sociology. I began to see how my own training and research in criminology and socio-legal studies, specifically in the areas of youth crime, family violence and gender, intersected with my growing interest in the sociology of mothering. I was able to theorize this area of human experience that had become so significant to my life. When I later reflected on the course I realized, however, that save for a children's book I read on the first day of class and a few cute anecdotes I had not incorporated my own mothering experiences into the course in any meaningful way. Why, I wondered? Had I not realized how connected my mothering was to my pedagogy? Perhaps. Then, I still held to the bizarre notion that the most important things I could teach my students were core concepts like "maternal thinking" or "second shift." I distanced my own experiences—the conflicts and contradictions and messiness—in favour of a more linear, precise, and intellectual rendering of the sociology of motherhood. How academic of me!

Between 2006 and 2008 I would go on to co-author my first book, publish articles in refereed journals, and give presentations to both public and academic audiences. All the while, however, I wrestled with a very pressing need to figure out how I could make my mothering front and centre in my academic life and how my home and family life could seamlessly merge into my professional one. I came to what I now find a silly and naïve conclusion: I am both a mother and an academic—at the same time! I was all out—never masking my mothering. I would bring my kids along to social justice presentations, intent upon showing them both what Mommy does and teaching them to have a social conscience. I think my dress too mirrored a more relaxed and (some may argue) less professional style. The "Cool Mom Clothes" masked how I was anything but relaxed for that first year back from maternity leave. I wanted to be the one looking after my pre-school children, but still held to the notion I had created about what an academic looks like, and how an academic mom should act. Then, in the fall of 2007 I got pregnant again.

Almost as soon as I had peed on a stick I had already started figuring out how unbelievably wonderful the following maternity leave would be. This time I would get it right. I thought I could finally strike the perfect balance between work and motherhood. I would write children's books, capturing the phases of babyhood, toddlerhood, and beyond with the expertise of an academic, but also the experience of a mother. My oldest starting kindergarten, my middle one turning three and a new baby at home—it would be perfect! I could write. I could be with my kids. Oh, the joy, the wonderment ... the unrealistic expectations I had and how unprepared I was for what was about to happen next!

In the midst of all the mental gymnastics in February 2008, I got the shock of my life when I was told at a routine ultrasound to confirm my dates, "there is no heart beat." I had a miscarriage. I will save a long and sad story of heartbreak and healing. Suffice it to say—this rocked my world. This loss made me realize how much more motherhood is to me than something I do, it is part of *who* I am and has radically transformed my sense of being in the world. In May 2008, I attended my first Association for Research on Mothering (ARM) conference and presented a paper based on my experience with early pregnancy loss and the social censure around miscarriage. I would experience two more miscarriages over the year that followed and had more opportunities to bridge the gap between theory and practice as I searched for explanations and found myself at two more conferences discussing miscarriage from the dual vantage point of scholar and mother.

MAYLAH GRACE

On June 28th 2010 at 6:44 pm my daughter, Maylah Grace, came into the world. Her name means miracle, and she is ours. Her journey to us was a harrowing one, an adventure I didn't plan. Especially in the last month as her due date approached (and passed!) I anticipated the joy and awe I would feel when she arrived. The intensity of the emotions I experience(d) is indescribable. She is so amazing. I have arranged a reduced workload and will be able to be her primary caregiver for most of the first year of her life. This situation is not ideal, as my institution only financially compensates me for 12 weeks of maternity leave. In moments of calm clarity (which are few and far between with two school-age boys and a baby in the house), I acknowledge and am so grateful that I am able to be an academic and a mother, without having to sacrifice either for the sake of the other entirely. But I now acknowledge that something *does* have to give. I am not willing to let it be my children. The lesson I have learned in all of this is how much of these two inter-related journeys I do not control. I can send away a paper and it can be rejected. I can take my child to his first day of school and he can want me to stay longer than I do. I have finally come to terms with and accept that my CV is not going to look as impressive as I once hoped it would. In this phase of my academic journey I have small children and their needs are many times going to take priority over my work. There have been and will be times, as well, when my teaching or my writing or my research will require that I am unavailable to lay with them before bed, for instance. This next year I will continue to reflect upon what matters at work and at home and I will make plans and goals for after my maternity leave. This time around I hope to be able to more fully embrace the mothering moments—whether that moment is a cuddle with my daughter, a car ride with my kids to hockey, or the first day of school. In turn, I hope I can do the same with my work life; that is, when I return to it. For now there are three little beings that need me to be their mom; there are school supplies to label, new clothes to buy, lunches to prepare, a vaccination appointment to attend, a play date to accompany my kids to (all real things on my Mom's to do list), etc. This time around the "first day of school" is going to be all about them!

I didn't get a doctorate so that I could be a Mom. However, it is my position as an academic mother that enables me the opportunity to be with my kids in the manner I choose. I did not get a Ph.D. to be a Mom … or perhaps I did.

15.

Integrating the Personal and the Professional

Reflections of a Full-Time Academic Mama in the Early Childhood Years

RACHEL EPP BULLER

Throughout American institutions of higher learning, including my own graduate program in art history, the perceived pinnacle of achievement for graduates is to land a tenure-track faculty position at a university that, for the price of teaching a few classes, allows you (or indeed, requires you, for advancement) to continue your own scholarly research. But toward whom is the tenure-track model geared? And is a tenure-track position really the best and only option for graduates from a doctoral program? Particularly in our current economic climate, as more people return to graduate school while colleges and universities simultaneously slash faculty positions and even whole programs of study, it makes sense to look at job options in addition to or outside of academia. Extended online discussions abound regarding the benefits of earning a graduate degree and working in an outside field, while a recent book interrogates the Ph.D. seeker to determine, "So what are you going to do with that?" (Basalla and Debelius). <versatilephd.com>, formerly a listserv titled "Wrk4Us," is a bulletin board-style website devoted to alternative career possibilities for academics, or 'recovering academics.' A 2009 editorial in the *New York Times* called for an "end to the university" (including its tenure system) as we know it (Taylor), an opinion that then generated heated debate on the *Chronicle of Higher Education* website and an issue that continues to gain editorial attention. One of the biggest problems with the current system of tenure and promotion is that it still assumes a nineteenth-century model of professorship. This model presumes that its faculty is comprised of either single men or married men whose wives assume full responsibility for home and family so that the man might fully live the life of the mind. Multiple recent edited collections, including *Mama, Ph.D.* (Evans and Grant), *Parenting and Professing* (Hile Bassett), and *The Family Track: Keeping Your Faculties While You Mentor, Nurture, Teach, and Serve* (Coiner and George), address in detail the myriad ways in which the establishment of academia sets up serious obstacles for those who wish to maintain both family and professional lives. There is much to be said for trying to change the system from the inside, but if the system is designed to work only for a select few, it seems reasonable that we should investigate other options as well. My essay explores some of the possibilities that exist for academic mothers outside the tenure system. Using my own situation as an example, I will argue that the alternative career path of the independent scholar can offer many more and diverse work options and provide far more flexibility than can the tenure track. Following some explanation of my journey to reach this point, I will outline how pursuing writing opportunities, interdisciplinary connections, and grant funding can afford academics the freedom to step off the tenure track. I will also detail how this unconventional path has allowed me to integrate my personal and professional worlds in concrete, dynamic, and critical ways.

REASONS AND RATIONALES

How did I get to this place and why does it continue to make sense for me? To begin with, I discovered, like so many scholars before me, that in academia, there is never a "good" time to have children. Do you attempt to manage this during graduate school, or wait until after completing your degree? Do you put your career on hold? Do you try to have one parent at home, or do you look into fulltime daycare? Can you afford either option? Does your employer grant parental leave only to the mother, or to the father as well? Can you take family leave if you're adopting a child? The reality is that, unlike most businesses, the majority of American colleges and universities have no set family leave policy, instead forcing individual faculty members to work out some sort of leave on a case-by-case basis within their own school or department.[1]

I earned my Ph.D. in 2004, birthing our first child ten months after passing my comprehensive exams, and our second, five days after defending the dissertation. But after graduation? That's when things got interesting. I now had two small children, and I was no longer a student.

Was I suddenly a stay-at-home mom? What about my years of academic training? In the post-partum haze, it felt as though the situation was happening *to* me, out of my control. Emerging from that haze, though, I recovered my agency and actively pursued a solution that would include both work and family. In the years since I finished school, my partner and I have negotiated a workable balance—sometimes trading off who works and who stays home, who travels for work at which time, while maintaining our shared commitments to raising children and developing professional lives.

A disclaimer up front: making this work is not always a lucrative proposition, though it is getting to be more so; were I a single parent, my choices might well be different, simply for financial reasons. And yet, I must honestly assess the decisions my spouse and I have made, none of which were based on financial gain. After having children, we moved to be closer to extended family and took a 40 percent pay cut in the process. While we recognize that we operate from a position of educated privilege, usually able to get by on one income, we also make creative choices and significant sacrifices in our financial balancing act.

In 2007, journalist Leslie Bennetts published *The Feminine Mistake,* a well-researched book that details the clear financial costs to women who step off the career track in favor of family, either temporarily or permanently. "It has become inescapably clear that choosing economic dependency as a lifestyle is the classic feminine mistake" (Bennetts xxiii-iv). To others, our financial and work choices no doubt look like not just feminine mistakes but general economic mistakes. With eyes wide open, we have both stepped off career tracks that would have led us to prosper more quickly, hoping to embrace the early childhood years before they slip away entirely. Even now, as two of three children have entered school, we discuss the ways in which our work choices will change in the coming years.

I in no way embrace the new cult of domesticity that Bennetts and others detail as having spurred so many of my generation to devote themselves entirely to home and hearth with no thought of a career, but I have found it far more fulfilling to chart my own course, making conscious decisions as a family about who works when and developing a variety of work alternatives, regardless of the more gradual rise in financial gain. Bennetts repeatedly notes the gender bias attached to the much-promoted-by-the-media concept of "having it all": "No one ever questions a man's right to have a family as well as doing meaningful work; nobody ever talks about men 'having it all' just because they've managed to sire children and hold down a paying job" (Bennetts 152). Countering the many stories she cites of women who regret, too late, the decision to forego a career, Bennetts also profiles cases in which individuals and couples devised creative solutions to managing life in between the media extremes of "opting out" and "having it all." Following Bennetts' lead, I provide some highlights from my journey so far of ways in which one mama-scholar is making it work outside of, or in addition to, academia. Based on my own experiences, I will argue that, rather than "opting out" or "having it all," the independent scholar can negotiate a path that moves within and around academia with a freedom that comes from the simultaneous development of alternative work opportunities.

WRITE, WRITE, AND WRITE SOME MORE

For academics not on the tenure track, it may be vital to your professional success, and perhaps to your own sense of professional self-worth, to maintain an active publishing life that will then be reflected in your curriculum vita. Book reviews are an easy commitment: they are quick to write, easy to find a venue for publication, and help to keep you abreast of current scholarship. Many academic journals welcome new book reviewers and will gladly send you books (to keep), if only you will write 500-750 words about them. Don't be afraid to look to smaller journals or even to ones that are related to your own field in an interdisciplinary way. In the past few years, I have written book reviews for *Woman's Art Journal, German Studies Review, The Space Between: Literature and Culture, 1914-1945*, and *Journal of the Association for Research on Mothering*. In my specific field, many publications also welcome exhibition reviews. For the past two years, I have been contributing regular exhibition write-ups to *Review*, a regional arts publication that actually pays (gasp!) its writers.[2] While most academic journals cannot pay their contributors (and indeed, in art history, authors may even have to pay out-of-pocket to have images reproduced), more popular-audience periodicals, and even local newspapers, may be willing to pay for good writing. It's often just a matter of persistent inquiry, along with a decent writing sample.

Another avenue for short, paid writing is the academic encyclopedia.

Thematic encyclopedias have exploded onto the publishing scene in recent years. As these are generally large, expensive volumes that are marketed primarily to libraries, publishers are able to pay contributors in varying amounts, depending on the length of the articles written. (A copy of the encyclopedia can sometimes be requested as an alternative form of payment, if desired.) As with book reviews, don't fear looking outside your immediate field. Many thematic encyclopedia projects have such a wide scope that there may well be entries specific to your discipline. I have contributed art entries to *The Encyclopedia of Sculpture* (Boström), *The Encyclopedia of Prostitution and Sex Work* (Ditmore), and *American Countercultures: An Encyclopedia of Non-Conformists, Alternative Lifestyles, and Radical Ideas in U.S. History* (Misiroglu). Calls for authors generally include a listing of the available entries and specific information regarding publication timeline and payment.

A more lucrative form of writing, if you can get it, is the textbook. In art history, this can include writing for general survey textbooks or for more specialized, upper-level texts. In addition, as universities strive to diversify their offerings without adding (or even when cutting) faculty, art history can be integrated into other humanities courses as well. Several years ago, I contracted as an author and art editor for a new edition of the textbook, *Patterns in Western Civilization* (Trulove, Woelfel, Auerbach and Epp Buller). The Humanities and Western Civilization professors heading up the project wished to broaden the scope of their course to include not just history but also art history and music history, so they wrote their own textbook. This book was required reading (read: required purchasing) for the university's 20,000 undergraduate students and the publisher marketed the textbook to other colleges and universities as well. Writing about works of art in such an interdisciplinary setting helped me in my own thinking about the work, shedding light on the art through specific historical and literary connections.

Publishers of survey textbooks that will be used widely in university teaching look for good writers with innovative ideas. I recently participated in a roundtable discussion at a national conference, hosted by a prominent art history publisher. By paying participants for their input, the publisher hoped to get feedback on new and existing educational tools and generate discussion about potential new resources. Such connections with publishers are valuable on multiple levels: if you are interested in textbook writing, you become a known quantity and are more likely to receive a positive response to your inquiry; if you are teaching classes, publishers will send you not only exam copies of textbooks but also various new faculty and student add-ons to test out; if you are looking into curriculum development, you can have a significant voice in the publisher's process of shaping pedagogical materials.

MAKE CONNECTIONS

The work lives of contingent faculty members and independent scholars can be extremely isolating. If your work does not enable you to have a built-in community of work colleagues, it is important to put forth the extra effort to make personal and professional connections. On a very basic level, seeking out support from other scholars who are in similar situations can help you maintain a certain level of sanity. Simply knowing that you are not alone can be tremendously empowering. You may be able to find such a support group within your own local community or via contacts with graduate school colleagues; if not, there are ample opportunities for making virtual connections across the globe from your own computer.

Attending conferences, at least periodically, fosters community through the exchange of ideas. Participating in a themed panel can introduce you to others working on related topics. National conferences may offer sessions geared toward non-traditional professional situations. National conferences are also valuable for their frequent inclusion of a book fair. Making the rounds of the exhibitors' tables and talking with publishers about your current projects allows you to practice presenting (selling) your ideas and to get feedback on the feasibility of your proposed publication. Publishers can be generous in their advice, directing you to a specific colleague whose press might be well-suited to your work. If attending your discipline's national conference seems overwhelming by its size, look into getting involved with the smaller, regional branches of the organization. Such groups will welcome your active participation and you will quickly develop a regional network of colleagues.

When connecting with colleagues near and far, consider developing your own larger, multi-participant projects. This can include organizing a themed series of speakers for a local university, chairing a conference session, or proposing an edited collection. Invitations lead to reciprocity, such as paid speaking engagements and consulting projects. And who knows, the prospect of a tenure-track job, with little room for advancement, may eventually pale in financial comparison with your independent projects.

EXPLORE GRANTS AND OTHER FUNDING

In the beginning, though, the earnings of independent scholars vary widely, depending on the kind of work they are able to locate. Without guaranteed access to university or other institutional funding to support research, grants and fellowships can be a valuable source of income. Everyone knows about some of the "big names" in fellowships, such as the American Association of University Women or the Getty Foundation. For lesser known, and less competitive, fellowships and grants, consult blogs, websites, and grant databases. Grants devoted to specific fields of study will be less competitive than those offered by interdisciplinary organizations such as the American Council of Learned Societies. It is a widely held belief among scholars that funding begets funding: once your work becomes legitimized through the receipt of one grant, other funding institutions will look at your proposal more seriously and are less likely to reject it out of hand. I give significant credit for my recent receipt of a large, international grant to the several lesser-known grants I received as a graduate student, thereby proving me on paper as a known quantity.

Pursue avenues of funding in your local area as well. Do not assume, for example, that small institutions do not have the funds to reward your efforts. They may be willing to provide an honorarium for a public presentation, or to pay you as a consultant for organizing a public programming series. Know that most universities, libraries, museums, and other organizations have access to a variety of sources of institutional grant funding, whether from private local groups or from state and federal agencies. I recently worked with a small historical museum that regularly receives funding from the state Arts Commission as well as the state Humanities Council to support their exhibitions, part of which can be used to pay for programming.

Grant funding can allow for community-building opportunities as well as your own professional growth. Particularly in the recent economic downturn, many grant agencies are directing their funds to projects that might help stimulate local recovery. This year, I wrote a successful grant for a community-based mural project to happen in our town, much of which was aimed at facilitating community involvement and providing job training to emerging artists.[3] Through local and federal grant funding, I plan to initiate an artist residency program within our community, a program that will bring in artists from other areas for some dedicated time to create new work and to exhibit to a new audience. A key component of this residency program will be the availability of family accommodations and help with the logistics of family needs, rather than the usual residency requirement that the artists travel and work alone.

BRING IT ALL TOGETHER

Ultimately, what has facilitated my development of an alternate career path, even while opting out of the tenure-track system, is that I have sought to integrate my personal and professional lives, or at least to define a significant amount of overlap between them. The life of an independent scholar is perhaps necessarily fragmented, comprised of so many varied components as to seem overwhelming at times—a description that applies equally well to mothering. In my own life and work, mothering has provided the connection between my worlds. This has taken on a variety of forms, in both art history and art production. Somehow, the birth of our third child spurred me back to work on my own art. I was a studio art undergraduate, with a love of history and languages, which translated well into an art history graduate program. I gave up any thought of studio work during that time, but years later I felt compelled to take up printmaking once again, perhaps seeking a creative means by which to survive the often overwhelming years of pregnancy and nursing.

One tangible benefit of this return to art-making has been developing connections in the regional art community. Through a funded Artist Exchange mentoring program, I found artists to inspire me, to raise critical questions about my work, to act as a sounding board for ideas, and to function as a network of support. Because of this, I have continued to make prints that confront and speak to issues of mothering. My year in Artist Exchange resulted in a monumental series of prints entitled *The Food Landscape*, which have generated national attention through conference talks and exhibitions. These "food prints" visually narrated the end of my breastfeeding journey. *The Food Landscape* is a series of screen prints, one for each day, from the time my youngest began eating solids at nine months, until she weaned at 17 months. For each day's print, the foods she ate are employed as the actual inks, pressed through the screen to reveal their natural pigments. The prints chart her gradually changing nutritional intake: in the early months, the food-image takes up very little space on the page, but by the late months, as she nursed less and less, the food occupies most of the page. The image is an abstracted one, the curvilinear shape of her mouth recorded in a series of drawings I did while she nursed, but the striations of food have often evoked for me a physical landscape, as well as the details of her own culinary landscape. Month by month, the prints show the progression as the food gradually takes priority over the breast milk. In its finished form, each month of prints constitutes its own accordion-fold book. Shelves full of books, cataloging a period of growth.

More recently, *The Identity Series* marks the changes, overlaps, and transformations of identity that occur in the life of the family. Initially conceived as a grouping of representational portraits, the series later morphed into an abstracted idea of portraiture, taking as its formal basis one fingerprint of each member of our family. Printed individually, the fingerprints highlight unique genetic qualities; when layered, they can speak to the temporary masking of identity that occurs in the position of motherhood. In hand-stitched print blankets, issues of genetic difference overlap, literally and metaphorically, with larger implications of family position—individuality alongside and within familial identity. The most recent print "quilts" combine the fingerprints with fragments of the representational portraits, further playing on issues of identity and likeness. These visual memoirs of motherhood use traditional patchwork quilting patterns to draw on a lengthy history of women's artistic creativity and on my own Mennonite cultural heritage.

In art history as well, I seek to integrate my personal and professional interests. Happening upon the Association for Research on Mothering and Demeter Press coincided with a turning point in my scholarship, as I shifted my focus to issues of mothering, the maternal body, and parent-child collaborations in contemporary art. In conference papers, essays, and articles, such as for Amber Kinser's *Mothering in the Third Wave*, I examine the work of artists like Renee Cox, Mary Kelly, Jess Dobkin, Louise Bourgeois, Carrie Mae Weems, and many others (186-98).[4] Where there was for centuries a relative taboo on many aspects of motherhood in art, the topic has gained increasing art world legitimacy within the past twenty years. As in our larger culture as a whole, which has witnessed a flourishing in the publishing industry of books that look critically at mothering issues, contemporary artists across the globe find this difficult position a rich field for critical discourse. My current book project, *Reconciling Art and Mothering*,[5] collects essays by visual artists and art historians around the world who reflect upon their own reconciliations of the personal and professional. I was overwhelmed with initial responses to the project, underscoring the ever-timely nature of the topic.

CONCLUSIONS

As mothers and scholars, we need to be empowered by reminders that there is more than one single path to career success. The tenure system in higher education is an antiquated, gendered, and overcrowded model. As my spouse and I negotiate an acceptable back-and-forth of who works when in these early childhood years, we choose a life that, for now, balances relatively meager means in a small Midwestern town with the ability to spend days with our children and develop independent professional projects. We maintain strong connections to our fields while moving toward what Leslie Bennetts characterizes as "home equity," or gender parity within the world of domesticity. Clearly, our solution would not work for everyone, either ideologically or fiscally, but in rejecting the notion that personal and professional lives must be separate and distinct from one another, I offer up an alternative—to my children, my students, and my peers. There are clear paths to career success that depart from the institutional model. By writing, speaking, and publishing in diverse venues, exploring grant funding, and initiating any and all manner of independent, collaborative, or community projects, academic mothers and fathers can find professional fulfillment in ways that more fully accommodate or even integrate family commitments. I sometimes struggle against the idea (perhaps my own nagging worry) that I am not doing things the right way, even while I and others have forged clear alternatives. The payoff comes as I uncover the myth of the tenure-track necessity: my prints are being shown and sold, my international research will be funded despite my alternate path, and my family readily joins me in the adventures.[6]

[1]For more on this topic, see Coiner and George and, more recently, Evans and Grant.

[2]Formerly a glossy print publication, *Review* recently moved to an entirely online format. http://www.ereview.org

[3]The 2010 Kansas Community Mural Project was funded by monies from the National Endowment for the Arts, Mid-America Arts Alliance, and ARRA.

[4]Demeter Press, publisher of Amber Kinser's book, *Mothering in the Third Wave,* was founded by the pioneering Association for Research on Mothering (ARM). Although ARM was forced to close in spring 2010 due to lack of support from York University, it has since enjoyed a rebirth as the Motherhood Initiative for Research and Community Involvement (MIRCI) and will continue to publish ground-breaking motherhood scholarship through Demeter Press and through its *Journal of the Motherhood Initiative.*

[5]*Reconciling Art and Mothering* is forthcoming from Ashgate Publishing in 2012.

[6]Our family will spend much of 2011 in Berlin, funded by grants from the Fulbright Commission and the Gerda Henkel Stiftung, as I complete research for a new book.

WORKS CITED

Basalla, Susan and Maggie Debelius. *So What Are You Going To Do With That? Finding Careers Outside of Academia.* Rev. ed. Chicago: University of Chicago Press, 2007.

Bennetts, Leslie. *The Feminine Mistake: Are We Giving Up Too Much?* New York: Hyperion, 2007.

Boström, Antonia, ed. *The Encyclopedia of Sculpture.* 3 vols. New Brunswick, NJ: Routledge, 2003.

Buller, Rachel Epp, ed. *Reconciling Art and Mothering.* Farnham, Surrey, UK: Ashgate Publishing, forthcoming 2012.

Coiner, Constance and Diana Hume George, eds. *The Family Track: Keeping Your Faculties While You Mentor, Nuture, Teach, and Serve.* Chicago: University of Illinois Press, 1998.

Ditmore, Melissa Hope, ed. *The Encyclopedia of Prostitution and Sex Work.* 2 vols. Westport, CT: Greenwood, 2006.

Evans, Elrena and Caroline Grant, eds. *Mama, Ph.D.: Women Write*

About Motherhood and Academic Life. New Brunswick, NJ: Rutgers University Press, 2008.

Hile Bassett, Rachel, ed. *Parenting and Professing: Balancing Family Work With an Academic Career*. Nashville: Vanderbilt University Press, 2005.

Kinser, Amber, ed. *Mothering in the Third Wave*. Toronto: Demeter Press, 2008.

Misiroglu, Gina, ed. *American Countercultures: An Encyclopedia of Nonconformists, Alternative Lifestyles, and Radical Ideas in U.S. History*. 3 vols. New York: M. E. Sharpe, 2009.

Review magazine. http://www.ereview.org

Taylor, Mark C. "End the University As We Know It." *New York Times*. Web. 26 April 2009.

Trulove, Sarah Chappell, James Woelfel, Stephen Auerbach, and Rachel Epp Buller. *Patterns in Western Civilization*. Vols. 1 and 2. Boston: Pearson Custom Publishing, 2002 and 2003.

16.

Halving It Both Ways

Co-Parenting in an Academic Couple

KAREN CHRISTOPHER AND AVERY KOLERS

Thisessay explores our lived experiences as academic co-parents of two young children. Drawing from the theoretical framework of the university as a gendered organization, we explore how our tenure-stream faculty jobs have both bolstered and hindered co-parenting. The flexibility offered by faculty positions facilitates co-parenting—but has required our continual resistance to the culturally ascendant model of the ideal worker. We describe our divergent experiences of accommodation and resistance. We discuss strategies we have used to sustain co-parenting when working with mostly supportive colleagues, but within a largely unsupportive institution. Most notably, we have struggled with inadequate university policies that do not account for the everyday demands of caring for young children. We end with a brief discussion of the implications of our experiences to suggest that existing university policies and practices—while making some space for co-parenting—will often exacerbate gender and class inequalities among university faculty.

CO-PARENTING IN AN ACADEMIC COUPLE TO HALVING IT BOTH WAYS

At least in our house, the waking hours of young children are pretty much the working hours of the traditional full-time job: 9:00-5:00, with a few hours tacked onto each end. If we want to spend significant time with our kids, we can't work 9:00-5:00. So we don't. On a typical workday each of us works about eight hours, but does so in nonconsecutive blocks of time, much of which is spent at home. We are fortunate to be able to do so: tenure-stream academic work permits flexibility. This flexibility is offset, as everyone knows, by the fact that an academic's work is never really finished, and by the stiff competition for journal space and status in the profession. This situation is not conducive to spending long stretches of time with young children. But as we explain below, we are privileged workers within the university; we should represent a "best-case scenario" for co-parenting academic couples. If we can't manage this successfully, who can?

In this paper we explore our experiences of co-parenting as an academic couple. We first discuss how families and the university are gendered organizations. We discuss the "ideal worker" model and, in brief, the "intensive mothering" model and explore multiple ways they constrain co-parenting and favor inegalitarian families in the gendered context of the university. We then place ourselves within this framework and describe our attempts to challenge the gendered nature of university life. We conclude with several suggestions for changes in policies, institutions, and ideology that would foster co-parenting among faculty parents.

THE UNIVERSITY AS GENDERED ORGANIZATION: THE IDEAL WORKER MODEL

Drawing from Joan Acker, Christine Williams defines gendered organizations as those in which "cultural beliefs about masculinity and femininity are built into the [organization's] very structure" (9). In the United States, the "ideal worker" is one who works long hours with few if any breaks in employment for caregiving responsibilities (Williams, J.). But—as has been widely noted—someone still has to run the ideal worker's household. And despite women's steady increase in employment over the twentieth and into the twenty-first century, mothers today still perform two times as much child care and housework as their male partners, even when both work outside the home (Bianchi, Robinson, and Milkie). Clearly, it remains the case that men, but not women, are typically both entitled and expected to be ideal workers (Williams, J.). Thus, any organization that in effect assumes that its employees are ideal workers may fairly be described as a gendered organization.

The ideal worker can be a stern taskmaster for anyone, male or female, who seeks to share equally in parenting. Despite the recent increase in co-parenting, men are likely to find that formal and informal workplace sanctions hinder or penalize their efforts to be co-equal parents. Indeed, the informal sanctions that emerge from others' expectations and assumptions may even be greater for men than for women. For instance, men's co-workers will not typically expect them to leave work for daytime responsibilities such as school absences and doctors' appointments. Nor will men's supervisors take childrearing-associated productivity declines in stride. The departure from the gendered norm will be noted. That the workplace is gendered, and presupposes "masculinity and femininity," may thus be a source of significant stress not just for women but also for men.

The university constitutes a particular kind of gendered organization (Evans and Grant). Universities typically permit tenure-stream faculty a high degree of flexibility regarding the workday, but the tradeoff is that one is never really "off" work. Work follows us home at night, over the weekend, and on vacation. Most academics cannot temporarily "go part-time." Our jobs include three distinct functions—research, teaching, and service—each of which is hard to assess for either quantity or quality. So for purposes of employee evaluation, the university operationalizes "research and creative activity" into publications or grant dollars, and teaching into numbers of courses and students taught and numerical evaluations. (Service is neither quantified nor meaningfully rewarded.) These methods of assessment are imperfect at best, but may be most inadequate during what remain of an employee's peak childbearing years in the decade after the Ph.D.; during this time the ratio of new course preparations is high and the tenure clock—the clichéd "publish or perish"—demands output for its own sake rather than deep scholarship that might not be measurable by number of publications or monies awarded by grantmakers. Finally, at least at our university, annual reviews of work performance—which tie raises to these criteria—pit all faculty members within a department against one another for a limited pool of money. Co-parents whose numerically assessable productivity is temporarily compromised will be likely to miss out on pay increases that compound over their career. We already see this in the case of female faculty members; women earn on average almost $17,000 less per year than men across academia—a number that rises to almost $22,000 in Carnegie Research I universities (AAUP). It is likely that those who would be co-equal parents can look forward to this kind of wage penalty for both partners rather than just one.

More generally, academia itself is a highly stratified, transnational economic system that, like other such systems, expects its employees to structure their lives around it rather than vice-versa. Accordingly, the most desirable, tenure-track jobs typically require workers to relocate. The strong status-hierarchy among universities into which graduate students in top Ph.D. programs are socialized, combined with the straitened job markets of the past several decades, creates the vision of a career trajectory featuring occasional or even frequent "upward" moves. Those who desire such a career trajectory have added reasons to maintain their numerically assessable productivity at all times. Moreover, for the perhaps two decades when parents have dependent children, they must choose between postponing or altogether getting off this (aspirational) career trajectory, or uprooting their children. The same goes for visiting positions, teaching fellowships, summer institutes, and so on, which involve long stays away from home.

Clearly, then, both individual universities and academia as a labor system are stratified environments geared toward rewarding and reproducing "ideal workers." Because they presuppose that someone will be available to run the worker's household, universities are therefore gendered organizations, and academia is a gendered labor system. The gendered university is also created by inequalities in family life, to which we briefly turn.

Drawing from in-depth interviews of mothers and textual analyses of child-rearing manuals, Sharon Hays identifies an "intensive mothering" ideology—that mothers should be primary caregivers of children and that ideal childrearing is time-intensive, guided by experts, and emotionally engrossing. Intensive motherhood requires that mothers put the needs of their children above their own (8). Many scholars identify intensive motherhood as the culturally ascendant ideology of mothering in North America during the 1990s and 2000s (Arendell; Avishai; Douglas and Michaels; Johnston and Swanson). With its emphasis on the primary role of mothers in children's lives, intensive mothering is clearly gendered—mothers are expected to be far more involved with their children than are fathers.

Given the ubiquity of intensive mothering, when fathers are co-equal parents, both partners may need to struggle to avoid creating a doubly intensive environment—inventing "intensive fathers" alongside intensive mothers. Yet it will not do, either, to both become "ideal workers" and simply hire intensive help. Rather than fall into these traps, co-parents must challenge the gendered workplace. Next, we explore the strategies that we as co-parents have used to to do so.

NAVIGATING AND RESISTING THE GENDERED UNIVERSITY

Within the academic labor system, we are privileged along numerous axes: we are white, heterosexual—which, in Kentucky, allows us to be married—and entered tenure-track jobs in our late 20s, which gave us several years to focus on research before starting a family. We were also lucky to get two tenure-track jobs at the same university after only two years living apart. We had our first child in June 2005 and our second in July 2008. We both sent our tenure portfolios to outside reviewers in May 2005, which meant that our tenure files were essentially complete before the birth of our son. So far, we are also lucky to have two relatively healthy children. All of these advantages should be kept in mind when assessing our experiences within the gendered university, as our privileges and good fortune make us in many respects a best-case scenario.

Our aim is to be co-equal parents and co-equal workers. But the structure and policies of our university work against this aim in ways both large and small. Childbirth and adoption merit only six weeks' paid leave, and few other "family-friendly" policies kick in thereafter. At the time of our son's birth the university had no on-site childcare. (This has now changed.) As of this writing, our university had just institutional-ized a formal policy for stopping Assistant Professors' tenure clock for childbirth, but there are no such policies for tenure-stream faculty to either work part-time or temporarily take on "modified duties" due to caregiving responsibilities.

Further, these inadequate university-wide provisions engender arbitrary intramural inequalities among those who have children. For one thing, a sympathetic and savvy chair can use course releases and other ad hoc methods to cobble together halfway decent paid leaves; an unfriendly or naïve chair can make things even worse. The luck of timing, too, lays bare more arbitrariness: because we work on ten-month contracts, the university believes summer births are none of its business. This fiction determined our circumstances after each birth. Rather than return to the normal 3-2 teaching load when our son was seven weeks old, Karen took a semester of unpaid leave and returned to teaching when he was seven months old. Our daughter's birth coincided with Karen's year-long sabbatical. That she could engineer such leaves made possible months of bonding and breastfeeding. But some new parents manage to work out similar arrangements *with* pay, and those who do not become parents are of course able to use their sabbaticals for uninterrupted research. Breastfeeding alone consumed over 600 hours—the equivalent of 75 eight-hour work days—of Karen's sabbatical. The point is not that nursing should be replaced by paid work, but that mothers of infants are, to a substantial degree, forced to choose. Avery undertook summer teaching before the birth of each child in order to reduce the teaching load during the semester, permitting more availability for childcare. This obviously ate into summer research time. Further, because the university's inflexibility pushed Karen into an unpaid leave, Avery was able, for financial reasons, to take only a semester's sabbatical. To quantify it, this amounts to over eight months' research time given up.

Individual-level Strategies of Resistance

Initially, at least, it would have been easy to slip into traditional gender roles; in light of the University's attitude, both physiological factors and our cultural upbringing would have made traditionalism the path of least resistance. We have, however, adopted several practical strategies to avoid that path. Interpersonally, our most valuable strategy has been creating—and, of course, following—a schedule that budgets every half-hour of the children's day. The schedule grants us equal or nearly equal time for paid work and childcare. The egalitarian schedule presupposes that we both want to spend significant blocks of time on child care and on paid work, and codifies our commitment to equality in each. And in the workplace, the schedule serves as a "bad cop," preventing us from taking on what the schedule does not permit.

We occasionally have to remind ourselves that the heavy childcare demands of young children will ease once they both attend elementary school—and, just as important, that the sixty-hour work weeks that were normal before we had children constituted *over*work. At times we have both felt like "less serious" academics compared to our higher research productivity before having children. Even short breaks from research can lead to longer-term feelings of distance from our area of expertise. In this context, normal setbacks (such as rejected papers) can become amplified and lead to questioning of our ability to stay relevant in our respective fields. Junior faculty members with children undoubtedly experience more acute dilemmas, and more serious repercussions. We also arrange our work hours differently and more efficiently since having children; almost every moment of time in the office is now spent working (not socializing, taking breaks, or surfing the internet). As the opening paragraph of this essay suggests, we often fit our work into non-standard work hours—such as early mornings or late nights—when the children are asleep.

While our individual efforts have given us some success in co-parenting, the university functions as a gendered organization that, on balance, works against us in this respect. As stated above, the parental leave policies, and until recently, child care policy, are completely inadequate. Furthermore, when no one in a department has young children, the everyday functioning of the department takes on a childless character. Total flexibility is assumed; people are expected to be on campus or available at any and all times, and may be chided when they are not. Such tendencies may be no one's fault, but it falls to the co-parent to chafe against them before any change is likely. Both of us have had to speak up—at times loudly and repetitively—for such changes. Our department heads have usually been supportive of our efforts to shift the departments' cultures from childless to family-friendly. They let us organize class schedules to facilitate co-parenting; further, they schedule department meetings in advance so we can arrange child care, support our leaves, and generally accept that our family lives take up a substantial amount of our time. However, there is only so much they can do, since they have little control over the larger university policies and procedures that presume an "ideal worker."

Institutional-level Strategies of Resistance

On an institutional level, Karen previously chaired and currently sits on a university-wide "Family-Friendly" policies committee that is working to expand the piecemeal policies our university currently offers. This committee has succeeded in allowing employees to extend the tenure clock for caregiving reasons, and slightly increasing paid leave for childbearing and adoption (from three to six weeks), and is working on implementing more flexible schedules for university workers. The current administration has been receptive to such changes, and we are cautiously optimistic about some degree of continued progress.

These kinds of institutional changes are critical to allay the psychological and economic costs incurred by co-parents in the university. For example, policies that allow faculty to stop the tenure clock when they have heavy caregiving demands acknowledge the substantial time and energy that children (as well as dependent parents) take away from research and teaching. Moreover, policies that allow faculty to work part-time for periods in their career should help parents share paid and unpaid work more equally; of course, this strategy is possible only for parents who can afford to do so. Finally, research universities could devise strategies for assessing and rewarding service and teaching responsibilities as much as research—which would ease the pressure for an annual published output.

That teaching should count as much as research perhaps goes without saying. But it bears emphasizing that service is principally faculty governance; if there is no faculty governance, either the university goes corporate or it goes nowhere. Greater institutional support for faculty governance—for instance, a genuine possibility of promotion based on university service accomplishments—would benefit both the university and parents who want to shift in that direction temporarily while they have young children. More generally, the (re)establishment of a professoriate with dedicated teachers and dedicated faculty-administrators, in particular, would allow faculty members with young children to excel in ways that are congenial to their distinctive burdens, skills, and interests, which may of course change over time. Such a system would accommodate faculty parents and many others as well.

Faculty participation in shaping university policies and procedures is also crucial. As in other gendered organizations, those running the university tend to be male, and—due to class and/or gender privilege—to have no experience as working co-parents. Karen's experience on the Family-Friendly policy committee has shown that effective steps to erase administrators' knowledge deficit, such as cross-institutional comparisons, can have real impact. In addition, faculty can tap into their social networks across campus to show that the lack of a standard policy on issues like course releases after childbirth leads to inequitable treatment of faculty across different departments and units. More informally, faculty need to raise their voice in everyday interactions to have more say in standard university practices: scheduling meetings far in advance, not when parents are likely to miss them (such as mid-afternoon when schools let out, or early evenings, when families aim to eat dinner together), and allowing more child-care for campus events can make the campus more welcoming to all parents on campus. This will obviously be easier for those of us with the job security that tenure provides; therefore, the onus to stand up for family and/or personal time should fall most heavily on tenured professors.

Yet changing the gendered nature of the university is not sufficient for gender equality—and it is typically a long, slow process. Changes in family life need not be onerous or complex in order to challenge the "intensive mother" model. Admittedly, even when we consciously aim to resist gendered practices in childrearing, decades of traditional socialization work against most of us. But what might begin as small changes in family life—such as implementing an egalitarian childcare schedule or relying more on "community mothering" (see O'Brien Hallstein)—can also give parents both more resources for, and more of an interest in, changing their workplace. For example, if more men assumed greater responsibility for the care of their infants, they could better understand the need for policies that temporarily stop the tenure clock or allow more flexible schedules. And meeting up with other faculty parents could aid in organizing to bring these changes about. These feedback effects go in both directions: after the implementation of the Swedish policy of "daddy leaves"—under which couples forfeit a portion of paid leave unless fathers take it—Swedish men became much more involved in day-to-day parenting tasks. Thus, policy changes and changes in family life can reinforce one another.

CONCLUSION

We conclude with a caveat and a justification. First, the caveat: stratification of the academic workforce. Compared to tenure-stream faculty, part-time and term faculty have less flexibility, earn far less, get lower priority in teaching assignments and schedules, and may commute more, including to multiple different institutions for teaching jobs. They are also much more likely to be women. That they are not expected to engage in research or service may be cold comfort, adding insult to injury. Most of the changes we have suggested would not address the stark class inequalities among university faculty, and may in practice exacerbate them. Deans and chairs might, for instance, happily grant full-time faculty members' leave requests, since cheaper part-time faculty can be hired in their place. Because of the gender division between tenure-stream and other faculty, however, we have reason to hope that chipping away at the gendered university will also chip away at the stratified university. Unless these problems are addressed together, "family-friendly" policies risk being friendly only to the families of already privileged workers.

Finally, it may be objected that all these policy proposals cost money, and would just further subsidize the optional reproductive preferences of families who already receive significant tax and other incentives for parenting. It is true that tax policies already partly socialize the costs of parenting, and it is legitimate to wonder how socialized these costs should be given that they are often optionally incurred. But our proposals are less about how socialized or privatized these costs should be, than about how these costs should be socialized when they are. Current practices socialize the costs of parenting in ways that reward families for accommodating and reproducing gender stratification in the workplace and in the home. A gender-egalitarian workplace would, like the Swedish "daddy leaves," reward gender egalitarianism. And such a workplace—particularly a university—would be good for students and faculty, and for the quality of the work we do. Rearing children in a way that manifests gender equality is furthermore good for children; a generation of children reared this way would be a public good of the first order (see Folbre).

WORKS CITED

Acker, Joan. "Hierarchies, Jobs, Bodies: A Theory of Gendered Organizations." *Gender & Society* 4 (1990): 139-158.

American Association of University Professors (AAUP). "No Refuge: The Annual Report on the Status of the Profession, 2009-10." *Academe* 96.2 (2010): 3-80.

Arendell, Terry. "Conceiving and Investigating Motherhood: The Decade's Scholarship." *Journal of Marriage and the Family* 62.4 (2000): 1192-1207.

Avishai, Orit. "Managing the Lactating Body: The Breast-Feeding Project and Privileged Motherhood." *Qualitative Sociology* 30 (2007): 135-152.

Bianchi, Suzanne, John Robinson, and Melissa Milkie. *Changing Rhythms of American Family Life*. New York: Russell Sage, 2007.

Douglas, Susan and Meredith Michaels. *The Mommy Myth: The Idealization of Motherhood and How It Has Undermined Women*. New York: The Free Press, 2004.

Evans, Elrena and Caroline Grant, eds. *Mama, Ph.D.: Women Write about Motherhood and Academic Life*. New Brunswick, NJ: Rutgers University Press, 2008.

Folbre, Nancy. *The Invisible Heart: Economics and Family Values*. New York: The New Press, 2001.

Hays, Sharon. *The Cultural Contradictions of Motherhood*. Princeton: Yale University Press, 1996.

Johnston, Deirdre D. and Debra H. Swanson. "Constructing the 'Good Mother': The Experience of Mothering Ideologies by Work Status." *Sex Roles* 54 (2006): 509-519.

O'Brien Hallstein, Lynn. "Second Wave Silences and Third Wave Intensive Mothering." *Mothering in the Third Wave*. Ed. Amber E. Kinser. Toronto: Demeter Press, 2008. 107-118.

Williams, Christine. *Still A Man's World: Men Who Do Women's Work*. Berkeley: University of California Press, 1995.

Williams, Joan. *Unbending Gender: Why Family and Work Conflict and What to Do About It*. New York: Oxford, 2000.

17.

Great Expectations for Moms in Academia

Work/Life Integration and Addressing Cognitive Dissonance

MARTA MCCLINTOCK-COMEAUX

I N A 2009 INTERVIEW, First Lady Michelle Obama stated, "...Work-family balance isn't just a policy conversation; it's about changing the expectations of who we have to be as women and parents" ("Oprah Talks to Michelle Obama"). Amen, (super achieving, role model) sister. Women in academia have huge expectations for ourselves or we would not have survived the higher education marathon to the Ph.D., EdD, DSW, or MD. Women with gigantic career expectations do not leave them on the welcome mats of our homes. We shoulder them in our personal lives as mommies, partners, caregivers, friends, community members. Profound expectations, when combined with diligent work and commitment often have profound rewards. However, current societal expectations for mothers and workers require unflinching dedication to both, a feat that is humanly impossible. Thus, expectations at work and at home are set so high that they cannot be realized. Socialization often dictates (at least to some degree) internalized cultural standards. Thus the pressure to perform at a level beyond what is realistically possible as both paid workers and moms is inflicted not only from the larger society, but from internalized pressure. No matter how much academic mothers achieve in each arena, the ultimate feeling for many is still one of failure due to unmet (unrealistic) expectations.

This chapter begins with an explanation of my own navigation (thus far) through the journey of combining motherhood with academia. In a way this work is self-serving, as I hope the process of working through these theories will assist my own feelings about my work/life integration, but I hope my exploration through personal experience will serve the reader well, perhaps connecting similar experiences and perspectives.

This chapter next explores two contrasting theories regarding work/life integration. One, the expansive hypothesis, offers an optimistic, positive perspective on all that is gained from combining multiple roles, such as: academic, mother, partner, community volunteer, etc. A second theory, the scarcity hypothesis, asserts that a multitude of roles and responsibilities induces stress and struggle. I hypothesize that currently mothers in academia more often endure the scarcity hypothesis in work/life integration due to the overwhelming demands placed upon women in each of these roles. The ideal worker norm and intensive mothering theories, combined with gendered patterns that exacerbate expectations specific to women are explored to support my hypothesis. These competing pressures lead to *great (unrealistic) expectations*, and cognitive dissonance for academic moms. The chapter continues by exploring cognitive dissonance. The chapter concludes with strategies aimed to ease the struggle that exists for women trying to meet multiple expectations, including tactics to relieve cognitive dissonance and achieve cognitive consistency, altering family expectations, changing public discourse, addressing university expectations, and changing national policies. My experiences in combining work and family roles are woven throughout the chapter in an effort to connect theory to personal experience.

MY MOTHERHOOD/ACADEMIA STORY

I am now an academic mom who is trying to figure out how to make it all work. "It all" meaning having three boys ages six and under, one baby on the way, a partner whom I adore, a tenure track university professor position that combines my love of teaching and passion for social justice as the director of women's studies, friends whom I rarely get to see, and community work as a coach, board member, fundraiser, leader in my church, and activist.

My journey into examining work/family integration research began eight years ago as a doctoral student when I talked to a mentor about when was the best time to have children as an academic. A few months later, Mary Ann Mason and Marc Goulden's article "Do Babies Matter?" which explores the effects of kids on academics' careers was published and placed in my mailbox by that faculty member. Their findings were that yes, babies matter a whole lot (3). For married men they correlate with career benefits; for academic women, the correlations were not nearly as positive (Mason and Goulden 3). My reaction? I got pregnant. In the summer of 2004, I submitted my written comprehensive exams, delivered my first child two weeks later, then successfully completed my oral defense two weeks after his birth with baby, stroller, and Mom-in-law in tow. The next two years were spent teaching and conducting research for my dissertation on Tuesdays and Thursdays while my son was in childcare and Saturdays when my husband was home. All other days and in the evenings when my son was awake, I was the portrait of a devoted, nurturing, committed mommy. Because I felt that I was *losing* time with my son when I was not with him, I embraced every moment I had with him. I sang to him while we were in the car or out for a walk, I carried him, citing made up rhymes and showering him with affection while I folded laundry or vacuumed. Most often I was on the floor, engaged in every age appropriate activity I could think of. We built with blocks, worked on puzzles, sorted shapes, danced and sang. We went to music class, tumbling class, the park, the zoo and library story time. I hugged and cuddled him, provided supportive comment on his every movement and word. I loved being a Mom. I also felt guilty though. I felt guilty for the time that I did not spend with him, and I felt guilty that I enjoyed the time when I was not with him that I spent on my work. I felt guilty that I was not getting my dissertation finished fast enough and that I should spend more time conducting research, publishing, writing grants, and completing other professional tasks. No matter where I went, there was the guilt.

I continued my pattern of combining birth and deadlines. I distributed my dissertation to my committee November 2006, delivered my second child two weeks later, and successfully defended my dissertation in December 2006. Of course, next to enter, was the pressure of finding a job. During the early spring of 2007, I attended a full day academic job interview, armed with my breast pump, plenty of breast pads, and prayers that I would not leak milk onto my stylish new black interview blazer. I had to request two "pump breaks" during the interview day. These seemingly minor details were huge challenges at the time. I had to tell the male chair of the search committee that I needed the pump breaks, and I needed to find a room on campus where I could sit in privacy with an outlet for my pump.

A month later, I was with my husband, our two-year-old, and our four-month-old in our car ready to go into a hospital. Doctors had just determined there was nothing else they could do for my 27-year-old brother who had battled leukemia for 17 months. He was full of cancer cells with no other treatment options. At this moment is when the call came with the job offer. It was my ideal job. The priority of this tenure track position would be teaching, but I would also serve as the Director of Women's Studies. This outstanding offer came at a time when the delicacy of life and its limits came crashing down around my family and me. It was one of the moments in a lifetime where the importance of time with people we love becomes the focus. I had *always* known I wanted to be a mom, and especially at this moment of saying good-bye to my little brother, I feared letting time and moments slip away with my kids due to competing requirements of this new potential career. Could I really be the completely devoted mom I wanted to be and still have a paid job? Simultaneously, I love teaching. I love learning. I had dedicated myself to the Ph.D. degree so that I could have this career. I am a feminist to my core, thus the director position was a perfect match. The responsibilities of this job could not have been better for me. Could I really perform at the level that was required to be a successful academic? I told the Dean I appreciated the offer and that I would get back to her about the position.

Over the next four days, my entire family stayed together in my parents' home while my brother was in hospice care at their house. My mom hardly left my brother's side. This was not a surprise. My mom (with my Dad) raised eight children and devoted her life to motherhood. She was an intensive mother before the identity had a name and she thrived in the role. She was a mom who made our Halloween costumes, attended every sporting/dance/music event, kissed scraped knees, and always told us and showed us that she loved us unconditionally. When my brother was diagnosed with leukemia, she stopped her life as she knew it and moved to care for him in every way that she could for 17 months. This was my model for what it meant to be a mom. I did not know how I was going reach that bar she set for motherhood, while also working full time, but I knew I wanted to try. I negotiated on the phone with the Dean and accepted the offer. The next day, my beautiful, courageous, fun-loving brother passed on.

The next four months required grieving, finding and buying a home, packing, moving, unpacking, finding childcare, and starting two new careers (my husband found a great job as a principal in an elementary school).

During my first year as a faculty member, I worked out a teaching schedule where I did not have to make the long commute to work every week day, affording me more time with my kids. A gold star for my identity as a mom. I also coached soccer teams, joined the childcare center/preschool board of directors that my kids attend, volunteered for the leukemia and lymphoma society, and joined my church's leadership body. As a new tenure track faculty member, and someone who loves my work, I could certainly not allow my work performance to slide. I work long, full days when I make the commute into work and most nights after I put my kids to bed. That first year I got the Women's Studies program off the ground, profoundly increased the number of WST minors, planned and implemented an annual conference, updated course requirements, applied for grants, presented research and successfully taught a 3-3 load. I was exhausted, but holding it together.

At the end of my first year as an assistant professor, I became pregnant. My third little one was due at the end of November, prior to the end of the semester. My university does not have set policies for how to handle such situations (yet). I worked furiously to make certain every detail was set prior to my leaving to birth my child. Two weeks after his birth, I was calculating final grades for the semester. When my third child was six weeks old, I started the spring semester and from January through May, my unintentional mantra in my head was, "I can't keep doing this." I literally thought I was going to collapse from exhaustion. I was getting 3-5 hours of interrupted sleep a night, every night. I was trying to bond with my newborn, making certain my other two boys felt completely loved and valued, prepping three courses, planning and conducting a conference, and directing the Women's Studies program. It was crazy making to say the least.

In my third year as a tenure track faculty member I have grown the Women's Studies minor, created two new courses, successfully taught another 3-3 load, with the assistance of outstanding students I planned and coordinated more educational, dynamic programming than ever before, planned and implemented another successful conference, and I believe I have put Women's Studies "on the map" at my university.

The 2010-2011 academic year is the final full year before I submit materials for tenure. So, of course, when there is career pressure, what do I do? I get pregnant. At the time of writing, I am nine months pregnant with our fourth baby. This time, I plan to do things differently. To start, I will arm myself with knowledge of the profound challenges facing academic women both at work and at home, then plan a strategy for how I will move in a positive direction to change my own and others' expectations, which will also hopefully change my experience.

This chapter is one facet of my work toward increased sanity and decreased feelings of failure. No matter how hard I work, it is never enough to achieve my overwhelming expectations of myself as a Mom and an academic. So, as I try to understand my own struggles for work/life integration, I look for knowledge in how to conceptualize this task.

WORK/LIFE INTEGRATION: THE EXPANSIVE HYPOTHESIS

An optimistic perspective that highlights the benefits of combining multiple roles, such as motherhood and paid work, is the *enhancement perspective* (Marks 926). This theory suggests that time and energy are subjective. If we feel commitment and positive regard to our roles, then we will have abundant energy. Rosalind Chait Barnett expanded upon this idea, also emphasizing the quality and rewards from multiple roles, called the *expansion hypothesis* (Barnett 152). For academics, it is likely safe to assume that most people have a commitment to their work (due to the amount of work it requires to attain such a position); it is likely that we have profound interest in investing energy in our work. The expansion hypothesis asserts that there are abundant benefits both physically and mentally from having multiple roles, such as combining work and family responsibilities. There is research that documents the benefits of multiple responsibilities. Those who have multiple roles report lower levels of anxiety and distress (Thoits 270) and women who do not work for pay outside of the home report high anxiety, while those working for pay do not (Barnett and Baruch 144). Multiple roles have been found to enhance self-esteem, power, and social connections (Barnett 152). Paid work also results in feelings of being in control, increased autonomy, and improved social skills. In higher education, faculty often have control, at least to some degree, of the classes we teach and the issues we tackle in our research, which is likely to lead to greater career satisfaction.

Another benefit of academia is the flexibility of the work. While there are schedules and time sensitive commitments, a large part of the responsibilities, such as teaching preparation, grading, research, writing, can be done at various times in various locations. Flexibility of work hours is a factor that relates to stress (Perry-Jenkins, Repetti, and Crouter 987). The greater the flexibility one has at work, the lower the stress level will be for the employee. Another plus for academic moms.

The caveat with the expansion hypothesis is that there is a ceiling. If one has too many roles and responsibilities, the experience turns to being overloaded and overwhelmed, thus tumbling into *the scarcity hypothesis*.

WORK/LIFE INTEGRATION: THE SCARCITY HYPOTHESIS

Role multiplicity requires strategic juggling for faculty moms integrating work and home responsibilities. At work, most academics are balancing the tasks of class preparation, grading, writing grants, conducting research, writing papers, presenting at conferences, serving on department and university committees and much more. At home, most moms are *on task* with kids, reading books, playing games, doing puzzles, engaged in imaginative play, going to the playground, hitting baseballs, helping with homework, kissing scraped knees and heads, consoling after fights with friends, struggling with curfews, planning birthday parties and holiday celebrations, attending artistic and sports events in which kids are engaged, not to mention shouldering laundry, grocery shopping, meal prep, cooking, cleaning, dishes, etc. The scarcity hypothesis asserts that time is limited, and thus as the number of tasks increase that an individual must complete in a given amount of time, the stress also increases. This hypothesis also highlights the tension that occurs from competition of roles and responsibilities (Greenhaus and Beutell 77). If the tasks for one role absorb time and energy, it makes it difficult to complete other tasks, leading to increased stress. Research supports the scarcity hypothesis experience, particularly for women. "To move through the professional ranks (e.g., receive promotions, become a partner, get tenure), one is still expected to devote huge amounts of time and emotional energy to the profession, an expectation that renders career advancement and raising a family virtually incompatible-at least for women" (Coltrane 215). Joan Williams book, *Unbending Gender: Why Family and Work Conflict and What to Do about It* explores work/family negotiation and determines that women are especially likely to struggle with the conflict and scarcity because they are often responsible for the majority of childcare and household responsibilities while also trying to excel in careers. Williams believes that it is impossible for women to be successful at both, based on societal standards, specifically because of the *ideal worker theory*.

EXPECTATIONS AT WORK: IDEAL WORKER THEORY

According to Williams, the ideal worker theory applies primarily to professional and managerial level positions and developed as a result of the separate sphere family structure, based on a traditional, hetero-sexual, married couple model of the man at paid work and the woman at home. With this structure, the paid employee prioritizes work, and the spouse (usually the wife) is at home taking responsibility for the children and household. If the boss asks "him" to stay late for a project, he does not need to worry about getting kids off the bus, fed, or ready for bed. Someone else takes care of those details. A second important component of this theory is that the ideal worker is expected to work throughout her/his lifetime with no time off. For a woman who wants to and is able to birth biological children, this is an impossibility (Crosby, Williams and Biernat 677). Such women literally cannot meet this standard. A third important component of this model is that the ideal worker's career takes priority. The ideal worker changes jobs as needed to move up the career ladder. If that requires changing hours or geographic location, the family adjusts to accommodate the ideal worker's career needs.

While this theory was based on a traditional, heterosexual, married household, the rules are still applied to all professionals and managers, regardless of family structure. The majority of married and dual parent households now have both adults working for pay outside of the home, however, expectations for dedication to careers have not wavered. In fact, they have escalated. The number of hours worked throughout the year continues to increase for those in "white collar" jobs such as academia (Jacobs and Gerson 20). Faculty report on average at least 50 hours dedicated each week to their paid jobs (Jacobs and Winslow 5). The stakes are especially high during the first few years in academia when on the tenure track. Tenure requirements are structured well for families who have a traditional model with one adult (specifically men) earning the income and the other devoting full time to children and the household (Williams 68), but not for academic moms.

In a culture that has immense expectations for performing dedication to work, it seems impossible for those trying to balance work and family life to be successful. As a tenure track faculty member, I feel this immense pressure. Simultaneously, I do not want these career goals and pressure to overshadow my dedication and prioritization of my family and my role as a mom. In fact, I feel immense pressure to prove my relentless dedication to my children and to being their mom.

EXPECTATIONS AT HOME: INTENSIVE MOTHERING

Mother is a significant identity for many women. Motherhood is a life event for women that is idealized in dominant culture. However, there are significant performance expectations and assumptions for moms that are beyond human possibility. The *maternal bliss myth* by Deirdre Johnston and Debra Swanson describes "that motherhood is the joyful fruition of every woman's aspirations ... (and) any maternal unhappiness and dissatisfaction (is attributed to) failure of the mother" (22). Cultural expectations for quality parenting are specifically based on sex. Taking on the quality mothering role is all encompassing, assuming that moms are completely devoted to their children and always responsive to their needs (Kobrynowicz and Biernat 587). Expectations for extreme dedication to the mothering role have been titled *intensive mothering* (Hays 6). Intensive mothering is a gendered model wherein mothers are to spend "...copious amounts of time, energy, and material resources on the child. A mother must put her child's needs above her own. A mother must recognize and conscientiously respond to all of the child's needs and desires, and to every stage of the child's emotional and intellectual development" (Hays 8). Overwhelmingly, the dominant cultural messages in the United States embrace and smother women with this overwhelming mothering ideology (Johnston and Swanson 21). Mothers' interpersonal time with their children is about three times the amount that fathers spend (Williams 124). Expectations for Dads have increased and father involvement in care giving has increased (Coltrane 217) however mothers and fathers are still not held to the same standards in caregiving expectations.

It can be assumed, given these findings, that a woman who does not experience eternal joy, is not completely encompassed, and is not emotionally absorbed in her role as a mom is falling short of the expectations for motherhood. How do women meet these expectations while also meeting the ideal worker expectations? The sad answer is, she physically cannot do both, and there are often consequences.

THE GENDERED EFFECTS OF COMBINING ACADEMIA AND MOTHERHOOD

Tenure track faculty members are required to meet research, teaching, and service requirements as specified by a university. Faculty members typically have five to six years from the commencement of her or his position to prove her or his ability to perform, thus "amping up" the ideal worker demonstration. For women, this timing of the greatest career pressure to perform often coincides with the time of greatest "time on task" as parents, when birthing and then caring for young children. Countless colleagues worked hard to align their timing of getting pregnant with semester or summer breaks (I admit to attempting this timing as well). There is no "good" time to have a baby in the middle of the semester if trying to simultaneously perform as an ideal worker. This is especially true when universities do not have clearly defined policies for how such circumstances are handled. How can one prove her ideal worker status when her baby is due week five of a fifteen-week semester?

There are consequences for mixing parenthood with the academic arena, but it seems to be a problem specific to women. Men are more likely than women to have tenure track and tenured academic jobs, to have published peer reviewed research and to have higher rank and salaries. Women are more likely to drop out of academia and are less satisfied with jobs and potential future within their jobs (Baker).

Gender representation discrepancies in academia are not surprising as research demonstrates that there is discrimination against academic moms. Personal and career capabilities of moms are often presumed lower than all men and women without children. Pregnant women are less likely than non pregnant women to be hired (Bragger, Kutcher, Morgan and Firth 223). Being a mom decreases the likelihood of being contacted for a job, but the same is not true for dads (Firth 898). Moms, as compared to dads, are assumed to be less competent (Friegen, Biernat, Haines and Deaux 748). Mothers earn far less wages for the same jobs as fathers (Crosby, Williams and Biernat 676) and "the mere anticipation that a woman will adopt the motherhood role is sufficient to elicit negative work-related evaluations" (Friegen, Biernat, Haines and Deaux 751). Stereotyped expectations for moms' potential are lower, which results in career consequences. Thus, it is likely that career moms must outperform others, and exceed all expectations to disprove the myths about mothers' paid work performance to prove their dedication to the socially constructed ideal worker role.

Academic moms endure conflicting messages that to be a "good" mom, they must perform complete dedication to children, yet to be a solid academic, they must demonstrate complete commitment to their work. These competing expectations inflict stress and an uncomfortable state of cognitive dissonance.

COGNITIVE DISSONANCE

A common human desire is to have consistency among beliefs, thoughts, opinions, and behaviors. A disconnect between one's attitudes and behaviors often results in cognitive dissonance, a feeling of discomfort that one experiences in the midst of the conflict (Festinger 260). The severity of the discomfort usually relies upon the quantity of disconnections, and the extent of the mental and/or emotional ties one has to each of the beliefs (Festinger 179). The amount of discomfort may also be influenced by the effort exerted in the various competing priorities (Festinger 262). Goals and identities that require exceptional time, effort, and dedication are likely to provoke more extensive stress when they contrast with other identities that required similar commitment. For example, a university faculty member who has earned a Ph.D. completed countless years of academic work to achieve that identity. Similarly, one who has a child makes a profound commitment to the time, energy and responsibilities required to be a parent.

The ideal worker theory imposes expectations that one demonstrates complete commitment to work. To achieve the highest expectations of motherhood, being an *intensive mother*, one must demonstrate complete commitment to that role as well. When one attempts to simultaneously embody these identities and meet these expectations, extreme cognitive dissonance is inevitable. Thus, academic moms are left with a quandary. How can we comfortably live among the tension of seemingly incompatible identities, responsibilities, and expectations?

RESPONDING TO COGNITIVE DISSONANCE: SEEKING COGNITIVE CONSISTENCY BY MAKING INTERNAL CHANGES

Those who experience cognitive dissonance are motivated to alleviate the discomfort (Festinger 263). Moving away from cognitive dissonance results in moving toward cognitive consistency, a state where one feels more at peace and less tension in her thoughts and feelings.

There are several strategies for relieving cognitive dissonance, some of which include 1) changing an attitude or belief that is in conflict with one or more of the others; 2) learning new information that counteracts the original beliefs; 3) decreasing the importance of the conflicting thoughts and/or feelings; 4) making different choices that alleviate the conflict; 5) increasing the appeal of one's current state by highlighting the benefits of the current thoughts, feelings, and experiences and exposing the negatives that would occur if one had made different choices. (Festinger 264-265). These options focus on the behaviors of the individual and some may be effective in decreasing internal stress and improving well-being.

I have considered these options for myself and considered (and in some cases attempted) at least one option of how I would put them into practice in my own life. It seems that strategies one and two (changing an attitude or belief and learning new information) need to be implemented jointly, as changing an attitude or belief does not happen on its own. For example, I want to "change my belief" that to be a successful academic and a successful mom I would have to dedicate 100 percent commitment to both. To make this change, I try learn new information that there are other women who are successful at both, while also dividing their time. I have talked to friends and their children in families where women had both successful professional careers and their kids rated them as "amazing" and/or "cool" moms who "were always there for them," (this statement was made even if they literally weren't "there" as the kids attended childcare several days a week or the family had a nanny while their moms were at paid jobs). There are examples of women (and specifically academics) whose employers have recognized their outstanding work via promotions and tenure, while simultaneously their kids give their moms high marks. Acquiring information that there are kids out there who rate their moms as excellent, regardless of the unrelenting cultural messages of the full dedication required to be a good mom, gives me hope that some of my most important critics, my own kids, might have the same feelings and reactions about my performance as a mom. Thus, I can *change my mind*. To address number 3, decreasing the importance of the compelling and conflicting thoughts or feelings, I have created my own "theory of relativity" where all of my concerns and stresses are relative to other matters or more specifically, other people.

So, when I begin to get consumed with feelings of insecurity and stress about work/life integration, I focus on others who have more severe challenges related to debilitating diagnoses, kids with severe genetic/developmental delays, or national/international issues that truly compromise people's health and well being. My cognitive dissonance, at least for a time, fades to the background as my work/life dissonance seems less compelling. In addressing number 4, making different choices that alleviate the conflict, I am attempting a new strategy in how I handle the birth of my fourth child and my responsibilities as a faculty member. I will take the full eight weeks of medical leave that my doctor prescribes. I will return to my paid work with a quarter-reduced course load for the spring semester by teaching one fewer class. The classes I do teach will be online. This approach slightly reduces the amount of time and commitment that will be required, and also affords me greater flexibility, a benefit that has been shown to reduce stress. Finally, I often try to increase the appeal of my current life by imagining what my life would be like if I made different choices (number 5). While I never imagine the "what if" I did not have children, I do sometimes consider "what if" I stopped my career as an academic. I am confident that I would be disappointed with myself, less satisfied, depressed, and frustrated. I know that I would be less content in my Mom role and my "performance" as a Mom would be greatly compromised. I know that when I think realistically, although the grass at my feet sometimes seems burned out and worn, I do not want the "green grass" of the neighbors who have made the choice to be home full time, as that is not what is in the best interest of my family or me.

Addressing the cognitive dissonance would be an important accomplishment and one that would alleviate some of the stress that arises from multiple, demanding, conflicting thoughts, feelings and behaviors. However, making change beyond our cognitions and including changing our expectations of our families, our universities, and our policies, is likely to result in longer term, more extensive changes and allow academic moms to move from the experience of the scarcity hypothesis to the expansive hypothesis.

SEEKING THE EXPANSIVE HYPOTHESIS BY CHANGING EXPECTATIONS
CHANGING FAMILY EXPECTATION

At a baby shower I attended recently, some of the women in the room participated in a conversation, laughing and joking about how they loved when they were pregnant and when the baby was born because their husbands (the women in the conversation were all heterosexual, married women) actually cooked, changed diapers, helped with the other children, and helped around the house. All of these women have paid careers and children in the home. Why in the world would expectations for equal participation in care for children and the home end after pregnancy and the development of a newborn? Mothers report more stress than fathers and mothers report the highest levels of work family conflict as compared to all other groups (Duxbury and Higgins 31, 33). Women do the majority of the childrearing, and we also take on the majority of the household responsibilities. Expectations for us in the home are overwhelming.

In traditional role segregation, men take on primary responsibility for tasks that require intermittent time, such as home and car maintenance, cutting the grass, shoveling snow, etc. Women most often have primary responsibility for tasks that require more consistent time and energy, such as cooking, doing dishes, cleaning, bathing and feeding kids, etc. A shift has occurred in the past several decades, in that men are contributing more to caring for children and the household than their fathers did, but still not nearly equal to what women are doing (Coltrane 217; Jacobs and Gerson 30). What is in the best interest of families is when both people in the couple are involved in caretaking and household duties, and the assignment of roles is based on skills and interest rather than gender. To address gendered caretaking tasks, Williams recommends employing equally shared parenting (244, 257) wherein the adults distribute caretaking jobs in ways that are equitable and that tap into the skills and interests of each adult rather than relying upon socialized cultural, gendered dictates.

To change expectations for household tasks and childcare, we first need to document where we are. My suggestion for changing expectations is in four parts. One, each member of the couple, during a typical week, create a grid documenting the amount of time spent on each household, caretaking, and career task each day of the week. Two, each person make a list of the tasks they enjoy and in which they excel, then a second list of the tasks they abhor. Three, each member of the couple shares her/his grid and the list of tasks she/he enjoys with her/his partner. Four, the couple works collaboratively to delegate tasks in a way that maximizes shared time, workload, and interest/ability in the task. This process will highlight incongruence and change expectations for more equitable distribution of responsibility, and hopefully maximize satisfaction and happiness for the individuals and the couple.

CHANGING THE PUBLIC DISCOURSE OF MOTHERS' AND FATHERS' ROLES

One of my husband's most frustrating experiences in life happens almost every time he takes our kids out by himself. I am not talking about tantrums, but rather about other people's comments. Several times on each occasion, others make comments such as, "Oh, Daddy is babysitting today" or "Wow. Daddy is out all by himself. That is so brave." How is it that a father caring for his children is considered a "babysitter?" These comments signal the cultural expectations that exist for parenting roles. "Mommy" would rarely be used in either of those incidences. These comments suggest that dads are unwilling or unable to be a primary parent.

A second strong signal of our expectations is how we integrate the word "help" when we discuss familial roles. In the earlier example of the women at the baby shower discussing their husbands' increased "help" indicates that the household and childcare roles are her responsibility, and he may do more or less to support her. We often use similar language with reversed genders discussing income when we talk about "her" income "helping" in paying the bills, signaling that his income is primary and her paid work adds a given amount to the standard. If we change language and change minds from presupposing gender related responsibilities and instead allow families to freely determine the best structure and function for their families, it is likely that we will change the burdensome expectations, especially for moms.

CHANGING UNIVERSITY EXPECTATIONS

Joan Williams articulates the ideal worker theory and highlights the struggle for women who want to have kids and have successful careers (1). For academic women, this can be especially challenging. Some parts of the dilemma can be solved if universities have clear, family friendly options for faculty. Some of the most elite universities have changed their expectations and have adopted family friendly policies. The University of California (UC) has a range of options available to all faculty, but they were developed to meet the needs of women faculty who most often are responsible for caretaking duties. The UC system has implemented 1) Active Service with Modified Duties for those who are preparing for or experience responsibility for at least 50 percent of childcare with the birth or adoption of a child. This option is not full leave, but it decreases career responsibility for a given amount of time without penalty; 2) Tenure clock stoppage; 3) Flexible Part Time Options; 4) Up to 4 months paid leave "disability"; 5) Unpaid leave for up to one year (University of California Family Friendly Edge). Similar policies have been implemented at The University of Michigan (Family Friendly). Stanford implemented $5,000-$20,000 annual childcare grants for junior faculty (Jaschik) and many other universities have recognized the need to provide family friendly options.

The old outdated standard was that each employee needed to figure out for her/himself how s/he would adjust to meet the needs of her/his university. Top institutions now realize that to be competitive in recruiting and hiring top faculty, they must shift their expectations of themselves and demonstrate their flexibility in attempting to meet the diverse needs of their employees.

CHANGING PUBLIC POLICY: UNIVERSAL CHILDCARE AND PAID FAMILY LEAVE

Two policy changes that would provide immense relief for academic moms are universal childcare and paid family leave. We had universal childcare in the palm of our hands until President Nixon vetoed the bill. If we can get such a bill to the president's desk once, we can do it again. There are outstanding activist organizations, such as Momsrising.org, that are working toward these types of policy changes.

The United States is one of only four countries that does not offer paid leave to new moms. How can this be in the world's "super power?" Imagine the superpowers that would be unleashed if families could afford quality childcare and could free our minds from the stress and worry about who, what, when, where our kids will be taken care of. To make these crucial policy changes, expectations of how we care for each other in this country and expectations of the resources our government should provide need to change.

In February 2010, it seemed that paid leave was on the horizon, as President Obama's budget included funding to assist states in paying paid family leave (washingtonpolicywatch). Currently there is still no further an indication that this plan will come to fruition. However, the fact that it became an item on the budget for the current administration indicates that this issue has the potential to become a priority.

CONCLUSION

Academic moms are pressured to perform at the highest level with complete commitment to multiple roles. At home, we endure intensive mothering expectations where we must perform unwavering devotion to our children and home. In our careers we are blasted with the ideal worker norm where we are required to demonstrate around the clock availability and a relentless production of research, service, and out-standing teaching. Simultaneously competing priorities result in cognitive dissonance, an uncomfortable tension that exists when our feelings and beliefs do no match our behaviors. The dissonance is connected to the work/life integration theory, the scarcity hypothesis, which asserts that trying to embrace multiple roles produces stress due to our limited time and limited energy. There are alternatives to living with cognitive dissonance, the scarcity hypothesis, stress, and guilt that so many of us endure. We can make changes to move toward cognitive consistency, a more peaceful and less tense state. This will also move us toward the expansive hypothesis, where we focus on the multitude of benefits we enjoy from our various roles.

Changing our minds and behaviors can relieve some of the cognitive dissonance. We can learn new information, decrease the importance of stressful thoughts, make different choices, and focus on the benefits of the life choices we have already made. Changing our family expectations by examining how our time and energy is allocated in the household and dividing tasks more equitably can move us toward more realistic demands and less stress in the household. Changing our language so that we have less gender bias can be a sign for ourselves and others that moms and dads do not have pre-determined roles unless we allow it to happen. Changing our university policies so that they are clear and support all who are working to integrate work and life demands will ease the stress for moms who are each trying to figure it out on their own. It will also legitimize the reality that academics have responsibilities outside of their careers and hopefully alleviate some of the ideal worker norm expectations. Finally, changing public policy will change the work/family experience. Having paid family leave and paid childcare alleviates the financial and time burden so many families endure. Making that change will also bring the United States to equal status of almost every other industrialized country in the world regarding work and family policy.

Changing expectations is not an easy task. It is a process that must occur among multiple arenas, including within our selves, and it will be a huge challenge. However, if there is one thing that we have proven as academic moms, it is that we are prepared to take on a challenge. Perhaps one day we will even meet the challenge of our own great expectations.

WORK CITED

Baker, Maureen. "Choices or Constraints? Family Responsibilities, Gender and Academic Career." *BNET: The CBS Interactive Business Network.* 2010. Web. 4 January 2011.

Barnett, Rosalind Chait. "A New Work-Life Model for the Twenty-First Century." *The Annals of the American Academy of Political and Social Science* 562 (1999): 143-158. Print.

Barnett, Rosalind Chait and Grace Baruch. "Women's Involvement in Multiple Roles and Psychological Distress." *Journal of Personality and Social Psychology* 49 (1985): 135-145. Print.

Bragger, Jennifer, Eugene Kutcher, John Morgan and Patricia Firth. "The Effects of Structured Interview on Reducing Bias Against Pregnant Job Applicants." *Sex Roles* 46 (2002): 7&8, 215-226. Print.

Coltrane, Scott. "Elite Careers and Family Commitment: It's (Still) about Gender." *The Annals of the American Academy of Political and Social*

Science 596 (2004): 214-220. Print.

Crosby, Faye. J., Joan C. Williams and Monica Biernat. "The Maternal Wall." *Journal of Social Issues* 60.4 (2004): 675-682. Print.

Duxbury, Linda and Chris Higgins. "Work-Life Balance in the New Millennium. Where are We? Where Do We Need to Go?" *Canadian Policy Research Networks Discussion Paper* W12. (2001): n. pag. Web. 20 March 2011.

"Existing Elements of the Family Friendly Package for UC Ladder-Rank Faculty." The University of California Family Friendly Edge. Web. 2 May 2010.

"Family Friendly: Policies, Programs, Services, and Benefits for Faculty at The University of Michigan." Work Life Resource Center. Web. 2 May 2010.

Festinger, Leonard. *A Theory of Cognitive Dissonance*. Stanford, CA: Stanford University Press, 1957. Print.

Firth, Michael. "Sex Discrimination in Job Opportunities for Women." *Sex Roles* 8.8 (1982): 891-901. Print.

Friegen, Kathleen, Monica Biernat, Elizabeth Haines and Kay Deaux. "Mothers and Fathers in the Workplace: How Gender and Parental Status Influence Judgments of Job-Related Competence." *Journal of Social Issues* 60.4 (2004): 737-754. Print.

Greenhaus, Jeffrey H. and Nicholas J. Beutell. "Sources of Conflict between Work and Family Roles. *Academy of Management Review* 10 (1985): 76-88. Print.

Hays, Sharon. *The Cultural Contradictions of Motherhood*. New Haven, CT: Yale University Press, 1996. Print.

Jacobs, Jerry A. and Kathleen Gerson. *The Time Divide: Work, Family and Gender Inequality*. Cambridge, MA: Harvard University Press, 2005. Print.

Jacobs, Jerry A. and Sarah E. Winslow. "The Academic Life Course, Time Pressures and Gender Inequality." *Community, Work & Family* 7.2 (2004): 143-161. Print.

Jaschik, Scott. "The 'Family Friendly' Competition." *Inside Higher Education* (April 25, 2007): Web. 2 May 2010

Johnston, Deirdre D. and Debra H. Swanson. "Invisible Mothers: A Content Analysis of Motherhood Ideologies and Myths in Magazines." *Sex Roles* 49 (2003): 1-2, 21-33. Print.

Kobrynowicz, Diane and Monica Biernat. "Decoding Subjective Evaluations: How Stereotypes Provide Shifting Standards." *Journal of Experimental Social Psychology* 33 (1997): 579-601. Print.

Marks, Stephen. "Multiple Roles and Role Strain: Some Notes on Human Energy, Time and Commitment." *American Sociological Review* 42.6 (1977): 921-936. Print.

Mason, Mary Ann and Marc Goulden. "Do Babies Matter?" *American Association of University Professors* (2002): n. pag. Web. 28 April 2004.

MomsRising.org. Web. 2 May 2010

"Oprah Talks to Michelle Obama." *The Oprah Magazine*. n.d. Web. Oprah.com. 22 February 2009.

Perry-Jenkins, Maureen, Rena L. Repetti and Ann C. Crouter. "Work and Family in the 1990s." *Journal of Marriage and the Family* 62 (2000): 981-998. Print.

"Paid Family Leave Included in Obama's Budget." Washington Policy Watch. Web. <washingtonpolicywatch.org>. 1 February 2010.

Thoits, Peggy A. Multiple Identities: Examining Gender and Marital Status Differences in Distress. *American Sociological Review* 51 (1986): 259-272. Print.

Williams, Joan. *Unbending Gender*. Oxford: Oxford University Press, 2001. Print.

3. Possibilities

18.
Autonomy in a Chilly Climate

Authority, Self-Confidence, and Resistance

SYLVIA BURROW

I DID NOT EXPECT TO BE a mother and an academic. I was happy that I did not become a mother when I was a graduate student, even though I was in a child-friendly Philosophy department. I would look at our well-organized professors and graduate students who were successful at parenting in academia and think, "if they can do it, maybe I can too!" But I made the right judgement in leaving a bad relationship and put my focus completely on my career. I defended my dissertation while beginning my first sessional position, graduating at the end of that academic year and then moving countries again for the next sessional position. I quickly landed a tenure-track job where I wanted to be in Canada. Now I have a solid relationship and a toddler. I am happy to be a mother but confused about my status as an academic. Am I taken as seriously by my students, my colleagues, or upper administration as I was before I became a mother? The president of our university welcomed me at the annual Christmas party by asking me if I would raise my daughter as a feminist. I wonder how this question might be taken politely. At the same time, my feminist consciousness raises concerns about the implications or innuendos of his comment. My experience as an academic philosopher raises deeper concerns about autonomy. In this essay I consider how status and authority affect autonomy and hence, career success for academic mothers. My account appeals to philosophy but its implications extend well beyond this academic discipline.

Women in philosophy encounter masculine values and ideals that are interwoven into both philosophical argumentation and discourse. Janice Moulton shows that philosophy values combative, aggressive forms of argumentation, which she calls *adversarial argumentation*. Her work has since been expanded upon to show that metaphors of masculine aggression help shape and define the ideal model of philosophical argumentation (Rooney 2010, 1994; Haslanger; Burrow 2010). In this essay I consider argumentation to include any form of discussion aimed at cooperative or persuasive ends, following Christopher Tindale.[1] Argumentation is distinct from *discourse*, which may have no aim or purpose beyond mere communication. I show that argumentation and discourse are *gendered* according to masculine and feminine norms and values. My point is that masculine ideals and values underwrite philosophical argumentation and discourse. This should come as no surprise since philosophy is, and has been for quite some time, dominated by men. Feminist philosophers have shown that philosophy is a chilly climate for women and have continued for several decades to point out that the numbers of women in philosophy remains startlingly low, even while the presence of women in other academic disciplines has risen (Garry; Crasnow; Haslanger; Penaluna). Much of the feminist response to the chilly climate aims to change the conditions in philosophy to be more inclusive to women and especially marginalized women. But little, if any, of this work on the chilly climate addresses harms to *autonomy* that women academics or academic mothers experience. I discuss autonomy here in its broadest sense as self-governance expressed through choice formation and pursuit. I plan to show that philosophy's masculine-dominated climate undermines women's autonomy, illustrated by the case of academic mothers. I extend this account to those areas of academia dominated by masculine values and ideals, arguably most disciplines.

In the next section I explore how academic mothers encounter difficult choices between family and career commitments that work against mother academics counting as ideal academics. The third section shows how academia's oppressive social conditions threaten autonomy through undermining self-confidence and hence forms of self-appreciation such as self-trust, self-respect, and self-worth. The fourth section shows that philosophy has a competitive and combative atmosphere that reveals masculine values and ideals of aggression creating a chilly climate for women. I argue in the final section that this chilly climate is similarly evident in other academic disciplines dominated by masculine discourse. The chilly climate endorses masculine interests and values at the cost of feminine interests and values, hence it works against women's choices to be both academics and mothers. Whether academic mothers subordinate family commitments or subordinate our academic commitments, we are exposed to masculinist assumptions about what it means to be a serious academic. Hence, we need to work at being taken seriously as academics; that is, to be regarded as academics with status and authority. Pressure, reproaches, and judgements from others in academia suggesting that academic mothers are not serious academics can undermine autonomy through damaging self-confidence, self-respect, self-worth, and self-trust—the very grounds for autonomy. My aim in this paper is to draw out how such chilly views of status and authority constrain academic mothers' autonomy. Loss of autonomy is harmful in itself but it also weighs heavily on the possibility for both career success and personal integrity.

CHOOSING BETWEEN FAMILY AND CAREER: THE DOUBLE BIND

A recent report by Robert Drago *et al.* shows that more women than men in academia practice behaviours aiming to minimize, hide, or neglect family commitments in order to improve their appearance as ideal academics, especially if those women are mothers. The authors also note that academic mothers often return to work soon after childbirth, have less children than non-academics (either one or two), or space their second child's birth well apart from the first (Drago *et al.*). These sorts of actions aim to limit childcare responsibilities to open up more time to pursue academic career goals. But this approach receives mixed results, exemplified in the following cases. Deborah Ross, a single mother, picked up her daughter after school and took her to events like Girl Guides. She was granted her request of no afternoon or evening classes by her department chair. What Ross didn't expect was that she would be so bitter for having given up so much of her academic interests to meet her parenting demands. After years of successful teaching and research, Ross's application for full professor was turned down while similarly successful male junior colleagues received that promotion. While Ross thought that her department's accommodations would give her a good balance between personal and academic life, it cost her promotion. She later expressed regret that she chose time with her daughter over her career in the years before tenure (Ross 40). Rebecca Efroymson asked to have a part-time academic status that allowed her to be in the office from 10:00 am to 2:00 pm. Even so, she was embarrassed to tell her fellow academic scientists that she could not make an 8:00 am meeting because she knew she would be at the "Mommy and Me" exercise classes she did with her son. Heidi Newberg took half-time status after receiving tenure, but needed to pay a nanny to do 40 hours of work per week. While her status was part-time, her hours were much longer. She tried to educate her colleagues that she is paid less to do less work but could not ignore the resentment directed at her for "not working as hard as everyone else" (Newberg 96). University administrators echoed the view that she was "unproductive," a view emerging around the time she requested part-time status. She later reflected on this similarity of timing, wondering if perhaps the real problem was that she requested a workload decrease to have time to care for her four children (97).

Whether an academic mother alters her family commitments or her work commitments, such choices can be difficult because pressures to be a "Serious Academic" work against being an academic and a mother. I call "Serious Academics" those that have endless time to devote to their academic lives at the cost of their personal lives. Serious Academics are never torn between family commitments and work, not pressured by the demands of a breastfeeding infant, a busy toddler, or a special needs child. Academic mothers are continuously choosing between how much to give up of their personal life for the sake of their career (see for instance Evans and Grant). Those that give up personal desires to have more children or spend more time mothering may experience regret over lost family opportunities for the sake of career progress. Those that aim to modify their workload to accommodate family commitments can experience regret over serious repercussions to their career status or progress. Choices can be agonizing, resulting in guilt and regret that one has managed to be neither a good academic nor a good mother. Sometimes the choices *seem* obvious, but this need not alleviate later worry or regret. Marla McIntosh, a full professor, reflects on her academic success and her position as associate dean. She chose to leave her children under others' care while she focussed on her career. She did not find it hard to make this decision, rationalizing that "because of who I am and who they have become, my family gained more than they lost by having a working scientist mom" (McIntosh 53). But after stepping down as associate dean, she regretted the choice for full-time care for her children and wished that she had worked part-time through the early years of her children's' lives. While weighing our decisions, we are never certain exactly how things will turn out. As in Ross's or Newberg's case above, professors might think that they have an accommodating chair or dean but find out much later than those "accommodations" leave deep scars in their careers. Or, as in McIntosh's case, professors might feel they have given too much to their careers at the expense of mothering.

Experiencing merely *difficult* choices does not indicate more of a problem for academic mothers than it does any other academic challenged by administration, colleagues, or any sort of personal situation. What makes the limitations on choices for academic mothers problematic is that academic mothers experience limitations on choice. Moreover, these limitations introduce harms to academic mothers that are difficult to escape. As feminist theorists have long recognized, when social or political structures systematically limit or harm persons because of their membership to a certain group or groups, those members experience oppression. Double binds are exemplary forms of oppression. In a double bind, either of two options pose limits or harms that seem inescapable. In this essay I show that academic mothers experience double binds and other forms of oppression that impede career success. But this is not my main goal. My main aim is to argue that oppression against academic mothers impedes success because it undermines *autonomy*. Threats to academic mothers' autonomy are not merely threats to the capacity to choose between caregiving interests and career success. As I show below, autonomy is central to the self's wellbeing in an overarching sense. Autonomy is damaged if positive self-regarding attitudes such as self-trust, self-esteem, self-respect, or self-confidence are sabotaged. Suffering loss in any of these areas of self-appreciation can alter or fragment integrity through cutting away the ground upon which one stands up for one's commitments. So on my account, undermining academic mothers' autonomy comes with serious personal costs extending well beyond any damage to one's career or family possibilities.

SERIOUS ACADEMIC MODEL: A CHALLENGE TO ACADEMIC MOTHERS' SELF-CONFIDENCE

Philosophy has traditionally cast autonomy as the defining feature of persons who are wholly self-determining and completely independent beings. Feminist philosophy overturns this idea in light of a relational view of the self that recognizes that persons are *not* wholly independent beings. We are attached to other persons in varying forms of relations that contribute to who we are: mothers, sisters, friends, aunts, employers, nannies, and so forth. Relational autonomy aims to capture that relational view of the self. It understands autonomy as a capacity developed *through* our social relations or otherwise affected *by* our relations to others (for a discussion, see MacKenzie and Stoljar). This essay expands the latter view to show that autonomy can be limited by others through their ability to affect those self-regarding attitudes necessary for autonomy. My view is that oppressive social conditions in academia erode core elements needed for autonomy through undermining women's status and authority.

Recent feminist work on autonomy reveals a newly emerging view that certain forms of self-appreciation ground autonomy, notably self-trust, self-esteem, self-worth, and self-respect. I will outline this view and then add a further component, self-confidence, as necessary to those grounds for autonomy. Trudy Govier explains *self-trust* as a core component of autonomy. Trust in another is typically founded on our view of others' motivations and competencies; it includes a willingness to rely or depend upon others, even though we are aware that they may not act as we expect. Self-trust includes similarly positive beliefs about one's own motivations and competencies, as well as a willingness to rely or depend upon oneself that accepts the risks of one's decisions and one's own vulnerabilities (Govier 104-06). Self-trust is necessary to autonomy because deliberating and choosing on the basis of one's own values, beliefs, and judgement requires trusting one's beliefs and competencies to form judgements and values (111). Without self-trust, a person cannot think and decide for herself and thus, cannot function as an autonomous being. Govier ties self-trust to *self-esteem* to show that self-esteem is necessary to autonomy. On her view, self-trust requires basic self-esteem since self-trust requires a positive sense of one's own motivation, competencies, and so forth. Basic self-esteem is basic self-acceptance, which supposes that one is a worthy and adequate person (113). This view of self-esteem is similar to Paul Benson's (1994) view of *self-worth* as a regard for oneself as competent to answer for one's own conduct in light of others' demands. We can see a parallel between these ideas of self-esteem and self-worth and that of self-respect. *Self-respect* relies on an evaluation of one's own worth because we respect what we consider worthy in ourselves. But there is a more basic sense in which we are self-respecting. Robin Dillon explains basal self-respect as a basic valuing of oneself as a worthy person, captured in our "primordial interpretations of self and self-worth" (Dillon 1997: 241). Dillon shows that damaged basal self-respect focuses on our shortcomings and insecurities. This focus on ourselves results in a "moral indulgence" of only regarding other persons insofar as they affect our sense of security and worth. In contrast, secure basal self-respect permits persons to see the independent moral value in other persons and things (242). The social and political point Dillon makes is that oppressive circumstances such as those that tell women we are "worth less" erodes basal self-respect in destructive ways, harming possibilities for self-construction, self-valuation, and self-perception (248). It is implicit to Dillon's account here and elsewhere (1992, 1997, 2004) that oppressive circumstances eroding basal self-respect seriously undermine autonomy. Without basal self-respect it is unclear how we are supposed to form judgments, make choices, and act as a person worthy of thinking and deciding for herself. Basal self-respect, like self-esteem and self-trust, seems essential for autonomy.

Autonomy can be undermined by social and political forms of oppression. Oppressive practices eat away at our ability to trust our judgements and to view ourselves as worthy to choose and act according to our beliefs and values. In a similar vein, those who experience damaged self-trust, self-esteem, or self-respect may not be able to withstand others' reproaches, criticisms, or views of oneself as incompetent or otherwise inadequate. Lacking self-appreciation diminishes resistance and resolve to act against oppressive circumstances, which diminishes autonomy. But more than self-appreciation is necessary to autonomy. I consider self-confidence to ground self-appreciation (see Burrow 2009). Self-confidence is opposed to self-doubt: to doubt oneself is to lack self-confidence. Without self-confidence, we cannot resist pressures working against self-esteem, self-respect, and self-trust. Self-confidence is necessary to self-trust because doubting our judgements or beliefs signals a lack of trust in our ability to decide or act. So too, without self-confidence, self-esteem and self-respect are undermined because each is opposed to doubting our self-worth. So on my account, self-confidence is central to resisting those pressures working against self-appreciation and hence, autonomy.

As we saw above, academic mothers can face criticisms from colleagues for taking time away from work, for adjusting their workload or schedule, or for allowing themselves time to care for their children. I suggested above that judgements, pressures, or reproaches from colleagues, chairs, deans, or administration suggest a similar theme, namely that academic mothers are not Serious Academics. Underlying this view is that academic mothers are somehow less competent or adequate than they were before they became mothers, and certainly not as competent or adequate as the ideal scholar. Views such as this undermine autonomy if they erode self-esteem, self-worth, or self-respect. It is likely they will do so because experiencing such negative pressures, whether overtly or covertly, tends to undermine self-confidence. Doubt begins to creep in: Am I compromising too much of my work now that I am a mother? Have I lost focus on my career while I single-handedly manage a household? Can I function as I once did now that I am tired all the time or stretched too emotionally thin with multiple family commitments? Even the most self-possessed person can encounter dents in her self-confidence as an academic. My point is that academic mothers have many more pressures working against their confidence than other academics; hence, academic mothers encounter more pressures threatening autonomy than other academics. Costs to academic mothers' autonomy are not merely personal costs. Academic mothers whose autonomy is diminished by harmful attitudes and practices face very real dangers to their careers. At stake lie promotion, grant, tenure, and job placement decisions, each of which may be affected by prevailing attitudes that undermine status and authority. Below, I look at how women's success in academia seems to be seriously impeded by a chilly climate that threatens both status and authority.

THE CHILLY CLIMATE: PRESERVING THE MASCULINE IDEAL ACADEMIC

It has long been recognized that academia is a chilly climate for women (Sandler and Hall; Menges and Exum; Holloway; Feldthusen; Aisenberg and Harrington; Acker and Feuerverger; Settles, Cortina, Malley and Stewart). In this section I argue that the chilly climate is especially oppressive for mother academics. The fallout of the chilly climate might best be captured in what is commonly called the "leaky pipeline." The leaky pipeline describes the increased absence of women in academia as we travel through our degrees toward tenured positions. My own discipline of philosophy has a terribly leaky pipeline. Women earned 31 percent of bachelor's degrees in philosophy in 2006-7, compared to 41 percent in history, 45 percent in mathematics, 60 percent in biology, and 69 percent in English (Penaluna). Women in philosophy received 12 percent of Ph.D.s in 1969-1970, increasing to 27 percent 30 years later; over the last ten years the numbers have remained steady, with 25-30 percent of women receiving Ph.D.s in philosophy (Crasnow). This proportion of women in philosophy receiving doctorates remains lower than other disciplines, which see on average 41 percent of women receiving doctorates (Crasnow). And women in tenure-track positions in philosophy have rested at a low 21 percent for the past several decades (Dillon 2009). So while women in philosophy earn a low 31 percent of bachelor's degrees, an even lower 21 percent of academic philosophers will be women. Such leaky pipelines are not limited to philosophy. As women advance through their degrees to employment, the numbers decline in many other disciplines. The leaky pipeline winds through the sciences, technology, engineering, and mathematics (Gouldon, Frasch and Mason). And it is present in the social sciences, including political science and its subfields of international relations and multidisciplinary international studies programs (Hancock and Baum). The leaky pipeline is part of academia. It is a symptom of much larger problem in which, I suggest, men's interests and values take priority over those of women.

We might say that academia is not just an ivory tower but rather plainly a phallic tower: it appears that academia is not simply dominated by a white presence, it is infused with *masculine* values, interests, and attitudes. Janice Moulton explains how many positive concepts are associated with masculine interests in her discussion of aggression within professional contexts. When aggression is attached to men in professions like politics, law, sales, and management it takes on positive associations with power, activity, ambition, authority, competence, and effectiveness (Moulton 149). These qualities are valued as masculine qualities. Philosophy exemplifies an academic discipline dominated by masculine standards and ideals. Sally Haslanger argues that philosophy values masculine interests at the expense of women. Haslanger points out that philosophy defines itself through dichotomies that neatly map onto to gender dichotomies. Dichotomies in philosophy such as rational/emotional, objective/subjective, and mind/body frame philosophy as rational, objective, and concerned with issues of the mind (beliefs, knowledge, and so forth). These qualities are associated with masculine ideals of philosophy as seminal, rigorous, and penetrating; and what philosophers do: target, attack, and demolish an opponent (Haslanger 213). If masculine values of aggression, power, and so forth are exemplars of good philosophy and good philosophers, then women will find it difficult to produce good philosophical arguments and be respected and appreciated as good philosophers. Notice that this difficulty has nothing to do with any empirical features of women. The frustrations and limitations women philosophers face arrive from ideals and values demoting, dismissing, or denigrating that which is not masculine. This environment is very chilly for women.

The chilly climate for women in philosophy is typically sustained through a competitive, combative atmosphere that Haslanger describes as "hypermasculine." She asserts that women who succeed in philosophy are good at conforming to accepted masculine norms (which requires sublimating important parts of one's identity) or are simply adept at adjusting to a dysfunctional environment (217). Any or all of these adjustments may occur without *recognition* that one resides within a chilly climate. My own experience did not require altering my identity to feel at home in a masculine environment. I grew up in a house dominated by a masculine presence, pursued degrees solely in philosophy and concomitantly was (and still am) active in martial arts training, a clearly male-dominated activity. I did not sense a chilly climate because I was so immersed within those masculine contexts. When I became sensitive to feminist issues I gained a new feminist lens, seeing that I embraced many masculine values and ideals. I quickly set about turning the tables. I forged friendships primarily with women, detached myself from many masculine forms of debate, and welcomed advanced teachings in the gentle, fluid motions of karate as the art of no combat. My aim was (and is) to create a welcoming space for the feminine in academia and in my life more generally. Now, as a tenured professor, I mentor female students, teach feminist philosophy, and exemplify non-combative forms of reasoning in the classroom. But I did not always feel free to overtly engage in these activities. Until I recently received tenure I was not exactly *clandestine*, but in many ways *subtle* in my manoeuvrings toward less chilly spaces in academia. Accepting that cases like my earlier self exist, Haslanger seems correct to say that women in academia conform or otherwise adjust to a masculine environment, but she does not say much about *how* women might adjust to a chilly climate. Below, I sketch out how women might take on masculine modes of argumentation and discourse to conform to a masculine environment, showing that doing so aims to increase status and authority but, because of oppressive attitudes towards women, this approach *undermines* status and authority.

I appeal to philosophy because it is a discipline primarily concerned with argumentation and persuasion, although my conclusion extends to other academic disciplines valuing masculine discourse and argumentation.

MODEL OF THE IDEAL ACADEMIC CHALLENGES ACADEMIC MOTHERS' AUTONOMY

Not so long ago in philosophy's dusty past, Ernest Sosa described "serious philosophy" as what is rational, objective, and knowable by any rational mind. We saw above that this depiction of "serious philosophy" in fact describes that which is gendered *masculine*. I submit that presumed masculine qualities of the "serious philosopher" also describe the Serious Academic, who toils endlessly in the hallowed halls of academia to the exclusion of most else. Such academics can focus on their work because they have no family commitments—or ignore them if they do. One mother and academic scientist reports recently that she was at a farewell party for a colleague where the department chair gave a speech in which he characterized the departing man as "the ideal faculty member" because he always worked late into the night every day, seven days a week (Baizer). One might think that this model is outdated, a picture of the past better replaced with model scholars who rake in grants, publish solidly, and who also hang their children's scribblings on their office walls and sometimes leave early to pick up their kids. I do not think so. Those academics who display their children's artwork in their offices are usually men, precisely because they enjoy the "daddy privilege" of being Caring Serious Academics while women are simply seen as Not Serious.[2] And if anyone is leaving early to pick up their children it is typically mothers, but they won't announce that fact for fear of not being regarded as Serious Academics.

If I try to capture my sense of discomfort upon returning to academia after a year's maternity leave, it might be that I no longer felt that my colleagues regarded me as a Serious Academic, or even a lower-case "serious academic." I introduce this last term to reclaim the idea of being a serious scholar without necessitating the extreme view of Seriousness that we have seen. I call a "serious academic" someone who is actively involved in teaching and research and is happy to spout off details of her latest academic thoughts and problems. This sort of academic colleague may not be so Serious but is at least a common presence who attends many (although never all) academic talks or functions and is usually involved in some sort of research project in addition to a standard teaching load. I fit this model. But for the first year or two since having my daughter I have not typically been asked questions about my research, teaching, or anything else academic for that matter. I am asked about my daughter. It is hard to shift topics from one's child to one's work but I have often inserted comments about my academic life to my academic colleagues after a small anecdote about my daughter. In doing so, I aim to reclaim my status as a serious academic before my colleagues. I am not too sure if it is working. That is largely due to the fact that I am not available for many of the casual conversations my colleagues enjoy in the course of a typical academic workday. I isolate myself in my office whenever I am not teaching in class so that I can catch up on my work *so that* I can leave at a reasonable time. I estimate that I do as much work now, or more, than I ever did in my long, sprawling days as an unpartnered, pre-mother academic.

My case seems to be part of a larger pattern. Stereotypes presume that academic mothers with young children produce less research and are thus less likely to receive tenure (cited in Hancock and Baum). I acknowledge that mothers typically have a higher parenting workload than their male partners.[3] Yet I disagree with the stereotype of academic mothers' lower research productivity. Hancock and Baum's () research shows that young children (under age five) are *not* a statistically significant factor in women's research productivity. I suggest that the reason why children under age five—even though these are the years demanding the most parenting time—do not detract from research productivity is because mothers are streamlining and condensing their workload to ensure they can publish at a reasonable rate (comparable to pre-mothering publishing rates). Anecdotal evidence supports this view. Gayle Zydlewski points out that a colleague in her department was a mother but "She and I could barely find time to talk, since when we were on campus we needed to pack our time full with research and then get home to our children!" (138). Academic mothers are very often successful researchers. Nevertheless, academic mothers will find it a largely futile task to be regarded as Serious Academics or even lower-case serious academics.

I expect that academic success hinges upon being taken seriously in academic contexts, in being seen as a legitimate authority who can offer convincing arguments for one's position. Persons with authority are not questioned or belittled; their arguments are taken as legitimate *because* they are persons with authority. If what counts as having legitimate authority presumes masculine ideals and values, then women rejecting those standards of masculinity lose authority. Rebecca Hanrahan and Louise Antony show that possessing authority is just a matter of *not having to prove* that one's authority is legitimate. "Because I said so" can be a legitimate form of authority, depending on who the speaker is (Hanrahan and Antony 74). Hanrahan and Antony fail to mention how *status* is an important determinant of legitimate authority, but we can understand its role more clearly by considering that Serious Academics possess legitimate authority because they have a certain status in the academic community. I expand on these points below, relating masculine ideals and values promoted in the chilly climate to challenges to women's possibility to maintain or claim status and authority. Women academics who are also mothers will experience these and further challenges that deeply undermine the possibility of attaining the status of a model academic.

Academic mothers fail to possess legitimate authority if their status is challenged by sexist assumptions. An academic is not so Serious once she has a baby in her arms or a child to retrieve from school. She fails to meet the ideal of the Serious Academic once she reveals that she has commitments outside of academia that matter to her. Once this happens, a curious consequence seems to be that her status is lowered in comparison to her colleagues. One can only presume that a devaluing of the feminine is at work here. Feminists have long recognized that what is feminine is typically devalued in the workplace, in the home, and in society in general. Mothers are quickly and easily associated with that which is feminine, which we might assume is because children bear witness to the female power of reproduction, a decidedly feminine trait. When status is challenged, legitimate authority hangs in the balance. "Because I said so" shows legitimate authority for speakers who have a status with good standing in their communities. It will not work to demonstrate authority if one's status is undermined because of sexist assumptions or stereotypes downgrading one's status.

It is not surprising that women's status and authority is routinely challenged in academia. Students ask questions of or make comments to women professors they would never dream of saying to professors who are men. Antony gives an illustrative example:

> Antony: What is the counterexample that convinced Frye that her first definition of *sexism* is inadequate?
> Student: I don't see the point of this definition-and-counter-example thing. (Hanrahan and Antony 59).

Students belittle, deride, and challenge their women professors in student evaluations (I have heard of snide comments about women professors' style of dress or hair cut, or their quality of voice as somehow counting against their ability to teach). Women in academia can find their presentations at conferences, department meetings, and so forth challenged in a similarly unrelated fashion. While Hanrahan and Antony outline many ways in which sexist assumptions about women undermine authority, we can see that those sexist assumptions implicitly assume a masculine model of the ideal academic—along with attendant masculine values and ideals about good argumentation.

We saw earlier that philosophical argumentation favours aggressive, adversarial forms of reasoning. Adversality is revealed in metaphors such as "verbal sparring," "cutting to the point," "thrusting the point home," "going for the jugular" and so forth. Adversarial argumentation supposes a battle between two opponents, spurring philosophers to assume that one's points are constantly under threat and need to be defended against possible or real attacks. Good philosophical argumentation refutes real or imagined opponents and so is immune to counterexamples or other forms of opposition. As Janice Moulton points out, such argumentation dismisses as plausible those forms of reasoning that might be cooperative, friendly, problem-solving endeavours, or other forms of working out ideas with others (Moulton 157). My view is that having authority as teachers, colleagues, and researchers turns on women's ability to present reasoned arguments that are judged according to masculine standards of legitimacy. I argue elsewhere that women face significant difficulties developing and maintaining authority as academic philosophers because good philosophical argumentation presupposes masculine forms of discourse (Burrow 2010). Masculine discourse is usually direct, forceful, and favours aggression and adversality; feminine discourse emphasizes connection, intimacy, inclusion, and problem solving. Correspondingly, masculine discourse strategies often employ insults, monologues, interruption, stonewalling silences, direct disagreement, and so on. Feminine discourse strategies often use strategies prompting communication, such as questions (*do you see? right? okay?*) questioning intonations at the end of sentences, hedging assertions (*I guess, sort of, kind of*), passive or indirect speech, empty adjectives (*cute, adorable*), or diminutives (*little, tiny, itsy bitsy*) (see, for instance, Christie; Coates; Mills; Lakoff 5).[4]

Women in academia face a double bind that holds as much for philosophy as it does other academic contexts dominated by masculine discourse and so, implicit masculine ideals and values. Expressing oneself through feminine discourse undermines authority yet, transgressing femininity and adopting masculine discourse fails to deliver authority in the same way it does for men. The first half of the double bind can be explained as follows. Expressing oneself using hedging assertions, indirect speech, or questioning intonation reveals a lack of assurance in one's view. Women adopting such feminine discourse strategies will thus be frustrated in their efforts to be taken as authorities by their colleagues and students. The second half of the double bind follows from considering that women can *transgress* feminine norms of discourse and adopt masculine discourse strategies (which can be done with the hope of being taken seriously by colleagues or students). But women adopting masculine discourse may still be questioned, belittled, or derided. Valuing authority of a dominant group is typically accompanied by denying authority to subordinates who lack, or stereotypically lack, those markers of authority of the dominant group (Addelson). Taking on masculine forms of discourse may not be enough to have authority because women transgressing feminine norms of discourse often face demands to prove their reasoning, frequently and indiscriminately. But we saw above that legitimate authority entails that we need not defend our reasoning indiscriminately or whenever another decides to challenge it. Having authority entails that there is a place where defence of one's reasoning is not needed.

One might think that such challenges to authority need not undermine the possibility for women to be regarded as serious academics: women who strive to be serious academics simply need to be *better* armed with masculine qualities, such as masculine discourse strategies (interrupting, hogging the floor, swearing, so forth) or masculine argumentation techniques (targeting opponents with counter-examples, thrusting their points home, and so on). But it is difficult for women to be taken seriously by employing such techniques because we are likely to be seen as "harsh," "aggressive," "rude," "cold," or plain "bitchy." These qualities are not those esteemed in the ideal scholar and they detract from, rather than promote, status and authority. Slurs and insults to one's character inherently demote women's status while at once undermining legitimate authority. Authoritative legitimacy hinges on being the sort of person who *has* authority. Bitches do not have authority because their arguments are simply a result of bitchiness and not a credible position and so too for other negative character traits attributed to women. Thus, adopting masculine forms of discourse or argumentation is likely to undermine status and authority. So even those women who manage to successfully tread the masculine world of academia will not easily be regarded as serious academics. The alternative, adopting feminine discourse or argumentation, invites derision or condescension because what is feminine is devalued and derided in academia, as the chilly climate shows.

The chilly climate is more than an issue of gender balance in terms of numbers of women in academia. It is deeply and disturbingly a matter of masculine interests and values suffocating feminine modes of being. In such a climate, women struggle to be taken as seriously as their male counterparts and so must continually work to attain the status and authority much more easily granted to men. At stake lie many sorts of academic decisions, including whether or not one gets an academic job in the first place or receives tenure, promotion, grants, or similar markers of academic success. My point is that women's success in academia largely relies on whether or not women possess status and authority as arguers. In a climate in which status and authority are routinely challenged or questioned, more than just academic success is at stake. Persistent, or perhaps simply multiple, challenges to status or authority undermine self-confidence. Success in academia relies upon success in one's ability to argue, whether in teaching, service, or research settings. Challenging this ability questions one's standing as an academic. In this climate, self-doubt works against those self-appreciating attitudes necessary to autonomy. Self-trust, self-esteem, and self-respect can all falter as one doubts one's abilities to live up to the standard of the "Serious Academic" or even the lower-case "serious academic." As we saw earlier, doubt diminishes one's capacity to form and act on choices because it undermines one's capacity to value and uphold one's beliefs, commitments, and values. Women in academia encountering challenges to authority and status and who experience self-doubt see their capacity to have and express autonomy undermined by this chilly climate. Academic mothers can encounter diminished autonomy for the same reason other women in academia do, but academic mothers have more challenges undermining autonomy *because* they are mothers.

Academic mothers face a serious double bind because of oppressive stereotypes about mothers. On the one hand, academic mothers may choose to minimize, hide, neglect, or otherwise conceal their childcare or family commitments so as to appear to be serious academics. But once a woman's standing as a mother is revealed to her colleagues, sexist stereotypes undermine her authority if she is not taken as seriously as her non-mothering counterparts. Success as a researcher is a primary marker for success as an academic, no matter how much talk one hears about success in teaching and service as necessary to academic success. And so, an academic mother needs to resist stereotypes depicting her as a less serious researcher than her colleagues. At the same time, she is likely to experience self-doubt undermining autonomy if she wonders if she can pull off motherhood and the large demands of a full-time academic position (which is the only position a serious academic occupies). On the other hand, an academic mother might decide to alter her academic commitments to allow her more time to focus on her childcare or family commitments. While she may be just as, or more, productive than her colleagues on a similar schedule, she will fight against stereotypes assuming that she is not a serious academic. Her status as an academic can be overshadowed by the stereotypical view that, if she is primarily a mother and secondarily an academic, she cannot be serious about her academic work. Hence, academic mothers face a deeply constraining double bind. Whether we subordinate our family commitments or we subordinate our academic commitments, we need to strive to be taken seriously as an academic—to be regarded as an academic with status and authority. In either case, we are exposed to masculinist assumptions about what it means to be a serious academic. Women find it difficult to live up to such expectations and be taken seriously, but academic mothers are bound by sexist assumptions about mothering that further undermine the possibility they will be regarded as serious academics.

CONCLUSION

In this essay I have indicated how academia constrains autonomy for academic mothers. Autonomy is eroded in environments pressing us to question or otherwise doubt our choices. If self-confidence is undermined because of self-doubt then self-trust, self-esteem, and self-respect each risk diminishment. In any of these cases it becomes difficult to trust our judgements, beliefs, and values. Consequently, self-doubt erodes our capacity to make and act on choices. Autonomy is thus critically diminished in environments fuelling self-doubt. I have shown that academia proves one such environment for academic mothers. This conclusion does not deny that academic mothers may have a strong self-confidence and flourish despite pressures working against autonomy. But I suppose these cases the exception rather than the rule. Self-doubt, criticism, or worry easily creeps in when academic mothers try to balance careers and family life. If academia supported mothering practices without implicit or explicit repercussions, then mothers' choices would not nearly be so difficult. But academia upholds a model of the ideal academic supposing masculine expectations, aims, and values. In this chilly climate, mothers try to achieve to be, and be regarded as, academics with a status and authority worthy of others' respect. At stake lies the possibility for academic success, which is typically determined through colleagues' decisions about jobs, promotions, tenures, and so forth. These are the academic costs I have focussed on in this paper. Personal costs are also at stake, but I can only give a brief indication of them at this point.

Costs to self-confidence, self-esteem, self-trust, and self-respect are not simply costs to autonomy. Undermined self-confidence and self-appreciation deliver personal consequences to one's well being or happiness. We cannot derive happiness from our decisions or actions if we are plagued by worry, doubts, or fears as we question our choices, wonder why we made them in the first place, or receive criticisms, reproaches, or admonishment by others for having made those choices. Such responses erode basic feelings of self-worth and self-respect. When this happens, it is difficult to maintain personal integrity. I agree with Cheshire Calhoun's analysis of integrity as a matter of standing for one's commitments before others. I argue elsewhere (Burrow 2012) that the ability to assert one's values, beliefs, and the importance of one's goals and projects is critical to having and maintaining integrity.

I have illustrated above some of the ways academic mothers may compromise commitments so as to succeed in academia. We might alter the number of children we have, our family commitments, or our appearance of being mothers so as to be taken seriously. These decisions are not usually made lightly. They compromise integrity if they entail that we give up or significantly alter our commitments because of outside pressures. I indicated above those pressures resulting from sexist stereotypes about ideal academics. *Resisting* those stereotypes is essential to standing for one's commitments as an academic mother.

In academia's chilly climate, academic mothers need to build a protective layer reinforcing our confidence that our choices are worth respecting and deserve to be taken seriously, just as *we* do. Until academia becomes less chilly, many women will limit or postpone motherhood in order to be regarded as ideal academics. Those who do secure accommodations to allow them to be productive and have children ask for what is legitimate (maternity leave, parental leave, adjusted teaching schedules, part-time status, and so forth) still suffer if they do not meet the model of the Serious Academic. We can suppose that women desiring to become mothers might foresee many of the sorts of difficulties raised in this essay and opt out of academia instead. Opting out is one way of avoiding a masculine environment that undermines mother academics' autonomy. BBut I would rather see academia become more inclusive of women and mothering so that our autonomy is not undermined by an oppressive chilly climate. Perhaps academic mothers and their allies can forge new models of the ideal academic that allows academic mothers to be serious academics, even if we put our children's drawings on our doors or even if we reduce our academic load to attend to family commitments. Resisting pressures against autonomy is part of *cultivating* autonomy, so through resisting dominant stereotypes and ideals, academic mothers can advance or regain their own autonomy. But the burden should not rest on those oppressed to challenge oppressive social and political structures. Academic allies need to join mothers to urge changes making academia less chilly to both women and mothers, which requires challenging implicit masculine values and ideals built into the view of the ideal academic.

[1]Tindale recognizes persuasion as part of argumentation but still upholds agreement as the main aim of cooperative argumentation.

[2]Drago *et al.* describe "daddy privilege" as a practice both men and women regard as unfair, that involves circumstances wherein men are viewed as leading a healthy, balanced life when admitting caregiving commitments in the workplace, while women *are seen as less than ideal* workers for similar admissions. Daddy privilege emerges from the closer

application of the norm of motherhood to women, and the presumption that men tend to be ideal workers.

[3]Hancock and Baum reference Scheibinger and Gilmartin's research on mother scientists in academia. It shows that women assume a disproportionate share of child care (women scientists do 54 percent of parenting labour in their households, and men scientists do 36 percent, where "parenting labour" refers to physical, psychosocial, and intellectual responsibilities).

[4]My discussion of typical gender patterns in discourse should not suggest that men always use masculine discourse or that women always use feminine discourse. I maintain that gender is performed through language and behaviour and is not tied to one's biological sex. Thus, those who are gendered as men may transgress typical gender roles through taking on feminine speech or behaviour; those who are gendered as women may transgress typical gender roles through taking on masculine speech or behaviour.

WORKS CITED

Acker, Sandra and Grace Feuerverger. "Doing Good and Feeling Bad: The Work of Women University Teachers." *Cambridge Journal of Education* 26.3 (1996): 401-22.

Addelson, Kathryn. "The Man of Professional Wisdom." *Discovering Reality*. Ed. S. Harding and M. Hintikka. Dordrecht, Holland: Kluwer, 1983. 165-186.

Aisenberg, Nadya and Mona Harrington. *Women of Academe: Outsiders in the Sacred Grove*. Amherst, MA: The University of Massachusetts Press, 1988.

Baizer, Joan. "Extreme Motherhood: You Can't Get There from Here." *Motherhood, the Elephant in the Laboratory*. Ed. E. Monosson. Ithica: Cornell University Press, 2008. 31-34.

Benson, Paul. "Free Agency and Self-Worth." *Journal of Philosophy* 91.12 (1994): 650-68.

Burrow, Sylvia. "Bodily Limits to Autonomy: Emotion, Attitude, and Self-Defence." *Agency and Embodiment*. Ed. L. Meynell, S. Campbell and S. Sherwin. Philadelphia: Pennsylvania State University Press, 2009. 126-144.

Burrow, Sylvia. "Protecting One's Commitments: Integrity and Self-

Defence." *International Journal of Applied Philosophy* (in press, 2012).

Burrow, Sylvia. "Verbal Sparring and Apologetic Points: Politeness in Gendered Argumentation Contexts. *Informal Logic* 30.3 (2010): 235-62.

Calhoun, Cheshire. "Standing for Something." *The Journal of Philosophy* 92.5 (1995): 235-60.

Christie, Christine. *Gender and Language*. Edinburgh: Edinburgh University Press, 2000.

Coates, Jennifer. *Women, Men and Language*. New York: Longman, 1986.

Crasnow, Sharon. 2009. "Women in the Profession: The Persistence of Absence." *American Philosophical Association Newsletter on Feminism and Philosophy* 9.1 (2009): 8-10.

Dillon, Robin. "Self-Respect: Moral, Emotional, Political." *Ethics* 107.2 (1997): 226-49.

Dillon, Robin. "Strategizing Changes in the Culture and Ideology of Philosophy: an Introduction." *American Philosophical Association Newsletter on Feminism and Philosophy* 9.1 (2009): 2-4.

Dillon, Robin. "Toward a Feminist Conception of Self-Respect." *Hypatia* 7.1 (1992): 52-69.

Dillon, Robin. "'What's a Woman Worth? What's Life Worth? Without Self-Respect!': On the Value of Evaluative Self-Respect." *Moral Psychology: Feminist Ethics and Social Theory*. Ed. P. DesAutels and M. U. Walker. Lanham, MD: Rowman and Littlefield, 2004. 47-68.

Drago, Robert, Carol Colbeck, Kai Dawn Stauffer, Amy Pirretti, Kurt Burkum, Jennifer Fazioli, Gabriela Lazzaro, and Tara Habasevichch. "The Avoidance of Bias Against Caregiving: The Case of Academic Faculty." *American Behavioral Scientist* 49 (2006): 1222-47.

Efroymson, Rebecca. "Part-Time at a National Laboratory: A Split Life." *Motherhood, The Elephant in the Laboratory*. Ed. E. Monosson. Ithica: Cornell University Press, 2008. 102-107.

Evans, Elrena, and Caroline Grant, eds. *Mama, PhD: Women Write about Motherhood and Academic Life*. Piscataway, NJ: Rutgers University Press, 2008.

Feldthusen, Bruce. "The Gender Wars: 'Where the Boys Are'." *Breaking anonymity: The chilly climate for women faculty*. Ed. T. C. C. Collective. Waterloo, ON: Wilfrid Laurier University Press, 1991. 279-314.

Garry, Ann. "What is on Women Philosophers' Minds?" *American Philosophical Association Newsletter on Feminism in Philosophy* 9.1 (2009): 4-7.

Gouldon, Marc, Karie Frasch, and Mary Ann Mason. Staying Competitive: Patching America's Leaky Pipeline in the Sciences. 2009. Web. <http: //www.americanprogress.org/issues/2009/11/women_and_sciences.html>.

Govier, Trudy. "Self-Trust, Autonomy, and Self-Esteem." *Hypatia: A Journal of Feminist Philosophy* 8.1 (1993): 99-120.

Hancock, Kathleen and Matthew Baum. "Women and Academic Publishing: Preliminary Results from a Survey of the ISA Membership." *International Studies Association Annual Convention*. New Orleans, LA, 2010.

Hanrahan, Rebecca and Louise Antony. "Because I Said So: Toward a Feminist Theory of Authority." *Hypatia* 20.4 (2005): 59-79.

Haslanger, Sally. "Changing the Ideology and Culture of Philosophy: Not by Reason (Alone)." *Hypatia* 23.4 (2008): 210-23.

Holloway, Marguerite. "A Lab of Her Own." *Scientific American* 269.5 (1993): 94-102.

Lakoff, Robin. *Language and Women's Place*. New York: Harper and Row, 1975.

MacKenzie, Catriona, and Natalie Stoljar, eds. *Relational Autonomy: Feminist Perspectives on Autonomy, Agency and the Social Self*. New York: Oxford University Press, 2000.

McIntosh, Marla. "Costs and Rewards of Success in Academia, or Bouncing into the Rubber Ceiling." *Motherhood, the Elephant in the Laboratory*. Ed. E. Monosson. Ithica: Cornell University Press, 2008. 51-55.

Menges, Robert, and William Exum. "Barriers to the Progress of Women and Minority Faculty." *Journal of Higher Education* 54 (1983): 123-44.

Mills, Sara. *Gender and Politeness*. Cambridge: Cambridge University Press, 2003.

Moulton, Janice. "A Paradigm of Philosophy: The Adversary Method." *Discovering Reality*. Ed. S. Harding and M. Hintikka. Boston: Kluwer Academic Publishers, 1983. 149-164.

Newberg, Heidi. "Less Pay, a Little Less Work." *Motherhood, The Elephant in the Laboratory*. Ed. E. Monosson. Ithica: Cornell University Press, 2008. 93-97.

Penaluna, Regan. "Diversity in Academe." *The Chronicle of Higher Education* October 11, 2009. Web. <Online http://chronicle.com/article/Wanted-Female-Philosophers/48729>.

Rooney, Phyllis. "Recent Work in Feminist Discussions of Reason." *American Philosophical Quarterly* 31.1 (1994): 1-21.

Rooney, Phyllis. "Philosophy, Adversarial Argumentation, and Embattled Reason." *Informal Logic* 30.3 (2010): 203-234.

Ross, Deborah. "Careers Versus Child Care in Academia." *Motherhood, the Elephant in the Laboratory*. Ithica: Cornell University Press, 2008. 35-40.

Sandler, Bernice, and Roberta Hall. *The Campus Climate Revisited: Chilly for Women Faculty, Administrators and Graduate Students*. Washington, DC: Association of American Colleges and Universities, 1986.

Schiebinger, Londa, and Shannon Gilmartin. "Housework is an Academic Issue: How to Keep Talented Women Scientists in the Lab, Where They Belong." *Academe* (2010). Web. <http://www.aaup.org/AAUP/pubsres/academe/2010/JF/feat/schie.htm>.

Settles, Isis, Lilia Cortina, Janet Malley, and Abigail Stewart. "The Climate for Women in Academic Science: The Good, the Bad, and the Changeable." *Psychology of Women Quarterly* 30.1 (2006): 47-58.

Sosa, Ernest. "Serious Philosophy and Freedom of Spirit." *The Journal of Philosophy* 84.12 (1987): 707-26.

Tindale, Christopher. *Acts of Arguing*. Albany, NY: State University of New York Press, 1999.

Zydlewski, Gayle Barbin. "Finding the Right Balance, Personal and Professional, as a Mother in Science." *Motherhood, The Elephant in the Laboratory*. Ed. E. Monosson. Ithica: Cornell University Press, 2008. 135-139.

19.

Being and Thinking Between Second and Third Wave Feminisms

Theorizing a Strategic Alliance Frame to Understand Academic Motherhood

D. LYNN O'BRIEN HALLSTEIN

> An alliance frame, then, seeks to provide a mechanism for healing for the subject of ... feminism through which she may take responsibility for her own complicity in contemporary and historic relations of ruling, not to feel bad or guilty, but to truly heal the violence through which our ancestors, and by extension, our current generation, relate to one another through segregation and separation. (Rowe 22)

ALTHOUGH MY FORMAL ACADEMIC TRAINING mainly focused on second wave feminisms[1] because I was a graduate student in the late 1980s and early 1990s, both my career and mothering have primarily unfolded within third wave feminisms. As a result, I live and think as a feminist maternal scholar and mother with one foot squarely in second wave feminism: feminism of the 1960s and through the 1970s that was primarily but not exclusively organized by and around white, middle-class women, and is generally marked as ending with the failure of the Equal Rights Amendment (Dow; Evans).[2] My second foot, however, is in the anti-essentialist third wave feminism that initially emerged in the mid-1990s[3] but is continuing to develop within third wave intersectionality:[4] contemporary feminist theorizing that attends to the multiple and intersecting axes of power that form identities and upon which instances of oppression and resistance are enacted. I am, in short, a feminist academic mother who thinks and mothers betwixt and between second and third wave feminisms.

Having one foot in each wave, however, can be quite challenging, particularly because much third wave intersectional thinking decenters the second wave's foundation in gender and the centrality of feminism in social justice work. Consequently, I have begun to wonder if it is theoretically possible to align my current third wave commitments to anti-essentialism and the idea that identities and instances of oppression/resistance are formed and enacted within multiple axes of power with my second wave commitments to centering my being and thinking around both gender and feminism as I work for social justice for all mothers, but especially for academic mothers. While my particular interest in exploring the one-foot-in-both dilemma may be unique to me, all post-second-wave[5] academic mothers are also deeply implicated within both second and third wave feminisms, because they are the first group of second wave beneficiaries who are living and mothering within the third wave. In short, all academic mothers are living within an historic moment that is also betwixt and between second and third wave feminisms. And, as such, we need to understand better the theoretical issues at stake as we explore academic motherhood.

In this chapter, then, I suggest that, as feminist maternal scholarship continues to employ different theoretical perspectives to explain and understand contemporary maternity more generally and academic motherhood more specifically, it is essential that we explore the contemporary tensions that exist between second and third wave feminisms and the possibilities of an alliance between the two for all academic mothers, regardless of whether or not any particular woman identifies as a feminist or not. The remainder of this essay attempts to sort through my particular intellectual "one-foot-in-both-second-and-third-wave-feminisms" dilemma as a way to explore the possibilities an alliance perspective might offer our theoretical understandings of academic motherhood and as a means to think more carefully about how we understand contemporary maternity as second wave beneficiaries and third wave academic mothers.

More specifically, I ask and answer the following questions: Can I continue to center on the second wave's focus on gender and feminism, while simultaneously incorporating third wave intersectional thinking as a feminist maternal scholar? And, if so, theoretically, what issues must be explored and provisionally resolved within both feminist maternal scholarship and intersectional work, between second and third wave feminisms? In addressing these two questions, I argue that an alliance or partnership between feminist maternal scholars and intersectional thinkers requires feminist maternal scholars to incorporate more intersectional principles into our analyses of contemporary maternity if we hope to move beyond the additive approach to understanding women's lives and to begin to acknowledge the intra-women oppression that permeates contemporary maternity. Conversely, I also argue that intersectional work must recognize that the ideological and material reality of contemporary maternity requires a strategic centering on gender and feminism, capital "F" feminism. Moreover, I also suggest that an alliance perspective requires an eradication of the younger-older, matrophobic generational structure that undergirds third-wave intersectionality. Finally, I conclude with a preliminary discussion of what a future alliance, grounded in a politics of accountability, must entail theoretically as we begin to develop specific strategies of resistance against the barriers that impede academic mothers.

FEMINIST MATERNAL SCHOLARS: FORGOING THE ADDITIVE APPROACH AND INTRA-WOMAN OPPRESSION

An alliance between feminist maternal scholars and intersectionality requires feminist maternal scholars to attend more to the multiple and intersecting axes of power that form identities and upon which oppression and resistances are enacted and to attend more explicitly to the intra-woman oppression that undergirds contemporary maternity. Even though I argue elsewhere (*White Feminists*), that feminist maternal scholars—feminist scholars who explore feminist counternarratives to the ideology of "good mothering" as a way to explore and develop maternal agency[6]—are in the vanguard for acknowledging diversity among mothering practices, the approach tends to be more "additive" still rather than interconnected in recognizing axes of power. So, for example, key texts (see O'Reilly; Kinser) continue to primarily separate mothering practices as "lesbian mothering," "African American mothering," "single mothering." Or, alternatively, texts are devoted to specific kinds of mothering, i.e., "queer mothering." While these texts are laudable for shifting feminist maternal scholarship away from second wave essentialism—generalizing white, heterosexual middle-class women's experiences to all women—it is still primarily an additive approach to recognizing the differences among women, particularly in terms of mothering practices, and, as a result, continues to reveal the lingering vestiges of second-wave thinking.

Today, there is also no doubt that the additive approach—simply adding race or class to gender—is problematic because women's identities are shaped differently across axes of power. So, for example, Kimberle Crenshaw, who is now widely credited with first using the term *intersectionality*, argued that understanding women's experiences within the legal system, particularly in the context of violence against African American women, is necessary because "the violence that many women experience is often shaped by other dimensions of their identities, such as race and class" (1242). Or, as Patricia Hill Collins also argues, race, class, social class, gender, and sexuality "form mutually constructing features of social organization, which shape [individuals'] experiences and, in turn, are shaped by [individuals]" (299). As a result, feminist maternal scholars need to actively resist the additive approach and instead adopt a more robust intersectional approach to understanding how women's lives are shaped across axes of identity formation within the context of maternity.

At its core, intersectionality resists the additive approach because of its roots in anti-essentialist feminisms. As scholars such as Leslie Heywood and Carissa Showden argue, third wave intersectional analyses emerged as a direct response to the essentialism critiques leveled first by women of color and lesbians of white second wave feminism. In doing so, third wave intersectional thinking shifts the epistemological focus of feminist thinking. In particular, as Showden argues and is worth quoting in length:

> While intersectionality is not itself a "politics," it is an attempt to shift the epistemological standpoint of feminism, providing a new subject position from which feminist critique is articulated. The position from which knowledge is articulated can have dramatic implications for the kinds of politics that are then seen as viable and valuable. So as intersectionality shapes feminist activism, new possibilities for collations become visible, and the specific goals or political projects of feminism are fruitfully reconceived as well. (167)

This means that, as intersectional analyses see various components of identity as interdependent and co-determinative rather than additive and discrete and, unlike much second wave politics that focused on women's group identity as women, it also shifts the epistemological ground of politics to coalitional politics based on interlocking yet always shifting and changing forms of oppression and axes of identity.

In addition to providing feminist maternal scholars a more robust approach to theorizing women's identities, intersectional thinking challenges feminist maternal scholars to explore and challenge the power differences that exist among women. Indeed, one of the key implications of the anti-essentialist critiques that undergird intersectional thinking is the idea that women's social locations are quite different based on how race, class, gender, and sexuality intersect. One significant implication of the intersectional attention to the power differences among women is that intersectionality requires feminist maternal scholars to attend more to the intra-gender oppression among women within maternity. Indeed, maternity—both institutionalized motherhood and women's actual mothering practices—is deeply implicated in unacknowledged privilege and oppression among women as a result of social location. So, for example, one of the hallmarks of contemporary western cultures, especially the U.S. and Canada, is the autonomy many women now enjoy as result of the large-scale social and ideological changes initiated by second wave feminisms. This autonomy,[7] however, is often at the expense of other women based on economic, race, and/or class privilege.

Contemporary maternity, in fact, is a premier example of the power differences at play in women's newfound autonomy. Aimee Carrillo Rowe, for example, quoting Sherene Razak initially, argues:

> "autonomous women derive their autonomy on the backs of other women. A mesh of material relations surrounds our capacity to be autonomous—other women who are our babysitters, domestic workers, secretaries...." I would add that this mobility is both enabled on the backs of those women whom women of privilege can literally afford to hire, but also through the hidden ways that mobility and access to privileged women is generated through the dislocation, forced relocation, and subordination of other women. (24)

The political economy that Rowe notes is especially true for many academic mothers, particularly for a privileged woman like myself—white, heterosexual, highly educated, and middle class. Indeed, my very autonomy is founded on my privilege—racial, heterosexual, and economic—and maintained by the other women who run the daycare programs my children attend, the cleaning ladies who clean my house, and the disposable income my family has to purchase the timesaving gadgets and services that maintain and sustain my family. Transnational mothering—mothers who leave their own children to work in the U.S. and other Western countries as nannies and/or domestic workers in order to support their own children back in their home country—is yet another example that is replete with intra-woman oppression. Thus, feminist academic mothers need to do more than just add on race, class, and sexuality, while also failing to account fully for the complex material relations at play among women, as we theorize both contemporary maternity generally and develop specific strategies for both empowerment and resistance within academia.

At the same time, however, an alliance between feminist maternal scholars and intersectional thinking is difficult because, when intersectionality shifts the epistemological ground of politics to coalitional politics based on interlocking yet always shifting and changing forms of oppression and axes of identity, much intersectional work decenters both gender and feminism and, like third wave feminism in general, is silent on maternity.

THIRD-WAVE INTERSECTIONALITY: DECENTERING GENDER AND FEMINISM AND FORGOING THE SILENCE

In terms of feminism, much intersectional work decenters feminism when working toward social justice. In fact, many contemporary intersectional thinkers and activists (Jervis qtd. in Rowe-Finkbeiner; Labaton and Martin; Rowe; Shah qtd. in Rowe-Finkbeiner) focus on social justice and see feminism as only part of that project. As a result, the focus on social justice shifts the center of intersectional analyses from "women's issues" to social justice for all. Julie Shah, co-director of the Third-Wave Foundation describes the third wave interest in social justice: "the third wave is self-defining for each individual. It's a group of women and men who are concerned about social justice for women and social justice in general" (qtd. in Rowe-Finkbeiner 93). Moreover, the focus of activism and politics shift away from "traditional" feminist concerns. In terms of feminism generally, as Vivien Laboton and Dawn Lundy Martin argue, "those issues that have traditionally been associated with the feminist movement—reproductive rights, domestic violence, date rape, and equal pay for equal work—are not the only issues that should define it [intersectionality]" (xxvii). While they then acknowledge that they are not suggesting that these "traditional" second wave issues no longer matter, they also argue that:

> we should not become so distracted by the core issues that we neglect other social justice concerns. The borders of feminism need to be split open, both so that we are freed from ideological rigidity and so that other identity claims or race, sexuality, class, nationality, and geography can move beyond being simply "tolerated" or "included." (xxvii)

Thus, intersectional thinkers believe the borders of feminism and the focus of social justice issues need to be expanded beyond the primary focus on traditional "women's" issues that drove many but not all second wave thinking and politics.[8]

Equally important, gender is also no longer always the central category of analysis. As Lisa Jervis, co-founding editor of the third-wave feminist magazine *Bitch* notes "gender isn't always the primary mode of analysis.... Anti-poverty work, international human-rights work, and labor are all issues that are feminist issues, but they aren't all about women" (qtd. in Rowe-Finkbeiner 103). Noticeably absent in the focus on social justice, however, is any attention to motherhood or mothering. Indeed, at this stage of its development, there is almost a universal silence on both in third wave intersectional analyses. In *The Fire This Time* (Labaton and Martin), for example, there is not one mention of motherhood or mothering, a pattern that scholars (Henry *Not My*; O'Brien Hallstein, *White Feminists*) have shown is also part of early third wave writing. Thus, as third wave intersectional analyses decenter gender as the central analytic category, while also decentralizing feminism, it also continues the early third wave silence on maternity.

Nonetheless, I agree with much of this third wave theorizing; in particular, as noted earlier, I accept that identities and instances of oppression/resistance are formed and enacted within multiple axes of power. I maintain, however, that once the multiplicity of identity, oppression, and resistance are acknowledged, the difficulty resides in developing ways to analyze and discuss these multiplicities. Clearly, many third wave feminists have responded to this difficulty by shifting their focus from "women's issues" to a broader concern for social justice. I believe that it is this move that is deeply problematic for how we theorize maternity because of the ongoing material reality of gender in maternity generally and within academic institutions specifically. Thus, even though an alliance between feminist maternal scholars and intersectionality, between second and third wave feminisms, must attend to interlocking forms of oppression, as I argue next, our specific historical moment requires a strategic focus on gender and an ongoing centering on feminism when advocating for social justice for mothers.

OUR SPECIFIC HISTORICAL MOMENT: THE IDEOLOGICAL AND MATERIAL WEIGHT OF MATERNITY

While it is fact that women's lives as unencumbered women—women without children—are different today because of the large-scale social and ideological changes brought about by second wave feminisms, gender continues to have ideological and material weight in the context of maternity, which is also a core point of the "Introduction" of this book. Ideologically, there is a systematic and sophisticated post-second wave backlash ideology at work within the context of maternity. In using the phrase *post-second-wave backlash*, I draw on Ann Braithwaite's recent extension of Susan Faludi's groundbreaking work *Backlash*. Braithwaite argues that a Faludian understanding of backlash entails recognizing how contemporary backlash simultaneously integrates feminism in the service of blaming feminism for any difficulty women experience in managing their post-second wave lives as mothers. Indeed, as I have argued (*White Feminists*; "Public Choices") institutionalized motherhood, via the contemporary ideology of good mothering—intensive mothering[9]—is a new post-second-wave ideology of "good" mothering that utilizes and harnesses women's gains as second wave beneficiaries in the service of re-establishing mothering as the most important part of contemporary femininity. As a result, contemporary intensive mothering is utilizing feminist gains in the service of constraining women's lives and re-confining women to mothering. And, as such, today's intensive mothering now positions all women as "second wave beneficiaries"—women who have benefited from and taken advantage of second wave feminist successes regardless of whether or not any particular woman[10] actually views herself as a feminist or has actually had access to the gains—and demands that all women bring their new found (or potential) gains in education and professional skills to their mothering.

One significant consequence of this backlash ideology is that contemporary maternity remains a unique problem for feminism with a capital "F" to address because *it is feminism* that is under "attack" in the backlash ideology. As a result, while feminism may only be part of a larger push for social justice for third wave intersectional thinkers—feminism "has become one of many investigatory means," (Labaton and Martin xxxi)—feminism with a capital "F" remains a primary focus for contemporary backlash against all people, but especially against feminists and mothers, regardless of what we think about the need or not for feminism. Consequently, within the context of maternity, feminism—capital "F" feminism—must remain central if we hope to forestall the erosion of feminist gains, if we hope to help women step out of and resist a primary means of gender-based oppression today, and if we want to resist the real ideological barriers to mothers' agency. Thus, if we hope to advocate for social justice for academic mothers, then, it is key that we do so specifically as feminists because the very gains—in education and professional arenas especially—many women, but especially third wave feminists assume and celebrate,[11] are most threatened within the context of maternity, a context that intersectional thinkers fail to even address.

The Prices[12] of Motherhood

In addition to the ideological constraints of our post-second wave intensive mothering, scholars such as Ann Crittenden, Judith Warner, Joan Williams and Williams and Nancy Segal have shown how contemporary motherhood constrains women's lives socially, legally, materially, and politically such that motherhood continues to have the material weight to constrain and penalize women *as mothers*,[13] particularly in an American context. Ann Crittenden argues in *The Price of Motherhood*, for example, that even though many contemporary unencumbered American women have gained much economic, legal, and social equality with men, once children come, traditional gender roles tend to emerge and women become the primary parent for the caregiving and early education of children. That women are the primary caregivers of children, as scholars suggest (Crittenden; Hays; Williams) is true across race and class differences. Thus, even though there are different costs for women based on race, class, and sexual orientation, women as a group experience gender oppression as women once they become mothers, even as variables such as class and race continue to position mothers differently in relation to one another.

Penalties for motherhood are also deeply embedded in U.S. academic institutions, norms, and practices. Recent studies of both academic women and mothers (Mason and Goulden, "Do Babies Matter?"; Mason and Goulden, "Do Babies Matter (II)?"; Wolfinger, Mason and Goulden) and contributors to this text (Beard; Ennis; Wyatt-Nichol et. al.; Wood) reveal that gender discrimination more generally and specifically against academic mothers continues to be widespread in academia. Indeed, even though more and more women are completing Ph.D.s and are entering the academic "pipeline," academic mothers do not have gender equity with male academics, including male academics who also have children. Mary Ann Mason and Marc Goulden ("Do Babies (II)"), for example, argue that "Even though women make up nearly half of the Ph.D. population, they are not advancing at the same rate as men to the upper ranks of the professoriate; many are dropping out of the race" (11). The primary reason women are dropping out or "leaking out of the pipeline" is because having children penalizes academic mothers far more than it does academic fathers, while sometimes having children even benefits academic fathers. Mason and Goulden ("Do Babies (II)") even wryly argue "'Married with children' is the success formula for men, but the opposite is true for women, for whom there is a serious 'baby gap'" (11). More pointedly, in their earlier essay, Mason and Goulden also note "there is a consistent and large gap in achieving tenure between women who have early babies and men who have early babies [having a baby prior to five years after a parent completes his or her Ph.D.], and this gap is surprisingly uniform across the disciplines and across types of institutions" ("Do Babies Matter?" 24). They also note, "surprisingly, having early babies seems to help men; men who have early babies achieve tenure at slightly higher rates than people who do not have early babies" (24). The opposite is the case for women who have early babies. Thus, Mason and Goulden ("Do Babies Matter?") find that women with early babies often "do not get as far as ladder-rank jobs" and often make family-work choices that "force them to leave the academy or put them into the second tier of faculty: the lecturers, adjuncts, and part-time faculty" (24). Thus, even though academic institutions are primarily progressive and liberal institutions, academic motherhood continues to be replete with discrimination based on motherhood.

The Maternal Wall

As such, academic mothers bump up against what Joan Williams describes as the *maternal wall*.[14] The maternal wall is a metaphor to describe the marginalization and disadvantages mothers face specifically at work. In *Unbending Gender*, Williams argues that the maternal wall is a result of persistent family-life gender roles that continue to position women as the primary caregivers of children rather than fathers. Williams also argues that the maternal wall is composed of professional practices that marginalize and discriminate against anyone who takes parental leave and anyone who takes on the traditional feminine role of caregiving. Because, however, women continue to be primarily responsible for caregiving of children, the maternal wall affects far more women than men. Specific work (Mason and Goulden, "Do Babies Matter?"; Mason and Goulden, "Do Babies Matter (II)?"; Williams *Unbending;* Wolfinger, Mason, and Goulden) done within academic settings confirms that the maternal wall underlies much of the penalties academic mothers face in academia.

This inequality for mothers, ironically, is justified on the grounds that women "choose" children and thus are responsible for the "choice" they made to become a parent. In other words, a key hallmark of second wave feminism—the right to choose to control reproduction—is being used to penalize women once they become mothers. Indeed, the second wave feminist rhetoric of choice is being simultaneously acknowledged and used against women once they become mothers, in yet another example of the strength of the ideological backlash against feminism in general. Crittenden also argues, and Sara Hayden and Lynn O'Brien Hallstein's (*Contemplating Maternity*) recent edited volume reveals, one of the central problems with "the rhetoric of choice" is that it fails to recognize the ongoing material weight of gender—the structural and ideological forms of power embedded in social, legal, and economic systems that penalize women once they become mothers. Thus, the rhetoric of choice not only ignores the power structures embedded in both the larger society and specifically within academia, it also ignores the very real material ways that maternity is being used both to penalize women once they become mothers and to erode systematically the changes to women's lives brought about by second-wave feminisms.

Neo-Traditional Families

The combined material effect of the post-second wave backlash and the prices of motherhood culminate in a new but very old form of gendered family life that is emerging in both contemporary culture and within academic families. Miriam Peskowitz has described this change as creating *neo-traditional families*. Neo-traditional families appear to be new because women's lives as unencumbered women have changed but the basic foundation of pre-second wave family roles and responsibilities still hold: mothers continue to be primary caregivers of children. Neo-traditional families are especially dangerous for academic mothers. Indeed, Nicholas Wolfinger, Mary Ann Mason and Marc Goulden suggest that it now clear that family formation accounts for the lower percentage of women in tenure track positions and is a major factor for why academic mothers "leak out" of the tenure pipeline (1595). In other words, while the second wave brought women's liberation—the newfound autonomy of women that we all celebrate, academic mothers and especially third wave feminists—there has *not been a mothers' liberation*. Indeed, as Peskowitz puts it: "the gains for women in the past decades have not meant a similar gain for mothers" (66).

In light of the ongoing gender oppression within the context of maternity and the reality that 90 percent of women[15] will become mothers at some point in their lifetime, the fact that there has been no call to advocate for social justice for mothers by third wave intersectional thinkers is deeply troubling. Indeed, if social justice is so important to intersectional thinking and contemporary mothers are so obviously in need of social justice, why has third wave feminism more generally and intersectional thinkers specifically been silent about the need for social justice specifically for mothers? Exploring this question is central before an alliance between feminist maternal and intersectional scholars can develop.

YOUNGER-OLDER GENERATIONAL STRUCTURAL PROBLEMS

Intersectional theory is silent on maternity because it emerges out of third wave feminism's general use of a younger-older generational structure between second and third wave feminisms. Even though third wave feminism is a term for a dynamic, sometimes contentious, body of thinking and activism within contemporary feminism, it is generally viewed as the "next generation" and "next wave" of feminism that followed second wave feminism. As scholars such as Astrid Henry, Leslie Heywood, Lynn O'Brien Hallstein, and Carissa Showden note, third wavers are usually "younger" women and describe themselves as the "younger" generation in relation to second wave feminists who are seen as the "older" generation of women. This generational divide is central to early 1990s third wave feminism. So, for example, in their 1997 academic collection *Third Wave Agenda*, editors Leslie Heywood and Jennifer Drake argued that their text explores a different kind of feminism, one that presents a "generational perspective, gathering voices of young activists struggling to come to terms with the historical specificity of our feminisms and with the times in which we came of age (the late 1970s through the late 1980s)" (2).

The younger-older, generational difference continues to be central to many intersectional thinkers. Indeed, in *The Fire This Time: Young Activists and the New Feminism*, editors Labaton and Martin consistently describe the contributors as "young women (and men)" or as "young feminists." In fact, the language and focus on younger-older—we as "younger" and as the "next generation"—permeate the "Introduction" and text. So, for example, Labaton and Martin also write:

> One of the luxuries that our generation has enjoyed is that we've reaped the benefits of all the social justice movements that have come before us; we have come of age in a world that has been shaped by feminism, queer liberation movements, antiracist movements, labor movements, and others. Consequently, many young women and men not only have an understanding of the interconnection of social justice issues but also see them as inextricable from one another. (xxvi)

Thus, it is clear that, even though intersectional thinking is a "new" form of third wave thinking, it continues to draw on the younger-older, next-generation structure that was central to the early third wave. Understanding this historical linage and its matrophobic consequences are essential to think through an alliance between second and third wave feminisms.

Historical Lineage of the Younger-Older Generational Structure

While many third wave feminists may believe that a younger-older structure between the second and third wave is new to them, it is not. Indeed, as Henry has argued, 1960s and 1970s second-wave feminists also employed a younger-older structure that simultaneously identified and disidentified with first-wave feminism. In terms of legitimating themselves, initially, women in the mid-to-late 1960s saw the 1960s New Leftists and civil rights movements—liberal and radical social movements focused on political activism and mass protests—as the geneses of second wave feminism (Henry *Matrophobia and Generations*; Klatch; Umansky). Or, as Henry puts it, "While many women were certainly aware that a women's movement had existed in the previous century, it was not this earlier movement but rather the New Left and civil rights movements of the 1960s that were initially perceived as the forerunners to this new feminism" (*Matrophobia and Generations* 18).

As 1960s and 1970s feminism evolved, however, 1960s and 1970s feminists began to identify with the feminist Suffrage movement of the late 1800s and early 1900s. In fact, the Suffrage movement began to be seen as the historical precedent for and legitimation of 1960s and 1970s feminism. Women participating in the leftist organizations needed legitimacy because, as scholars such as Benita Roth, Sara Evans, and Lauri Umansky argue, a central struggle 1960s women faced within the left was convincing both women and men to place gender issues on the New Left's agenda. Moreover, Henry also argues that "the second wave's identification with the first wave granted feminists in the 1960s a group identity: women involved in the historic struggle for women's rights" (*Matrophobia and Generations* 10). Consequently, the identification gave second wave feminists a historical group of foremothers with whom to compare themselves, a group identity, and legitimacy within the Leftist and civil rights movements.

At the same time that second wave feminists identified with first wave feminism as a way to legitimate the second wave, these feminists also disavowed or disidentified from first wave feminism. In fact, Henry argues a key event that defined the future of the second wave and was, simultaneously, a pinnacle disidentification moment occurred during the 1969 inaugural of Richard Nixon. Various women's groups organized a separate women's event for the counter inaugural rally being organized by the National Mobilization Committee to End the War in Vietnam in Washington, D.C. In planning the demonstration, members of New York Radical Women organized a "give back the vote" for which Suffragettes had struggled. Organizing a give back the vote emerged because, as Henry argues, many second wave feminists believed that the focus on the vote in the late nineteenth and early twentieth centuries was the downfall of that feminism because "first-wave feminists had not fought for 'real emancipation' but rather had allowed themselves to be placated by 'sop'" (*Matrophobia and Generations* 21). In other words, rather than focus on large-scale institutional change, Suffragettes emphasized on and were placated by an "easy" goal: "simply" gaining the vote for women. This moment of disidentification with the first wave allowed the second wave to articulate what was a "better" and new focus for the second wave. Thus, strategically situating feminism both with and against the Suffragette movement allowed 1960s feminists both to identify and disidentify with the first wave, such that "the 'dead' suffrage movement was defined as conservative, misguided, and over, so the 'new,' 'real' feminism of the present could be posited as truly radical and thus, ultimately, a better kind of feminism" (Henry, *Matrophobia and Generations* 21).

As I have argued (*White Feminists*) elsewhere, the younger-older, identification-disidentification strategy of second wave feminism is deeply problematic because it entrenches the fear of becoming like the mother—matrophobia—within the wave metaphor itself and between generations of feminists. Disidentification is matrophobic because, as scholars such as Judith Butler, Diane Fuss, Astrid Henry (*Matrophobia and Generations*), and I (*White Feminists*) argue, it is an identification or disavowal *against something or someone*. As such, disidentification is a negative process of identifying against something or someone, or as not like something or someone. A similar negative process is also at work in matrophobia. In summary, because the fear of mothering is an identification against something—the fear of becoming like the mother; "not like her"—it is also a negative identificatory process against the mother. Both Henry (*Not My*) and I (*White Feminists*) have argued second wave feminists also employed a matrophobic disidentification strategy with the first wave, which is fundamentally built into the generational structure and wave metaphor that second wave feminists employed to justify themselves.

This disidentification[16] also permeates the younger-older generational structure between second and third wave feminisms generally and inter-sectional thinking specifically and further entrenches matrophobia in the wave metaphor and an ongoing silence on maternity for several reasons. First, as scholars (Henry *Not My*; O'Brien Hallstein *White Feminists*) have shown, the younger-older cross-generational structure reinforces a mother-daughter relationship between the second and third waves when third wave feminists position themselves as the next generation against older second wave feminists. This intergenerational younger-older, mother-daughter structure emerges because many young feminists remain within an imagined mother-daughter relationship precisely in order to give themselves a position from which to speak—as anti-essentialist third wave daughters rather than essentialist second wave mothers.[17] Consequently, as with the third wave in general, contemporary third wave intersectional thinkers continue to entrench matrophobia within feminist analyses, the wave metaphor, and the intergenerational structure when they define themselves as the younger women and/or the younger daughters in relation to second wave mothers.

Doing so also encourages silences on maternity because it creates a feminist subject position or location of critique that is fearful of mother-ing—that is built on matrophobia. As with the younger-older generational structure, embedding matrophobia within the primary feminist location of critique is also not new to third wave feminists and in fact is a linger-ing legacy of second wave feminism. Marianne Hirsch ("Feminism"), in fact, suggested matrophobia was embedded in second wave feminism's preference to organize around and critique the larger culture from the standpoint of sisters. Indeed, Hirsch was the first to suggest, and Henry's (*Matrophobia and Generations*, *Not My*) and my (*White Feminist*) more recent work also confirms, matrophobia played a key role in white second wave feminism's rhetorical preference for organizing around the metaphor of sisterhood, which also became a feminist subject position or location of critique from which to explore culture.

In "Feminism at the Maternal Divide," Hirsch argued retrospectively that the metaphor of sisterhood provided:

> the possibility of mutuality and reciprocity. The metaphor of
> sisterhood, though still familial, can describe a feminine mode
> of relation, an ideal and alternative within patriarchy. It could
> help women envision a life and a set of affiliations outside of

> the paradigm of mother/child relations and the compromises
> with men that motherhood seems to necessitate. It can liberate
> feminist women from our anatomy and from the difficult stories
> of our own mothers' accommodation, adjustment and resigna-
> tion. "Sisterhood" can free us, as we were fond of saying, "to
> give birth to ourselves." (356)

Thus, while a powerful location of critique or feminist subject position,
the sisterly subject position that developed was fundamentally built on
privileging mutuality and reciprocity *between women* rather than any
reciprocity between mothers and children or mothers and daughters.

As a result, the sisterly perspective was fearful of acknowledging the
maternal or mothering and, hence, expelled both from the sisterly location of critique. As Hirsch first argued in *The Mother-Daughter Plot*:
"To say that 'sisterhood is powerful,' however, is to isolate feminist
discourse within one generation and to banish feminists who are mothers to the 'mother-closet'" (164). Consequently, expelling or separating
mothering from the sisterly perspective is matrophobic in its fear of
mothering and, equally important, divides and separates feminists from
one another. As a result, Hirsch extended Adrienne Rich[18] by arguing
matrophobia was also a problem *within* academic feminism, including her own earlier work on the mother-daughter relationship. Indeed,
Hirsch concludes that matrophobia "exists not only in the culture at
large, but also within feminism, and within women who are mothers, ourselves, who have spent a good part of our [academic] careers
thinking about motherhood" (365). Thus, even when feminists were
addressing motherhood, they did so employing matrophobic perspectives or locations of critique.

More recent work also confirms (Henry *Matrophobia and Generations*, *Not My*; O'Brien Hallstein *Matrophobic Sisters*; O'Reilly) that
the matrophobic fear of mothering as a location of critique for feminist
analyses, even by feminists who actually have children, continues to
play a problematic role in contemporary feminist analyses. In fact,
like second wave feminists, at the epistemological level and as a new
location of critique, distance and separation from maternity and/or
silence on maternity are also embedded in third wave feminism generally because the intergenerational structure is matrophobic. Clearly,
then, the strategic choice that second wave feminism made in relation

to developing a wave metaphor within feminism laid the foundation for an intergenerational and matrophobic relationship between first wave foremothers and second wave sisters, a relationship that continues between so-called second wave mothers and third wave daughters.

The twin rhetorical moves[19] of identification and disidentification, then, also fuel the new epistemological foundations of third wave intersectionality. In short, I am suggesting that, rather than challenge the matrophobic generational structure that has undergirded second wave feminisms, intersectional analyses are continuing to perpetuate it, which also encourages silence on maternity. At the most basic level, then, the generational structure that intersectional thinking employs and further entrenches must also be resisted if there is to be a fruitful alliance between feminist maternal scholars and intersectional scholars. Consequently, we need an alliance perspective between generations of feminism that heals the separation and division that preclude the possibility of an alliance between second and third wave feminisms, between feminist maternal scholarship and intersectional thinking. We require, as Rowe suggests, an alliance frame, then, that "seeks to provide a mechanism for healing for the subject of … feminism through which she may take responsibility for her own complicity in contemporary and historic relations of ruling, not to feel bad or guilty, but to truly heal the violence through which our ancestors, and by extension, our current generation, relate to one another through segregation and separation" (22).

CONCLUSIONS

The primary interest here was to begin to explore the theoretical issues raised when considering an alliance between feminist maternal scholarship and intersectional thinking, an alliance between second and third wave feminisms. That we have these sorts of theoretical discussions remains imperative to academic feminists. While much motherhood studies laudably draws on feminist academics' experiences as mother, implicitly, I have tried to suggest and explicitly show that being and thinking as an academic mother still requires that *we think very carefully* about what kinds of feminisms and which ideas we utilize as we try to understand and build strategies to resist the barriers of contemporary maternity generally and academic motherhood more specifically.

Detailing the actual practice of such an alliance frame in light of the theoretical discussion here, however, requires much more sustained attention. Even so, it is clear to me at this specific historical moment we need an alliance between the second wave's commitment both to capital-F feminism and gender analyses and the third wave intersectional insistence that analyses recognize the interlocking connections among race, class, gender, and sexuality when advocating for the social justice mothers need now. To do so, however, does not require "old" ways of thinking but instead new ways of thinking that are informed by both the past and present, by both my intellectual "feet." Rather than engage in the kind of essentialism that drove much second wave work, for example, we need to employ the kind of strategic essentialism described first by postcolonial feminists. Indeed, as some postcolonial writers (Sandoval; Spivak) argue, because culture is not fully free from colonial thinking and colonial forms of power—we are between the old and new—we need to challenge remaining colonial ways of thinking and forms of power at the same time that we recognize new postcolonial forms of thinking and power. As a result, they advocate for a strategic essentialism—a conscious and reflexive centering on gender—as a political praxis to recognize simultaneously both the vestiges of lingering colonial power structures and new postcolonial power.

In the same way, within the context of our post-second-wave maternity, we can and must also employ the same kind of strategic essentialism or, as Fuss (*Essentially Speaking*) puts it, "the risk of essentialism" in order to recognize, simultaneously, new and old gender roles for women. In other words, just as postcolonial feminists recognize we are between new and old gendered power configurations, we too can build a feminist maternal praxis around a provisional strategic essentialism on gender as we try to erode the specific barriers to women's agency in the context of motherhood. This feminist praxis would center strategically on gender in adhering to social justice for mothers, particularly in terms of challenging the prices of motherhood and neo-traditional families that continue to undergird academic institutions. That we do so is especially imperative in the context of academic motherhood if we hope to gain more gender equity because family formations continue to create barriers for academic mothers' success in the academy. As Mason and Goulden put it, "A true measure of gender equity in the academy would look at both career and family outcomes" ("Do Babies Matter (II)?" 14). To put it another way, until both the underlying male-organizing system that shapes academia and neo-traditional family formations are eradicated, we must utilize strategies and politics that allow us to advocate for mothers, risking essentializing strategies and politics.

What I am advocating, then, is a politics of accountability among feminists and between second and third wave feminists, between feminist maternal and intersectional feminists. Indeed, building an alliance frame between feminist maternal scholarship and intersectional thinking would require feminist maternal scholars to develop, as Rowe describes, a *politics of accountability*. A politics of accountability among women and between feminist generations would allow all contemporary feminists, but especially someone like myself, whose autonomy is built on the labor of other women, to take responsibility for my own complicity in power relations. Doing so would also help facilitate the kind of mutual responsibility[20] between generations of feminists that I have argued (*White Feminists*) can purge matrophobia from the generational structure. Finally, as noted earlier, intersectionality is not itself a "politics" and instead shifts the epistemological standpoint of feminism, providing a new subject position from which feminist critiques are articulated. An alliance built on a politics of accountability between feminist maternal and intersectional thinkers, then, would also embed a feminist praxis within the alliance. In short, a politics of accountability can draw upon second and third wave feminist ideas in ways that heal the matrophobic younger-older generational structure that segregates and separates generations of feminists, feminist maternal scholars and third wave intersectional thinkers.

Feminist academic mothers, then, can begin to build intellectual alliances that strategically center on gender and make feminism central, while also recognizing interlocking power axes also embedded in contemporary maternity. More specifically, an alliance perspective would eschew the additive approach to recognizing women's different social locations, the intra-woman oppression that permeates contemporary maternity, attend to the multiple and intersecting axes of power, and forgo the younger-older matrophobic generational structure that all currently make alliance building difficult. This, then, then would allow me to resolve my one-foot-in-second-and-one-foot-in-third-wave-feminist dilemma by insisting that second and third wave ideas can be simultaneously employed as we begin to develop strategies to seek social justice for mothers both within and outside academia.

[1]I was lucky enough to be raised within second wave feminism. Born to leftists parents in 1963, both my parents participated in 1960s and 1970s second-wave feminism and raised all of their children to be feminists. As a result, unlike many feminist thinkers who were introduced to feminism in graduate school, I started my graduate training well versed in feminist ideas and political action. Thus, my connections to second wave feminism are more than just intellectual. Second wave ideas are part of my being as a feminist.

[2]While my family participated in both second wave feminist and civil rights protests and intellectual discussions, it is important to note that we primarily, however not exclusively, participated in what is now understood as white second wave feminisms. See Benita Roth.

[3]Initially, the early 1990s was considered the beginning of the third wave. However, recent academic work suggests third wave ideas began to appear in writings and discussions focused on the intersections of feminism and racism in the mid-1980s, primarily by women of color. These early writings called for a "new subjectivity" or feminist "voice" that honored race due to the overwhelming focus on white women's issues in much of the media-represented second wave feminism and the failure to attend to race by many white second wave feminists. This focus was articulated initially by some of the key activists in the second wave: Cherrie Moraga, Gloria Anzaldua, bell hooks, Chela Dadoval, Audre Lorde, Maxine Hong Kingston and other feminists of color. Focusing on race continued, mostly in academic circles, until the Anita Hill Clarence Thomas hearings. The Hill-Thomas hearings, conducted by the United States Senate Judiciary Committee to investigate professor Anita Hill's allegations of prior sexual harassment by Hill, was televised live in October 1991. Although the hearings had no legal significance and Thomas was eventually confirmed, many mark the hearings as the symbolic beginning of a new discussion of gender inequity and sexual harassment in America, which continued long after the hearing was over in both academic and popular circles. As a result, 1991 is often credited with the initiating a new conversation—a third wave conversation—about feminism and feminist ideas, in both popular and academic circles. There is little dispute, however, that by 1992 the term *third wave feminism* came into public consciousness or at least the political left, when Rebecca Walker, daughter of Alice Walker, founded the Third Wave Direct Action Corporation in 1992 with Shannon Liss, which later became the Third Wave Foundation in 1998. The

non-profit institution cultivated young women's leadership. At the same time, key third-wave texts—including one that Walker edited—were written in the early 1990s and are now recognized as central to the development of third wave feminism. Thus, there is no dispute that, in the early 1990s, feminism resurfaced both within media and academic circles and many women, especially young women, became reengaged with a new kind of feminism.

[4]While it is true that key second-wave thinkers— Audre Lorde, Combahee River Collective, Kimberle Crenshaw, bell hooks, and Iris Marion Young—began to describe intersectional analyses as early as the 1970s, the term *intersectionality* was not used until Kimberle Crenshaw coined the term in 1994 in her landmark essay, "Mapping the Margins: Intersectionality, Identity Politics, and Violence Against Women of Color." Thus, my interest in this essay is the contemporary third wave rendering of intersectionality rather than the early work that may or may not be included in the third wave understanding of intersectionality. For clarity, I acknowledge that some of the critiques I level against third wave intersectionality may not be relevant to the work that began in the second wave. I thank to Karma Chavez for pointing out potential lineage issues and the inappropriateness of some of my critiques in relation to the earlier work on intersectionality.

[5]Here, I am specifically drawing on the understanding of post-second wave that was detailed in the introduction.

[6]Drawing often on Adrienne Rich's groundbreaking distinction between institution of motherhood and the potential of mothering to be empowering to women if women are allowed to define mothering themselves, contemporary feminist maternal thinkers argue mothering itself is not necessarily oppressive and instead it is the socially constructed patriarchal institution of motherhood—the ideology of good mothering and institutionalized practices that encourage that ideology—that oppresses women and disallows women from defining mothering themselves. Consequently, feminist maternal thinkers view maternal agency as both the ability to define mothering outside of institutionalized motherhood and the ability to influence the larger society to work towards social justice for both women and children.

[7]Indeed, celebrating their autonomy is central to third wave feminism in general but especially third wave intersectional thinkers.

[8]While it is true that some third wave intersectional thinkers might not

drop women's issues and instead approach those issues differently, i.e., insisting, rightfully, that poor women of color in the U.S. have different needs surrounding reproductive rights than white, middle-class women in the U.S., my concern here is with the third wave intersectional thinking that downplays focusing on women's issues while also decentering gender. Again, I thank Karma Chavez for pointing out this important distinction in her review of an early draft of this essay.

[9]Sociologist Sharon Hays coined the term *intensive mothering* and argues that it is an ideology of child rearing that "requires not only large quantities of money but also professional-level skills and copious amounts of physical, moral, mental, and emotional energy on the part of the individual mother [and] is a relatively recent historical phenomenon" (4). Feminist academics (Douglas and Michaels; Hays; O'Reilly) now argue that it rests on at least three core beliefs: 1) children need and require constant and ongoing nurturing by their biological mothers who are single-handedly responsible for meeting these needs; 2) in meeting those needs, mothers must rely on experts to guide them, and 3) mothers must lavish enormous amounts of time and energy on their children. In short, mothers should always put their children's needs before their own. Thus, even though not all women practice intensive mothering, as Hays argues, it is the *proper* ideology of contemporary mothering that all women are disciplined into, across race and class lines, even if not all women actually practice it.

[10]While intensive mothering focuses specifically on educated professional women, uneducated women are also penalized because of their lack of education, their inability to bring professional-level skills and education.

[11]Here, I want to be clear that much of the kind of autonomy I describe is deeply tied up with race, class, and sexual privilege, i.e., the autonomy that white, heterosexual, highly educated, women enjoy.

[12]Below, I draw extensively on Ann Crittenden's book *The Price of Motherhood*, where she first described the various costs of motherhood to women. Because I want to make the point that there are many "prices" to motherhood, I pluralize the costs, even though Crittenden does not.

[13]In arguing that maternity constrains all women's lives, I acknowledge that different women's lives are constrained differently in relation to their social location. So, for example, women have very different concerns and real material constraints depending on how women are located in

and constituted by racial, class, sexual, and national dynamics in the context of maternity. Even so, as I have been arguing throughout this essay, women as a group share gender oppression in the context of maternity, while some of that oppression is different based on any particular woman's social location.

[14]The term *maternal wall* was coined by Deborah J. Swiss and Judith P. Walker in their 1993 book *Women and the Work/Family Dilemma: How Today's Professional Women Are Confronting the Maternal Wall*. John Wiley & Sons, 1993.

[15]Joan Williams makes this claim in her book *Unbending Gender*, 2.

[16]For my more extensive analysis of the long-term consequences of disidentification between second and third wave feminists, see my book *White Feminists*.

[17]For more detail on the third wave's preference to organize as daughters, see both Henry's (*Not My*) work and my book *White Feminists*.

[18]Rich was the first to explore matrophobia in the context of the mother-daughter relationship and motherhood in her book *Of Woman Born*.

[19]I coined the term *twin rhetorical moves* in my earlier work on the matrophobic consequences of the intergenerational structure. See *White Feminists* for more detail.

[20]A mutually responsive relationship between feminist generations allows feminists to forgo matrophobia because it is grounded in ongoing connection, the loop of empathy, and efforts to self-repair between generations. See "Chapter Five," *White Feminists*.

WORKS CITED

Braithwaite, Ann. "Politics of/and Backlash." *Journal of International Women's Studies* 5.5 (June 2004): 18-33.

Butler, Judith. "Against Proper Objects." *Feminism Meets Queer Theory*. Eds. Elizabeth Weed and Naomi Schor. Bloomington: Indiana University Press, 1997. 1-30.

Collins, Patricia Hill. *Black Feminist Thought: Knowledge, Consciousness, and the Politics of Empowerment*. New York: Routledge, 2000.

Crenshaw, Kimberle. "Mapping the Margins: Intersectionality, Identity Politics, and Violence Against Women of Color." *Stanford Law Review* 43 (1990): 1241-1299.

Crittenden, Ann. *The Price of Motherhood: Why the Most Important*

Job the World is Still the Least Valued. New York: Henry Holt and Company, 2001.

Douglas, Susan J. and Meredith Michaels. *The Mommy Myth: The Idealization of Motherhood and how it has Undermined Women*. New York: Free Press, 2004.

Dow, Bonnie J. "Review Essay: Reading the Second Wave." *Quarterly Journal of Speech* 91.1 (Feb. 2005): 89-107.

Evans, Sara. *Tidal Wave: How Women Changed America at Century's End*. New York: Free Press, 2003.

Faludi, Susan. *Backlash: The Undeclared War against American Women*. New York: Crown, 1991.

Fuss, Diane. *Identification Papers*. New York: Routledge, 1995.

Fuss, Diane. *Essentially Speaking: Feminism, Nature, and Difference*. New York: Routledge, 1989.

Hayden, Sara and D. Lynn O'Brien Hallstein. *Contemplating Maternity in an Era of Choice: Explorations into Discourses of Reproduction*. Lanham, MD: Lexington Press, 2010.

Hays, Sharon. *The Cultural Contradictions of Motherhood*. New Haven: Yale University Press, 1996.

Henry, Astrid. *Matrophobia and Generations of Feminism*. Diss. The University of Wisconsin-Milwaukee, 2000.

Henry, Astrid. *Not my Mother's Sister: Generational Conflict and Third-Wave Feminism*. Bloomington: Indiana University Press, 2004.

Heywood, Leslie L., ed. *The Women's Movement Today: An Encyclopedia of Third Wave Feminism*. Westport, CT: Greenwood, 2006.

Heywood, Leslie and Jennifer Drake, eds. *Third Wave Agenda: Being Feminist, Doing Feminism*. Minneapolis: University of Minnesota Press, 1997.

Hirsch, Marianne. "Feminism at the Maternal Divide: A Diary." *The Politics of Motherhood: Activist Voices from Left to Right*. Eds. Alexis Jetter, Annelise Orleck, and Diana Taylor. Hanover: University Press of New England, 1997. 352-368.

Hirsch, Marianne. *The Mother/Daughter Plot: Narrative, Psychoanalysis, Feminism*. Bloomington: Indiana University Press, 1989.

Kinser, Amber, ed. "Introduction: Thinking About and Going About Mothering in the Third Wave." *Mothering in the Third Wave*. Toronto, Canada: Demeter Press, 2008. 1-16.

Klatch, Rebecca E. "The Formation of Feminist Consciousness Among

Left- and Right-Wing Activists of the 1960s." *Gender and Society* 15.6 (Dec. 2001): 791-815.

Labaton, Vivien and Dawn Lundy Martin, eds. *The Fire This Time: Young Activists and the New Feminism*. New York: Anchor Books, 2004.

Mason, Mary Ann and Marc Goulden. "Do Babies Matter (Part II)? Closing the Baby Gap." *Academe* 90.6 (Nov.-Dec. 2004): 10-15.

Mason, Mary Ann and Marc Goulden. "Do Babies Matter? The Effect of Family Formation on the Lifelong Careers of Academic Men and Women" *Academe* 88.6 (Nov.-Dec. 2002): 21-27.

O'Brien Hallstein, D. Lynn. "Matrophobic Sisters and Daughters: The Rhetorical Consequences of Matrophobia in Contemporary White Feminist Analyses of Maternity." *Women's Studies: An Interdisciplinary Journal* 36.4 (June 2007): 269-296.

O'Brien Hallstein, D. Lynn. "Public Choices, Private Control: How Mediated Mom Labels Work Rhetorically to Dismantle the Politics of Choice and White Second Wave Feminism." Eds. Sara Hayden and D. Lynn O'Brien Hallstein. *Contemplating Maternity in an Era of Choice: Explorations into Discourses of Reproduction*. Lanham, MD: Lexington Books, 2010. 5-27.

O'Brien Hallstein, D. Lynn. *White Feminists and Contemporary Maternity: Purging Matrophobia*. New York: Palgrave, 2010.

O'Reilly, Andrea. Ed. *Mother Outlaws: Theories and Practices of Empowered Mothering*. Toronto, Canada: Women's Press, 2004.

Peskowitz, Miriam. *The Truth Behind the Mommy Wars: Who Decides What Makes a Good Mother?* Emeryville, CA: Seal Press, 2005.

Rich, Adrienne. *Of Woman Born: Motherhood as Experience and Institution*. 2nd ed. New York: W.W. Norton, 1986.

Roth, Benita. *Separate Roads to Feminism: Black, Chicana, and White Feminist Movements in America's Second Wave*. Cambridge: Cambridge University Press, 2004.

Rowe, Aimee Carrillo. "Subject to Power—Feminism Without Victims." *Women's Studies in Communication*, 32.1 (Spring 2009): 12-35.

Rowe-Finkbeiner, Kristine. *The F Word: Feminism in Jeopardy: Women, Politics, and the Future*. Emeryville, CA: Seal Press, 2004.

Sandoval, Chela. "U.S. Third World Feminism: The Theory and Method of Oppositional Consciousness in the Postmodern World." *Genders* 10 (1991): 1-24.

Showden, Carissa R. "What's Political About the New Feminisms?"

Frontiers, 30.2 (June 2009): 166-199.

Spivak, Gayatri Chakravorty. "Can the Subaltern Speak?" *Marxism and the Interpretation of Culture*. Eds. Cary Nelson and Lawrence Grossberg. Urbana: University of Illinois Press, 1998: 271-313.

Swiss, Deborah J. and Judith P. Walker. *Women and the Work/Family Dilemma: How Today's Professional Women Are Confronting the Maternal Wall*. Hoboken, NJ: John Wiley & Sons, 1993.

Umansky, Lauri. *Motherhood Reconceived: Feminism and the Legacies of the Sixties*. New York: New York University Press, 1996.

Warner, Judith. *Perfect Madness: Motherhood the Age of Anxiety*. New York: Riverhead Books, 2005.

Williams, Joan. *Unbending Gender: Why Family and Work Conflict and What To Do About It*. Oxford: Oxford University Press, 2000.

Williams, Joan and Nancy Segal. "Beyond the Maternal Wall: Relief for Family caregivers who are discriminated against on the Job." *Harvard Women's Law Journal* 26 (2003): 77-162.

Wolfinger, Nicholas H., Mary Ann Mason, and Marc Goulden. "Stay in the Game: Gender, Family Formation and Alternative Trajectories in the Academic Life Course." *Social Forces* 87.3 (March 2009): 1591-1621.

20.

The Cost of an Education

Exploring the Extended Reach of Academe in Family Life

AMBER E. KINSER

L
AST SPRING I WAS SITTING BY A SMALL LAKE near the beach trying to put my ideas together for this chapter when my cell phone
rang. It was my daughter, who is now in college at the university
where my partner and I teach. Her thoughts were scattered but the gist
of the call was that her best friend's mother, who also was my co-worker
and about my age, suddenly died of a brain aneurism. I sat and stared out
at the lake, breathless at the thought of mothers leaving their children,
stripped mid-stride in their mother journeys of their right to keep teaching
and learning, cut off mid-job, right in the middle of their motherwork.
A week later I stood in the lobby of this woman's church waiting to be
received by her family among hundreds of other family, friends, and
community members. As I stood, I watched the "celebration of life"
DVD they prepared in her honor playing on the flatscreen in the lobby,
an extensive collection of photo stills that paid tribute to this mother's
life and loves and relationships. I cried as I watched it from my place in
that long line as it snaked through the lobby and I thought about the
deep, deep loss for this family. And then I found myself thinking about
me, flashing through my nineteen years or so of mothering and what I've
accomplished or haven't, how well I did any of it, what my own funeral
DVD might say about me and my choices. What crystallized for me in
these reflections about living and mothering is the way my academic life
so heavily impinges upon, is intricately interwoven with, so profoundly
shapes, injects, my experience of being a mother. What strikes me in
particular is the tension produced when life in the academy rubs against
the world outside it, both for mothers and their children. The language,
practices, and worldviews that are afforded credence and that find company

in academic contexts have little resonance or companionship in other contexts. My academic mothering, it seems, has limited street cred.

In thinking about whether the term "academic mothering" is really what I mean, I've come to confront the fact that my mothering practices are very much guided by academic and particularly feminist theory; by my own research and writing agenda; by the seasons and tides of the academic year; by the surveillance that I perceive to be directed at my family from those in academe and those ostensibly outside it—a gaze made particularly piercing because: my children have attended the K-12 "lab school" that is located on my university campus and their daily proximity meant they were often under foot in my office and at campus events; my partner and our relationship are quite visible on campus and he is a faculty member in the department over which I am chairperson; and, given my position as Director of Women's Studies for ten years, our rather accessible family life was surely scrutinized to determine what kinds of people all that feminism produces, perhaps in the hopes that it produces very flawed people, proving that feminist theory is "just" theory. So I think that, for me, and perhaps for many, "academic mothering" is not an inaccurate identifier. Further, the relationship between academe and motherhood for me is an intimate one that sits at the core of who I am and who my children are, as feminists, as social actors, and as citizens. It isn't just my job; it is, in many ways, our life. And that life insinuates itself into multiple arenas, extending far beyond academe. For me, it extends into three arenas for making meaning in particular.

First, academe is a place where I cultivate and grow and tend my feminism, so my practices of mothering have roots and are nourished there. But these practices also have roots that are grounded in many other areas as well (my childhood, my adult partnerships, economics, my children's personalities, to name a few) that entangle themselves with the feminist ones and compete for prominence in our family life. Feminist mothering has been a complicated affair. Second, academic training has situated me among knowledges with which most mothers are unfamiliar and many are even uncomfortable. So what I know and how I mother are frequently at least awkward and at worst a site of contestation between me and the mothers that surround me. Third, my academic feminist mothering of my children situates them among knowledges with which most of their friends and peers are neither familiar nor comfortable, nor able to argue intelligibly for or against. Even my kids find such knowledges confounding and feel pushed by them into the margins in many ways and some of this I find troubling. I explore here these three facets of the relationship between my academic training and my mothering practices, with particular attention to how academe situates my family in our larger social world and the possibilities in academic family life for living fully and without apology.

It's an awkward piecing together, the academy and the "real world," a distinction that is faulty but no less tossed about on a regular basis in university culture. And it's awkward for several reasons, not the least of which relates to the *kind* of thinking that is cultivated in that culture—a seeking out of questions that don't have answers and the mapping of a quest to find them, titillation by the quizzical and the rush to make sense of same. Academics seek out the chaos but less to dance in it than to order it.

WINDMILLS: ACADEMIC TRAINING AND INTERRUPTED MYTHOS RESISTANCE

There is a scene in the 1987 film *Broadcast News* in which the protagonist, a network news producer played by Holly Hunter, is working to orchestrate a critical decision about whom to send out on assignment. The decision is not hers to make in this scene, but she intervenes in her supervisor's process and tries to influence its outcome anyway. She does this sort of thing throughout the film and in this instance her supervisor turns to her, frustrated by her presumptuous intrusions and says snidely, "It must be nice to always believe you know better, to always think you're the smartest person in the room." She looks at him, perplexed by his so thoroughly missing her truth: "No," she says almost tearfully, "it's awful!" I relished this scene back then and think of it frequently now because I identify sharply with the angst of it. I love it partly because it nailed the protagonist's character flaw so perfectly, so supremely, and I love it partly because I identify with her struggle. Though I hardly think of myself as the smartest person in the room, one of the tricky facets of being an academic is that often enough you *do* feel like you're the only one there who knows what's going on, at least in your particularly trained area. And when that area is the institution of motherhood and the cultural constructions of family reality and women's lives, knowledge, and experience, you are knowledgeable about something that the families around you also know a great deal. And they are much invested in what they know. Your knowledge, though, is of a different kind, one that is grounded in more than personal experience, belief in biological imperatives, religious investments, or an N drawn from your immediate social world. Once you've stepped outside of academic circles, sometimes it really is awful to be the only one in the room who knows in this way.

Somehow the Sartrean notion of "dreadful freedom" holds particular salience for me when reflecting on this. It's a dreadful thing to know that the ways that motherhood is currently constructed are of human design and as such could be re-designed; it is dreadful to have to confront the fact that if the oppressive elements of our worlds remain oppressive it is because human beings have chosen to act or not act in ways that ensure this. We really do, as individuals and in solidarity with others, have immense freedom and power to create the world we believe ought to be. Knowing this and yet never quite creating that world is a source of dread and anxiety for many, which are more acutely felt by them when in the company of people whose worldviews deny this freedom and power, who live, as Sartre says, "in bad faith." I feel like I am in such company most of the time. Raising children with knowledge that most of the mothers around me, that most of those who parent my son's friends and peers don't have is in many ways awful, dreadful. Raising my children to hold that same knowledge, surrounded by children who do not, has proven at times, for my kids, dreadful.

I know from my understanding of the complex relationship between feminism and mothering; from my own growing up with full-time employed lower middle-class parents; from theorists and historians like Sharon Hays and Stephanie Coontz, who show that family practices of a given time are grounded in transient cultural norms and no thing that is universal; and from recent research synthesized by Po Bronson and Ashley Merryman, Lenore Skenazy, and Pamela Paul among others that much of the prominent ideology about what children need and parents ought do is just so much nonsense. But somehow none of this can compete with the more resounding cultural message that embracing any of this knowledge is just "wrong, wrong, wrong" as Paul says (227) and that for it we'll be eternally sorry, sorry, sorry.

It is true, as Lenore Skenazy has argued, that mothers today are parenting in a time when their images of family are viscerally textured with graphic television violence and sensationalized news drama about risk for kids, even though the statistical risk of "stranger danger" is unbelievably small. It is true that parents can hardly help fretting over the threat ostensibly posed by Halloween candy poisoners, frightening costumes, and masks that block vision and promote the spread of bacteria. It is a stalwart (and lonely) person who maintains that these "threats" do not demand parental intrusion into and micromanagement of yet another holiday and yet another formerly kid-directed activity, even though we do not have evidence that Halloween candy or masks or costumes have proven dangerous. It is true too that consumerist ideologies make it difficult for parents to trust themselves if they don't have some mediating product or expert to ensure success or safety, and it is true that the fear of lawsuits that plagues schools, towns, and organizations shape the public standards that no less direct our private lives, guiding as they do what kind of play parents will allow on their property, or what tale they can envision themselves reciting to the police officer or judge about why they thought making allowance X for their child was a good idea. And it is true that the way we "fetishize children and family," to use Pamela Paul's phrase, is intricately and systematically interwoven with consumption in ways that are significantly more likely to generate "abstainer's remorse" than buyer's remorse (211, 76). So *why* I and the parents that surround me feel compelled to parent in particular ways is not surprising. But *how* to not let this parenting mythos hold deterministic sway over my own life, especially in light of the fact that I seem to be just about the only parent in my immediate social world that sees these as mythology and lore rather than incontrovertible and impermeable truths, is the great conundrum of my life. Many of the parents of my children's friends are not "higher" educated and if they are, their academic knowledge is not in the area of mothering or parenting, certainly. I'd wager they, like many, believe that my academic knowledge is just so much nonsense, not "real world," the result of having my head in the books rather than my mind on the kids.

So what good—what close-range, personal, familial, identifiable good—I wonder sometimes, lots of times even, is the knowledge and awareness I hold if I'm the only one in the room, on my block, at the soccer game, in the parent-teacher meeting, who holds it? Being an academic who studies and writes about mothering means, among many things, that my children and I find ourselves teetering, off-balance from mothering and being mothered on the proverbial edge. And this feels perverse in light of the fact that the family life I'm advocating is not edgy at all, or even special, maybe not even interesting. Kids are not perpetually at risk; childhood is not perpetually fraught; kids are not so fragile and not, to invoke Skenazy again, "complicated cakes we have been given to make, and if we don't follow the recipe exactly...the whole thing will collapse" (25). Kids do not benefit from early edutainment videos; they are not better prepared for college because they were exposed to Mozart in utero or Baby Einstein 'curriculum' before kindergarten, as the studies reviewed by Bronson and Merryman show. Protecting self-esteem by lying to children about what constitutes "winning" athletic competitions or by telling them their mediocre work is just as worthy of unbridled praise as their stellar work does not, research shows, make them higher academic achievers, or stronger contenders in the marketplace, or better naviga-tors of the information age (Bronson & Merryman). It does, however, encourage them to "stew in adorable incompetence" (Skenazy 73) and it does discourage us from being disgusted by that. Praise and esteem building and having parents perpetually in the stands, whether literal or figurative does not, as it turns out, produce confidence and competence. It produces dependence and self images utterly contingent on the responses of others. But most parents won't have any of that. So here my children and I remain, on the edge in a not particularly edgy family.

Part of the difficulty for parents in releasing ourselves from the hold that our children have on our lives, or many of us believe they must, is explained in bell hooks' argument that parents regard their children as "property," as a "possession" (145). We see them as demonstrating who *we* are more than as separate, individuating selves, possessions that we cannot bare to share with others and expose to other worldviews because our kids are ours, ours, ours. And another part of the difficulty is our own insecurity stemming from a world that seems so far beyond our grasp, an economy so sickly and volatile and unassuring, international warfare so far beyond our comprehension, and the conspiratorial relationship between workplace and consumerist ideologies so pervasive that it has parents working, working, working to support even just what we deem to be the most necessary spending, spending, spending. But we really can release ourselves from these choking constrictions; we really can seriously entertain the notion that the world is safer than we imagine, that our kids don't benefit from our micromanagement, that we finally have very limited control over who they become but much influence on the world in which they are becoming. My students and I hold these truths to be self-evident and my family so holds them too. And then we leave the classroom and we leave our house and find that we are renegades, swearing that we see what seems wholly invisible to others, all of us appearing as mad Don Quixotes lancing windmills that we swear are dragons.

TENDRILS: ACADEMIC FEMINISM AND WAYWARD IMPACT

Like the walk of a police officer, which looks the same whether she is in or out of uniform, and like the tone of my son's kindergarten teacher, which sounded the same whether she was talking to five-year-olds or their parents, I suspect that the social performance of academic life is affected with its own predictable movements and scripts—its own texts and subtexts that are difficult to cast off once one leaves the classroom or the library. I suspect that my mothering practices are affected with the habits of explicating and exemplifying, with me providing more background information than my audience is interested in, with the high expectation that they'll eagerly refine their critical skills ever more sharply. It is probably unreasonable to hope that I do this any less as a mother than I do as a teacher or writer.

The difference though is that, as a teacher or writer, I seldom see the nuanced misreads my audiences bring to my work. I do see the major errors in my students' writing—errors that may just as likely indicate their misread as my own pedagogical or rhetorical mishaps—but I don't see any long-range impact of my training on their lives. Further, I am not their primary teacher, their housemate, or their emotional caretaker, so my impact is less profound and in any case more difficult to measure in any depth or breadth. The impact of my teaching/training/mothering of my children, however, is another matter, though perhaps not entirely. I can see the tendrils of academic feminism and how they have twined their way around elementary and middle and high school life, and its shoots and sprouts are not as innocuous as they may seem. On the subject, for example, of how to reconcile my lessons about male dominance and my critiques of masculine culture with my lessons about human equity and dignity, I have reason to believe I may have faltered.

I tried to teach that women and men, as generic groups, are of equal worth, that being male or female isn't what determines human value. But a more (painfully) honest look at what I've modeled reveals I'm afraid, a different picture. The message that no group has greater value by virtue of its sex is a tricky one to transmit effectively when one is simultaneously and persistently tagging just one of those groups for overestimating its own value, for in fact meticulously de-valuing the other group, for being the culprit, the victimizer, the oppressor, and when one is pointing out examples, as professors do, whenever she can which, given that I live with this particular audience, is all the time. I never said, in fact, that men are the problem. But this may be precisely what my children heard in any case. While I do feel like I have been able to distinguish for myself patriarchy bashing from "male bashing," to separate critiques of male privilege as a system from criticism of men as a group, I don't know that I have effectively communicated this distinction to them, and I find this disheartening.

As my son is an early teen, I have some data to examine, but little that is usefully longitudinal. I don't know yet what he takes from the endless parade of books and films and artwork and conversations about women that move into and out of our home as part of my academic work and consequent aesthetic interest. What does he take from my commentary "on the regular," as Joan Morgan writes, about women's lives, from my pleading on the regular that he choose not to be like "lots of boys" on this front or that, from my being cited on local television and local print news and his teachers mentioning to him that they saw the feature, and his knowing that the thrust of it most certainly implied a critique of masculine worlds? What does he take from the fact that, until I saw a Lifetime movie about the topic, I had never talked, much less thought, about teen pregnancy in boys' terms; I never even thought about *him* keeping or not keeping the baby. I am reminded here of Morgan's bold discussion of men's reproductive rights, of how, for example, feminism is loathe to admit "that the struggle for independence and reproductive choice also grants women the power *to control the lives and destinies of unwilling fathers via their bodies*" (170, italics in original). I wonder if my mothering is as equality based as I thought; as I meant. And I wonder more importantly how it shapes his conduct in, say, the middle school lunchroom, in his Facebook posts, in the text messages he forwards.

If males are suspect or the problem ipso facto, if an individual's worth *is* grounded in large part on their sex, if girls are the ones done (badly) to, and boys are the ones doing it—if this is the message he understands despite my intent—then I've terribly misconstrued the meanings of agency and power and how they function for everyone, and if I've botched the meanings of these two fundamental concepts, then I fear I've failed feminism and my children at their core. And my academic knowledge will prove "just" academic.

Even in places where the knowledge my son and I share is solid, and grounded in equity, and taught and learned well, the costs are high. When he was in third grade, for example, I told him to pick out a book for us to read and he chose his book on the human body, turning, not surprisingly, to the chapter on reproduction. It was fascinating looking at those pictures of male and female anatomy, seeing the penis and testicles and uterus and vagina, and actually spending time matching images he had not seen or did not remember to the words he already knew. The discussion of the uterus gave me an opportunity to talk about the menstrual cycle and what it's about, as well as about his own birth and how it was, as a C-section, different from his sister's. He was completely intrigued. So intrigued in fact that he was talking about it the next day in school to a boy on the playground. I know this because his teacher found out about the conversation when the boy he was talking to came unraveled over talk about "periods" and "where babies come from," and ran screaming around the playground, cupping his hands over his ears, and then reported the discussion to the teacher. The teacher called the parents of all ten students to tell them this kind of conversation was happening and that she was concerned about it. I told her that I felt it was perfectly appropriate that two boys were having this discussion; she said that other parents have not had this "talk" with their children yet; I told her I thought that was pathetic but that perhaps now they would, and that while they were at it they might also teach their children how to walk away from an exercise of free speech with which they were not comfortable or how to counter it with their own exercise of same. I told her that if her purpose in calling was to have me tell my son to stop having this conversation, then I would not be accommodating. She said my son claimed he was not part of the conversation, but I assured her that he was. And I made clear that I wasn't going to undo eight years of teaching him a healthy attitude about the body by thwarting his intrigue now. She was not happy. My son was ostracized for days.

For a few months afterward, every time I had a conversation with another adult, my son was convinced I was talking about his playground sex discussion, no matter what efforts I made, prior to and after this event, to assure him that I find such discussion important and interesting and healthy, and that their fear of informed sex talk was the problem, not our comfort with it. Yet the teacher and the class parents, and their children too no doubt, did not agree. Nor were they able to distinguish between my son's playground discussion, and another boy's repeated comments to the girls in the class that he wanted to see them naked and wanted to have sex with them. My son's healthy and accurate knowledge about sex and the body—a knowledge that for us is unquestionably rooted in my academic work—marked him as dangerous. The twist, of course, is that his understanding of these matters and his openness about sexuality conversation might well make him one of the least "dangerous" boys at school. I seriously had no doubt, given the opportunity to compete with any and all boys at his school in a "sexuality bee," that he would have brought home the knowledge trophy. But we would have been alone in our celebration of that victory; the trophy would likely have ended up in his closet rather than proudly on display on his trophy shelf.

My choice to raise him with academic feminist sensibilities has consequences that weighed on him even in third grade, and did that, in fact, as early as kindergarten and on through middle school, and continues now, in high school. It has often been argued in feminist circles, and wisely so, that raising children *not* feminist has consequences as well, with troublesome outcomes that will ripple across their lives. Feminist living and the struggle against oppression can produce "ugly imprints left on cheeks that have turned the other way too many times," as Morgan writes (68). So I could not teach my son about sex and the body without also teaching him what it means to hold a knowledge that the world may find suspicious, and without teaching him how to protect himself against how people react when they hold someone suspect. I imagine he hasn't quite learned the latter. I wonder if it is even a lesson anyone ever really learns. I believe that other parents find me a suspicious character, and I don't even know now, in my late forties, how to protect myself against their silent slings and arrows.

MESSES: ACADEMIC LIFE AND IMMUNITY RESISTANCE

The academy is, if nothing else, an environment of unrest in the face of unanswered questions, a context of thinking, thinking, thinking through until things make sense. I bring this unrest into my mothering, expecting constructions of motherhood to make more sense than they do, children's reactions to be more explicable than they are, parenting outcomes to demonstrate more connection to my intention than they can. As I sat in session with my therapist recently, contending with my terror that because my daughter is now at college the foundation for living that I wanted to lay with her has been lain, and that if there are flaws in its design they'll probably have to be lived with rather than fixed; wrestling with the fact that the photographs that might comprise the "celebration of life" DVD at my funeral won't look at all like those of my co-worker, replete with family frolic, a single marriage, the same home for 30 years that my partner built, many family photos to mark the many family passages and lots of fun, fun, fun; sparring with the question of whether I should have done more family frolic and less academic training and career-building, more "hands-on" mothering and less writing about mothering, my therapist yanked me into place with a principle I thought I already learned years ago in AA. "You think all your thinking makes you immune." I peek out from my tears and perplexity. "You think that if you study motherhood and analyze it and dissect it and write books about mothering and argue on its behalf that you will release yourself from the fear of inadequacy that mothers face generally and most people face regularly. You think that if you just knew enough about it you could do it without fear or doubt or regret." *That's sort of the idea, yes,* I thought. It's the futile but enduring hope of the academic mindset. I was cast back to my AA meetings where I confronted this already. In those days I couldn't figure out why I just couldn't figure out my drinking problem in a way that helped me stop having a problem. Surely, I've insisted, in recovering and mothering, someone as mindful as I am, as educated as I am, could "figure this out." And surely all of my intellectual work can save me some of this other, gut-wrenching emotional work, this wretched learning and re-learning of the same cliché lessons over and over; surely it can give me the will to dance in family messiness or, better yet, the tools to clean it up. Surely we can think and talk and write our way to a better world, where we are lancing dragons that look, to more of us, like—guess what—dragons. Actually, I won't relent to the impossibility of that last one; in fact I suspect that thinking and talking and writing are the very things that offer the greatest possibility for freeing us.

I do, however, put perhaps undue faith in their ability to create order and sense in my social world, in my family, in my mind. These are not, alas, outcomes that we acquire and then bask in. Nor is recovery, nor freedom from fear, doubt, or regret in mothering, nor the comfort of being surrounded by fellow parents of like mind. These are slippery things, always slithering from our grasp, demanding that we keep grabbing for them, clawing at them even. I do feel sometimes like I'm grasping for assurance and clarity and some sense that the academic life my family lives is a good and affirming and justified one. What I get is dirt under my nails and sore joints and bit of lost footing for all my efforts and not much of what I was grasping for. But I did choose the academic life with purpose (though I didn't know back then that I was choosing it for anyone but myself), and I did pursue feminism with intention, and I did put persistent effort over the years into being mindful about my mothering choices. In my graduate school days, I saw academe as a haven from a harsh world, a refuge from religious and social imperatives, a secure and predictable community of people and ideas like me and mine. To be sure, it has functioned in these ways at some level, which is why I love it. But mostly it's been as messy as any other workplace, and more so since it spills out into my personal and social lives and into those of my children. As a result, we find ourselves feeling perplexed when people don't know what we know and don't care to; alone more often than we like, and much more edgy than we truly are. Our greatest struggle at times is finding the will to continue positioning ourselves in this way, though by now the academic life is so central a component to our lives and who we are that a greater struggle perhaps would be living some other way.

WORKS CITED

Bronson, Po and Ashley Merryman. *Nurtureshock: New Thinking about Children*. New York: Twelve, 2009.

Broadcast News. Written, directed by James L. Brooks. Twentieth Century Fox Film Corporation, 1987.

Coontz, Stephanie. *The Way We Never Were: American Families and the Nostalgia Trap*. New York: Basic, 1992.

Hays, Sharon. *The Cultural Contradictions of Motherhood*. New Haven, CT: Yale University, 1996.

hooks, bell. "Revolutionary Parenting." *Feminist Theory from Margin to Center*. Cambridge: South End Press, 1984. 133-47.

Morgan, Joan. *When Chickenheads Come Home to Roost: My Life as a Hip-hop Feminist*. New York: Simon & Schuster, 1999.

Paul, Pamela, *Parenting, Inc. How the Billion-Dollar Baby Business Has Changed the Way We Raise Our Children*. New York: Times Books, 2008.

Sartre, Jean Paul. *Being and Nothingness*. Tr. Hazel E. Barnes. New York: Philosophical Library, 1948 [1943].

Skenazy, Lenore. *Free-Range Kids: Giving our Children the Freedom We Had Without Going Nuts With Worry*. San Francisco: Jossey Bass, 2009.

21.

Basketball, Skating, and Scholarship

Or, How to do Research from the Bench, the Rink, and the Car

ELIZABETH PODNIEKS

ABOUT TWO YEARS AGO MY SON, then ten, and my daughter, then eight, almost simultaneously entered the world of competitive sports. Zachary began playing basketball for three different associations—his school team, a "rep" league, and a skills academy; and Emily went from being a casual to a serious figure skater, one whose training includes off-ice gym and ballet classes. All of this means, of course, that as parents my husband and I have necessarily become committed to and co-opted by these activities. We spend on average six days a week in the early mornings, afternoons, and evenings driving Zachary and Emily to their respective practices, games, tournaments, and competitions, each parent paired off with one of the kids. In addition to being a mother and a wife, I am also an Associate Professor of English. While I have two perfectly functional offices—one at my university and one at my home—my work space of necessity has become the court and the rink, as well as my parked car. The gyms and arenas are located far enough away from our home so that the most efficient use of time is to sit and wait during practices and warm ups. More importantly, we generally want to stay, especially for the games and competitions, as we enjoy watching our kids in action just as they love us being there.

Consequently, I prepare lectures, mark essays, and draft book chapters either at the frigid arena, bundled up in winter clothing whether or not it is cold outside, or in a sweaty school gym, where the air is sticky and stale. With my makeshift desk—a clipboard on my lap—I squeeze into the hard, chilled seats at the rink, or I perch awkwardly on courtside benches and bleachers. Sometimes, daylight depending, I revel in the luxury of my parked car, where the seat is plush and the space secluded, but short

394

of idling the engine to run the heater or air-conditioner, I freeze or boil in seasonal turn. The repetitive strains of music to dances like the Dutch Waltz, Canasta, and Fiesta set the tempo of my reading, while urgent shouts like "pass the ball" and "box out" are my white noise. I am as familiar with the work of Dwayne Wade, Dwight Howard, Steve Nash, Joannie Rochette, Patrick Chan, and Tessa Virtue as that of Adrienne Rich, Sharon Hays, Andrea O'Reilly, and Sara Ruddick. Moves like hustle, drive, drift, dunk, foul shot, flip jump, toe loop, sit spin, spread eagle, and death spiral have become, for me, metaphors for the intersections of motherhood and scholarship on the run.

In this chapter, I explore the impact that becoming and being a mother has had and continues to have on my academic career, specifically my role as a scholarly editor and writer in helping to shape motherhood as a literary and cultural discourse. Further, I discuss how my roles as an Associate Professor and maternal scholar have influenced my life as a mother. My analysis is guided by overlapping questions such as the following: what do the projects and specific authors I choose for scholarly investigation indicate about my own interests as a mother? How does my construction and representation of maternal literary figures reflect and contribute to the ways I construct, imagine, and understand myself as a mother? What is the relationship between the decisions and value judgements I make as an editor and those I make as a mother myself? How do I assess the mothering practices and aesthetics of the literary mothers I research, and how do those assessments signal my own maternal biases and perspectives? And how do I find and accept as a workable balance my desires to both parent and research within an academic's flexible schedule—one which permits me to spend hours sitting courtside and rinkside facilitating the passions of my children, while concurrently demanding that I use that time on career productivity?

In considering some of these questions here, and in trying to reconcile the seemingly often opposing realities of my professional and personal identities and roles, I draw on theories and conceptions of intensive mothering, "good" and "bad" mothers, the "new momism," and liminality. I position myself as one of the mid-career faculty mothers identified by Maike Ingrid Philipsen in *Challenges of the Faculty Career for Women: Success and Sacrifice*. Although we as a group continue to struggle with work/family balance just as early-career women do, the issues which cause anxiety—like securing tenure—have "shifted," and we have "developed coping strategies and somewhat more definite 'lines in the sand' that demarcate what [we] are willing to do, and what [we] decide to give up" (81). Ultimately, I consider myself to be an empowered academic mother and maternal academic, such that my research in modernist life writing, popular culture, and motherhood studies impacts in positive and rewarding ways with my life as a mother.

MOTHERHOOD AND SCHOLARSHIP ON THE RUN: THEORETICAL CONTEXTS

One of the works I have been using to ground my research on mothering over the past few years is *The Cultural Contradictions of Motherhood.* Author Sharon Hays focuses on the concept of "intensive mothering" which "is a gendered model that advises mothers to expend a tremendous amount of time, energy, and money in raising their children" (x). Hays qualifies that her study is grounded in middle-class conceptions of parenting, in that "the model of the white, native-born middle class has long been, and continues to be, the most powerful, visible, and self-consciously articulated" one (21). As a "white, native-born middle-class" professor, I perhaps not surprisingly find myself practicing and assessing my maternal behaviours within the ideological framework of intensive mothering. Historicized to a 1940s American culture of at-home mothering prescribed via child rearing manuals and parental "experts," this ideology persists today despite the reality that over 50 percent of mothers with dependent children are in the workforce, and regardless of an entrenched late-twentieth century "me" generation focused on individuality and egoism which is at odds with the selflessness typically expected of mothers (x).

Intensive mothering, which consistently privileges the needs of the children over those of the mothers, is predicated on the devotional self-sacrifice traced to the late eighteenth century and the growing impact of Rousseau's notion of the innocent, noble child needing to be shaped by the moral or "good" mother. Indeed, the "good mother" is defined by her willingness to forego material goods and services for herself in order that she may provide these things for her children instead (Hays 126-27). In general, the ideology of "good" mothering, flourishing from the mid-nineteenth century to our present day, insists that the mother "lavish affection on the child; she must also be constantly vigilant in maintaining her own virtue and using the proper methods to instill like virtue in her child," practices which are "not only emotionally absorbing but also labor-intensive" (Hays 32).

Likewise, in *The Mommy Myth: The Idealization of Motherhood and How It Has Undermined All Women*, Susan J. Douglas and Meredith W. Michaels locate these tenets of intensive motherhood in what they define as the discourse of "new momism," which is "a set of ideals, norms, and practices, most frequently and powerfully represented in the media, that seem on the surface to celebrate motherhood, but which in reality promulgate standards of perfection that are beyond your reach" (4-5). The new momism arises from media images that have bombarded us from the 1980s to the present, such that "Women have been deluged by an ever-thickening mudslide of maternal media advice, programming, and marketing that powerfully shapes how we mothers feel about our relationships with our own kids and, indeed, how we feel about ourselves" (7). The new momist ideology insists "that no woman is truly complete or fulfilled unless she has kids, that women remain the best primary caretakers of children, and that to be a remotely decent mother, a woman has to devote her entire physical, psychological, emotional, and intellectual being, 24/7, to her children" (4).

The new momism, like intensive mothering, posits a "good" mother who fulfills these ideological expectations while her antithesis is branded the "bad" mother, as showcased in *"Bad" Mothers: The Politics of Blame in Twentieth-Century America*. Editors Molly Ladd-Taylor and Lauri Umansky make the relationship between the two clear in that today, "[v]estiges of the Victorian ideal of motherhood persist: the 'good' mother remains self-abnegating, domestic, preternaturally attuned to her children's needs" while the "bad" one does not (6). From the twentieth century on, we are told, mothers in the United States (and I would argue the western world in general) have been classified stereotypically as "the welfare mother, the teen mother, the career woman who has no time for her kids, the drug addict who poisons her fetus, the pushy stage mother, the overprotective Jewish mother," and dismissed as unfit to parent. While some women may certainly be guilty of "real violations of parental duty," overall "mothers get blamed for everything, pure and simple" (2).

My engagement with scholars like those noted above has alerted me to some uncomfortable truths: in many ways *I* am an intensive mother,

I subscribe to new momism, and *I* aspire to be the "good" mother. Growing up in a middle class family, raised by a single mother (my father passed away when I was thirteen) who is now a Professor Emeritus, and educated at a school for girls, I cannot recall ever questioning that I would have both a profession *and* children. Although I became an academic before becoming a mother, as soon as I had children I did begin to wonder how I would, realistically, "do it all." My mother had "intensively" raised two children while teaching a full course load, but I wasn't sure if I possessed her enormous strengths and energies. I had been working as a first-time sessional or contractual instructor when I became pregnant, and soon after learning the news I was informed that my application for a two-year Post-Doctoral Fellowship was successful. My son was born shortly after the grant's official start date. I do not think it even occurred to me to defer the award: I wanted the financial aid, and since I had just begun building my academic portfolio I feared that if I stepped "off" the career path for a few years I would never find my way to the tenure "track" or "stream."

I thus read and wrote whenever the slightest opportunity presented itself to me, in sleep-deprived and frantic fits and fragments. At the same time, I revelled in my new motherhood and wanted to be with my son more than anything. As he got a bit older I found my way to a group of women (some were on maternity leave, others had decided to quit their jobs to work as stay-at-home moms) who met almost daily at a variety of playgroups and baby classes. I was drawn to this community because I needed to get out of the house for external stimulation, just as I had no intention of falling into—or being condemned to—the category of the clichéd "bad" "career woman who has no time for her kids," as noted by Ladd-Taylor and Umansky. Along the way the cultural models of what I would later recognize as intensive mothering and the new momism seemed to reflect, legitimize, and promote many of the choices I wanted to and was prepared to make as I defined and honed my goals and ambitions as a mother in the academy.

Flash forward to the present moment, when my children have committed themselves to their own goals and ambitions—as athletes.[1] Having early on set out to be the "good" mother, I now willingly offer them my intensive "time, energy, and money" (Hays x). I spend almost all of my so-called "free" time organizing *their* itineraries; virtually all of my energy is devoted to *their* fulfilling pursuits; and my paycheck is sucked into the vacuum of *their* program fees and expenses. I have had to quit my yoga classes because I can't fit them into any one day, and instead I watch my children workout; other than my stand-up lecture hours which are beyond my control, I plan all of my reading and research around (and within) my children's packed schedules; and while I might deny the purchase of an expensive pair of shoes for myself, I dole out a small fortune on children's sports gear with nary a glance at the price tag.

Intensive practices such as these reflect, significantly, those of the academic mother. Philipsen introduces us in her study to several faculty women who sacrifice "care of self" as they try to "do it all." One professor, for instance, admits that in trying to prioritize teaching and mothering, "what goes in that prioritization is nothing for myself," such that "'exercise has gone pretty much out the window,' and so have quiet meditation and journaling." Another confesses not only that she "gave up hobbies and things she enjoys doing in her free time such as the gym or working on scrapbooks" (29) but also that she plays with her children until their bedtime, at which point she "reverts back into the academic mode" and works long into the night (32)—as I often do. Although Philipsen is here writing about early-career or pre-tenured faculty, she confirms that the balancing efforts required to maintaining a scholarly and a maternal life speak to academics across the board (97).

In a new momist haze I seem to donate or "devote," to quote Douglas and Michaels, my "entire physical, psychological, emotional, and intellectual being, 24/7, to [my] children" (4). I am also caught "between two rather powerful and contradictory cultural riptides," taking to heart the new momist's dictum: "Be more doting and self-sacrificing at home than Bambi's mother, yet more achievement-oriented at work than Madeleine Albright" (11). Ironically, though, as an aspiring Albright—in my case, as a full-time tenured professor—I focus my research in large part on analyzing, critiquing, and undermining the very myths, stereotypes, and ideologies that led to and inform intensive mothering and the new momism. How can I be, and how can I do, both of these things? In the next section of this chapter, I explore via an overview of my own scholarship some of the ways I simultaneously embrace and reject these tenets. My interests have always been centred on women's texts and issues, but once I became a mother I repositioned my projects in a maternal direction.

MOTHERING MY RESEARCH

While writing my dissertation on the literary aspects of modernist women's diaries, I came upon the figure of Emily Holmes Coleman, an American poet, novelist, and diarist, whose massive journal, which comprises some 19,000 manuscript leaves, had been purchased by the University of Delaware. After completing my Ph.D., I was granted permission by Coleman's executor, Joseph Geraci, to edit a portion of the diary for publication. While a treatment of Coleman's biography is beyond the scope of this chapter, of particular note here is that after giving birth to her only child, John Coleman, on January 6, 1924, she developed what was referred to as toxic exhaustive psychosis and she was institutionalized in the Rochester State Hospital for two months. Two years later, in 1926, she, along with her husband and son, moved to Europe where she wrote the surrealistic, autobiographical novel *The Shutter of Snow* (1930) based on her experiences with post-partum depression.

I began editing the diary when my husband and I, both of us native to Canada, had the opportunity to live in England for a year. I was newly married with no children and eager for adventure, and so I was easily caught up in Coleman's bohemian, Anglo-American modernist life in 1920s and '30s France and England. Sifting through the hundreds of photocopied pages from her archive that I had packed for my trip, I focussed on those entries that illuminate the artistic, literary, and cultural milieu of the period. I privileged Coleman's accounts of her development as a poet and novelist, and her encounters with the "famous" figures of the expatriate scene. My interest in her son, John, was limited to the role he played in *The Shutter of Snow*, which fascinated me as a literary work of modernist experimentation. And although I had included in my transcription a few passages about him here and there to maintain narrative flow, I had regarded him as a peripheral figure and not really worthy of scrutiny. I hardly contemplated Coleman as a mother, either; what, for example, was her buying peanut-butter for a four-year-old child compared to her meeting with the great T. S. Eliot? My perspective was encouraged by Coleman herself. Her quest for artistic autonomy led to the dissolution of her marriage and her increasing lack of interest in being a hands-on mother, and when John was two-and-a-half years old, she sent him to live with his nanny, Nina Donn: in exchange for financial support, Donn and her husband, Russian exiles, agreed to raise John alongside their own two children in a Paris suburb.

In the earliest stages of my editing, I had accepted these details about Coleman's maternity within the context of modernism, the collective term for disparate aesthetic, cultural, and political movements impacting the western world from around 1890 to 1940, and which reflects the urge by writers, artists, and the like to "make it new" by rejecting the perceived conservatism of the Victorian past. While middle-class domestic and maternal ideologies continued to support the heteronormative structure that had been established from the eighteenth century on of the married mother who remained at home with her children, many modernists repudiated this model as they advocated for and promoted "new" ways of being and thinking as a mother. Coleman, for instance, engaged in a so-called radical or unconventional lifestyle that included divorce; sexually promiscuous relationships; living away from her son for long periods of time; and the affirmation that she lacked a maternal "instinct." In short, she was everything that the intensive mother would not be.

Returning to Canada and to university teaching I put the diary on hold. After giving birth, I struggled to use my (Post-Doc) time at home with a newborn to take up Coleman's text during the brief intervals of his nap-time. With my own baby sleeping next to my desk, it was with a tremendous shock that I began noticing in the original diary manuscript countless references to John, which I had ignored in my initial transcribing of the material. It was also with a great shock that I found myself regarding Coleman with distaste: no longer to be admired as a talented representative of a challenging artistic movement, Coleman had become for me in my maternity a seemingly "bad" mother because she ostensibly *gave up* her child. What kind of a mother would forsake her son for her art? The intensity of love I felt for *my* son was influencing my interpretation of Coleman. Clearly, being a new mother had touched a nerve, and forced me to confront an awkward reality: as a scholar who for years has sought theoretically to understand and champion the lives of modernist women, I was now in practice assessing Coleman according to stereotypical assumptions about how a woman should perform her traditional, scripted roles, and assessing her according to the dictates of intensive mothering—dictates to which I found myself suddenly and surprisingly ascribing.

My involvement with Coleman's life and text coupled with my becoming a parent threw into relief how easily the labels "good" and "bad" may be assigned to mothers and mothering. The fact that I had been, even in those first moments of motherhood, trying frantically to incorporate my own professional writing into my child-rearing while heaping blame on Coleman for doing the same had evidently been lost on me. If Coleman seemed to me a "bad" mother, surely, I see now, others could say the same of me as a mother who was "negligently" scribbling away during her infant's precious nap, hoping desperately that he would stay sleeping so that I could finish a section of work uninterrupted?

The more I invested in Coleman, the more experience I gained as a mother (having given birth a second time); and the more I strove to accommodate my career as a professor (having been promoted to the tenure stream) with raising my two children, I came nearer to understanding some of what Coleman might have gone through as a woman who also wanted to write. While editing the diary, I saw a Call for Papers by Andrea O'Reilly for a special issue of the *Journal of the Association for Research on Mothering* (*JARM*) on feminist mothering. I had never heard of the journal or its organization The Association for Research on Mothering (ARM), but the discovery of them solidified and legitimized my nascent critical and theoretical preoccupations with both Coleman's and my own maternal identities. I submitted a proposal for that special issue of *JARM*, and the article which I then developed was published under the title "'The One True Thing in My Life': Mother-Son Relations in the Art and Life of Emily Coleman." Writing that first article on mothering coupled with my exposure to ARM initiated the profound shift in my academic career towards motherhood studies.

In preparing the final version of the diary manuscript over the last few years, I have been alert to the ways that my own biases and perspectives can so seamlessly intrude into the arranging of Coleman's narrative; and I have been careful to *re*read her at the nexus of modernism and maternal theory. I have become sensitized to the fact that although she resisted defining herself according to her child she nonetheless loved him profoundly. She frequently wrote about him in her diary, and communicated regularly through letters and periodic visits, building a unique and long term relationship with him that thwarts or undermines the sustainability of a "good"/ "bad" dichotomy. In appreciating how John is so central to the diary and to Coleman's life I transcribed him back into "my" selected text whenever he appears in the original manuscript. As I have taken on other projects over the years I have been transcribing maternity, as it were, into almost all of them such that the articles and chapters I write, along with the conferences I attend, are grounded in motherhood studies.

My article on Coleman's mother-son relations was also delivered as a paper in 2004 at ARM's annual conference, and it is there that I met in person ARM's founder and director, Andrea O'Reilly. My research had alerted me to the fact that there was a dearth of scholarship on mothering in literature, and I suggested to Andrea that we put together a collection of essays on the topic. After several years of labour, the collection was published as *Textual Mothers/ Maternal Texts: Motherhood in Contemporary Women's Literatures*. The book examines fiction, poetry, and autobiography from three different but often interconnected perspectives: daughter-centric (the daughter writes about the mother), matrifocal (the mother writes about her own experiences), and matrilineal (the grandmother's, mother's, and child's voices are multiple and connect across generations). The matrifocal narrative, which affords unprecedented agency to mothers, also guides Philipsen in her vital study *Challenges of the Faculty Career for Women*, for she articulates the highly underexamined and underrepresented subject position of the maternal academic "across their professional life span"—that is, early, mid and late career (2). In like manner, taking the time in this present chapter to contemplate the intersections of my own maternal and scholarly positions in a matrifocal manner allows me to recognize the matrilineal directions of my work as well: I think back through my mother (to echo Virginia Woolf) while using my research as a means of communicating with my children, points I will return to later on.[2]

The chapter I contributed to *Textual Mothers* is on another modernist figure, Zelda Sayre Fitzgerald, wife of author F. Scott Fitzgerald and mother of Patricia Frances Fitzgerald Lanahan ("Scottie"). Like Coleman, Zelda Fitzgerald often rejected the demands of parenting in favour of her artistic pursuits and, coupled with the fact that she spent much of her adult life in a variety of psychiatric institutions, was unable to mother in traditional ways. Fitzgerald appealed to my scholarly curiosity because here again was a writer—as well as a dancer and artist—who negotiated her maternal and creative desires and frustrations in a variety of textual forms, such as her autobiographical novel *Save Me the Waltz* (1932). I turned to her as a subject just as I was becoming increasingly overwhelmed with the need to produce scholarly research while concomitantly responding to my children's bourgeoning passions for extracurricular activities.

In *Save Me the Waltz*, Fitzgerald depicts a mother who leaves her husband and child to study ballet, but on the eve of her stage debut is literally poisoned—by an infection in her foot—so that she cannot perform, and she begrudgingly returns to the domestic fold, to the satisfaction of her husband and child. Fitzgerald was in fact offered a professional dance contract but inexplicably turned it down. Since the blood poisoning is one of the only fictionalized elements of the novel, it is possible to argue that Fitzgerald was projecting onto her persona what she knew would be her own fate; that is, she would be punished for daring to pursue a career at the expense of motherhood. In trying to find a means to resolving some of Fitzgerald's tensions—and thus recuperate for her, and generate for myself, a maternity that can be accommodated within professional spheres—I came to appreciate that her role of mother, however unconventional, formed a central feature of her identity, as it did for Coleman. I thus theorize, for instance, that *Save Me the Waltz* is a matrifocal text in which Fitzgerald boldly confronted the cultural conditions which divided her selfhoods, and that her preoccupation with motherhood registers how in her artistic productions and life she was able to form and redesign significant, if ambivalent, ties with her daughter.

While I find parallels between Fitzgerald's maternal focus within her disparate endeavours and my own efforts to inscribe motherhood in my work, I know that my position as a woman in the twenty-first century is drastically different from hers in the early twentieth century. Fitzgerald, like many of her contemporaries (including Coleman), relied on childcare provided by the nannies she was able to employ, but she received little if no psychological support for her career choices and goals by her society or family.[3] Indeed, as an adult reflecting on her mother in 1979, Scottie Fitzgerald Lanahan told an interviewer that she felt Zelda Fitzgerald, who died in an asylum fire just before turning 48, stands as "a tragic figure" in her failed efforts to "break out of traditional bounds" and fully realize herself as an author, dancer, and artist, whereas today women are afforded more "freedom," as Lanahan put it (479).

And yet, Hays, and Douglas and Michaels, respectively emphasize that our present "freedoms" are undermined by the "mommy wars," those battles fuelled and fought from the late 1980s on by the seemingly opposing teams of stay-at-home and mothers employed outside the home. In like manner, Philipsen provides ample evidence testifying that female faculty consistently feel thwarted by "the incompatibility of their personal lives with the design of an academy that continues to be based on the assumption that the successful academic has a wife at home" (3). Philipsen further provides a corollary to my reading of *Save Me the Waltz* such that, while Fitzgerald shows us how mothers would be punished for pursuing a career, Philipsen exposes how female faculty are penalized for daring to pursue motherhood at the expense of tenure, promotion, and publications.[4]

My engagement with the autobiographical narratives of Fitzgerald and with Philipsen's subjects throws into relief how my own story is one of privilege. For instance, under the heading "The Hostile Institution: 'A Very Old and Very Patriarchal Model'" (91), Philipsen uncovers multiple examples of mothers who feel unsupported by their universities, colleges, and colleagues, experiencing hostility, resentment, alienation, and promotional setbacks, leading many to keep their motherhood in the proverbial closet. In contrast, because my English Department has experienced a massive growth over the past ten years after a two-decade hiring freeze, the majority of my colleagues (more than half of whom are female) are my age or younger, and over 60 percent of them are parents, facts which lead to an environment in which I feel respected and visible as a mother.

Further, I am fortunate to have an emotionally and financially supportive husband, one who takes a place in Philipsen's section "Partners as Enablers: 'It is Really What Makes Possible the Mosaic That We Live'" (86). As a (non academic) professional who has at least as many business obligations as I do, my husband fills his Blackberry with as many "appointments" at the court and the rink as at board rooms and meetings, his car (like mine) equally packed with sporting equipment as with documents and files. I am the one most often "on duty" to cover the period between after school and dinner time, and thus I seem to prove the notion underpinning both intensive mothering and new momism—that the mother is the central force in child rearing[5]—but it is the flexibility of my job's schedule which led us to such an arrangement rather than the implicit or explicit assumptions that a mother's time is less (or more?) valuable. In addition to my husband, my mother is another enabler who has been on hand to assist us in all facets of our parenting. Retired from teaching, she remains an active researcher, and yet she makes herself available to her grandchildren every chance she has—and every time I ask for help.

Overall, my experiences are echoed by Philipsen's summary that "Mid-career faculty, much like their early-career colleagues, have enablers in their lives that help them be successful, and they employ a wide array of coping strategies to deal with barriers to what they would consider a successful balance of their personal and professional lives" (109).

My strategies for balance, as discussed throughout this chapter, include incorporating motherhood as theory and practice into my scholarship, and so after completing the *Textual Mothers* book I sought new maternal projects. I have been teaching courses in popular literature for several years; I am a celebrity gossip junkie; and as my children have become older they are increasingly and inescapably immersed in all facets of popular and media culture. It was thus inevitable that I began thinking of how motherhood plays out in all of this, the result being my next edited collection, *Mediating Moms: Mothers in Popular Culture.* My contribution includes a chapter on celebrity mothers like Angelina Jolie and Britney Spears. Intrigued by the fact that the "new momism" is marketed especially through the "celebrity mom profile" (Douglas and Michaels 110-139), I found in Jolie and Spears the perfect examples by which to investigate how the discourses promoted by and in the media today articulate some of the same directives upheld by society in the early twentieth century and which threatened women like Coleman and Fitzgerald.

Jolie and Spears are positioned by the media as antithetical "good" and "bad" mothers. Jolie is the new momist poster girl as she appears to us as a sexy madonna with six children who is also partnered to the handsome Brad Pitt and maintains a blockbuster film career, while Spears serves as the cautionary tale of the white-trash divorced mother whose multiple stints in rehab have dimmed her popstar's shine and threatened her custody of her two boys. These celebrities illuminate the ways that the media indiscriminately idolizes and vilifies mothers, keeping them under constant surveillance and judging them according to the degrees to which they fulfill the dictates of new momism. As Douglas and Michaels posit, "Motherhood has become a psychological police state" with all mothers vying for a place on the podium of success: "Intensive mothering is the ultimate female Olympics: We are all in powerful competition with each other, in constant danger of being trumped by the mom down the street, or in the magazine we're reading" (6). The celebrity mom profile sets the terms for the ultimate Olympics, blasting us with the fantasy that the famous mother has endless financial and emotional resources to pour into her children while maintaining a fascinating career and vital personal life. In contrast, of course, the mother who inhabits the "real" world is more likely to be exhausted, cash-strapped, tied to an unglamorous job, and neglects care of the self (Douglas and Michaels 116).

While I obviously have no stake in the lives of figures like Jolie and Spears, I do have an interest in how my identity as a mother is implicated in their mediated maternal portraits, and so I use their celebrity mom profiles to gauge, clarify, and assess my own responses to the ideologies of intensive mothering and the new momism. As a figure so blatantly manufactured and commodified by the media (and by herself), Jolie embodies the dictates of new momism taken to the extreme end of the continuum. In her superstar supermom profile, these dictates are writ so large as to be rendered absurd, their premises and promises exposed as a fabricated, romanticized, and wholly unrealistic vision of the contemporary mother. By the same argument, the celebrity profile that turns figures like Spears into anti-moms condemned for their maternal transgressions are surely just as magnified and distorted by the media. In both cases Jolie and Spears serve as enablers who open up a middle space where "real" mothers like myself who are neither supergood nor superbad reside, and within which our everyday heightened maternal aspirations mingle with, merge, and negotiate with our (supposed) limitations.

Since I have been working to be the "good" mother, my readings of maternal celebrity culture have led me to wonder about my own aspirations to bring home the gold, as it were. I mentioned earlier how I had initially judged Coleman to be a "bad" mother while other women could equally have labelled me one for my persistence in trying to squeeze academic work into my infant's day. In like manner, my present status as a self-identifying intensive mother might be called into question not only by other mothers but also by my children. I spend endless hours at the court and the rink, but I am not *always* watching my kids, not always fully focussed on *them*. I may be there, but I am usually there *working*. I miss baskets scored by my son because I am checking references, and I fail to look up from a book in the moments my daughter lands her double jumps. Moreover, I do not romanticize my experiences at the gyms and rinks as the new momist might. I often feel that if I have to endure for one more second the thumping sounds of a ball as it is dribbled across the court or listen to one more piece of insipid ice dance music I will go completely mad; desperate to escape the confines of athletic venues, I am impatient with my kids at the end of their sessions and deny them post-activity chat sessions with their friends; and I snap at them in the car on the way home if they do not seem eternally grateful for every single thing I am doing for them. With performances such as these, I am not likely to earn points or win a gold medal in the "good" mother event, but in learning to recognize that my inscriptions of the prevailing maternal ideologies are ambivalent ones I gain valuable perspective on my sense of self as an intensive and new momist mother.

Taken together, I have positioned Jolie and Spears, like Coleman and Fitzgerald, within and against the discourses of intensive mothering, the new momism, and the "good" and "bad" mother in ways that allow me to reflect on my own status as a professor mother located in what I call a liminal scholarly maternity, as I will discuss in the final section of this chapter.

CONCLUSIONS: "BETWIXT AND BETWEEN" MOTHERHOOD AND SCHOLARSHIP

In *Women's Lives: The View from the Threshold*, Carolyn G. Heilbrun considers women—especially literary women—as being in a state of transition, one that she likens to "a threshold experience," or "liminality." As she defines it, "The word 'limen' means 'threshold,' and to be in a state of liminality is to be poised upon uncertain ground, to be leaving one condition or country or self and entering upon another" (3). Heilbrun's work is especially relevant to my discussion here in that she traces the conception of a liminal position to feminist revisions of modernism, in which female authors in the moment of resisting patriarchy "found themselves betwixt and between, neither altogether here nor there, not one kind of person or another, not this, not that. They found themselves in a state of liminality" (8). As a scholarly mother and maternal scholar, I too find myself in a state of liminality. Heilbrun contends that "The threshold was never designed for permanent occupation" and "those of us who occupy thresholds, hover in doorways, and knock upon doors, know that we are in between destinies" as we search for alternatives to patriarchal structures and mandates. And yet, this threshold at our present moment in time "is the place where as women and as creators of literature, we write our own lines and, eventually, our own plays" (101-102). The threshold is where I acknowledge and seek to reconcile the divisions between my personal and public roles, and write the script to my own story as a faculty career mother. The court, the rink, and the car are the spaces that symbolize my liminal existence where I am "poised" as a mother and an academic in mid career, with children who are themselves on the threshold of adolescence, maturity, and independence.

The notion of being "betwixt and between" resonates with Hays' discussion about maternal ambivalence generated by the "mommy wars," previously mentioned. Hays summarizes that in one corner are the "supermoms" who "regularly describe stay-at-home mothers as lazy and boring," while in the other corner we have the "traditional moms" who "regularly accuse employed mothers of selfishly neglecting their children" (132). Such a divide renders neither side victorious, for *both* groups "experience and express some ambivalence about their current positions, feeling pushed and pulled in two directions" (145). This state of feeling "pushed and pulled" parallels my liminal condition of being "betwixt and between." As an academic I am simultaneously identified as a paid worker and a stay-at-home mother, rendering me "not one kind of person or another, not this, not that," according to Heilbrun's definition. For example, because of the professor's flexible hours I am able to attend Pizza Day lunches, sign up for field trips, and pick up my kids from school when it ends at 3:30, so that many mothers I see at these times assume that I do not have a career. However, depending on my university duties my children must sometimes attend their after school care program and I pick them up by six o'clock—at which point I am "recognized" by other late-arriving professionals to be a paid working mother. In a related manner, the mothers who see me most afternoons with my brief case in tow at the court and the rink likely position me "betwixt and between" a downtown office and a suburban home.

I am further "betwixt and between" in that many of my friends in fields like law and medicine (who are respectively holed up in corporate firms for eighteen hours a day or are "on call") as well as those who are stay-at-home moms equally assume that as an academic I work only "part time." *Both* sides think I have it good, *both* sides think I am lucky: I get the stimulation of intellectual pursuits and I enjoy quality time with my children. To the outside observer, I put in only minimal hours on the job (your first class doesn't start until 10:00 a.m.?! You teach only nine hours per week?!) and I have four months of every year "off." Neither side fully appreciates that an academic is always—and feels the pressure to be always—working and that our jobs follow us everywhere (Philipsen 22, 38), as mine does to the court, the rink, and the car. In short, the academic's career is itself a liminal one, "neither altogether here nor there" (Helibrun 8), and neither full time nor part time by traditional 9:00 to 5:00 standards. As one of Philipsen's interviewees put it, professors "enjoy the freedom to work themselves to death" (23)—and, it could be argued, so do intensive mothers.

There are times, to be sure, when I feel "stressed near the breaking point" (Philipsen 97), and I know I cannot sustain forever this intensive existence as the "portable professor," as I tend to think of myself. Heilbrun's liminal space is not "designed for permanent occupation" (101-02) and I anticipate leaving this condition and "entering upon another" (3) as my children's needs and identities shift in the coming years. For now, though, I accept and even relish my liminal status, and I fall in with the mid-career faculty described by Philipsen who have, despite obstacles, "learned to capitalize on enabling conditions, often informally created, and use a wide array of coping strategies to deal 'with it all'" (126). In this same spirit I slide into the late-career category as well, identifying with those faculty who "have reached a point at which they seem relatively happy with the balance between their personal and professional lives." Philipsen acknowledges: "By no means do late-career faculty members agree on how the relationship between their professional and personal lives out to be defined. But the majority is able to define it in ways *they* see fit"—one of the ways being "to merge the two spheres of their lives" (127-28), which is the strategy that I have been employing by deliberately turning the court, the rink, and my car into functional and productive work spaces. One late-career professor reflects my experiences when she speaks to Philipsen about

> a "very permeable membrane" between her professional life and her life outside academe. They are "deeply interwoven," she says, "because my professional and personal life cover the same territory in terms of my interests, in terms of my community involvement. . . . There is no real stark distinction between my work and my private life in many ways." Her life is a "continuum,"

she elaborates, "rather than a separate category of boxes." And so she has gotten to that place in her life, she insists, where she finds it possible to have both a satisfying career and a fulfilling personal life. (129)

It is precisely in the "betwixt and between" that I am able to satisfy my twin urges to participate in the academy and in the lives of my children.

I am quite certain that it is due to my own mother that I have been able to conceive of this place of conditional balance. Growing up I was immersed in her academic world; she had entered the teaching profession via her practical career as a nurse, with a Bachelor of Science degree, but when my father died she went back to school and earned first a Master's degree and then a Doctorate. Remarkably, my mother and I were writing our Ph.D. dissertations at the same time, and we defended them (from the same institution though different faculties) in the very same week. Just as remarkable is the fact that I am now, by coincidence, employed at the same institution as she was and where she remains a Professor Emeritus. She has garnered an international reputation for her work on the prevention of elder abuse, and was honoured in being made a Member of the Order of Canada. She is my inspiration, mentor, and role model. In conversation as in action my mother and I move seamlessly from the topics of scholarship to parenting; through our ongoing academic and (grand)maternal lives, we connect and are reinforced by matrilineal strands.

In the same way, I am (I hope) forging these same bonds with my children. They have come to accept that my availability at disparate times of the day is predicated on my ability to bring my work along, and they are learning to show respect for and are taking an interest in that work—just as I show respect for their focus on and commitment to their athletic goals, among other things. They are beginning to see themselves reflected in the subject matter that directs my research just as my research impacts how I respond to them. Drafting versions of this chapter at—where else?—the basketball court, the skating rink, and in my car, I register the plethora of ways my life as a mother intersects with my career. As an academic and a mother, I exist in the interstices of my university and my home. As a maternal academic I have the privilege to work *on* what I work *at*—mothering. Such is my compromise, my liminal stance, my gesture of reconciliation.

[1]Between the time of my grant ending and my children entering school full time—my husband and I carefully chose a school that had a comprehensive after school care program—we employed a nanny for three years who served as one kind of "enabler" to my career, a term with broad meanings mentioned by Philipsen throughout her study and which I will touch on later.

[2]Woolf noted in *A Room of One's Own* that "we think back through our mothers if we are women" (83).

[3]Emily Coleman's husband, Loyd (*sic*) Coleman, convinced that she had literary genius, encouraged her to spend as much time away from the family domicile as needed in her artistic quest which, as noted she did, to the ultimate detriment of their marriage.

[4]See for instance pages 33, 38, 39, 43, 44, 45, 140, 144.

[5]See Hays (8, 21); Douglas and Michaels (4), for instance.

WORKS CITED

Coleman, Emily. *The Shutter of Snow*. London: Virago Press Ltd, 1981 [1930].

Douglas, Susan J. and Meredith W. Michaels. *The Mommy Myth: The Idealization of Motherhood and How It Has Undermined All Women*. New York: Free Press, 2004.

Fitzgerald, Zelda Sayre. *Save Me The Waltz*. *The Collected Writings of Zelda Fitzgerald*. Ed. Matthew J. Bruccoli. Tuscaloosa: University of Alabama Press, 1991. 1-196.

Hays, Sharon. *The Cultural Contradictions of Motherhood*. New Haven: Yale University Press, 1996.

Heilbrun, Carolyn G. *Women's Lives: The View from the Threshold*. Toronto: University of Toronto Press, 1999.

Ladd-Taylor, Molly, and Lauri Umansky. "Introduction." *"Bad" Mothers: The Politics of Blame in Twentieth-Century America*. New York: New York University Press, 1998. 1-28.

Lanahan, Eleanor. Scottie: *The Daughter Of ... The Life of Frances Scott Fitzgerald Lanahan Smith*. New York: HarperCollins, 1995.

Philipsen, Maike Ingrid. *Challenges of the Faculty Career for Women: Success and Sacrifice*. San Francisco: Jossey-Bass, 2008.

Podnieks, Elizabeth. "Baby, Boo-Boo, and Bobs: The Matrilineal Auto/

Biographies of Zelda Sayre Fitzgerald, Frances Scott Fitzgerald, and Eleanor Lanahan." *Textual Mothers/ Maternal Texts: Motherhood in Contemporary Women's Literatures*. Ed. Elizabeth Podnieks and Andrea O'Reilley. Waterloo: Wilfrid Laurier University Press, 2010. 439-462.

Podnieks, Elizabeth. "'The Bump is Back': Celebrity Moms, Entertainment Journalism, and the 'Media Mother Police.'" *Mediating Moms: Mothers in Popular Culture*. Ed. Elizabeth Podnieks. Montreal: McGill-Queen's University Press, 2012.

Podnieks, Elizabeth. "'The One True Thing in My Life': Mother-Son Relations in the Art and Life of Emily Coleman." *Journal of the Association for Research on Mothering* 8.1,2 (2006): 252-69.

Podnieks, Elizabeth, and Andrea O'Reilly, eds. *Textual Mothers/ Maternal Texts: Motherhood in Contemporary Women's Literatures*. Ed. Elizabeth Podnieks and Andrea O'Reilley. Waterloo: Wilfrid Laurier University Press, 2010.

Woolf, Virginia. *A Room of One's Own*. London: HarperCollins, 1977.

22.
Academic Mother Crossing Linguistic and Cultural Borders

MASAKO KATO

I N THIS CHAPTER, I will explore what it means to be a mother in academia, and in particular, the relationship of identity and ideology between researcher and the researched. In doing so, I will focus on the issue of *uchi*/*soto*. In fact, the chapter stems from my own experiences of being overwhelmed by the dichotomy of *uchi* and *soto* when I conducted my dissertation research. The *uchi*/*soto* kind of dualistic positioning of researcher in relation to the researched is not new; it is similar to an insider/outsider issue. Nevertheless, because *uchi*/*soto* is the organizational key of various aspects of Japanese social domains, including Japanese interpersonal relationships, and because it is situationally changing, it became quite critical to me at every stage of research. That is, *uchi*/*soto* did not merely determine a position between me (i.e. a Japanese mother researcher) and my informants (i.e. overseas Japanese mothers) in our first encounters but kept challenging my mother-researcher identity and my ideological orientation toward motherhood until the end of research.

Through reflecting on my field experience, I aim to demonstrate how being a mother and a linguistic anthropologist affected my research on motherhood among Japanese mothers in the US. I further explore how these dual roles helped me to understand my position of dissertation student and mother during the research, and how ultimately, it enhanced my sense of self as an academic mother. I conclude that being an academic mother was much more complex than just the balancing act of work and family. It suggested a constant exploration of identity and ideology throughout my research which was indeed encouraging and enriching.

BEING A MOTHER-RESEARCHER AT HOME

I am a linguistic anthropologist and a mother of three children. For me, these two professions merge smoothly together, rather than colliding with each other, and combine to make my whole/seamless identity. My sense of such self is quite solid in my mind.

However, this sense of self becomes considerably naïve in practice (or in reality). In everyday life, my children, with whom I spend most of my day, interact with me as Mommy and have no idea that I am something else. I show no outward sign of being anything else, such as a linguistic anthropologist, even though I often find myself exercising discourse analysis on their language exchanges in my mind. Yet, it is not the case that they know nothing about the other side of me. The oldest and middle children know my "non-Mommy" side as "work." When I sit at my computer working at home, they do not bother me because they know that I am not ready to give them help. For them, "work" is "something Mommy does" apart from spending time with and taking care of them. "Work" is something serious to which they have no access, unlike anything else that Mommy possesses and that they have all kinds of access to.

"Work" sometimes makes Mommy different from her usual self; when she goes to work, she wears a suit and make-up. Thus, "work" is something that makes Mommy estranged from them. Therefore, they do not really like it. Even the youngest, who knows nothing about it, shows some kind of resistance against the term "work." While I do some work at home during the day (which is unusual), if she comes to me, I usually say, "Mommy is busy working." She replies back to me, "No. Work no!" However, of course, they have no idea what the work is. Needless to say, the children find no connection between "work" and being a linguistic anthropologist. I do not at all have to juggle the roles with my children. They are so small that I do not blame them about not understanding that I am more than Mommy.

WAS I *UCHI* (INSIDE) OR *SOTO* (OUTSIDE) OR WHAT?

In April 2004, I began my dissertation research to investigate the diversity and complexity of Japanese mothers' expectations and their practices of motherhood in New York City. In order to unravel the dynamics of their bilingual motherhood, I collected the data through ethnography, participant observation, and I also tape recorded and/or videotaped conversations of Japanese caregiver-child pairs, and conducted interviews with mothers. During my fieldwork, I lived in the city and met 21 mothers and a father and their children in different locales, including their homes and my home; at play dates, cultural events, music classes, and playgrounds. At this time, my oldest daughter was about one year old. She was a gem in many ways, inspiring me to take on the research and giving me respite from it, but I must admit that I was frantic as an academic mother who was attempting to balance motherhood and academic work.

Before launching my dissertation research, I kept wondering how my informants, Japanese expatriate mothers, would perceive me. Am I one of them, or an outsider, or what? Recruiting participants is not always a straightforward task for researchers, but recruiting Japanese mothers was even more complicated and challenging for me, a "Japanese mother" researcher.

As a Japanese woman born and raised in Japan, and who had read literature on Japanese culture and communication, I was quite familiar with the binaries of *uchi/soto* (inside/outside or in-group/out-group). Japanese scholars have identified that the *uchi/soto* concept is linked to aspects of self and society in Japan. They point out that *uchi/soto*, along with other paired terms, including *ura/omote* (back/front) and *honne/tatemae* ('private'/'public'), underlie conceptions of Japanese social situations and communication (Bachnik and Quinn; Doi). *Uchi*, *ura*, and *honne*, existing on one side, represent one's private, intimate, and informal aspects of self and invoke in-groupness in communication, whereas *soto*, *omote*, and *tatemae*, existing on the other side, represent one's public, aloof, and formal aspects and invoke out-groupness. Although *uchi* and *soto* shift according to contexts, interactions in *uchi* relations are considered to be informal space in which one can express inner and intimate feelings and those in *soto* relations to be formal spaces in which one can express public or emotionally restrained feelings.

Thus, as *uchi/soto* overlapped with the well-known insider-outsider positioning of anthropologists, I vaguely knew that the *uchi/soto* boundary would somehow establish my position in relation to mothers; but would they consider me as *uchi* or *soto*? I supposed that they would view me as *soto* if I was identified as a researcher, and that they would view me as *uchi* if I was identified as a Japanese mother. Moreover, I supposed that establishing *uchi* relations with mothers, indicating social solidarity, was inevitable in continuing my research. Recognizing the potential difficulties of recruiting participants and collecting data when viewed as *soto*, I went into the field with little confidence about how to manage my positions.

BEING A MOTHER-RESEARCHER IN THE FIELD

When I was in the field conducting my dissertation research, being a mother and linguistic anthropologist was a much more complicated issue. It was not because I had to struggle to balance academic work and domestic work, but because I had to negotiate my multiple identities, namely a mother identity and a researcher identity. That is, I was always cautious to phrase which profession should come first when I introduced myself to prospective informants in our first meetings. The two roles did not readily go in tandem—they were often contradictory—and thus were a somewhat awkward combination to the informants, Japanese expatriate mothers. In the field, I constantly wrestled with such questions as "How should I introduce myself?" "If I begin by identifying myself as a linguistic anthropologist, rather than as a mother, will they see me as an irresponsible mother who prioritizes the profession over motherhood?"

In the early stage of this research, I ended up emphasizing my position as a researcher. The major reason for this was that, at the beginning, I was so desperate to find participants that I took every chance to introduce my research, thus identifying myself as a researcher. Another reason was that I wanted to be honest with participants and let them know that I would possibly take advantage of collecting data as a researcher. Of course, I told them that I was a mother raising children in the same situation as they were, anticipating that my position as a mother would aid my access to them by decentering my researcher position. In addition to introducing myself as such, I usually marked this role distinction with my language use. When I took a researcher role, I tended to use formal and polite forms of Japanese, whereas I used casual and familiar forms when I emphasized my mother role, just being like friends. While I certainly shifted linguistic forms during conversations, I was more conscious than usual about my language use and pushed myself to use more formal and polite forms in order to keep my researcher demeanor. I applied this underlying logic, even when I created distance from participants by presenting myself as a researcher and implying out-groupness. I reasoned that if I showed honesty and sincerity to them, I could win their understanding and obtain their willingness to participate in my research. Nevertheless, my anticipation turned to disappointment. One mother said that she could not participate because she had nothing special to tell that could help my research. Even mothers who were personally close to me declined to participate because they explained, "it is embarrassing (that my things go public)." Thus, I was trapped by their restricted and aloof reactions to my research inquiries and stumbled upon mothers' discomforts and rejections about participating in my research.

This discouraging experience came to a great extent from the above *uchi/soto* categorizations, as many anthropologists of Japan have discussed (Hamabata 6-25; Kondo 9-48). Unlike those American scholars who were baffled with these binary dimensions, I am native Japanese, born and raised in Japan. Yet, I too had difficulty understanding how *uchi/soto* worked in the fieldwork setting. In my case, I was probably too conscious of the role boundary between mother and researcher; I improperly imagined my two positions in research to be independent, thinking they should be utilized as one or another, and discounted the contextual contingency of the role alignment. This mistake led to the creation of a barrier between the participants and me. It was I who made the erroneous assumption that my positions as researcher and mother were dualistically compartmentalized. It should be unsurprising that mothers saw me in a dubious light, viewing me not as either an insider or an outsider, but as having an awkward existence. Their understanding of me was worsened by my "native Japanese" identity, for unlike "foreign" researchers, I was expected to be able to flawlessly traverse these role boundaries.

Time passed and I became timid with little successful recruitment of participants. Still, I needed to move on. I started to approach the informants by not clearly demarcating my roles. That did not mean that I hid or told lies about my "researcher" and "mother" identities. Rather, I made both my roles available to participants. During interviews, I did not prioritize either role but shifted between them at the mercy of situations, conversations, and topics, as I always do in everyday interactions with my Japanese friends. Accordingly, I paid no attention to my language use; I assume that I shifted linguistic styles according to participants and contexts, but not based on my distinct roles. As *uchi/soto* moves in social interactions, the choice of linguistic formality and politeness varies and is contextually negotiated based on age, class, region, gender and so forth. Indeed, it was these flexible roles and contexts, as opposed to my prescribed identities, that were significant in allowing my research to move forward.

It appeared that I had learned how *uchi/soto* would work in recruiting participants and establishing my relationship with them, and that I effectively managed my mother and researcher identity. Nevertheless, there were other issues concerning my identity. The label "Japanese mother" did not give me enough credit with the mothers of Japanese in the field.

BEING A JAPANESE MOTHER

Existing literature about parental roles in Japan indicate that mothers identify themselves and are identified as primary caregivers, while fathers are put in the most important role as economic providers (c.f. Imamura 13; Lebra; Shwalb, Kawai, Shoji, and Tsunetsugu). Even in contemporary Japan, which has seen a drastic increase in employed women, the maternal role of women remains idealized and highly revered. While such emphasis on women's roles as primary caregivers is common in other cultures, Mariko Fujita suggests three notions that construct the ideology of mother in Japan: (1) the mother is the best care-giver and educator of children; (2) mother-child bonding is the most natural and fundamental human relationship; and (3) no other job is better or more suitable for women than mothering (75-76).

Being a Japanese mother outside of Japan does not mean that they are simply being caregivers. My informants expressed their motherhood through many kinds of roles, including being a linguistic minority, a responsible linguistic and cultural transmitter, and a maintainer of gender identities (Kato). The most important role that mothers were assigned was that of Japanese language transmitter. With little practical help from their husbands, Japanese mothers strive to teach their mother tongue, Japanese, to their children who are growing up in the bilingual context.

The majority of my informants reported that their low proficiency in English limited their participation in the host country, with significant influences on their roles as mothers. In particular, those whose children were school-age confronted this linguistic issue on a daily basis, as they dealt with matters pertaining to their children's American education. The linguistic issue often led to them feeling left out by English speaking mothers, and to feeling uncomfortable when talking to their children's American teachers.

Moreover, in juggling two cultures, mothers faced the spectrum of gender roles in Japan and the U.S., and actually came to enhance the Japanese ideology of motherhood by their own experiences of living outside the home country. The lack of linguistic and cultural resources made the maternal role of Japanese mothers outside of Japan more conservative by strengthening the normalized division of labor.[1]

Under such circumstances in which the ideology of motherhood was solidified in the foreign context, my identity of "mother" did not work as an advantage for me to conduct research. While I negotiated/managed my multiple identities throughout my dissertation research, the negotiation of my "mother" identity became tricky when I positioned myself in relation to my informants over the issue of motherhood. As I explain further below, because of our different orientations toward motherhood, the relation between researcher and researched was again put into a question even beyond the first phase of the *uchi/soto* concern.

DIFFERENT ORIENTATION TOWARD MOTHERHOOD

Apart from my researcher identity, we, my informants and I, shared a lot in common. We were Japanese nationals and mothers who were rearing our children in a foreign country—the United States. We were all responsible for taking care of not only our children's welfare but also their linguistic and cultural development, while managing our own foreign statuses. I predicted that this shared identity in the challenging situation was an asset for (at least) making contacts with them. Undergoing bilingual motherhood experiences together, I considered it encouraging to share some similarities of the experiences, which in turn positioned me as an insider. I rarely imagined, however, that my "mother" identity would, in fact, prevent me from being connected with them. I mistakenly thought it would be a "connection" maker. I did not imagine that it would push me aside or out of the group by highlighting our differing orientations toward motherhood: the self-effacing orientation versus the self-assertive orientation. Self-assertive motherhood suggests mothers' commitment to autonomy and flexibility whereas self-effacing motherhood suggests mothers' dedication to their children and families. Interviewing them, I observed mothers in my research of the self-effacing orientation toward motherhood, whether they completely accepted it or not. Indeed, this difference brought me back to the issue of *uchi-soto* and problematized my relations with them in the field again.

When I noticed that my motherhood was in conflict with that of the mothers, I assumed that it would not be a help or it might even become a harmful obstacle for my research, in that it would alienate me from them, and would label me as a "deviant" mother, putting me in a marginal position of motherhood. I ceased making this orientation visible in the meetings with them, although that orientation in fact played a great part in my sense of self as more than a mother-researcher and gave me a critical lens for my research.

In fact, exploring "motherhood" served as the site of struggle/negotiation of my orientation toward it vis-a-vis the mothers' orientations; my motherhood became an insecure arena in the face of their normative ideology of motherhood. I could not bring and exercise my own position alone into the field; my position was often affected by my informants through such ideology. Namely, my research on this topic challenged me not only as a researcher but also as a mother because mothers of this study probed and judged my motherhood. They asked me: "What kind of mother are you?" "What is your motherhood like?" "What do you think about being a mother in a foreign context?" etc. With these questions, it was not too difficult for me to reflect back on my own research and my own position within it, leading to contemplation on myself and my motherhood.

At the same time, there were occasions during which I felt frustrated by the mothers who were attached to the self-effacing motherhood, specifically the cultural "good wife and wise mother" ideology. For example, I had a conversation with one mother about her Japanese husband's involvement with child care at home. She said that he was usually helpful, pointing to the fact that he helped to give their child a bath in evenings. But one day, when she automatically asked him to do so as usual, he suddenly told her that she should not count on him every single time because he sometimes did not feel like doing it. In retrospect, she reported that she was first shocked to hear his remark, but then that she felt sorry for him because he worked hard outside of home. I understood from this conversation that this mother was influenced by the traditional division of labor: husband as breadwinner and wife as homemaker. I, holding the self-assertive motherhood, was frustrated considerably by her story.

I found myself anxious to tell these mothers, "Look! There are different ways of mothering out there!" Of course, I did not. I knew that I could not and should not force my personal and academic orientation onto my informants and that I should refrain from this in order to understand their real voices and real lives as uninfluenced by my views as possible. Simultaneously, I asked myself reflexively, "Am I an outrageous wife?" demanding that my husband share domestic work and child care on a daily basis; and "Am I a harsh mother?" putting her small children into daycare to work on her dissertation? Accordingly, my way of mothering emerged to weigh heavily on me. It emerged as significant because it defined the relations between me and the mothers. It also emerged as significant because it gave me a critical perspective on the motherhood of the research. This was how I came to understand what being an academic mother means. In other words, I came to understand that being an academic mother not only involved the practical issue of balancing work and home but it also affected the ideological part of my research; it challenged a great part of my motherhood and gave me new insight and inspiration on motherhood that could have been overlooked during fieldwork. It was just such an ideological tension that urged me to reflect on myself and explore my motherhood and my research. Moreover, the tension, I suppose, came from the fact that I was in academic motherhood.

CO-CONSTRUCTING MOTHERHOOD

I believe that these dialogues with mothers constructed the knowledge of motherhood and actually made it possible for me to create the ethnographic account of my dissertation by providing a bridge between subjective and objective viewpoints. In my dissertation, I describe an occasion in which three mothers and I sat around a table and had a talk about "our" bilingual motherhood in one of their apartments:

> ...while our children were playing, we had a heated discussion about what we had been doing in terms of their Japanese language development. We talked about how we had dealt with difficulties in bilingual motherhood, how we were managing current hardships, and how we should expect and handle forthcoming ones. The discussion lasted about 30 minutes, which was a fairly long meeting for having had our children around. One of the

mothers said that this kind of meeting helped her to digest her blurred concerns about bilingual motherhood. Another mother said that she found it important to have an opportunity to discuss such issues with other mothers of children of a similar age, because it forced her to think of unexpected things and let her prepare for them. Clearly, it was easiest for me and mothers of preschoolers to mutually create a sense of comradeship or *uchi* ("in-groupness"), in which one feels free to express her inner feelings. (Kato 45-46)

After this gathering, I felt connected with these mothers and believed that this discussion was the best I had experienced in terms of eliciting their personal and subjective experiences. In this context, the differing expectations toward motherhood did not bring us to conflicting positions but intertwined and created the process in which we mutually constructed our understandings about motherhood. Further, this was the moment when I transcended the researcher-researched boundary and managed to integrate various identities and ideologies in the field.

Thus, in working with my informants, I was compelled to deal with both the cultural binary of *uchi/soto* and the ideology of motherhood. The issues of motherhood and *uchi/soto* were not parallel to each other. Instead, they intersected. And this intersection puzzled me in my relation to the informants, complicating the relationship between researcher and the researched. It should be noted that the relationship was never fixed at any point. It was clearly a process that we negotiated together during the whole period of my fieldwork. Therefore, I shifted my roles by participating in various social contexts with my informants and, importantly, I was given a chance of exploring different angles to better understand the "motherhood" of my research, and to complete my research project.

I would not say that *uchi/soto*, acceptance/rejection in this case, worked one way or the other. The two occupied a continuum, their boundaries situationally constructed and constantly shifting (Bachnik 7). "Using these terms invokes a complex series of gradations along a scale of detachment and engagement, distance and intimacy, formality and informality" (Kondo 31). I believe that no mothers completely accepted me or rejected me, regardless of our experiences of and orientation toward motherhood. That is, depending on how they contextually defined me, they accepted part of me and rejected part of me, deciding also how to present themselves to me. I too shifted the boundaries of *uchi* and *soto* in relation with them depending on contexts, how I wanted to present myself and my motherhood and how I thought they viewed me. My participation and relationship with mothers was negotiated constantly in our relationship. As I learned in the early phase of this research, there was no real insider and only inside. To be an insider greatly varied in conducting research in the field. Indeed, "fieldwork is nothing but a long series of negotiations and compromises between our expectations and standards and those of our hosts" (Duranti 92). Therefore, the relationships between the mothers and me were all established by "us" and our contexts.

Thus, the fieldwork experience taught me that the boundary of mother-researcher was an irrelevant construction. By offering me an opportunity to get to know not only them but also each other, the fieldwork experience made me recognize my sense of self as an academic mother, which was no longer explained by the simple binary of mother-researcher. With the mothers, I constantly negotiated and compromised in terms of identity and ideology, and placed myself in a dialectic movement between insider and outsider, thus affecting my data collection and interpretation. The outcome of such interactions was my dissertation, the "bilingual mother-hood" they and I experienced, which proved to me that being an academic mother was an evident and enriching field experience.

MY LIFE AS AN ACADEMIC MOTHER

Although I have stated all the pains and challenges of conducting my research, I should acknowledge that it would not have been possible to finish this dissertation project without having the mother-linguistic an-thropologist identity. Indeed, while I was engaged in this research project, motherhood and work fused collaboratively to enhance each other, un-like what is implied by the well-known expression regarding academic motherhood, "juggling/balancing motherhood and work."

In fact, having experienced *uchi/soto* throughout the different stages of my research, I found that academic motherhood suggests not just conflict of work and family obligations as usually discussed, but as in my case a conflict of different ideologies of motherhood. Dealing with *uchi/soto* taught me that there was always a series of negotiations over motherhood and work, between researcher and researched, in various levels and different aspects of the research process. In my particular case, role negotiation and ideological negotiation between me and my informants were highlighted. This negotiation proved to be an interactive process of learning. Such negotiation offered me a new awareness of my roles and allowed me to explore and reflect on both my motherhood and my academic motherhood. This research experience made it clear to me that motherhood and work were not opposites in conflict, but were in a dialectical relationship as they affected and challenged my views about both sides. Because of my identity as a mother, I was able to deeply engage with this particular research project. I, as a mother, remained interested in others' viewpoints about motherhood, and my personal experiences as a Japanese mother in the U.S. allowed me to access the full subtlety of their motherhood experiences. Because of my identity as a linguistic anthropologist, I was able to reach deeper insights about my personal motherhood by having toward it both an objective and subjective stance. This meant, though, that being a mother and being a linguistic anthropologist often became blurred, and it made me feel I was always working in the field. This also risked mixing the voices and views of the informants with my own. Certainly, it was difficult to separate being a mother from being a linguistic anthropologist, being subjective and objective, and being personal and public, but such to-ing and fro-ing helped to strengthen and diversify my perspectives on my research project and my life as an academic mother. This continued to influence and shape my dissertation research, and as a result, I believe in the integration of academic work and mother work, and identify my life as an academic mother.

[1] For further discussion of bilingual motherhood among Japanese mothers, please see Kato.

WORKS CITED

Bachnik, Jane M. "Introduction: *Uchi/Soto*: Challenging Our Conceptualizations of Self, Social Order, and Language." *Situated Meaning: Inside and Outside in Japanese Self, Society, and Language*. Eds. Jane M. Bachnik and Charles J. Quinn, Jr. New Jersey: Princeton University Press, 1994. 3-37.

Bachnik, Jane M. and Charles. J. Quinn, Jr., eds. *Situated Meaning: In-*

side and Outside in Japanese Self, Society, and Language. New Jersey: Princeton University Press, 1994.

Doi, Takeo. *The Anatomy of Self*. Tokyo: Kodansha International, 1986.

Duranti, Alessandro, ed. *Linguistic Anthropology*. Cambridge, UK: Cambridge University Press, 1997.

Fujita, Mariko. "'It's All Mother's Fault': Childcare and the Socialization of Working Mothers in Japan." *Journal of Japanese Studies* 15 (1989): 67-91.

Hamabata, Matthew. *Crested Kimono: Power and Love in the Japanese Business Development in Modern Japan*. Ithaca, NY: Cornell University Press, 1990.

Imamura, Anne. E. *Urban Japanese Housewives: At Home and in the Community*. Honolulu: University of Hawaii Press, 1992.

Kato, Masako. *Bilingual Motherhood: Language and Identity among Japanese Mothers in New York City*. Ph.D. Dissertation, CUNY Graduate Center, New York, 2009.

Kondo, Dorinne. *Crafting Selves: Power, Gender, and Discourses of Identity in a Japanese Workplace*. Chicago: University of Chicago Press, 1990.

Lebra, Takie S. *Japanese Women: Constraint and Fulfillment*. Honolulu: University Press of Hawaii, 1984.

O'Reilly, Andrea, ed. *Feminist Mothering*. Albany: SUNY Press, 2008.

Shwalb, David W., Hisashi Kawai, Junichi Shoji and Kinya Tsunetsugu. "The Middle Class Japanese Father: A Survey of Parents of Preschoolers." *Journal of Applied Developmental Psychology* 18 (1997): 497-511.

23.

Mothers In Law

Re-thinking Equality to Do Justice to Children in Academia

ISABELLE MARTIN AND JULIE PAQUIN

IN THEIR NUMEROUS BATTLES to improve their conditions, women have found law to be both an important obstacle to overcome and a powerful tool to effect social change. Indeed, feminist "victories" have often consisted in the striking down of discriminatory laws limiting women's freedom or the adoption of legislation allowing them to fully benefit from this freedom. Women's fights against discrimination and the social policies put in place in the aftermath of those fights are in great part what made access to the academic universe possible for women and mothers.

The importance that the legal discourse has taken on in framing the very issues that women face is well illustrated by the omnipresence of the word "rights" when time comes to discuss the conditions of mothers and women in general. In such a context, women's legal victories are contingent on their capacity to express themselves in terms that the law recognizes as legal.[1] A good part of our training as lawyers consisted in developing this ability to frame complex personal and social issues as legal problems to be resolved by courts or to be addressed by legal reform. We came to realize that the development of this ability may come at a price, as one's acquaintance with the law as an academic and political language may deprive her of the words needed to express, in her own voice, the personal needs behind the legal demands. Being mothers brought to light our incapacity to translate our personal experiences in terms that could resonate in the academic universe and to develop arguments for change. As academics, we found ourselves unable to express our voice as mothers. As mothers, we came to realize that belonging to the legal academia severely restricted our capacity to devise appropriate solutions to social problems, and to our own.

We chose to express this divide between the legal discourse and our experience of mothering by juxtaposing legal perspectives on work-life conciliation issues with our own life experiences. This will strike some as an unusual way to discuss legal issues. In the legal discipline, narratives usually form the primary material on which law is superposed: personal accounts are translated in legal terms, and not the reverse. But law acknowledges the power of narratives to question its own capacity to fulfill its aspirations to justice. In the anti-discrimination context, in particular, the "acknowledgement of the fluidity of groups boundaries, through the telling of stories of the interdependence of the self and other, of we and them" (Benhabib 70) may lead to the transformation of exclusionary patterns. In this essay, we draw upon on our experience as mothers to advocate for a reconsideration of the current Canadian legal conception of equality in a way that would allow for the full recognition of the relational aspects of parenthood as well as provide innovative ways to support academic mothers and transform academia itself.

MOTHERS' RIGHTS TO EQUALITY: ARE CHILDREN "DISADVANTAGES"?

In legal terms, the inclusion of mothers into the academic universe is first and foremost a matter of achieving equality. Formal legal protection against discrimination arose essentially in the aftermath of World War II. At the international level, the 1948 Universal Declaration of Human Rights was the first document to recognize equality rights as human rights. In Canada, human rights legislation was passed mainly in the 1960s and 70s; the right to equality is now guaranteed by the Canadian Charter of Rights as well as numerous statutes adopted at the provincial and federal levels.

The objectives pursued through the recognition of equality rights were twofold. First, human rights legislation made it impossible for law-makers to provide for different treatments on the basis of a variety of specific grounds of discrimination. The objective was to "treat everybody the same" and even the playing field, thus allowing women and members of other discriminated groups to join white, able-bodied men in their race to personal achievement. The second objective was to prevent unfair individual decisions based on prejudicial beliefs and stereotypes. It was believed that, with "neutral" laws and institutional practices in place, any discriminatory act that remained was to be attributed to the prejudiced attitudes of individuals, and not conceived as a systemic problem.

It is only in the course of the 1980s that tribunals came to recognize that neutral legislation and practices could nevertheless have a discriminatory impact on certain groups of people. In 1989, the Supreme Court of Canada unequivocally recognized that "every difference in treatment between individuals under the law will not necessarily result in inequality and, as well that identical treatment may frequently produce serious inequality" (*Andrews* 164) and proceeded to replace the traditional "formal" equality by the notion of "substantive" equality. Under this new logic, the right to equality does not mean treating likes alike, but remedying the disadvantages deriving from individual differences. An integral part of the new "substantive equality" is the duty to adopt special measures to accommodate individual differences, including, in certain cases, the adoption of "positive discrimination" measures such as affirmative action programs. Traditionally disadvantaged people do not only have the right to enter the race: they are even allowed to put their starting block ahead of others' so that they have a chance to win.

In the case of mothers, "substantial equality" entails remedying the "disadvantages" deriving from childbearing and the fulfilling of maternal duties. The 1990s saw the introduction of paid parental leaves and subsidized day-care services generally presented as an instrument to fight sex discrimination in the workplace and protect women's choice to become mothers. Although it is hard to say whether these programs were actually motivated by the desire to achieve substantial equality or by the economic need to keep women at work,[2] it is clear that, in any case, they did have a positive impact on mothers. But they also point to the inherent limitations of the concept of substantive equality to improve the lives of mothers.

A major one concerns the reliance of substantive equality on the notion of a traditional disadvantage as a basis for intervention. Vindication for social change through equality rights and social policies entails a process of self-categorization as a traditionally marginalized group. In the vast majority of human rights statutes, sex constitutes the only prohibited ground of discrimination on which mothers can base their claims. From this perspective, mothers are to be protected first and foremost because they are part of a larger disadvantaged group, i.e. women. To the extent that mothers are entitled to protection, it is because their condition derives from the inalterable, biological fact that it is women, and not men, who bear children. The role of law is thus to alleviate the negative impact of childbearing and, to a certain extent, the care of very young children, on the career paths of women.[3]

This approach relies on a conception of specific conception of motherhood in which babies are essentially a temporary "burden" from which women should be relieved so that they can be as free as men: provided with maternity leaves and access to cheap childcare, women do not have to hesitate anymore between staying home with the kids and going back to work. The same can be said with respect to parenthood more generally. Although some Canadian jurisdictions have included "family status" as a prohibited ground for discrimination distinct from sex in their human rights legislation, this recognition has had a very limited impact in practice, with courts intervening only where "substantial family obligations" (*Health Sciences*, par. 39) going far beyond the normal duties of average parents. Although a child's severe illness or the need to respect the access rights of divorced parents may justify some accommodation from a parent's employer, granting the same rights to "normal parents" of "normal kids" would entail the risk of causing "disruption and great mischief in the workplace" (*Health Sciences,* par. 38).

Viewing children as handicaps or disadvantages for women has important implications with respect to how the "problems" of women are framed and solved. Categorization is by definition a reducing process; it freezes people into a single-trait identity and risk reinforcing stigma and stereotypes (Minow). Moreover, the discourse of equality rights, with its unavoidable division between majority and minorities, draws progress as a one-way process where traditionally excluded victims are handed majority's privileges. Not only is this a recipe for capture or even backlash[4]: it presupposes that the minority has nothing of value to share.

The primary aim of the social policies adopted in Quebec is not to ensure that children are well taken care of, but to protect their mothers' right to work. While childcare provided by professional educators in recognized facilities is heavily subsidized (about 35 dollars a day per child), mothers who choose to stay at home receive no compensation for the loss of income that their decision entails. In addition, only fulltime daycare services are subsidized, turning women who need them less than five days a week into cheaters "stealing" the places of the families with "real" work responsibilities. The provision of child care by "professional" caregivers paid by the State subtly leads to a devaluation of the parental role, making it harder for parents to justify, and be totally comfortable with, their decision to raise their children themselves rather than exercise their fundamental right to go back to work. In return, the mere existence of such social policies contributes to fuelling the idea that, once baby starts to walk, maternal duties are basically a set of chores to be performed between 6:00 pm and 8:00 am. Conversely, women whose kids attend daycare facilities close to work no longer have a reason to leave before 6:00 pm! Ultimately, then, the provision of services like 7:00 am to 6:00 pm daycare in order to compensate for the "disadvantages" faced by mothers contributes to generating expectations that mothers should be as "productive" and available as non-mothers (and men) as soon as their children enter daycare.

To outsiders, the system in place in Quebec may easily look like an ideal out of reach. As insiders, though, we also note that this ideal system is not so perfect. The "lucky" mothers of Quebec might have the right (and often the obligation) to work, but they often can exercise it only at the cost of exhaustion and guilt. An additional hurdle faced by legal scholars and professionals concerns the culture of law firms and faculties, which limits the type of accommodations that institutions are ready to make, and that mothers feel entitled to obtain or ask for. After years of training to fight for their rights to be treated the same and get admission in the boys' club, women with kids are generally more than satisfied with getting permission to pump their milk in the toilets and take their babies to the office or conferences from time to time.

Isabelle learned this at her expense when she tried to juggle her duties as a mother and her job as a lawyer and, later, as a graduate student:

> *I was working in a union defending the rights of workers, but couldn't find any argument for my right to leave the office at five to pick up the kids at daycare when everyone else stayed on. I entered graduate studies in law, like many other women, looking for another kind of universe, one in which having a meaningful work did not make it impossible to be a parent. Being a graduate student allowed me to set my own objectives and spend with my children the time I felt they needed. It made it easier to take a day off to care for a sick child. In many cases,*

however, the flexibility of the academic world is quite limited when time comes to respond to the needs of parents. For example, there were a number of interesting reading groups and seminars that I would have liked to attend during my graduate studies. But most of them were set after five o'clock, conflicting with the strict schedule of daycare facilities. I managed to attend some of them, taking advantage of the few times when my husband could leave "early" (at 5 pm) from his work in a law firm. When a Ph.D. support group was set to meet from 4:00 to 6:00, I ventured to suggest that the meetings should rather be held at lunchtime, in order to allow students with family obligations to attend. The organizers replied that they had set the time with a view to accommodating the larger number and couldn't change it (the consultation they conducted must have been confidential because I had never heard of it). The only group that happily accommodated my request was the feminist reading group.

For Julie, it is the realisation that children are not less demanding as they grow up that prompted her reflection on the feasibility of conciliating an academic career with the care of three children:

My decision to have children during my studies rather than after securing an academic position was based on two major reasons: I wanted to be available to my children, and, more importantly, I wanted to become a mother, period. Already in my thirties and facing fertility issues, it would not have been wise to wait any longer. I first gave little thought to the impact that this decision could have on my future career. I would go to "academic career day" panels and listen to those young women professor explaining how they managed to take care of the kids between 8 and 8 PM and then go back to work till midnight, and I would think: "if they can do it, why not me?" My main concern was to be able find a job, despite the time I had 'lost', leaving my resume quite empty for the last few years.... I was in any case shortly reassured by a former professor and mentor of mine, whom I asked whether I should made potential employers aware of the existence of my children: "sure, you should," he said, "faculties prefer to hire women with kids rather than women that will spend

*half of their first years in the position on maternity leave." At
first, I found this remark rejoicing: I really could hope to become
a professor! It is only much later that I started wondering what
it really meant for my future as an academic mother....*

BEYOND SUBSTANTIVE EQUALITY

By convincing people that they can solve most work/ family conciliation
issues, the social policies implemented in Quebec have allowed policymak-
ers and employers to eschew the larger and more fundamental question
of the place of children in our society. But the province of Quebec and
its universities have not suddenly become child-friendly places. For most
Quebecers, children belong to the playground, daycare and classrooms;
where their presence does not disturb the natural order of things. In this,
the people of Quebec are perfectly in line with the substantive equality
paradigm, under which women do have rights even if they have children, but their children do not have the right to have present mothers.
Paradoxically, resorting to the powerful language of women's rights and
reasonable accommodation forecloses the possibility of the institutional
transformation required to take into account of the actual needs and
preferences of children and their parents.

The failure of the substantive equality approach to recognize fully
the needs of mothers AND their children does not, however, necessarily
entail the total abandonment of the notion of equality itself. We want to
argue that, to the contrary, it represents an opportunity to reconceptualise
equality in more transformative ways, for two main reasons. First, the
guarantee of equality presents the considerable advantage to constitute
a firm legal ground to vindicate the full recognition of the impact of
motherhood on women's career and the appropriate remedies. And,
conversely, the resonance of motherhood, and parenthood generally,
makes family-work conciliation an ideal ground to start developing the
new paradigm needed to fully realise substantial equality.

In our view, the legal issue at play is not the notion of equality itself,
but its close association with the concept of disadvantage. The traditional
view of the role of equality consists in alleviating the disadvantages that
limit one's capacity to choose freely between different roads to happiness.
Once such choices are made, however, it is to the individual to bear its
consequences.

In the last 50 years, widespread access to contraceptive methods has led to the view that motherhood is not a matter of fate anymore, but a matter of individual choice. With children spending ten hours a day in daycare representing the new social norm, it becomes even easier to see motherhood as a personal decision whose cost must be borne by the person who made it, either in the form of "double shift" work or of a prolonged pause in her professional career. Quebec women now have as much the right to be parents as to engage in spouse swapping or stamps collecting, i.e. as long as it does not interfere with the increasingly excessive demands of their career. This seems to be particularly true within legal academia, where the "choice" paradigm combines with an intensely competitive work ethos. Despite discourses emphasizing the value of inclusiveness and diversity in law schools and society, parenthood, and more particularly motherhood, is generally perceived positively only to the extent that it evidences the capacity of the woman concerned to fulfill the expectations of her colleagues as well as others, despite her "personal situation."

It seems more and more evident, though, that the claim to achieve balance through the provision of professional care-giving services misrepresents the nature of parenthood. Motherhood, as well as fatherhood, is first and foremost a lasting relationship with a child with his own needs and demands. And such relationships take time to create and nurture. The full recognition of the relational aspect of motherhood (and fatherhood) leads to the reconsideration of the kind of accommodation that parents need. The availability of day care services matters, of course, but an even more fundamental point might be one's capacity to have a say on the organisation of her work.[5] In line with this recommendation, many European countries have granted legal rights to employees to request for flexible hours of work or even a reduced work load.[6] One possible collateral benefit of such a change would also entail would be to put an end to the enduring discrepancy between the terms and conditions of part-time work and full-time work, which has a noted disproportionately negative impact on women workers.

More broadly, moving from a conception of equality focusing on the alleviation of "disadvantages" to one which recognizes that such "disadvantages" often arise from the creation and maintenance of fundamental relationships entails abandoning the notion of accommodation in favour of a new paradigm of profound institutional transformation. The recognition that some tasks cannot be delegated—workers can buy their meals and hire cleaning ladies, but they cannot escape the tasks inherent to the non-professional, relational aspects of their identity: as spouses, children, parents, citizens, and individuals—entails for institutions to provide them with the space and time they need to fulfill their multiple personal obligations, including toward their mental and physical health. Conversely, it opens the door to the recognition that the vast majority of professional activities involve the creation and maintenance of positive "working" relationships.

INSTITUTIONAL TRANSFORMATION AND WHAT IT MEANS FOR LAW (AND OTHER) FACULTIES

In view of the current economic context and the increasing pressures it exerts on all human "factors of production," institutional transformation looks like a battle hardly worth fighting for, and more even so in the academic world. The "natural selection" system in place in universities also constitutes a considerable obstacle to the reinvention of the academic world. As soon as they enter graduate school, future candidates to academic positions are expected to prove they are worthy of academia by filling the "research experience" of their CVs with peer-reviewed publications and participations at prestigious conferences, and gain significant teaching experience. This clearly disadvantages mothers, whose limited availability and mobility and numerous family obligations force them to concentrate almost exclusively on their research. This also ensures that the "chosen few" who make it as academics are fully committed to the system as it is, and will reproduce the model of the perfect academic as a stressed out, exhausted, overachiever fantasizing about his next sabbatical and seeing his situation as a dream one for brilliant, independent minds. This includes the few mothers who, due to their exceptional nature and/or favourable circumstances, managed to succeed in academia.

And yet, academia may be just the right place to start. The complaints of young professors, both male and female, make it clear that the performance standards of universities now exceed the capacity of most normally constituted human beings. As studies of mother academics indicate, the separation between the professional and the private lives of academics is also at the source of the dissatisfaction of a large number of women academics, who would like "to be recognized for the ways their mother role informs their professional role and the ways their professional role makes them better mothers." (Swanson and Johnston 6-7). In addition, the seemingly increasing tensions between the diverse tasks of academics —research, teaching, and service—and the introduction of new learner-centered teaching approaches call for new ways to conceptualize academic work with a view to increasing the level of integration and complementarity between the different aspects of the job.

The adoption of a "mothers' perspective" on academia would entail considering the academic function not as a fixed identity, but as a position within a very special web of relationships. In the same way as mothers do not exist independently of their children—it is the very existence of those children who turn women into mothers, and it is the continually evolving mother-child relationship that gives motherhood its true meaning—relationships are what give academic work its purpose. Professors would be superfluous if they could simply be replaced by podcasts from the world's most famous experts. The creation and maintenance of relationships with students is at the core of what it means to be a teacher. It is the physical presence of professors and students within the very same walls that turn universities into places of mutual discovery and learning. It is through relationships that children and students learn, and that mothers and teachers learn how to nurture, guide and teach them.

Being mothers has a profound impact on our conceptions of learning, the role of teachers and the meaning of success. For both of us, maternity was from the very start associated with the need to cope with special circumstances over which we had no control. As a baby, Isabelle's firstborn son needed a physiotherapist to teach him things that other babies were naturally doing by themselves:

> *The first words the physiotherapist told me were: "My role here is to take him as he is and to help him go as far as he can." This expression of acceptance of my son's strengths and weaknesses combined with her professional dedication to use her knowledge as best as she could in order to help him taught me a new way to look at people. It helped me develop a balanced attitude toward my son, one that combines understanding and pushing him toward personal accomplishment. And I think that it's important to realize that, however gifted university students*

may be, they also follow their own personal path during the learning process. The role of professor is to accompany them and to help them move on to a deeper understanding, to give them the structure of learning and make knowledge available to them, so they can learn to walk their own path. This made me realize that the reason why academia is sheltered from the «real world» of relentless production and marketing requirement is precisely to allow for all the paths to be explored, without regard to the interests of the powerful or the popularity of particular views. In the same way as the purest music doesn't come from a desire to please listeners, the best research is driven by personal intuition. Accepting that some children will never follow the "normal" path helps us to appreciate and nurture the distinctiveness of each of us.

The learning disability from which Julie's son suffers also led her to reconsider her relationship to the traditional schooling system:

My older son has moderate dysphasia and ADHD, which make it hard for him to meet the demands of traditional teachers. But he really wants to learn, and we discovered that he is quite able to learn, when the right conditions are in place. I see my job as a mother as to create those conditions. The difficulties met by my son forced me to change how I see learning, achievement, and success. I now know that learning is first and foremost a process of discovery and self-discovery in which the learner, and not the teacher, is the main actor. I know that learning is a journey, and that the destination, and the time it takes to get there, matters less than the travel. I know that teaching something does not require knowing it as much as knowing the person to whom I teach it. I realize how much learning is instrumental in the building of self-esteem, and how self-esteem is essential for learning. More than everything, I understand that one's real achievements rarely show on a CV. I hope these realisations make me a better mother for my son, and for his siblings. I know they turned me into a more engaged citizen, and a better researcher. Of all the teachers I have had in my life, my children are the ones to whom I owe the most.

Although we tend to see it as a job made mostly in isolation from others, academic research is also relational in nature. One reason why research takes place in public institutions as universities is because it is seen thought to serve a social, rather than purely instrumental, function. Academic research continues to be funded because the possibility to do independent research is said to contribute to the development of a better society. As researchers, university professors are to follow their own path, to shed their personal light on social problems and disciplinary challenges. But the social relevance of academic work ultimately depends on one specific condition, i.e. the capacity of researchers to be in relation with the society in question during the whole process of discovery (and self-discovery) that lies at the core of academic research. And yet, academics tend to conceive of their social role in terms of an obligation to "disseminate" findings and serve on faculty committees or as experts on boards of directors. Such conceptions fail to recognize both the relational aspect of 'service' as well as the social value created by different forms of unpaid, volunteer work.

Seeing academic work in relational terms not only leads to a more balanced and inclusive conception of the relationship between teaching, research, and service, but entails a profound reconsideration of what it means to "perform" as an academic. Creating and sustaining relationships take time, openness to dialogue, and availability. Professors need time to know their students and explore with them the diverse ways in which their teaching could be bettered in order to appeal to a wider and more diverse audience. One's capacity to listen to and live with others is also key to the quality of one's overall contribution to society. This contribution is not restricted to paid work, but includes all the work that we do as teachers, parents, citizens, neighbours, friends, grandparents, sisters, coaches, etc., in any relationship that gives meaning to our lives.

TRANSFORMING UNIVERSITIES: INITIAL IDEAS

Despite the many advantages of the institutional transformation we advocate for, one might wonder whether such transformation, although desirable, is feasible in practice. Is it reasonable at all to contemplate transforming universities in order to make room for all the relationships that give them their true value? We believe that it is. To make our point, we would like to suggest a small number of measures that could be put in place relatively easily in universities.

A first step would be to remove barriers to entry to graduate school for mothers and parents generally. Part-time graduate studies should be possible, and a different time limitation should be available for doctoral students with family obligations. It should become possible for students to have children without being considered less committed or productive than their colleagues. We also notice that funding opportunities are often restricted to students who follow standard paths to success. Adjustments to current approaches to funding should also be made in order to recognize the distinctive worth of diverse personal trajectories and the particular needs of certain types of students.

Secondly, the normalcy of the full-time paid work paradigm should be reconsidered. In some way, academic work is already done part-time: half teaching, half research, plus some community service. Professors should be allowed to reduce their working load by concentrating on either teaching or research for a while, without being penalized. This would allow for a deeper immersion and more intense investment in teaching, to the benefits of students, or research. In return, part-time workers should not be perceived as less committed workers whose real life lies elsewhere, but evaluated as any other workers, on the quality of their work. It is worth noting that this formula would not entail additional expenses: on the contrary, two happy part-time profs are very likely to produce more than one overworked one, for about the same price!

Thirdly, the notion of "community service" should be extended. Many universities are self-contained entities that would benefit for a breath of fresh air. Rather than sitting on departmental committees, professors should have the opportunity to connect more closely with the world by spending time outside the walls of the university. Neighbourhood associations, primary and secondary schools, sports clubs, environmental committees, and support groups are only some of the organizations to which profs could bring valuable contributions. Involvement with such organizations would allow profs to pursue a variety of interests, invest in diverse relationships, and strengthen the connection between academia and society.

The institutional transformation of universities would not only benefit parents and their children, but more largely all those who cannot find the time to make and sustain the connections essential to their health and happiness as individuals. It would also pave the way to more respect for individual differences, and more inclusiveness among professors and students. Universities would benefit from the variety of perspectives needed to constitute a place of real debate, dialogue, and discovery. Society would benefit from the increased presence of academics in public debates and community organisations. The "separate spheres" would finally merge, allowing the mothers in us to work hand in hand with the academics we want to be to take all of us from where we are and take us altogether as far as we can go.

[1]On society as a separation of discourses, see generally Luhmann; Teubner.

[2]See the opinion of Chief Justice Dickson in *Brooks* v. *Canada Safeway Limited*: "Combining paid work with motherhood and accommodating the childbearing needs of working women are ever-increasing imperatives. That those who bear children and benefit society as a whole thereby should not be economically or socially disadvantaged seems to bespeak the obvious."

[3]For example, about a third of the leave available to parents is reserved to biological mothers and is not available to women who adopt.

[4]Capture denotes the "subtle forms of institutional ... resistance to transformative legal norms," while "backlash represents a more explicit rejection of the transformative norms" (Sheppard 399). As Sheppard notes, the phenomena of capture is quite common in the domain of reconciling paid work and family obligations.

[5]This recommendation goes along the lines of the recommendations made in a Report prepared the Federal Labour Standard Review (Fudge).

[6]Some regimes allow only small-child parents to benefit from this regime, while others grant any workers a restricted right to request it (Fredman 44).

WORKS CITED

Andrews v. *Law Society of British Columbia* [1989] S.C.R. 143.

Benhabib, Seyla. *The Claims of Culture, Equality and Diversity in the Global Era*. Princeton: Princeton University Press, 2002.

Brooks v. *Canada Safeway Limited*, Supreme Court of Canada, [1989] 1 S.C.R. 1219.

Fredman, Sandra. *Control Over Time and Work-Life Balance: Comparative/Theoretical Perspective.* Ottawa: Human Resources and Social Development Canada, 2005. Available online: <http://www.hrsdc. gc.ca/eng/labour/employment_standards/fls/research/index.shtml>.

Fudge, Judy. *Control over time and Work-Life Balance: A Detailed Analysis of the Canada Labour Code, Part III.* Ottawa: Human Resources and Social Development Canada, 2006. Available online: <http://www. hrsdc.gc.ca/eng/labour/employment_standards/fls/research/research17/ page00.shtm>.

Health Sciences Association of British Columbia v. *Campbell River and North Island Transition Society* 2004 B.C.J. 922; 2004 BCCA 260.

Luhmann, Nicklas. *Social Systems.* Stanford: Stanford University Press, 1995.

Minow, Martha. *Not Only for Myself : Identity, Politics and the Law.* New York: New Press, 1997.

Sheppard, Colleen. "Individual Accommodation versus Institutional Transformation: Two Paradigms for Reconciling Paid Work and Family Responsibilities." *La Charte des droits et libertés de la personne: Pour qui et jusqu'où?*" Ed. Tribunal des droits de la personne and Barreau du Québec, Cowansville: Yvon Blais, 2005. 379-404.

Swanson, Debra H. and Deirdre D. Johnston, "Mothering in the Ivy-Tower: Interviews with Academic Mothers." *Journal of the Association of Research on Mothering* 5.2 (2003): 1-10.

Teubner, Gunther. "Altera Par Audiatur: Law in the Collision of Discourses." *Law, Society and Economy.* Ed. Richard Rawlings. Oxford: Oxford University Press, 1997. 149-176.

24.

Liberalism's Leaky Legacy

Theory and the Narratives
of Graduate Student Mothers

JAMIE HUFF, SARAH COTÉ HAMPSON, AND CORINNE M.
TAGLIARINA

N 2007, THE UNIVERSITY OF CONNECTICUT (UConn) enacted a
policy providing graduate students with six weeks of paid maternity
leave. The enactment of the policy, itself the result of agitation on
the part of graduate students, demonstrates that graduate students at
UConn were demanding a greater focus on parenting and family policy.
Nearly two years after the policy went into effect, we interviewed 34
graduate students about the maternity leave policy, family-related policy
in general, and their own experiences with pregnancy and childbearing.
Our interviews demonstrate that pregnancy and mothering presents
graduate students with a complicated situation in which the academy's
liberal basis made effective policy a difficult achievement. We argue
that the public-private split in liberalism pushes mothers in academia
away from the top rungs, which diminishes their unique and important
viewpoint.

The chapter proceeds in four sections. First, we outline our methods, which involved gathering data from 24 in-depth interviews of
graduate student women at the University of Connecticut. In section
two we begin our argument, describing the split between academic
and "private" family life. We also discuss the public-private split's
theoretical basis in liberalism and how our interviews show evidence
of this split in academia. In section three, we sketch how departmental
norms stem from a vaguely-worded university-wide maternity leave
policy and the public-private split. Finally, in section four, we describe
how the public-private split creates different specific market pressures
for mothers. We also use this section to outline the positive aspects of
graduate student mothering in order to determine whether a market

failure is occurring when academia excludes graduate student mothers. We conclude by stressing the importance of making room in academia for graduate student mothers.

METHODS: NARRATIVES OF MOTHERHOOD

Part of our project's aim is to evaluate UConn's recent graduate student maternity leave policy and its relation to the "pipeline" of women in academia. Additionally, part of its aim is to test whether strong theoretical patterns related to the public-private split that have been noted in other literature can be found in the experiences of graduate student women at UConn. Both of these goals require empirical evidence. To this end, we conducted interviews with 34 graduate students at the University of Connecticut, men and women, parents and non-parents, about their knowledge of the policies pertaining to graduate student parenting at UConn and their experience as a parent and a graduate student at UConn. Our 34 interviews include 10 men and 24 women. In this chapter, we focus specifically on the responses of women, 20 of whom were mothers. We also sent a broader survey to all of the graduate students at the University of Connecticut through the primary graduate student listserv. Though information from the survey is not included in this chapter, we did use the survey to recruit participants for the in-depth interviews which are used here. Additionally, we posted flyers around campus and put leaflets in the graduate student mailboxes of all departments on campus with graduate programs requesting participants for the interviews. The majority of interviews were conducted in person and were recorded, and then transcriptions were made from the recording. A few interviews had to be conducted over the phone due to location difficulties, and those interviews were not recorded, but the interviewer took notes, verifying specific quotes when necessary.

We designed a semi-structured interview guide, beginning by asking the interviewees to tell us a little about themselves and their families. We had two separate interview guides for parents and non-parents, although they shared several questions, such as asking about the knowledge of the maternity leave policy. After a few introductory questions to allow the interviewee to become comfortable, we asked the parents questions about their experience as being both parents and graduate students at UConn. We had several specific topic areas we wanted to cover in the interview, but frequently in the process of telling their stories, the interview subjects discussed many of the topics on their own. If necessary, we followed up by asking questions about how they were treated by faculty, advisors, departmental administration, fellow graduate students, and undergraduates. We also wanted to know about how they managed to balance their academic responsibilities and family life. We asked about how being a parent had changed their academic work, for the better or for the worse. Finally, we asked about their knowledge of UConn policies for graduate student parents, and what policies or institutional changes would be most helpful to them as graduate student parents. We ended the interviews by asking if there was anything else they wanted to share with us, which elicited several stories we never would have thought to ask about, and highlighted the interesting nexus between employee and student that graduate students inhabit. The interviews tended to be between 30 minutes and an hour long, with a few lasting up to three hours.

The non-parent interviews were considerably shorter and tended to be more structured, because the interview subjects had less of a story to tell on this subject. We interviewed non-parents because we were interested in the difference between how non-parents see the experience of being a graduate student parent and the actual experience of current graduate student parents. We also wanted to know how non-parents take the various pressures of academia into account when making personal life choices, such as becoming a parent. We asked the non-parent participants questions about whether they would be comfortable having a child in their department at UConn if they found out they (or their partner) were pregnant. How did they think being a parent would affect their life in academia and their future career choices? We asked about people in their department with children and their observation of that experience. We also finished by asking about their knowledge of the policies in place at UConn for graduate student parents, and what policies they thought would be helpful. Again, at the end of the interview we asked participants if there was anything about their particular experience with this subject that they wanted to share.

The interview data for this study is presented in narrative form, with all names changed. The interpretive method in political science has long held the significance of speech as "action"—as something that, once it is "out there" is at once interpreted by others and simultaneously shaping their interpretations. Paul Ricoeur suggests that this speech gains meaning as a "text" once it is uttered, and its meaning is contingent upon its interpretation. Ewick and Silbey similarly suggest that storytelling both creates, shapes and passes on meaning for the storyteller, but also that its interpretation by others is significant in either shaping and maintaining hegemonic ordering, or in subverting it by offering antidotes. In addition, the authors point out, narratives can play a role in identifying where inequalities exist. They write: "Narratives are likely to bear the marks of existing social inequities, disparities of power, and ideological effects" (Ewick and Silbey 222).

This final feature of narrative makes it a useful tool for research into traditionally oppressed groups, therefore narrative is commonly used in feminist methodology, both as a means of identifying patterns of domination and as a means of allowing women's voices to be heard. This second element is especially important for feminist methodology. Feminist critiques of positivist research have a long tradition, articulating that positivist studies have historically excluded women in terms of the selection of research topics and subjects, given an "illusion of objectivity" that meant that the exclusion of women in these ways appeared "scientific," and that these practices had a fundamental impact on women's lives, despite the frequent exclusion of their perspective (Jayaratne and Stewart 86). Therefore, "a deep suspicion of quantitative methods as having concealed women's real experience has motivated much preoccupation with, and advocacy of, qualitative methods as methods which permit women to express their experience fully and in their own terms" (Jayaratne and Stewart 88). It is therefore the intention of this paper to allow the interviewed women's voices and their perspectives on the subject of mothering in graduate school to speak for themselves.

FINDINGS: PUBLIC ACADEMICIANS, PRIVATE MOTHERS

"Being a parent and a graduate student has been its own type of hell," says Alison, a graduate student in the social sciences. Her department is notoriously demanding, combining a large teaching assistantship or teaching load with three courses each semester. This workload can overwhelm any graduate student, but for Alison the problem is compounded by her status as the mother of a young child. Alison also explains, "My department tries to be supportive, I guess … they know I have a son, some professors have let me bring him to class." However, that support on an individual level is not replicated in Alison's schedule. Alison goes on to say, "My partner and I have very different hours, so when I'm home I'm taking care of our son. I can't do additional work at home," and "Sometimes they schedule me to teach classes so that I'm not home until 9:30 at night, and we have to work around that." These scheduling issues show that Alison's department places her family squarely within the private realm, scheduling her time as if she is the same as any other single graduate student. While her department may view this blindness to her status as a mother as treating her equally, it results in an extremely difficult and hectic life for Alison. Alison's department is primarily concerned that she continues to attend classes and teach; yet, they fail to realize that to make this fully possible they may need to take Alison's family concerns into consideration.

All 24 of the female graduate students we interviewed, whether they were parents or not, implicated the split between work as public and family as private as a major concern. Katie, a graduate student in Education, said, "Men aren't asked to put their lives on hold for grad school." The "lives" Katie is referring to are private lives, or family lives, lives outside of academia. Katie's statement indicates that departments view the private life of the family as incompatible with graduate school, something to be placed on "hold" or kept to oneself. Another graduate student who was pregnant during her interview, Melissa, echoed this statement, saying, "No one wants to show that they have this other life." She went on to say:

> I think part of the reason I was so fearful of people knowing [about my pregnancy], I'm afraid that they'll assume that I can't do my job as well ... I can still function, I can still do these things, I'm perfectly capable, but I wish that the environment was so that I could be more honest and wouldn't have to put a show on. I understand having to put a show on in the classroom when I'm teaching, but when I'm in my office sometimes I just want to lie down. But I don't and I don't let anyone see me.

Melissa and Katie's narratives show that graduate student mothers often feel uncomfortable with how their departments might react if their child bearing and rearing becomes too public.

Other graduate students feared that having children would disadvantage them vis-à-vis their departments. Diana, a graduate student in the humanities who had not yet had children, said, "I think they're used to the single, young academic, and they hold us all to that model. And especially now that funding is an issue for departments, you don't want to make them mad or think that you're not serious." It seems that seriousness means being able to devote nearly all of one's time to research and teaching, not doing the work of mothering that may interfere. Amanda, a graduate student in the social sciences, said, "Sometimes I feel like I'm being a student 50 percent and I'm being a mother 50 percent, so I'm kind of doing both half-assed." Her language divides her time as "student" and "mother" into percents; she indicates that each role is separate and in competition with the other. Melissa also noted the practical concerns associated with parenting, saying,

> It's scary because the assumption is that ... your first priority should be school. The way that classes are scheduled and the way that TA-ships are given, the way the whole university functions is with the assumption that you're a standard, single, local, isolated graduate student who can just come into school at the whim of anybody's demand, and that you're always accessible and available.... I think women carry a big burden with that.

When departments focus solely on graduate students as workers, ignoring their concerns about families and parenting, they encourage the public-private split.

Our interviews thus uncover the connections between the normative assumptions of academia and a longer liberal legacy of public-private sphere divide. Both classical and contemporary liberal theory rests upon a public-private split, with the family and its caretaker relegated to the private sphere, seemingly separate from the public sphere of work, politics, and the market (Elshtain; Kelly, "Private Family"; Kelly *Domestic Violence*; Okin *Women*; Okin *Justice*). Susan Okin (*Women; Justice*) argues that when we introduce gender and the family into liberal theories of justice, these theories become unhinged. The liberal university system functions similarly to these theories of justice: direct discrimination based on sex is arguably not acceptable, but the statuses of the family, gender, and race within the university system are immune from the considerations of justice (Agathangelou and Ling). Departments like those of Alison,

Amanda, Melissa, Katie, and Diana have structured their rules and expectations on a model that does not consider the possibility of having graduate students who are mothers. Because departments consider families a private concern, departments like Alison's can continue to assign inconvenient and inflexible schedules without consideration to a student's family status.

UConn's graduate student maternity leave policy also falls under the rubric of the public-private split. While a six-week leave is guaranteed, the workload of the student during that period has been interpreted differently across departments. The policy only addresses official leave time—a very public issue. Iris Marion Young argues that another consequence of the public-private split is that it allows those within the public sphere to distance themselves from gendered or "messy" concerns. Other issues mentioned by our interviewees, such as childcare, issues with taking classes, or a designated space to pump breast milk on campus, are not covered by the policy. Two interviewees, Marie and Stacey, spent much of their initial time on campus after giving birth searching for an empty office in which to pump so that they could continue with their course schedules. These issues are private—they deal directly with the family, the child, and the mother as caregiver. As such, the liberal university can position them as beyond its scope of influence, even as they occur on the very public university campus.

POLICY FAILURE AND THE RULE OF NORMS

Traditional liberal notions of justice make direct discrimination impermissible but allow subtle pressures and norms to influence behavior. Unsurprisingly, for most of the women we interviewed, the legacy of the public-private split is clearly tangible in larger norms their departments establish. Whether deciding if having children in graduate school was a "good" idea or determining how much or how often to allow their family life to be visible at work, every woman in our study noted influential social cues within her academic environment. Some women pointed to direct comments from faculty members that affected their decision-making. Diana observed:

The weirdest thing was around the first time my husband and I started trying, I was talking with a faculty member in the hall-

way and out of nowhere she says, "Oh, and don't get pregnant now" like she was joking…. And it scared me that they would say something like that, you know, it made things very clear.

For other women, their impressions of departmental norms came from their observations of the experiences of other women who had previously had children in graduate school. Melissa recounted, "There are stories in this department specifically of professors approaching grad students who are pregnant and saying 'I really would have waited if I were you.' Things like that set the tone here and that's what made me so nervous. I've heard horror stories and I've heard about the support people do not get."

Many women who did not cite a direct discouragement from their department were still fearful of how professors and colleagues might react if they had children in graduate school. For women like Melissa and Katie, these fears stemmed from unstated impressions that they received from members of their department about what was expected of them. For Melissa, departmental attitudes indicated that she should fit into the mold of a young, single student. She said, "The assumption is that grad students should be young, and I'm 28…. [So for] some of us who are a little bit older than the incoming grad students, there's this disconnect. I think the assumption is that you shouldn't even be thinking about a family yet, which is why they're encouraged to wait." Katie's fears of her department's reaction were shaped by how the department treated others who have had children. "I don't want to become a dropout statistic," says Katie. She is afraid people will think: "Oh, she started grad school, but then she got married and had a baby and didn't finish."

Of the 20 women we interviewed who had children, all keenly observed how their departments reacted to their motherhood. Eight of these women told us they experienced overtly negative reactions from colleagues or faculty members. Katie, for instance, recalls how "I was talking to my advisor about my [dissertation] progress and he said 'ha ha, and then you got pregnant' which I now realize was a totally inappropriate comment." Seven of the mothers we interviewed perceived that people in their departments, whether faculty, administration or graduate students, felt uncomfortable talking about their pregnancy or their children As Beth relates, "I felt like I got weird vibes from people, like they were trying not to look at my giant pregnant belly or trying to pretend I wasn't pregnant…. I think it's something the department just isn't used to." Thirteen of the women we spoke to who had children expressed some positive reactions to their pregnancy and childbirth. Bethany, for example, says "the culture of our department is very supportive of when you have children. I informed my committee…none of them had anything negative to say." However, most of the women who cited positive experiences also cited negative or awkward experiences with other members of their department. Of the 20 mothers we interviewed, only five mentioned solely positive experiences with the attitudes and norms in their departments.

Unfortunately, the one formal policy at the disposal of those women who do not have positive experiences with their departments (the graduate maternity leave policy), does not offer solutions for women who choose to resist academic and departmental norms. This is due to the fact that the policy leaves the details of *how* a woman is able to take maternity leave—how her work will be covered, for example—to the individual departments to work out. This is in keeping with Michel Foucault's characterization of liberalism as the philosophy of how to govern the least. The vacuum left by the maternity leave policy is quickly filled by departmental norms.

Research on "legal pluralism" finds that the presence of norms and attitudes can shape individuals' interactions with law and policy. Catherine Albiston's study of the mobilization of FMLA rights by working women demonstrates how competing normative orders, particularly when housed in institutional or corporate settings, can establish myths and ideologies that hold significantly more power for the individual than the law.

Over time, the interconnected and mutually reinforcing systems of meaning among gender, disability, and work have come to form an invisible cognitive framework that gives meaning to leave for family or medical purposes … seemingly neutral features of work, such as attendance and time invested in work rather than productivity, have come to define "good workers" (Albiston 17).

The women are "bargaining in the shadow of the law," because they are caught between normative orders, and must negotiate between the law and the powerful ideological and market forces that compete with the law for legitimacy. She finds that, "In practice … legal conflict over leave rights may never arise because workers fear shift changes, bad relations with managers, or the stigma of termination if their employer retaliates. In addition, employers can...limit information about rights" (Albiston 41).

Claire's story highlights the significant role of a department's norms as part of its power in the bargaining experiences of graduate student women. Claire is a Ph.D. student in a department within the hard sciences with *no* female faculty and only two female Ph.D. candidates. Claire is raising a thirteen-year-old stepdaughter, but says she feels she could never have children of her own while pursuing her graduate work. Claire added, "A lot of that is not the department's fault. In any science field, in order to graduate you have to prove yourself to that field and if you need to take some time off for pregnancy, someone else is working on what you're working on and they will pass you, and then you have to start all over again." Claire was also unaware of any university maternity leave policy, and reiterated that she did not feel able to have her own child in graduate school anyway. Speaking further, it became clear that Claire has, to a great extent, internalized the normative ordering of her field, which is in direct tension with the university's policy of allowing women to take time off to have children:

> I think that women are groomed to ... be more emotional and more caring, and that's not something that's acceptable in our field. I'm not saying that people don't have a conscience, it's just that if you were to get upset over something, the way that women handle it and men handle it is very different, and when you're the only woman in a room, you can't handle it the way an average woman would handle it. So that's not exactly welcoming for anyone who's your average woman.

Again, Claire states that she blames the norms of her field for the restrictions that she feels, placing blame elsewhere than the department, despite the fact that it is actually her department that has the direct power over how much time she can devote to family life. Specifically, Claire mentions that her advisor, who is the only faculty member in her department who had children while in graduate school, is flexible with letting her take time to look after her stepdaughter occasionally, and allows her to make up the time later. Claire explains, "He is very understanding, but I wouldn't be able to work for anybody but him." Without this flexibility, Claire claims, she would not be able to complete her degree, and recognizes that with any other advisor she would have felt she had to leave the program with just her master's degree.

Jasmine is also working toward a Ph.D. in a field within the sciences, but her story could not be more different from Claire's. Jasmine was expecting her first child at the time of her interview, and was very positive about the attitudes and norms of her department. She says,

> I'm very fortunate to be grant funded right now. I was just talking with my advisor about the spring semester and whether I would be T.A.-ing or be on the grant and he's trying to work my school schedule around the things I'll be dealing with then, you know daycare and that sort of thing and I think it's going to work out really well. He's going to make me an R.A. so I can have a lot of flexibility.

Not only was Jasmine's department more accommodating, but administration had also made her aware of the graduate maternity leave policy and gone *beyond* the policy's requirements to modify her schedule. Jasmine cites not only the department's actions *since* her pregnancy, but also the positive cultural norms, and dialogue that were transmitted to her before her pregnancy. Jasmine explains:

> I've seen my department be really accommodating to me and also to other people who've had children. I know they've shifted T.A.-ships around for people and things like that. I feel like they try to work with people. And especially since the university maternity leave is really short and they really have to help you work around that because it's not enough. I went to them and told them that I was really interested in seeing what I could do from home for a while … and they were really supportive.

For both of these women, the normative ordering of their departments was salient. In Jasmine's experience, the pre-existing norms within her department overruled any cultural biases that Claire felt existed in the sciences in general for women, allowing Jasmine to make choices that Claire could not. The graduate maternity leave policy, on the other hand, had a limited impact on these women's experiences. Claire was unaware of its existence and her statements indicate that she would not have felt able to invoke it. In Jasmine's case, the policy was a clear part of the department's recognition of her rights, but arguably not the only motivation for its actions, as demonstrated by its apparent willingness to go beyond the policy's requirements. Claire and Jasmine's stories speak volumes about the power of normative ordering and its ability to supersede the intentions of university policy. While policy has the potential to overcome problems stemming from the public-private split, it must address departmental norms in order to do so.

MOTHERS AND MARKETS: HOW THE PUBLIC-PRIVATE DIVIDE LEADS TO A MARKET FAILURE

Our interviews suggest that liberalism's public-private split also manifests itself in the market aspects of academia. Academia has become increasingly more concerned with the business side of the university, and universities use market logic to justify the exclusion of mothers who are unwilling or unable to devote as much time to their research as if they were non-parents, once again, attempting to avoid direct discrimination in favor of more subtle pressures. Claire, as quoted earlier, thought it was obvious that universities would prefer to hire someone without children because her time would not be divided. Another interviewee, Jane, who had her youngest child while working on a Ph.D., said that she thought that research universities would see children as a "conflict with my time." She added, "I also think I would have the need to prove myself and show that family wasn't interfering with my research agenda." Jane also said that she had "several discussions" with a member of her committee "about how being pregnant might impact my job interviews."

Bethany, a Ph.D. student in the humanities, had her first child while preparing for her comprehensive exams. When asked if she thought having a child would affect her career prospects, Bethany answered:

> It's a natural thing that you know that someone who is, say, single—unmarried no children—is going to have less demands on their time than someone who had one or two or more children. There's more splits and more demands on your time. Do I think people are consciously going to go "we're going to hire this guy 'cause he's single and not this person because they have

> *three children"? But I think we all have subconscious elements*
> *to our decision-making process that can affect who we choose.*
> *I think the most prudent act is not to advertise your parental*
> *status on the job market.*

Marie also saw potential difficulties in getting an internship as a mother or while pregnant, saying:

> *We know people who haven't worn their wedding rings to intern-*
> *ship interviews ... they don't really care about a man wearing*
> *their wedding ring because like, whatever, you'll still do your*
> *job—but if a woman wears her wedding ring, there's an assump-*
> *tion that you won't have the same amount of time and energy*
> *to devote to the position.... There is no way you can go to an*
> *interview if you're pregnant. They're going to take one look at*
> *your big belly and be like "we are not taking you." ...There's so*
> *much forethought about 'who can I look pregnant for' in terms*
> *of it being okay. Obviously if you start an internship and you're*
> *pregnant, or you start a post-doc and you're already pregnant,*
> *it's going to cause problems.*

Marie and Bethany's discussions of the difference between being a parent or not on the job market again stems from the public-private divide in liberalism. Non-parents are more desirable because they do not have a private life to interfere with their devotion to their public lives. Marie points out that not only is evidence of a private life undesirable to a potential employer, it is seen as especially detrimental to women, who are assumed to have more responsibilities within their private lives. Men are allowed the illusion of only having a public life, even with evidence of a private life, such as a wedding ring, but women are expected to hide their marital or parental status in order to demonstrate their commitment to their public, academic life.

Graduate students understand, and are made to understand by their departments, the possible consequences of being a parent in academia. The results are fairly clear: female academics with children have a harder time getting jobs. Wolfinger, Mason, and Goulden describe the leak in the pipeline between earning a Ph.D. and getting a tenure track job. They find that women earn 47 percent of Doctoral degrees, but only 35 percent of tenured or tenure track faculty are female. Wolfinger, Mason and Goulden report that "The SDR data show that women, especially those with young children, have disproportionately high chances of taking non-ladder teaching positions or leaving the labor force altogether" (392).

Because the academy uses liberalism to emphasize academics as individuals devoted only to their public life, mothers, who are not autonomous individuals in the traditional liberal sense (see for example Mackenzie and Stoljar), are in a disadvantaged position. Departments may view them as less productive than their male counterparts, believing that they are devoting "too much" time to private concerns. Fathers in academia are also expected to be autonomous individuals, but because historically they have been married and had wives as primary caregivers for their children, they are able to perpetuate the illusion of complete attention to their public lives.

As a result of both actual time constraints and discrimination based on the differences in private time constraints on mothers and fathers, mothers are underrepresented at the highest levels of academia. They either "opt out" by taking jobs at schools that focus less on research and more on teaching, leave academia altogether, or they do not have children. Six women that we interviewed explicitly mentioned looking for non-R1 jobs, primarily teaching jobs, because they wanted to be able to have a family life. Claire says that these market pressures to hire someone who will be the most productive are "why, of the women in [her] field, less than half have kids—much less than half."

However, recognizing that the jobs mothers are taking are highly constrained by the structure of the market, the absence of mothers from the highest levels of research-based academia poses a potential problem. The market structure of academia expects the same time commitment and productivity from all workers, regardless of family status, and mothers may be excluded from the highest levels because of time constraints, or because departments assume they will not be as productive.

If mothers are being unfairly discriminated against because they are not as intellectually productive as their male counterparts, the market is not operating properly. If mothers offer insights to academic research that would not be included if mothers are excluded, their systematic exclusion constitutes what economists refer to as a negative externality, a type of market failure. A negative externality is an undesirable, but unpredicted consequence of the way the relevant market is structured. A market failure occurs when the market does not operate efficiently. A negative externality is a type of market failure because all the costs are not calculated and allocated properly, leading to inefficiency. We argue that not only are mothers valuable academics, but that they often add a unique perspective to their work, which indicates that their exclusion from the highest level of the academic market is a market failure. The necessity of an open market without unreasonable barriers to entry is enough to justify changes in the market structure, specifically rethinking the traditional public-private divide, to allow mothers to advance further.

When we asked graduate student mothers about how their academic contributions have changed since having children, several common responses emerged. Out of the 20 mothers we interviewed, eleven of them discussed greater focus and clearer priorities as a result of becoming a mother. Nora said, "It makes you think differently. It makes you plan your day for sure, because I know I'm only going to have three or four half hour blocks to work on my dissertation, so it makes me think when I sit down at the computer and not just go, oh I'll check my Yahoo!Mail, instead I'm going, okay, what's the next step in my dissertation?" Claire also mentioned this point as well, emphasizing that even with less time, mothers can still be highly productive academics: "I think that it makes me more focused. Well, I don't have time to surf the internet, which, we all know, is about a quarter of the time of most grad students. So, while my peers might work eighty hours a week, I can do about sixty-five, because that extra time is not wasted." Beth, who was earlier in her Ph.D. program when she had her first child said, "As far as my graduate education it's been positive because it's made me focus a lot more, on what I want my life to be and what I want to do, and ultimately what I want my research to be. It's made me interested in finishing earlier. I think it's maybe made me grow up a little quicker as an academic." The mothers we interviewed were able to focus on their research and not waste time allowing them to accomplish more in less time, challenging the idea that mothers are necessarily less academically productive than non-mothers.

Three of the mothers we interviewed cited a better connection to the real world. Ellen said, "I think life experience is really important and often really lacking in academia, you know, the ivory tower being the classic metaphor. So I think that anyone who has that experience has something to offer." Melissa echoed this point and adds that academia "weeds out the people who care the most." Real-world connections keep research current and relevant, avoiding many of the problems of the ivory tower.

A related point that three other mothers discussed was that mothers tend to do research that other academics do not do, on children, parenting, women, and families. Pauline especially emphasized this point:

> *Because it's definitely a change I've noticed since I've had the baby that I'm just a lot more understanding and I'm a lot more willing to see the other side of things. The other thing that I've noticed is that I really do think it's going to change my research goals to work a lot more with mothers and children.... Policy has all kinds of unintended consequences and some of those, really, you can foresee. So if you're creating a policy and you don't incorporate an entire group—and something like mothers with children is a pretty darn large group—your policy is not going to—I don't want to say be as attractive—but the unintended consequences are probably more proportionately going to affect that group.*

Mothers, as a traditionally excluded group, are also more theoretically aware of how society and the state are structured and the unintended consequences of those structures. Pauline also added:

> *Every time you bring in a new group and you start to recognize new lifestyles that are not traditional to academia—and motherhood really isn't—and I mean women in academia is also, it's still not, you know, women just don't have as many Ph.Ds as men, it's just a fact. And when they [women] do [get Ph.Ds], they [women] get them [Ph.Ds] in English and the humanities and social sciences. So, sure, it brings in a different perspective that's important for us to understand. Especially in most of the social sciences.*

We agree with Pauline that bringing mothers and other underrepresented groups into academia provides a new and necessary perspective to academic research. The systematic, although possibly unintentional, exclusion of mothers from the highest level of academia as a consequence of the liberal public-private divide constitutes a market failure. Our interviews indicate that the experiences of mothers are fundamentally important to the mission of academia. Academia plays an important role in knowledge production and influences larger understandings of the world and individual's lives. If the class of knowledge producers is limited to those who are not parents, the knowledge produced may not take into account the full nature of relationships in the world. People exist in society, in relationships, and have claims on each other. Academia needs people whose lives reflect this reality to transmit their experience into the production of knowledge.

CONCLUSION: OVERCOMING SILENCE

If graduate student mothers are pushed out of academia or if their voices are marginalized, we lose a class of knowledge producers who may be likely to change many of the problematic practices of the academy. It is clear that graduate student mothers experience the consequences of the public-private split and that they recognize it as detrimental to their academic careers. They are also concerned about the practice of depart-mental norm-creation and question the notion of the ideal graduate student and the marketable new Ph.D. as single, young, and perpetually available for work. In the conclusion of her interview, Melissa said, "in terms of what the university is missing, it's missing reality, that's what it's missing. We're missing what real lives bring." Melissa's quote sums up the central problem that we found in the overlap between liberalism and the academy: the vacuum left between the public and the private, between policy and experience, allows the creation of expectations that exclude the reality of the family and mothering. However, graduate students and other academics with families are strongly motivated to change these expectations. Our interviewees expressed a strong interest in changing the academy for the betterment of academic mothers. Our study demonstrates that mothering while a graduate student is not only a source of problems, but can also be an instigator for the expression of agency as a researcher, teacher, and activist.

Though the public-private split is pervasive, our interviews provide insight into strategies graduate students can use to challenge it. Gradu-ate students are in a uniquely vulnerable position within the university system, and we draw the strategies we suggest from the experiences of our interviewees. First, we maintain that it is important for graduate students to be knowledgeable about any parental leave policies their universities may have. Not only should graduate students use these poli-cies, but they should also consider improving these policies if necessary, with the help of graduate student advocacy organizations, their graduate student senate, or unions. One interviewee, Melissa, specifically noted the need to raise awareness about the policy as she knew many other students and faculty in her department were unaware of it. This assertion matches our evidence. Only three of our interviewees had used the Graduate Maternity leave, and none of the interviewees knew about the leave prior to becoming pregnant. In a related survey we conducted of 308 graduate students at UConn, only 14 percent of survey respondents knew about the existence of the Graduate Maternity leave policy and only three percent had used the graduate maternity leave. Increasing awareness and use of the policy is crucial for creating more mother-friendly norms within departments.

Second, graduate student mothers can benefit immensely from coalition building. Our interviewees frequently used this strategy in a number of different ways—eight discussed maternity leave policy and norms with other graduate students who had had children and one even met with supportive faculty and graduate students to discuss how to best manage the challenges of having children as graduate students. Finding allies not only provides an avenue for producing more useful policy, but meeting with supportive faculty and students can provide a safety net for graduate students. Faculty members play an important role here; graduate students lack the benefits of tenure, the support of a union at most universities, and the power that comes along with faculty governance. Graduate students are not always in a position to advocate for themselves on their own, but supportive faculty have a better vantage point from which to help graduate students. Fifteen interviewees noted the importance of supportive advisors, committee members, department chairs, or other faculty members in making their experience as graduate student mothers more positive. As four interviewees directly pointed out, silence surrounds discussions of family in the academy. That silence *is* the public-private split. For graduate students, speaking through that silence is the first step in overcoming the public-private divide and supporting academic mothering.

WORKS CITED

Agathangelou, Anna, and L. H. M. Ling. "An Unten(ur)able Position: The Politics of Teaching for Women of Color in the US." *International*

Feminist Journal of Politics 4.3 (2002): 368-98.

Albiston, Catherine. "Bargaining in the Shadow of Social Institutions: Competing Discourses and Social Change in Workplace Mobilization of Civil Rights." *Law and Society Review* 39.1 (2005): 11-50.

Elshtain, Jean Bethke. *Public Man, Private Woman: Women in Social and Political Thought.* Princeton: Princeton University Press, 1993.

Ewick, Patricia and Susan Silbey. "Subversive Stories and Hegemonic Tales: Toward a Sociology of Narrative." *Law and Society Review* 29.2 (1995): 197-279.

Foucault, Michel. "The Birth of Biopolitics." 1979. *The Essential Foucault.* Eds. Paul Rabinow and Nikolas Rose. New York: The New Press, 2003: 202-207.

Jayaratne, Toby Epstein and Abigail J. Stewart. "Quantitative and Qualitative Methods in the Social Sciences: Current Feminist Issues and Practical Strategies." *Beyond Methodology: Feminist Scholarship as Lived Research.* Eds. Mary Margaret Fonow and Judith A. Cook. Bloomington: Indiana University Press, 1991. 85-106.

Kelly, Kristin. *Domestic Violence and the Politics of Privacy.* Ithaca, NY: Cornell University Press, 2002a.

Kelly, Kristin. "Private Family, Private Individual." *Social Theory and Practice* 28.3 (2002b): 361-80.

Mackenzie, Catriona, and Natalie Stoljar, eds. *Relational Autonomy: Feminist Perspectives on Autonomy, Agency, and the Social Self.* New York: Oxford University Press, 2000.

Okin, Susan Moller. *Justice, Gender, and the Family.* New York: Basic Books, 1991.

Okin, Susan Moller. *Women in Western Political Thought.* Princeton: Princeton University Press, 1979.

Ricoeur, Paul. *From Text to Action: Essays in Hermeneutics, II.* Trans. Kathleen Blamey and John B. Thompson. Evanston: Northwestern University Press, 1991.

Wolfinger, Nicholas H., Mary Ann Mason, and Marc Goulden. "Problems in the Pipeline: Gender, Marriage, and Fertility in the Ivory Tower." *The Journal of Higher Education* 79.4 (2008): 388-405.

Young, Iris Marion. *Justice and the Politics of Difference.* Princeton: Princeton University Press, 1990.

Contributor Notes

Lucy E. Bailey is an associate professor of social foundations at Oklahoma State University, also serving as a core faculty member in gender and women's studies. She is a feminist methodologist and activist with interests in diversity and higher education, foundations of education, and qualitative methodologies.

Carolyn Barber is an independent scholar living in New Jersey. She received her Masters in Environmental Studies from York University in 2005. She lectures part-time for the Human Ecology Department at Rutgers University and is Board President of her son's cooperative nursery school.

Laura J. Beard is a Professor in the Department of Classical and Modern Languages and Literatures and an Assistant Dean in the College of Arts and Sciences at Texas Tech University. She has a B.A. in English literature from Carleton College in Northfield, MN, and the M.A. and Ph.D. in Hispanic literature from The Johns Hopkins University, in Baltimore, MD. Her research and teaching interests include women writers of the Americas, Indigenous literatures and cultures, autobiographical genres, and contemporary critical theories. She is author of *Acts of Narrative Resistance: Women's Autobiographical Writings in the Americas* (2009).

Sylvia Burrow is Associate Professor of Philosophy in the Department of Philosophy and Religious Studies, Cape Breton University, Nova Scotia and a Scholar in Residence at the Canadian Centre for Ethics and Public

Affairs in Halifax, Nova Scotia (2011-2012). Her research advances feminist discussions of women's autonomy within different contexts to show that capacities of autonomy are (i) embodied; (ii) subject to limitations due to external forces and (iii) a function of certain substantive requirements such as self-trust, self-worth, self-confidence, self-respect and self-esteem. Recent publications explore women's autonomy in gendered discourse; embodied autonomy; and limits to autonomy for women in academia.

Margarita M. Cardona has spent the majority of her professional career in research administration, occupying positions in both government and academia. She is also currently pursuing a doctorate in public policy Her research interests include family-friendly policies, faculty professional development, academic freedom and the operation of institutional review boards.

Laurie J. C. Cella is an Assistant Professor at Shippensburg University in Pennsylvania. She has published articles in *Reflections: a Journal of Writing, Community Literacy and Service-Learning*; *Southern Literary Journal*, and *Frontiers: A Journal of Women's Studies*. Currently, she is co-editing a collection of essays with Jessica Restaino entitled *Unsustainable: Owning Our Best, Short-Lived Efforts at Community Work*.

Karen Christopher is Associate Professor of Women's & Gender Studies and Sociology at the University of Louisville. She has published on the topics of motherhood, employment, social policy, and poverty. Her most recent project explores employment and caregiving narratives among a diverse sample of Canadian and U.S. mothers. She can be contacted at 331 Gardiner Hall, Women's and Gender Studies, University of Louisville, Louisville, KY 40292. E-mail: k.christopher@louisville.edu.

Sarah Coté Hampson is a Ph.D. candidate in Political Science at the University of Connecticut, and serves as the Managing Editor of *Polity*. Her research interests include women and politics, feminist theory, law and society, public policy, and race, gender and ethnicity.

Karen Skivers Drake has over 20 years experience as senior level HR strategist, operations manager, consultant, coach and teacher. Her career has included roles in higher education and international organizations. Karen is passionate about her work with employee on-boarding, career management, engagement, diversity, work-life, women's careers and transition issues.

Linda Ennis is a psychoanalytic therapist in private practice and lecturer at York University. She has written and spoken extensively on her research in her area of expertise, on combining motherhood with employment, which was the first qualitative piece done in this area. Since she is, also, an early childhood specialist, she has appeared on television to discuss effective parenting strategies. She has, more recently, written contributions discussing the "empty nest," the "mommy track," and the implications of marriage, particularly on women.

Rachel Epp Buller is a feminist-art historian-printmaker-mama of three who investigates critical issues of mothering and the maternal body through prints and artist books, as well as through writing and curatorial projects. She is a contributor to Amber Kinser's *Mothering in the Third Wave* (2008), editor of *Reconciling Art and Mothering* (2012), and co-editor of *Mennonite Mothering* (2013). She holds a Ph.D. in art history.

Bethany Crandell Goodier joined the Department of Communication in 2001. She teaches courses on such topics as organizational communication, health communication, interviewing, business communication, and leadership. Dr. Goodier has been chair of the Department of Communication since 2010. Dr. Goodier's research interests include spirituality, organizational change, collaboration, leadership and health communication.

Jennifer Hauver James is Assistant Professor in the Department of Elementary and Social Studies Education at the University of Georgia. Her research, teaching and service are driven by her passion for preparing reflective practitioners engaged in education for critically-minded democratic citizenship. She uses narrative inquiry to understand and interrogate teachers' positionings in the discursive, institutional, familial and sociocultural contexts that shape, and often bound, ways of knowing and acting in schools. In particular, her work troubles prevailing mothering narratives of teaching that emphasize sacrifice, isolation and a discourse of protection, which tend to legitimize avoidance of difficult content and blur the public/private spaces of classrooms.

Jamie Huff is a Ph.D. student in political science and Women's Studies at the University of Connecticut. Her current research explores connections between critical legal theories, intersectionality, and cultural narratives of the U.S. South.

Masako Kato holds a Ph.D. in Anthropology from the Graduate Center, CUNY, USA. She is a mother of three children, ages four, six, and eight, and currently teaches part-time at Tsuda College in Japan. Her research interests include linguistic anthropology, language socialization, language and identity, and bilingualism.

Kerri S. Kearney is an associate professor of educational leadership at Oklahoma State University. Her professional experience is a hybrid of education and organizational consulting. She holds an M.B.A. and an Ed.D. Her research agenda focuses on the emotional impacts of human transition, other mothering, and visual methodologies in qualitative research.

Amber Kinser is Professor and Chair of the Department of Communication at East Tennessee State University, where she also recently held the position of Director of Women's Studies for ten years. She earned her Ph.D. from Purdue University in Communication with emphases in family interaction and gender studies. She is author of *Motherhood and Feminism* (2010) and editor of *Mothering in the Third Wave* (2008). Her work appears in *Encyclopedia of Mothering* and collections such as *Feminist Mothering* (2008), and *Mother Knows Best: Talking Back to the Baby Experts* (2009). She writes a weekly blog called "Thursdays with Dr. Mama" for the Museum of Motherhood; her blog and more are available at www.amberkinser.com.

Avery Kolers is Associate Professor of Philosophy at the University of Louisville. He is the author of *Land, Conflict, and Justice: A Political Theory of Territory* (2009) as well as articles on territorial rights, on philosophical issues in parenthood and procreation, and on ethics in institutions. He is currently writing on territory and on solidarity. He can be contacted at the Philosophy Department, University of Louisville, Louisville, KY, 40292. E-mail: akolers@louisville.edu.

Isabelle Martin (BA, LIB, LIM) and Julie Paquin (LIB, LIM, DEA, DCL) met during their doctoral studies at McGill University Faculty of Law. They were then in their thirties, and had already spent a few years working as legal professionals. They are currently mothers to a total of seven children aged from four to eighteen.

Marta McClintock-Comeaux, Ph.D., MSW, is the Director of Women's Studies and an assistant professor at California University of PA in the Department of Justice, Law and Society. She earned her doctorate in family studies from The University of Maryland and her Masters in Social Work from The University of Michigan. Her primary research interests include egalitarian couple relationships, relationship education programs, work/life integration issues, and more broadly, issues of social justice. She is a proud and grateful mom of four with her husband Patrick.

Joanne C. Minaker is Assistant Professor in the Sociology Department at Grant MacEwan University in Edmonton, Alberta. Her work raises questions regarding identity, power, choice, social exclusion, and social justice. Dr. Minaker's main areas of expertise are the sociology of motherhood and criminalized girls/women. Since earning her Ph.D. in Socio-Legal Studies from Queen's University in 2003 she has published widely, including a book, co-authored with Bryan Hogeveen, called *Youth, Crime, and Society: Issues of Power and Justice,* and various articles on mothering. Her current research involves exploring the meaning of marginalized young mothering through qualitative interviews and an edited collection (with Bryan Hogeveen) on *Criminalized Mothers/Criminalizing Motherhood.* She can often be found with her daughter (almost two) and amazing partner watching her sons (eight and six) play hockey in Edmonton rinks.

D. Lynn O'Brien Hallstein is an Assistant Professor of Rhetoric in the College of General Studies at Boston University. She is the author of *White Feminists and Contemporary Maternity: Purging Matrophobia,* co-editor of *Contemporary Maternity in an Era of Choice: Explorations into Discourses of Reproduction,* which won the Organization for the

465

Study of Communication, Language, and Gender's 2011 Outstanding Book Award for an edited volume, and she has been published in variety of academic journals

Andrea O'Reilly is Professor in the School of Women's Studies at York University and is founder and director of The Motherhood Initiative for Research and Community Involvement (MIRCI), founder and editor-in-chief of the Journal of the Motherhood Initiative and founder and publisher of Demeter Press, the first feminist press on motherhood. She is editor and author of 17 books on motherhood including most recently *Twenty-first Century Motherhood: Experience, Identity, Policy, Agency* (2010) and *The 21st Century Motherhood Movement: Mothers Speak Out on Why We Need to Change the World and How to Do It* (2011). She is editor of the first *Encyclopedia on Motherhood*. In 2009, she was the recipient of the CAUT Sarah Shorten Award for outstanding achievements in the promotion of the advancement of women in Canadian universities and colleges. She is currently beginning a research project with May Friedman on the Slutwalk Movement, tentatively entitled "Reclamation and Resistance: Feminism, Collaboration and the Building of the Slutwalk Movement." She is twice the receipient of the "University-Wide Professor of the Year Award" at York University. She is the proud mama of three fabulous and feminist adult children.

Julie Paquin is Assistant Professor at the Faculty of Law of University of Ottawa (Canada) and mother of three children aged four, seven, and nine years old. She holds a doctoral degree in comparative law.

Serena Patterson competed her Ph.D. in Clinical Psychology at Simon Fraser University in 1991, five years after the birth of her daughter. She currently teaches courses in Developmental Psychology, Women's Studies, and Equity and Social Justice at North Island College in Courtenay, British Columbia. She has served for a decade on the Status of Women Committee for British Columbia's Federation of Post Secondary Educators, chairing the committee from 2004-2006. She has published in the *Journal of the Association for Research on Mothering* and in *Canadian Woman's Studies/les cahiers de la femme*. She shares a clinical practice with her life partner Monika Grünberg, who also shares in parenting, dog care, community, academic and family life.

Elizabeth Podnieks, mother of two active athletes, is an Associate Professor in the Department of English and the Graduate Program in Communication and Culture at Ryerson University, Toronto, teaching and researching in the fields of motherhood studies, modernism, life writing, and popular culture. Her writing on motherhood includes a chapter on celebrity maternity blogs in *Mothering and Blogging* (2009), and entries in the *Encyclopedia of Motherhood* (2010). She is the co-editor of *Textual Mothers, Maternal Texts: Motherhood in Contemporary Women's Literatures* (2009), editor of the collection, *Mediating Moms: Mothering in Popular Culture*, which is forthcoming from McGill-Queen's University Press. She is the Area Chair for the Motherhood/Fatherhood Area of the Popular Culture Association.

From 1988-98, **Yvonne Redmond-Brown Banks** had two children, lost her husband, received her doctorate (Educational Policy and Administration, University of Minnesota), and became the only black female professor at her institution. She is now a professor of Education and Dean of Academic Support Services at Northwestern (Minnesota). Her research centers on remediation strategies, placement decisions, and equity policies for children in special education.

Corinne M. Tagliarina is a Ph.D. student in Political Science and Human Rights at the University of Connecticut. Her regional specialty is South Asia and her current research interests include the right to water, women's rights, and the institutionalization of rights.

Michele L. Vancour has a Ph.D. in Health Education from New York University, and is an Associate Professor of Public Health at Southern Connecticut State University. Her research interests involve work-family practices in higher education, maternal health, breastfeeding, and family-friendly initiatives for working parents.

Jill M. Wood earned her Ph.D. in Biobehavioral Health and Women's Studies at Penn State University, studying women's sexuality (particularly during the menopausal transition) and women's health (specifically menstruation and childbirth). A feminist qualitative researcher, Jill has published numerous articles on women's sexual desire, postmenopausal women's sexuality, young women's menstrual experiences, and the medicalization of women's health issues such as pregnancy and childbirth. Jill is currently a Senior Lecturer in the Women's Studies Department at Penn State where she focuses primarily on teaching undergraduates, as well as teaching graduate students about feminist pedagogy. Jill is the proud mama of three children, and above all else she enjoys spending her time watching them eat peas fresh off the garden trellis and contemplating questions like, "Mama, how can my foot be asleep if it doesn't have eyes?"

Heather Wyatt-Nichol, Ph.D., is an Assistant Professor and MPA Program Director in College of Public Affairs at the University of Baltimore. She has published book chapters and articles on a variety of different topics. Her research interests include diversity management, ethics, family friendly-workplace policies, organizational behavior, and social equity.